1996

BUSINESS, ETHICS, AND THE LAW

Paul F. Hodapp,
Editor

UNIVERSITY
PRESS OF
AMERICA

Lanham • New York • London

Copyright © 1991 by
University Press of America®, Inc.
4720 Boston Way
Lanham, Maryland 20706

3 Henrietta Street
London WC2E 8LU England

Library of Congress Cataloging-in-Publication Data

Business, ethics, and the law / Paul F. Hodapp, editor.
p.   cm.
1. Business ethics.   I. Hodapp, Paul F., 1943 .
HF5387.B877   1991
174'.4—dc20   90–26842 CIP

ISBN 0–8191–7888–8 paper

174.4
14687

Table of Contents

537.42

Curriculum

4-8-96

iii

152,362

PREFACE

My aim in this anthology is to provide students with materials whose value to them will increase after they leave college. I have not included materials which introduce or give background to business problems. I assume this text will be used to supplement other materials whose primary purpose is to give information and answer questions. Materials in this text are to raise questions, to challenge students to consider the reasons for one business policy rather than another.

I have also tried to find selections whose audience is not college students but business persons. Hopefully, these selections will encourage students to read and study business ethics problems after they leave college.

CHAPTER I

ETHICS IN THE LAW

INTRODUCTION

There are many common misconceptions about ethics and especially business ethics which is sometimes considered to be an oxymoron. Business is related to ethics as military is related to music. One common basis of this misconception that business and ethics should be contrasted is that business issues are considered easily known and determined, because there is a clear enforcement mechanism in the law, while ethics is considered a matter of personal opinion, because there is no social enforcement mechanism for ethics. Any business person who has had to pay large amounts of money for outside attorneys to decide whether a certain course of conduct is legal or not must question whether the enforcement mechanism of the law is quite so clear. Also, considering that the United States Bill of Rights is a part of the fundamental law of the land should cause one to pause before extolling the clarity and the enforceability of the law.

Before a statue or administrative regulation can be enforced against a business, there must be reason to believe that the regulation does not violate the Bill of Rights. But what is the meaning of the phrases in the Bill of Rights such as equal protection and due process of law? What is a reasonable search and seizure? How is one to decide these question in the democratic setting of business organizations without undertaking the task of ethics as a practical and human endeavor, i.e., without asking what interests should we as a society protect and how do we balance these competing interests against one another.

In thinking about the law in terms of the balancing of interests, we need to ask first whether some interests are so basic that they should never be subject to balancing. For example, when the First Amendment to the Bill of Rights speaks of Congress making no law abridging the freedom of speech, does that mean simply what it says? Is it an absolute prohibition on free speech by the government? What room is there left to balance the

1

right to free speech against the majority's interest? For example, as an employer, I may wish to express my strong anti-union opinions during an organizing campaign and I may wish to tell my employees what I will do for them if they do not unionize. Should Congress be able to prohibit my speech? Should the speech of Union organizers who stand just outside my private property accusing me of unfair labor practices and attempting to discourage my customers be prohibited or limited?

You should also consider whether any of the Bill of Rights has lost its point; whether some of the rights might be reinterpreted to be given new vitality or purpose. For example, does the First Amendment protection for the press continue to be valid, or has it become too costly in terms of other values in an age where the press is a large multi-media conglomerate which no more needs special constitutional protection than the steel industry? And if rights may be lost because their point has been lost, then rights may need to be added. One might wonder why economic rights are absent from the Bill of Rights. Should there be a constitutional right to life-time employment, to decent housing, to a fair wage?

Finally, one might question whether any of the rights outlined in the Bill of Rights should not only protect individuals from government but also be extended to protect persons from business. Should the due process, equal protection, free speech, and search and seizure rights be applied to the conduct of businesses? What would be the cost of such an extension in a highly competitive international market place?

If these questions have raised doubts regarding whether the law is as clear as it first appears, whether the distinction between law and ethics is so sharp, then we are in a position to begin to look at business ethics, not as an oxymoron, but as a tool to help us address the basic policy questions which confront a business.

QUESTIONS AND PROJECTS

1.   Which one of the rights in the Bill of Rights would you as a business person argue should not be there, and what other right or rights belong there and why?

2

2. Should the Bill of Rights, or some of them, be extended to protect private employees? If so which ones and why? If not, why not?

3. Are the rights in the Bill of Rights positive or negative rights? For example, to what extent should the government guarantee to each citizen the economic basis sufficient to have meaningful free speech?

The Constitution of the United States of America

ARTICLES

In addition to, and Amendment of,
The Constitution of the United States of
America

Article I

Congress shall make no law respecting an establishment of religion, or prohibiting the free exercise thereof; or abridging the freedom of speech, or of the press; or the right of the people peaceably to assemble, and to petition the Government for a redress of grievances.

Article II

A well regulated Militia, being necessary to the security of a free State, the right of the people to keep and bear Arms shall not be infringed.

Article III

No Soldier shall, in time of peace be quartered in any house, without the consent of the Owner, nor in time of war, but in a manner to be prescribed by law.

Article IV

The right of the people to be secure in their persons, houses, papers, and effects, against unreasonable searches and seizures, shall not be violated, and no Warrants shall issue, but upon probable cause, supported by Oath or affirmation, and particularly describing the place to be searched, and the persons or things to be seized.

Article V

No person shall be held to answer for a capital, or otherwise infamous crime, unless on a presentment or indictment of a Grand Jury, except in cases arising in the land or naval forces, or in the Militia, when in actual service in time of War or public danger; nor shall any person be subject for the same offence to be twice put in jeopardy of life or limb; nor shall be compelled in any criminal case to be a waitness against himself, nor be deprived of life, liberty, or property, without due process of law; nor shall private property be taken for public use, without just compensation.

Article VI

In all criminal prosecutions, the accused shall enjoy the right to a speedy and public trial by an impartial jury of the State and district wherein the crime shall have been committed, which district shall have been previously ascertained by law, and to be informed of the nature and cause of the accusation; to be confronted with the witnesses against him; to have compulsory process for obtaining witnesses in his favor, and to have the Assistance of Counsel for his defence.

Article VII

In suits at common law, where the value in controversy shall exceed twenty dollars, the right of trial by jury shall be preserved, and no fact tried by a jury, shall be otherwise re-examined in any Court of the United States, than according to the rules of the common law.

Article VIII

Excessive bail shall not be required, nor excessive fines imposed, nor cruel and unusual punishments inflicted.

Article IX

The enumeration in the Constitution, of certain rights, shall not be construed to deny or disparage others retained by the people.

Article X

The powers not delegated to the United States by the Constitution, nor prohibited by it to the States, are reserved to the States respectively, or to the people.

CHAPTER II

BUSINESS ETHICS

INTRODUCTION

The purpose of the first chapter was to show that ethical thinking, which involves the balancing of interests, has an essential role in the American Legal system. But you may still doubt whether ethical thinking is useful in business. You may think that business norms, for example, those prescribing dishonesty in business, lack an enforcement mechanism and lack the precision of other areas of business, e.g., accounting. Thus you might conclude that business ethics is still a matter of opinion about which there can be no rational discussion.

Such ideas are often popular, but I believe that they represent an incomplete truth. The problem is not that business norms lack sufficient precision for enforcement; business norms can be and are enforced by any business which chooses to adopt the procedures to make them enforceable. The difficulty is that business norms are not given by some external source. They reflect the conflicting interests of the constituents of a business, and must be made definite and enforceable to fit the many different forms and situations of business.

Increasingly large numbers of very successful companies are implementing codes of conduct for the company and its employees. Such policies represent an attempt to make ethical norms definite and enforceable within the company.

It still might be challenged that such ethical codes reflect only the opinion of the individual companies, or individuals within those companies. The answer to this challenge is both affirmative and negative. Affirmative, because in a pluralistic society there is no external source which gives definitive answers to ethical behavior; negative, because the companies are correct in believing that their codes are not merely the product of unreflected opinion. Companies spend a great deal of time and money to implement a code which fairly balances the interest of the company, its shareholders, its

7

employees, it distributors and suppliers, and the
communities in which the company is located.

Businesses recognize that plurality regarding values
is not the same as irrationality, that differences of
opinion do not mean that anything is permitted. In fact,
it is the very plurality of values which presupposes the
shared value of democratic fairness and consideration for
all the constituents of business in formulating business
codes. This not to say that business codes are
altruistic. They do serve valuable business purposes,
e.g., guaranteeing a workforce with a sense of commitment
to the company. But the fact that such codes serve
valuable business purposes does not entail that they are
not also valuable for the interests of the constituencies
of the business. A business cannot be antagonistic to
the interests of its constituents; they need to be
harmonized one with the another.

One final objection is that the norms of business
codes are mere platitudes which lack sufficient precision
so that employees can understand what behavior is
prohibited and what behavior is rewarded in order to
guide their behavior. Again, this question actually
reinforces the point that there is a shared value of due
process, that no one should be punished for behavior that
she could not have known was wrong.

There is no easy solution to the imprecision and
enforcement problems for business ethics. What is a fair
norm will vary from company to company. The solution to
the problem will depend upon the procedures within the
company, namely, establishment of company ethics
committees which will work to develop sufficiently
precise rules in a democratic fashion for the purposes
of that company.

Ethics subcommittees should be established at
various levels of the company in order to insure input
from all employees. Such democratic involvement may
serve at least to rule out culturally biased ethical
norms. A business ethics committee also should reflect
upon the constituents which are essential to the
efficient operation of any company. Such constituents

include not only the shareholders of the company but also it's employees, distributors, customers, and the wider community in which the company exists.

Each of these groups is essential to business. None of them is a mere instrument to be used by the others for its own purposes.

In light of these constituencies, each business will have to decide what specifically it wishes to accomplish in relation to each group. For example, does the company want a better educated, healthier work force? If it does, then it should set up specific attainable targets over a period of time to insure that the company is working towards this goal. The company should consider where it stands presently with respect to its workforce, and where it realistically wishes to be in three years or five years. Then realistic means will have to be discussed in order to define specific goals for each year.

Ethics committees do not guarantee successful business; there are forces in a complex society which have the effect of defeating ethical business practices. Some of these forces arise from an undue emphasis on one or more of the constituencies of a business. For example, what reasons might justify a company placing shareholder interest above those of the other constituents. Is there any justification for elevating shareholder interest in a very large corporation where the primary means of raising capital is by loans and not by the issuance of stock.

In conclusion, I have given you some reasons to think that business ethics can be made precise and enforceable. If you are not convinced, you should reserve judgement regarding the value of business ethics, until you have read more selections.

QUESTIONS AND PROJECTS

1. Following the outline of the institutionalizing ethics article, set out in detail an ethics committee for a business with which you have some familiarity.

2. Is it possible to create a meaningful societal audit for companies based upon specific goals and targets for each business constituent. If so, then construct such a social audit for a company with which you have some familiarity. If not, justify why you believe such a social audit is impossible or infeasible.

3. Is it possible to reconcile business ethics committees with the short term profit models discussed in the Hosmer article? If not, what is the justification for business' emphasizing short term profits? Should government legislate against takeovers which have the effect of forcing business to consider only short term profits?

INSTITUTIONALIZING ETHICS INTO THE CORPORATION

James Weber

Beyond its responsibility to oversee management, strategic planning, and shareholder dividends, the board must monitor the integrity of all the corporation's actions--its social integrity, its community activities, its affirmative action programs. The board should satisfy itself that the corporation is being a responsible citizen in these matters. The pressure in the 1980's will be to perform this overview role.

This challenge demonstrates the significance of the ethics issue to boards of directors. Major corporations are beginning to view ethical issues as a recognized part of doing business, thereby integrating or institutionalizing ethics into the corporate decision-making structure.

The term institutionalizing ethics is academic and may sound ponderous. But it has value. It simply means getting ethics formally and explicitly into daily business life, making it a regular and normal part of business. It means putting ethics into company policy making at the board and top management levels and, through a formal code, integrating ethics into all daily decision making and work practices for all employees.

A corporation may institutionalize ethics by three principal means: a company policy or code of ethics, a formally designated ethics committee on the board of directors, and a management development program that incorporates ethics into its curriculum.

From <u>MSU Business Topics</u>. Copyright 1981. Reprinted by permission of the Michigan State University Press.

Development of a Code

General Philosophy. The writers of the general policy statement should acknowledge, in the opening sentence, the difficulty of preparing a code and the need for constant review and revision. The policy statement should declare ethics a critical element of corporate concern and should define, as clearly and as simply as possible, the following terms: changing versus static values, business versus personal ethics, and illegal versus unethical actions.

A code also must consider ethical issues specific to the corporation.

The formulators of a code should be sensitive to the need to respond to the ethical dilemmas confronting the corporation. As the transnational Norton Company discovered, a universal code might need to be tempered due to differing local laws and customs. The observance abroad of U.S. laws (for example, the Foreign Corrupt Practices Act of 1977) by a U.S.-owned plant could result in a loss of sales and revenue to European competitors. The lost income must be weighed against the consequences of violating U.S. laws and the possibility of legal action. Solutions to these types of ethical dilemmas may not be reached easily, although projects such as the United Nations committee for developing a transnational code of ethics may help. Nonetheless, the framers of the corporate code must struggle with the attempt to resolve these matters.

Finally, the general policy statement of a code should promote ethics as a necessary value applicable throughout the corporate network, to every domestic and foreign plant and to every employee. To be institutionalized, ethics must be considered in daily business operations.

Areas of Concern. Following the general policy statement should be a section on matters of ethical concern for the corporation. Some possible areas are transnational responsibility, boycotts, government relations, community relations, environmental quality, energy conservation, labor disputes, antitrust compliance, interlocking directorates, false advertising, use of confidential information, product quality and safety, occupational safety and health, charitable contributions, political contributions, equal employment opportunity, gifts, favors, gratuities, bribes, personnel grievances, employee drug addiction, employee alcoholism, conflicts of interest, employee pilfering, accounting procedures, tax evasion, slush funds, company expense accounts, and embezzlement.

Drafters of the code should select areas germane to the company's daily operations and address the ethical component in these areas. The code should specify briefly how existing programs relate to the code, for example, affirmative action guidelines, occupational safety and health regulations, and environmental quality regulations. By including these, the corporation eliminates the potential problem of a conflict in responsibility between the ethics committee, which is the corporate enforcer of the company code, and the staff officer in charge of the specific program or regulation. The code should not and cannot be a substitute for existing programs. Rather, inclusion in the code would give greater emphasis to the programs, highlight their ethical nature, and avoid possible bureaucratic confusion.

Communication. The third major section of a code should be concerned with comprehensive communication. This could be achieved through periodic review of the code and through a general communique from the CEO to each employee. This communique should explain the code and request feedback. There should be a two-way flow of communication between the ethics committee, including the CEO, and middle management. A multilingual printing (especially for multinational corporations) and corporatewide distribution are essential. The firm should periodically review its code and corporate practices (probably annually), with participation of as many corporate levels as possible (especially middle management). The code should be distributed frequently to employees newly hired and acquired through mergers. Finally, a board-level ethics committee should be established, and communication of the code should be one of its primary functions.

Enforcement. The corporate code of ethics should give the ethics committee enforcement powers.

There should be a system of positive reinforcement. Incentives such as recognition, appreciation, commendation (already implemented in some firms), and possibly monetary rewards are examples. In cases of unethical behavior, there should be provision for the ethics committee to correct and punish. Within the limits of the law, the code should allow for investigation, judgment, and similar responses to violations.

In short, the code should be enforced through disciplinary measures delineated in a corporate policy statement and through positive rewards for ethical actions.

Ethics Committee Essential

Enforcement will be ineffective without a board-level ethics committee to further the involvement of ethics in daily corporate operations. It should provide the board of directors with a groups of advisors well versed in the ethical issues of the company.

Composition. The committee should consist of a balance of internal and external directors This balance is critical, as it has been recognized by the courts as desirable and beneficial to the corporate decision-making process.

In Fogel v. Chesnutt, a federal appeals court upheld a decision imposing liability on internal directors, but it observed that if they had reviewed their actions with external directors and secured the latter's advance approval, liability would have been unlikely. This case was heard under the Investment Company Act, which requires that external directors be on the board. However, this practice would seem sensible whenever external directors are available. A mixture of internal and external directors provides for a sense of realism and is viewed favorably by the courts.

14

The knowledge of the company possessed by internal directors and the independence of external directors should lead to a more effective ethics committee. There should be a sensitivity to the vested interest each internal director has in the company and in his or her particular department. The balance within the committee should temper any prejudices and help overcome the weaknesses.

Another area of consideration for an ethics committee is the role of the company's CEO, who should have at least an ex-officio role. The CEO should not simply be included because of his or her corporate position, but on the merit of personality, concern for ethics, and business skills. For example, Robert Cushman, CEO of the Norton Company, was found to be outstanding in all three areas by his board of directors and was asked to chair the firm's ethics committee.

In general, the size of the committee should be manageable (three to seven members); additional personnel may be invited to meetings to share their knowledge. Committee members should be selected by the board of directors on the basis of their concern for ethics, their ability to work with others having different opinions, and their expertise. Members should bring to the committee various abilities and approaches toward institutionalizing ethics in the corporation.

Resources. If a corporation is dedicated to institutionalizing ethics, the committee should be given adequate assistance, preferably through access to the regular staff or on an ad hoc basis. The primary function of the staff should be to assist the ethics committee in its activities--to communicate, investigate, and enforce the company code of ethics.

Functions. The ethics committee members should have eight primary functions: attend meetings to discuss ethical issues, probably semiannually; clarify the grey areas of ethics, as stipulated in the code; communicate the code to all corporate managers and employees; investigate possible violations; enforce the code through sanctions; reward or discipline code compliers or violators; review and revise the code based on annual corporate reviews by management and on the changing

15

business climate; and report to the board of directors on all committee actions.

Areas of Concern. The ethics committee should be concerned primarily with those issues included in the corporate code of ethics. The committee also should work with the staff of existing programs related to the code. It would be beneficial for the ethics committee to develop a working agreement with each representative of the company's social ethical programs such as the coordinator of the affirmative action program, the antitrust compliance legal expert, and so forth. This agreement should entail an exchange of research expertise and cooperation in any investigation of unethical practices.

Sanctions. The sanctions the ethics committee can apply should be delineated in the code of ethics and should enable the committee to fulfill its eight primary functions. If additional or different powers are necessary, the committee should submit the appropriate recommendations for code changes to the board of directors.

Pitfalls. There are numerous pitfalls the corporate ethics committee must avoid. For example, integrating ethics into corporate decision making should not be viewed as a short-term consideration; nor should ethics be seen as the sole criterion for the firm's decisions. Corporations should recognize ethics as one criterion for daily business operations, including legal, financial, and marketing decisions.

A company should avoid the false comfort of merely formulating and adopting a code of ethics. A code needs continuous change and revision; it should not be written, approved, and then filed and forgotten.

A code should be observed, and a company should avoid the pitfall of creating a committee that is inoperable due to its lack of sanctions.

Finally, the corporation that has begun to institutionalize ethics should avoid the pitfall of seeking immediate, tangible results. The integration of ethics into corporate decision making is a slow and

16

subtle process. The corporation should stand by its convictions and allow the institutionalization to occur.

Development of an Ethics Module

A corporation could further its efforts to institutionalize ethics by establishing an ethics training program within its management development program. Such a module need not be elaborate or expensive. The corporate ethics committee could determine the framework within which designated levels of managers would participate on a semi-annual or quarterly basis. A coordinator of these sessions may be called for.

Coordinator and Participants. The coordinator should be versed in basic ethical theory and in the ethical values pertinent to daily business operations. It may be profitable to recruit this individual from outside the firm to avoid any conflict of interest and to gain a fresh viewpoint. Participants could be selected by the corporate ethics committee from middle and lower management, with emphasis on those who appear to be moving up the organizational ladder.

Procedure. A procedure for these training sessions is outlined below. First, participants could describe ethical dilemmas they have confronted in their jobs. Second these descriptions could be sent to the coordinator a few weeks before the group meets to allow time to evaluate them. Third, the group could meet for a roundtable discussion of the cases. The ethical values involved in these dilemmas, the ethical conflicts evident to the managers, and alternative actions could be discussed. Fourth, the session need not formulate specific solutions, but develop ethical guidelines for the managers to consider when confronted with similar issues.

Top management should follow up these sessions by requesting evaluations from participants, including recommendations for additions to or deletions from the corporate code of ethics.

Advantages. The advantages of the training module have already been mentioned, but to summarize: (1) An ethics module within the management development program could aid middle and lower management by reviewing the ethical content of the decisions they must make each day; (2) the module could assist managers in discovering new or better ways to deal with these decisions; (3) the module could benefit the corporate ethics committee by pointing out areas in the code that need review or revision; and (4) the module could further institutionalize ethics into the corporate decision-making structure.

Summary

The business climate appears ripe for the institutionalization of ethics into each corporation's decision-making process. This can be done through the three principal means described in this article: a code of ethics, an ethics committee, and ethics training within the firm's management development program. While these methods have widespread application, each corporation is unique and should adapt these methods to its environment and size. This endeavor is essential if a firm is to become a responsible citizen. The 1980s will require this characteristic.

Note
1.   Charles W. Battey, <u>Tempo</u>, a Touche Ross publication. 26. No. 2, 1980.

THE INSTITUTIONALIZATION OF UNETHICAL BEHAVIOR

LaRue T. Hosmer

During the spring and summer of 1985, there were several highly visible and, to those of us concerned with business ethics, highly disturbing disclosures of inappropriate managerial behavior in large companies. General Electric, a firm with a reputation for excellence and one inevitably included on lists of "best managed" companies, pleaded guilty to a charge of defrauding the government on a missile-warhead contract. The defense fraud conviction cost the company $2 million in criminal penalties. In a lesser known but equally disturbing case, General Electric was fined $100,000 and told to absorb $900,000 of overcharges in a civil suit involving a satellite contract.

E. F. Hutton, one of the largest and most respected of the retail brokerage firms, pleaded guilty to a check-overdraft scheme that allegedly defrauded approximately 400 small banks. The intentional overdrafts gave Hutton the interest-free use of up to $250 million, and is said to have cost the banks as much as $8 million. The company was fined $2.75 million, and ordered to make restitution to the banks.

General Electric and E. F. Hutton were the most publicized of the 1985 investigations into fraudulent practices, but they were not the only examples that could be found. It has even been alleged that G. E. and Hutton were selected for prosecution because they were well known, and well respected, and "G. E. was sacrificed in some sense," John Van Naanen of the Sloan School of Management at M.I.T. is quoted as saying in the Wall Street Journal. "You could have found the same thing at a dozen other companies."

From the Journal of Business Ethics (1987) 439–447. Reprinted by permission of Kluwer Academic Publishers. Copyright 1987 by D. Reidel Publishing Company. Notes omitted.

Which are those other companies? Many of them are
defense contractors. In June, Rep. John Dingle of
Michigan released a list of firms accused of defrauding
the government in military purchases. The list had been
provided by the Pentagon Inspector General, and included
McDonnell Douglas for cost mischarges, Rockwell
International for labor overcharges, General Dynamics for
improper billings and cost mischarges, Boeing for labor
overcharges and product substitutions, United
Technologies for gratuity payments, subcontractor
kickbacks, cost mischarges and defective pricing. There
is no need to detail all of the allegations. It is
sufficient to say that all ten of the largest defense
contractors faced federal criminal investigations during
the summer of 1985.

Why has this occurred? This is the interesting
issue, for those of us concerned with the ethics of
management, and there have been a number of explanations
of varying sophistication. Mr. Lester Crown, Executive
Vice President of General Dynamics, member of the Board
of Directors, and representative of the family that owns
roughly 22% of the common stock of that company, blamed
the situation in his company upon the ineffective
auditing procedures employed by the Department of
Defense.

General Dynamics had been accused of adding $63
million of improper overhead expenses, including country
club memberships and dog kennel fees, to defense
contracts during the period 1979 to 1982. In
explanation, Mr. Crown said, "All these things were put
in for reimbursement. The D.C.A.A. (Defense Contract
Administrative Auditor) looked at them, then the
contracting officer. They then knocked out certain
percentages. That is either a very efficient or a very
lazy way. You end up, with the passage of time, throwing
more and more in, because you know a certain percentage
of it comes out in the end."

Mr. Crown felt that the major error made by General
Dynamics was not pressing for improvements in the
auditing methods of the Pentagon. "Is it (the Pentagon
auditing procedure) a right way? No, I don't think so.
It should be more specific about individual charges.

Perhaps we should have had the foresight and ingenuity to say it should have been changed."

Mr. Crown also added the familiar excuse that senior executives were unaware of the problem. "You aren't talking about ethics. I don't think anyone in the corporate office knew how these things were being charged. It was done on a local basis. The thing got sloppy, but not with any thought at the top." Mr. Crown did not explain why the internal auditing procedures at General Dynamics, nor the external auditing required by law and performed by Arthur Anderson and Company, had not revealed the problem prior to the Congressional investigation.

Another explanation blamed the non-competitive nature of the weapons procurement process, and the "anything goes" attitude that seemed to permeate that process. The New York Times, in an editorial, stated:

> General Electric is a household word. It is the nation's largest maker of electrical appliances. Its management techniques are studied worldwide. Its automated factories are models of advanced design. Yet this week it pleaded guilty to defrauding the Air Force of $800,000 by forging workers' time cards on a contract for upgrading the Minuteman missiles.
>
> What made a superb company stoop to picking the public's pocket, and for so petty a gain?
>
> Seeking the causes of crime outside the criminal may not be fashionable, but it's somehow hard to envisage a group of G.E. managers deciding out of the blue that it was a good day to rob the Air Force. They surely operated in a culture of sleaze and borderline morality in which such behavior is deemed acceptable.
>
> That's not the culture of General Electric, but it's coming more and more to look like the pattern of acceptable behavior among certain defense contractors. Though G.E. is the nation's sixth-largest defense contractor,

21

military work counts for only 18 percent of its business.

Despite recent attempts at reform, the Pentagon has destroyed competition, preferring sole-source contracts in which officials are free to alter and gold-plate weapons regardless of cost. The same officials then go to work for the contractors they cosset. Through contractor lobbying, Congress is made a party to a system greased by vast sums of money, in which weapons are procured by favors and influence, not by open competition.

The New York Times did not explain how open competition could be made applicable to the design of complex weapon systems that require extreme technological capability for development, and extreme asset specificity for manufacture. The New York Times also did not explain how, in essence, exactly the same pattern of fraudulent exploitation appeared at E. F. Hutton, in the retail brokerage industry that has no connection to defense and no lack of competition.

E. F. Hutton was paired with General Electric in the introduction to this paper to illustrate the impartiality of managerial dishonesty. Defrauding of customers, workers, suppliers and the public seems to occur in both the military and civilian sectors of the economy. We do not know the extent of the fraudulent practices in the civilian sector, of course, for we do not have the benefit of Congressional and Department investigations --except in the unusual instance of E. F. Hutton--but let me cite some anecdotal evidence. All of us who teach managerial ethics at Schools of Business Administration are occasionally contacted by former students, troubled about particular practices that seem to be accepted as ordinary business routines within their companies. These contacts often seem to be inspired by current news stories. Here are summaries of three recent contacts, obviously prompted by the publicity given to E. F. Hutton:

1. A prior student, working in data processing and operations management at the dividend disbursement section of a

22

large bank, said that it was common practice not to respond to the first inquiry from a company stock-holder regarding non-receipt of a dividend payment. Individual investors, particularly older people, lose their checks, or they move between winter and summer homes, and the Post Office may not forward their checks. Non-response to the first inquiry permits the bank to have the use of the funds for 45 to 60 additional days, until a second inquiry is sent.

2. A prior student, working in the purchasing department of an automobile manufacturer, said that it was common practice to delay payments to small parts suppliers beyond the normal 30 day terms. Smaller suppliers have no effective way of complaining, beyond discontinuing the business relationship. It is interesting that the E. F. Hutton overdrafts were drawn on smaller banks, that again had no effective means of rectifying the situation.

3. A prior student, working as a commercial loan officer in a large bank, said that while it was not a common practice, the bank would arrange, as part of their normal cash management services, to have customer checks drawn on accounts at remote locations; this, of course, delayed the actual payment of the funds, and increased customer bank balances. This person also said that customer overdrafts on those accounts were "accepted" as a cost of business. "E. F. Hutton is only one of many companies that has discovered this cheap form of financing" was the statement made to me, in confidentiality.

These three practices are, perhaps, not illegal, but they do have an adverse impact upon stockholders, suppliers and creditors without their consent, and consequently

23

there is an ethical element. Why do they occur, apparently without examination or concern at the companies involved? We have looked at two explanations --lack of auditing and lack of competition--that seem not to be applicable in the present instances. Let us look at a third--benefits to the corporation, not to the individual--from the <u>Wall Street Journal</u> that will serve to introduce the major argument of this paper:

> But, rules and lectures are ineffective against an excess of loyalty to an employer. Unlike former LTV Corp. Chairman Paul Thayer or Tennessee banker Jake Butcher, both of whom recently drew prison sentences for illegally using their positions to enrich themselves, the G. E. managers who have violated laws did so to bolster the company's fortunes, not their own.

The argument that unethical behavior is a consequence of an "excess of loyalty to an employer" and a desire to further the employer's interests, not the individual's, even at the expense of stockholders, suppliers, employees and creditors, in my opinion totally misconstrues the position in which many, if not most, middle level managers are placed today. There are personal benefits to unethical behavior in middle management. These personal benefits come from very specific provisions in the organizational structure and managerial processes currently used by large firms. Let us look at these "structural" causes of unethical behavior.

Most large companies, today, are diversified. In a landmark research project on corporate strategy (the first to use large scale data to relate economic performance to corporate strategy and organizational structure), Richard Rumelt of U.C.L.A. found that by 1969, 93% of America's 1000 largest firms were diversified operating in more than one industry). Subsequent studies have shown that the 93% figure has increased. In the major finding of his work, Prof. Rumelt confirmed the earlier historical analysis of Alfred Chandler that a divisionalized structure followed a diversified strategy, and he demonstrated that this strategy-structure sequence was related to the improved economic performance of firms within his sample.

The divisionalized structure, of course, divides a company into a series of product divisions, each of which is responsible for the financial performance of a given product or product line. A divisionalized structure of this type, at the date of the Rumelt study, was generally decentralized: authority for product, market and process changes was allocated to the divisional management who were also held responsible for economic performance.

There are two major problems with the divisionalized, decentralized type of organizational structure. Firstly, interrelationships between the divisions--in products, markets, processes or technologies--cannot be utilized as the basis for economies of scale or economies of scope due to the separate nature of the divisions. For example, three divisions all using fractional horsepower motors in their product designs, or all using industrial wholesalers for their distribution channels, have no incentive in decentralized structure to combine their activities. And, corporate management in the decentralized structure had no control over the divisional strategies until after an outstanding success or absolute failure had occurred. Changes in the management of diversification were needed.

General Electric led in the development of new methods for the management of diversity. G. E., of course, is almost the archetype of a diversified firm, with numerous products, multiple markets and various processes, and in the 1970's it was organized in a decentralized structure, with approximately 250 product divisions grouped by industry type and evaluated by financial performance. Corporate executives, however, were concerned that despite substantial sales increases and continual technical developments, profits remained almost constant in absolute terms, and actually declined as a percentage of sales. The corporate-level executives were also dismayed by their inability to influence the strategy of the product division competing in the mainframe computer market, which eventually resulted in a write-off of nearly $300 million in developmental expenses and facility investments. It was felt that a new method of strategic planning was needed, to combine related divisions and to control divisional strategies.

The strategic planning method developed by General Electric was termed a portfolio model since it evaluated each product-market-process unit in the company as an investment that could be increased, maintained, or decreased over time, similar to the portfolio or assortment of investments in stocks and bonds held by a mutual fund. The product-market- process units at General Electric were termed "strategic business units," or "SBUs"; they consisted of related product divisions that had an ability to act independently in an industry with known competitors through a clearly defined strategy. Because each SBU combined related divisions, functional executives within an SBU could achieve economies of scale and economies of scope through cooperative actions. Because each SBU acted independently within an industry (that is, without the need for relying upon input materials or output sales from other sections of the company), senior executives within the firm could hold the managers and staff of an SBU solely responsible for short-term performance. Because each SBU was dependent upon the corporation for finance, senior executives could review and direct the long-term strategy of an SBU through resource allocation, using a corporate planning model rather than a capital budgeting process. The 250 decentralized product division at General Electric became 73 semi-centralized strategic business units.

The central concept of the semi-centralized corporate planning model developed by General Electric was that each strategic business unit differed on two basic dimensions: the attractiveness of the industry, and the strength of the company within that industry. It was felt that each strategic business unit could be measured on those two dimensions, and then compared. As a result of the comparison, corporate resources could be channeled to the divisions that combined industry attractiveness and company strengths because these were felt to be the divisions with the greatest probability of competitive success and increased profitability.

The attractiveness of the industry was measured on a multiple factor scale that included such inputs as the overall size of the market, annual growth, historical profitability, competitive intensity, etc. See Figure 1 for a listing of the factors, and an example of the measurement process. The factors were weighted (by percentage) and then the business unit was measured (on a comparative rather than absolute scale of 1 to 5) for each factor to obtain an approximate value that could be summarized, and used to evaluate the competitive posture of the SBU.

	Weight	Measurement	Value
Overall size	0.20	4.00	0.80
Annual growth	0.20	5.00	1.00
Historical margins	0.15	4.00	0.60
Competitive intensity	0.15	2.00	0.30
Technological requirements	0.15	3.00	0.45
Inflationary vulnerability	0.05	3.00	0.15
Energy requirements	0.05	2.00	0.10
Environmental impact	0.05	1.00	0.05
Social/political/legal	Must be acceptable		--
	1.00		3.45

	Weight	Measurement	Value
Market share	0.10	2.00	0.20
Share growth	0.15	4.00	0.60
Product quality	0.10	4.00	0.40
Brand reputation	0.10	5.00	0.50
Distribution network	0.05	3.00	0.15
Promotional effectiveness	0.05	2.00	0.10
Productive capacity	0.05	3.00	0.15
Productive efficiency	0.05	2.00	0.10
Unit costs	0.15	3.00	0.45
Material supplies	0.05	5.00	0.25
R&D performance	0.10	4.00	0.80
Managerial personnel	0.05	4.00	0.20
	1.00		3.90

| | Company within the industry | | |
	Above average	Average	Below average
Above Average	Invest	Invest	Retain
Average	Invest	Retain	Divest
Below Average	Retain	Divest	Divest

Fig. 1. Factors, weights and measures for the General Electric planning matrix.

The strength of the business unit within the industry was also measured on a multiple factor scale that included such elements as market share, share growth, product quality, brand reputation, etc. Again, these factors were weighted and the business unit measured along cardinal scales to obtain a summary figure.

Owing to the subjective nature of the weights that were applied to each of the factors, and to the inexact method of measurements along comparative rather than absolute scales, the summary figures for the attractiveness of the industry and the strength of the company within that industry were not used directly to evaluate each business unit. That is, a strategic business unit that measured 3.45 X 3.90, as in the example in Figure 1, was not automatically considered to be "better", or more likely to receive funding for further growth, than one that measured 3.35 X 3.80, or even 3.45 X 4.00. Instead, all strategic business units were grouped along each dimension, with one-third below average, and then they were visually displayed on a simple nine-cell matrix, again illustrated in Figure 1.

Business units that were above average on one of the dimensions of the General Electric planning model, and at least average on the other dimension, were considered to be optimal candidates for corporate investment, and accelerated growth. Business units that were below average on one of the dimensions, and no better than average on the other, were felt to be prime candidates for disinvestment, and eventual sale or liquidation. The balance of the business units were destined to be maintained at approximately the existing sales level and capital supply until either the industry's attractiveness or the company's strength within that industry changed, leading then to increased investment and growth, or to gradual devestment, and sale.

The planning model proposed by the Boston Consulting Group, though considerably better known due to "catchy" phrases and an active promotional campaign, is in reality an offshoot of the one developed by the General Electric Company. The B.C.G. model, shown in Figure 2, avoids the problems of subjective weighting and comparative measures by assuming that a single statistic can serve as the surrogate for industry attractiveness, and that another single statistic can serve as the surrogate for the divisional strengths within the industry.

```
20.0  -
            _____

17.5  -

            Stars, with high cash     Problems, with low cash
15.0  -     generation and high         generation but high
            investment needs            investment needs
12.5  -

10.0        _____

 7.5  -

      -

 5.0  -     Cows, with high cash      Dogs, with low cash
            generation but low          generation and low
 2.5  -     investment needs            investments

 0.0  -
            _____
               4.0       2.0       1.00      0.50      0.25
```

Fig. 2. Market share and market growth relationships for the Boston Consulting Group planning matrix.

The Boston Consulting Group believes that the growth rate of the market, in percentage terms, can be used as a summary figure for the attractiveness of the industry, since high growth rates tend to be associated with high growth margins and low competitive pressures. High growth rates generally occur in the early stages of the product life cycle, before intensive competition affects industry prices, margins and profits. The Boston Consulting Group also believes that the share of the market, again expressed in percentage terms, can be used as a summary figure for the competitive position of the company within the industry because high market share tends to be associated with low production and distribution costs. The relationship between high market share and low competitive cost in the B.C.G. model is felt to be partially the result of the economies of scale that bring a constant decrease in average unit costs with each increase in annual production volume, but it is thought primarily to be the result of the experience curve that brings a continual decrease in average unit costs with each doubling of the cumulative production volume. The relationship between market share and market growth is generally portrayed in the B.C.G. model on a 4-cell matrix, with the familiar "star," "cash cow", "problem child" and "dog" categories.

What do "star", "cash cow", "problem child" and "dog" categories, or for that matter "above average", "average" and "below average" rankings have to do with unethical managerial behavior? They are determinant, given the uses of the strategic planning models by senior management. Think for a minute of the possibility of your business unit being ranked below average on either industry attractiveness or company strength; what will happen to that unit? Lack of investment, and a "wait and see" attitude on the part of corporate management is the best you can expect; disinvestment, and eventual sale or dissolution, is the most likely outcome. What will happen if your business unit is positioned in the dog category? Your unit will be, if we continue to use the B.C.G. barnyard lexicon, "harvested", generally through sale of the unit or dissolution or the assets.

Is it propitious to a person's career to be "harvested"? There is little empirical data here, but there is substantial anecdotal evidence, all of which

31

seems to indicate that the sale or dissolution of a business unit often brings personal trauma as executive teams are broken up, and a very real chance of dismissal in the subsequent cost cutting efforts.

Is it possible to avoid the "below average" rankings or the "cash cow" and "dog" categories? Yes, simply by maintaining quarterly profits as a return on investment at a "satisfac-try" level. In the General Electric planning matrix, profitability has a direct influence on the measurement of industry attractiveness through the input factors of historical margins and competitive intensity, accounting for 30% of the weightings. Profitability has an indirect influence on the measurement of company strengths through the input factors of product quality, brand reputation, promotional effectiveness and production efficiency, accounting for 35% of the weightings. The influence on company strengths is indirect because high profits are felt to be an indication, not a direct measure, of high product quality, good brand recognition, etc.

In the B.C.G. planning matrix, high profits are assumed to be the result of high market share and high market growth. Consequently, the markets served by a given strategic business unit are further segmented and redefined until the profit, growth and share figures are consistent. This is not as unprofessional as it may seem; the need for consistency forces detailed examination of market segments and growth rates, and provides a better understanding of the competitive position of a firm. For example, Mercedes-Benz has a very small share of the most rapidly growing luxury automobile market both in the U.S. and worldwide.

Can the managers within a strategic business unit alter the recorded profit of that unit, and consequently the position of that unit on the planning matrix? Yes, it is all too easy over the short-term. In the non-competitive defense industry, it is possible to change labor charges from a fixed-price to a negotiated-price portion of the contract, as was done by General Electric. Or, it is possible to switch wages from indirect to direct labor so that higher overhead rates may be allocated, as was done at McDonnell Douglas. Or, it is possible to simply add more overhead items, as was done at General Dynamics.

In the competitive brokerage, automotive supply and commercial banking industries, it is possible to change the amount of capital employed by a strategic business unit. Most companies now charge for both working capital and fixed capital, and those charges constitute a major expense item. By reducing the amount of capital recorded against a business unit, it is possible to improve both the numerator and the denominator of the return on investment ratio. (ROI--profits/ capital employed) The branch offices at E. F. Hutton, the dividend disbursement unit of the bank, the assembly division of an automobile company and the customers of the cash management service all were reducing the amount of capital charged to their organizational units, and improving their return on investment ratios.

What can be done to prevent these practices? They may or may not be illegal, but the ones we have discussed in the competitive industries do harm the smaller banks, the small stockholders, the smaller suppliers. No office manager at E. F. Hutton attempted a deliberate overdraft against Citicorp, and I think it safe to assume that no dividend disbursement officer has ignored the first inquiry from Morgan Stanley or Goldman Sachs. Lastly, my informant from the automobile industry admits that large suppliers are paid promptly. The Pentagon, of course, is not small, but apparently many defense contractors felt that the weapons procurement process was too complex and cumbersome for effective control of labor and overhead billings, and so provided an opportunity for exploitation.

What can be done? General Electric Company has taken three publicized actions since the conviction. They have strengthened the policy manual to ensure that strict accounting procedures are followed in government contracts. They have appointed an ombudsman authorized to investigate any allegations of wrongdoing within the company. They have issued a series of statements stressing that unethical behavior will not be tolerated. The Chairman of General Electric, John Welch, spoke out clearly on "abuses of integrity" in a story from the <u>Wall</u> <u>Street Journal</u>:

> Lest anyone doubt the seriousness of G.E.'s intent, Mr. Welch issued a stern warning in a videotape being shown to employees. Pressure to meet corporate goals won't excuse misbehavior, he says, adding that such pressures are intensifying as G.E. battles competitors around the globe. He also urges employees to come forward with their suspicions of wrongdoing. 'Whistle blowing, speaking out, telling it like it is, is part of what we're after', he says. 'I can assure anybody who wants to talk aboutabuses of integrity in this company that they will be welcomed'.

Will these actions be effective? In the article from the <u>Wall Street Journal</u>, it was stated that, "Workers at the Philadelphia missile-warhead plant where the fraud occurred confirm that G.E. is tightening accounting procedures and checking time-card charges to prevent falsifications. But they stress that plant employees were fully aware of correct procedures long before the fraud occurred."

The appeal of "whistleblowers" may be no more effective than the tightening of accounting procedures. All of the managers within an SBU are affected by the rankings of their unit. Most of the managers probably were not aware of the exact methods used to improve those rankings at G.E. and E.F. Hutton, and few of the managers actually participated in those schemes, but most probably were grateful. An "us against them" attitude has developed in the strategic business units at most corporations--the operating people being pushed for performance improvements against the senior executives and corporate staff doing the pushing--and I assume that the loyalties of the business unit people are reasonably well established. Gratitude and loyalty are powerful forces to add to the normal reluctance to inform on others.

What is needed to eliminate the structural forces that push managers towards unethical decisions and actions? I have two suggestions. The first is to

34

emphasize analytical rather than strategic planning. Planning, control and motivation are related--see Figure 3. Divisional strategic planning

	Strategic planning (method of competition)	Environmental assumptions Organizational resources Managerial intentions Strategic alternatives
Planning system	Program planning (allocation of resources)	Net present value Internal rate of return Cost-benefit analysis Competitive position analysis
	Budgetary planning (projection of results)	Revenue forecasts Expense estimations Numerical measures Descriptive standards Cost accumulation systems
Control system	Operational accounting (recording of performance)	Cost allocation systems Responsibility centers Transfer prices and shared costs
	Comparative evaluation (analysis of variances)	Organizational control Program control Management control Operational control
Motivation system	Organizational response (design of incentives	Perceptual response Financial response Positional response Personal response
	Individual response (actions and decision)	Personal influence Interpersonal influence Social influence Cultural influence

Figure 3.   Relationship of planning, control and motivational systems in corporate management.

that is based upon an analysis of the competitive conditions of the industry, the specific strengths and weaknesses of the firm, and the anticipated trends in the economy can be translated into more accurate resource allocations in the program planning stage, and more realistic achievement targets in the budgetary planning process. Strategic planning that avoids the company, industry and economy appraisal in favor of establishing arbitrary financial goals, following the directives of the senior executives, can lead to inappropriate resource allocations, unachieveable performance standards, and the temptation to cheat. Listen to this statement that describes directive rather than analytical strategic planning from a very recent issue of Business Week:

> Then Begel (Thomas Begel, Chief Executive Officer of the Pullman Company, which has just acquired Peabody International, a manufacturer of road graders, dump trucks and other construction equipment) can start improving Peabody. He wants to reach 5% after taxes, matching Pullman's. He also wants a return on equity of over 15%--quite a change from the 2% Peabody posted in the first half of fiscal 1985. First, though, Begel intends to "take a hard look at everything" Peabody has. "If there are any losers in there, they're going to become winners, or they're going to be consigned to oblivion", predicts Prezelski (Frank Prezelski, financial analyst at Shearson Lehman Brothers, the analyst assigned to the Pullman Company, who presumably made this statement after meeting with senior executives).

What are the "losers" at Peabody going to do? They compete with low margin products in slow growth markets against well established firms, both domestic and foreign. In any portfolio planning model, they would find themselves in the "below average" ranking or "dog" category. There are few legitimate means of increasing the return on equity quickly, given that competitive position. There are, however, numerous means of raising the return on equity that may or may not be what Thomas Begel and Frank Prezelski expect, and what suppliers, banks, employees and customers consider to be "fair".

36

My other suggestion, and this is certainly related to the need for more analytical and less directive strategic planning, is to change the corporate management style. The corporate management style at many if not most large companies today is to push: to push for greater revenues, higher profits, larger returns. No one says "and we don't care how you get them", but was that statement not previously implied at General Electric and E. F. Hutton, and is that statement not now implied at Peabody International?

It is very instructive that the problems at General Electric have occurred under the current C.E.O., John Welch, not with the prior C.E.O., Reginald Jones. Mr. Welch led the 1984 listing in Fortune's "The Toughest Bosses in America". He is known, according to that article in Fortune, as "Neutron Jack", referring to the alleged capability of a neutron bomb to save the buildings but get rid of the people. Mr. Jones, on the other hand, leads the individuals described in the new book by Harry Levinson and Stuart Rosenthal, C.E.O.: Corporate Leadership in Action. Here are two personal quotations, one from each source (Welch, Jones) that are very indicative of the management style of each individual:

> The role for the mediocre is clearly short-lived.

> G.E. has a unique culture. It's a family. We enjoy each other. We don't lose many in the family of G.E. people. We're so supportive of each other we try desperately to save an individual who has failed, by placing him in a job that better matches his capacities, in order that the individual can make a contribution to the organization. We save many people. There is a renaissance of these people in many instances.

There is a need for a corporate management style that pulls people to meet future competitive conditions by defining a common objective rather than pushes them to meet current financial projections by installing a comparative planning system. This management style is

37

termed "leadership", and it sets the moral standards for the organization by focusing on the integrity of common purpose. Let me close with two quotations on leadership and morality that I truly like, from Philip Selznick and Chester Barnard:

> Leadership is more than the ability to mobilize personal support; it is more than the maintenance of equilibrium through routine solution of day-to-day problems. Leadership is the ability to define the ends of group existence, to design an enterprise distinctly adapted to those ends, and to see that the design becomes a reality.

> Leadership in organizations is the power of individuals to inspire cooperative personal decisions by creating faith in common understanding, faith in the probability of success, faith in the ultimate satisfaction of personal motives, faith in the integrity of common purpose. Leadership is the moral factor in organizations; it creates the moral code for the organization.

Both Philip Selznick and Chester Barnard are saying clearly--though Chester Barnard says this with characteristically greater precision and elegance--is that common objectives create the values of a firm. This is a lesson that appears to have been lost in the current methodology of strategic planning.

CHAPTER III

THE MODERN BUSINESS MANAGER

INTRODUCTION

As a business student, you have decided that you wish to create a life for yourself as a business person. This chapter is to help you consider what it is that business managers do and what sort of life you are choosing when you chose a life in business, and whether that is a worthwhile life.

Since the time of the Greek philosopher Plato there has been an image of a decision maker as one using reason to resolve social conflicts and uncertainty. This rational model of decision making has also been applied to the business manager. On this view, business persons have goals which they accomplish and their performance can be evaluated with relative precision in terms of how well they accomplish these goals.

What if the business world is not so certain? What if the problems of the modern business managers are so complex, with information so scarce that rational problem solving are virtually impossible? How are the activities of managers different under this view of decision making?

I wish to suggest the hypothesis that as businesses become larger rational answers based upon full information become less and less likely. The certainty that one seeks in making decisions is not to be found in reason but in the loyalty of the other business persons which one gathers around one. If a business person cannot be assured of the right answers based upon reasons that can persuade any rational persons, then at least there can be persons around him/her who will be persuaded by the reasons given, who share assumptions about the processes to arrive at answers. On this view the key virtue of business persons is not reason but loyalty.

What then do business persons do all day. On this second view, they seek to cement a consensus regarding resolutions to problems. They persuade, cajole; they bring together persons who have a stake in the problem to a mutually agreed-upon solution. Certainly some

39

persons will be superiors and some persons will be inferiors. But the command is less important than the forged consensus. Obedience is less a virtue than loyalty. This is the situation in which justice is doing good to one's friends and harm to one's enemies. This loyalty is one product of the socialization processes of any company.

Loyalty within the company, however, conflicts with competition within the company. What are the psychological consequences of both loyalty and competition? Are managers placed in an impossible dilemma? On the one hand, they need the loyalty of others to get some certainty to their decisions making. On the other hand, many of these persons are competitors for an increasingly fewer slots for promotion.

One should also consider the effect of the dual emphasis on management loyalty and competition on minority hiring and promotion. If, as a subsequent article argues, women think differently than men about ethical matters is it possible women will lack the shared assumptions around which male loyalty is built? And if manager performance is evaluated around such loyalties, then can women ever perform as well as men? To the protest - but she can do the job as well as he can, the response is the rhetorical question - but what is the job?

If there are special problems which minorities face in becoming involved in a business system of loyalty, what can a business do to assist minorities to succeed in business in face of such loyalty, to insure that the investments business and society have made in the education in all of its citizens payoff? For example, should a system of mentoring be created for all employees?

But the more basic question remains. Why should business do anything at all if this is a competitive society where productivity is so clearly measured that those who fail simply do not meet the objective mark? Should not each person be allowed to meet that mark based upon his or her own abilities?

Consideration of business as a society based upon

40

loyalty also has interesting ramifications for the issue of whistle blowing. How should an employee deal with information that a product with which she is working may be defective? The others in the team believe that the product is not defective or that the harms associated with the product are justified by the product's benefits. But what if you remain unconvinced. Should you blow the whistle on your team? Aren't you assuming that there is a rational solution to this problem that you possess and others do not? Is the problem made more complicated by the fact that other members of the team tell you that there is information regarding the justification of the product which is simply not available to you? Is the company justified in discharging you, regardless of whether you are right or wrong on the grounds that loyalty is an essential virtue which you have challenged?

The questions remain, what if there is at the time no rational way to resolve the question of the defective product? What if business decisions are made by a process which stresses loyalty; and persons with shared assumptions are trying to do the best they can under conditions of uncertainty. If mistakes result then are they a cover-up or does the loyalty process create a presumption of favoring accepted decision making which has been successful before? None of this is to suggest that defective products are not a horror and that cover-ups do not exist. Rather I want you to begin to look at the problems of business from the inside, where there may not be easy decisions.

Recently there has been a great deal of discussion regarding the Japanese emphasis on loyalty and socialization as opposed to individuality. Do you think that Japanese companies place more emphasis on loyalty than American companies do? What management practices offer any possibilities for the resolution of the conflict between individuality and socialization?

In conclusion in this Chapter I have tried to help you to think differently about business decision making, to think of business not as an arena where questions are answered but as an arena where loyalties need to be forged in order to reach consensus about what problems should even be addressed. How will you deal with these problems in your career?

41

QUESTIONS AND PROJECTS

1. Imagine that you are a manager of a large subsidiary in the United States which is owned by a Japanese parent company. Describe how you would deal with the contradictions described in the Japanese management article. To what extent do you believe these contradictions would not exist in an American work place?

2. What are the virtues of the modern business manager? How might the complex of virtues necessary for success in business contribute to ethical dilemmas for modern managers?

3. Do you believe that the Japanese contradictions exist in your personal life? How do you resolve them? How do you expect to resolve them when you begin to work?

ORGANIZATIONAL SOCIALIZATION AND
THE PROFESSION OF MANAGEMENT

Edgar H. Schein

I can define my topic of concern best by reviewing very
briefly the kinds of issues upon which I have focused my
research over the last several years.   In one way or
another I have been trying to understand what happens to
an individual when he enters and accepts membership in
an organization.   My interest was originally kindled by
studies of the civilian and military prisoners of the
Communists during the Korean War.   I thought I could
discern parallels between the kind of indoctrination to
which these prisoners were subjected, and some of the
indoctrination which goes on in American corporations
when college and business school graduates first go to
work for them.   My research efforts came to be devoted
to learning what sorts of attitudes and values students
had when they left school, and what happened to these
attitudes and values in the first few years of work.   To
this end I followed several panels of graduates of the
Sloan School into their early careers.

When these studies were well under way, it suddenly
became quite apparent to me that if I wanted to study the
impact of an organization on the attitudes and values of
its members, I might as well start closer to home.   We
have a school through which we put some 200 men per
year--undergraduates, regular master's students, Sloan
Fellows, and Senior Executives.   Studies of our own
students and faculty revealed that not only did the
student groups differ from each other in various attitude
areas, but that they also differed from the faculty.

For example, if one takes a scale built up of items which deal with the relations of government and business, one finds that the Senior Executives in our program are consistently against any form of government intervention, the Sloans are not as extreme, the master's students are roughly in the middle, and the faculty are in favor of such intervention. A similar line-up of attitudes can be found with respect to labor-management relations, and with respect to cynicism about how one gets ahead in industry. In case you did not guess, the Senior Executives are least cynical and the faculty are most cynical.

We also found that student attitudes change in many areas during school, and that they change away from business attitudes toward the faculty position. However, a recent study of Sloan Fellows, conducted after their graduation, indicated that most of the changes toward the faculty had reversed themselves to a considerable degree within one year, a finding which is not unfamiliar to us in studies of training programs of all sorts.

The different positions of different groups at different stages of their managerial career and the observed changes during school clearly indicate that attitudes and values change several times during the managerial career. It is the process which brings about these changes which I would like to focus on today--a process which the sociologists would call "occupational socialization," but which I would prefer to call "organizational socialization" in order to keep our focus clearly on the setting in which the process occurs.

Organizational socialization is the process of "learning the ropes," the process of being indoctrinated and trained, the process of being taught what is important in an organization or some subunit thereof. This process occurs in school. It occurs again, and perhaps most dramatically, when the graduate enters an organization on his first job. It occurs again when he switches within the organization from one department to another, or from one rank level to another. It occurs all over again if he leaves one organization and enters another. And it occurs again when he goes back to school, and again when he returns to the organization after school.

Indeed, the process is so ubiquitous and we go through it so often during our total career, that it is all too easy to overlook it. Yet it is a process which can make or break a career, and which can make or break organizational systems of manpower planning. The speed and effectiveness of socialization determine employee loyalty, commitment, productivity, and turnover. The basic stability and effectiveness of organizations therefore depends upon their ability to socialize new members.

Let us see whether we can bring the process of socialization to life by describing how it occurs. I hope to show you the power of this process, particularly as it occurs within industrial organizations. Having done this, I would like to explore a major dilemma which I see at the interface between organizations and graduate management schools. Schools socialize their students toward a concept of a profession, organizations socialize their new members to be effective members. Do the two processes of socialization supplement each other or conflict? If they conflict, what can we do about it in organizations and in the schools?

Some Basic Elements of Organizational Socialization

The term socialization has a fairly clear meaning in sociology, but it has been a difficult one to assimilate in the behavioral sciences and in management. To many of my colleagues it implies unnecessary jargon, and to many of my business acquaintances it implies the teaching of socialism--a kiss of death for the concept right there. Yet the concept is most useful because it focuses clearly on the interaction between a stable social system and the new members who enter it. The concept refers to the process by which a new member learns the value system, the norms, and the required behavior patterns of the society, organization, or group which he is entering. It does not include all learning. It includes only the learning of those values, norms, and behavior patterns which, from the organization's point of view or group's point of view, it is necessary for any new member to learn. This learning is defined as the price of membership.

45

What are such values, norms, and behavior patterns all about? Usually they involve:

- The basic goals of the organization.
- The preferred means by which these goals should be attained.
- The basic responsibilities of the member in the role which is being granted to him by the organization.
- The behavior patterns which are required for effective performance in the role.
- A set of rules or principles which pertain to the maintenance of the identity and integrity of the organization.

The new member must learn not to drive Chevrolets if he is working for Ford, not to criticize the organization in public, not to wear the wrong kind of clothes or be seen in the wrong kinds of places. If the organization is a school, beyond learning the content of what is taught, the student must accept the value of education, he must try to learn without cheating, he must accept the authority of the faculty and behave appropriately to the student role. He must not be rude in the classroom or openly disrespectful to the professor.

By what processes does the novice learn the required values and norms? The answer to this question depends in part upon the degree of prior socialization. If the novice has correctly anticipated the norms of the organization he is joining, the socialization process merely involves a reaffirmation of these norms through various communication channels, the personal example of key people in the organization, and direct instructions from supervisors, trainers, and informal coaches.

If, however, the novice comes to the organization with values and behavior patterns which are in varying degrees out of line with those expected by the organization, then the socialization process first involves a destructive or unfreezing phase. This phase serves the function of detaching the person from his former values, of proving to him that his present self is worthless from the point of view of the organization and that he must redefine himself in terms of the new roles which he is to be granted.

The extremes of this process can be seen in initiation rites for novitiates for religious orders. When the novice enters his training period, his old self is symbolically destroyed by loss of clothing, name, often his hair, titles and other self-defining equipment. These are replaced with uniforms, new names and titles, and other self-defining equipment consonant with the new role he is being trained for.

It may be comforting to think of activities like this as being characteristic only of primitive tribes or total institutions like military basic training camps, academies, and religious orders. But even a little examination of areas closer to home will reveal the same processes both in our graduate schools and in the business organizations to which our graduates go.

Perhaps the commonest version of the process in school is the imposition of a tight schedule, of an impossibly heavy reading program, and of the assignment of problems which are likely to be too difficult for the student to solve. Whether these techniques are deliberate or not, they serve effectively to remind the student that he is not as smart or capable as he may have thought he was, and therefore, that there are still things to be learned. As our Sloan Fellows tell us every year, the first summer in the program pretty well destroys many aspects of their self-image. Homework in statistics appears to enjoy a unique status comparable to having one's head shaved and clothes burned.

Studies of medical schools and our own observations of the Sloan program suggest that the work overload on students leads to the development of a peer culture, a kind of banding together of the students as a defense against the threatening faculty and as a problem-solving device to develop norms of what and how to study. If the group solutions which are developed support the organizational norms, the peer group becomes an effective instrument of socialization. However, from the school's point of view, there is the risk that peer group norms will set up countersocializing forces and sow the seeds of sabotage, rebellion, or revolution. The positive

47

gains of a supportive peer group generally make it worthwhile to run the risks of rebellion, however, which usually motivates the organization to encourage or actually to facilitate peer group formation.

Many of our Sloan Fellow alumni tell us that one of the most powerful features of the Sloan program is the fact that a group of some forty men share the same fate of being put through a very tough educational regimen. The peer group ties formed during the year have proven to be one of the most durable end results of the educational program and, of course, are one of the key supports to the maintaining of some of the values and attitudes learned in school. The power of this kind of socializing force can be appreciated best by pondering a further statement which many alumni have made. They stated that prior to the program they identified themselves primarily with their company. Following the program they identified themselves primarily with the other Sloan Fellows, and such identification has lasted, as far as we can tell, for the rest of their careers.

Let me next illustrate the industrial counterpart of these processes. Many of my panel members, when interviewed about the first six months in their new jobs, told stories of what we finally labeled as "upending experiences." Upending experiences are deliberately planned or accidentally created circumstances which dramatically and unequivocally upset or disconfirm some of the major assumptions which the new man holds about himself, his company, or his job.

One class of such experience is to receive assignments which are so easy or so trivial that they carry the clear message that the new man is not worthy of being given anything important to do. Another class of such experiences is at the other extreme--assignments which are so difficult that failure is a certainty, thus proving unequivocally to the new man that he may not be as smart as he thought he was. Giving work which is clearly for practice only, asking for reports which are then unread or not acted upon, protracted periods of training during which the person observes work, all have the same upending effect.

The most vivid example came from an engineering company where a supervisor had a conscious and deliberate strategy for dealing with what he considered to be unwarranted arrogance on the part of engineers whom they hired. He asked each new man to examine and diagnose a particular complex circuit, which happened to violate a number of textbook principles but actually worked very well. The new man would usually announce with confidence, even after an invitation to double-check, that the circuit could not possibly work. At this point the manager would demonstrate the circuit, tell the new man that they had been selling it for several years without customer complaint, and demand that the new man figure out why it did work. None of the men so far tested were able to do it, but all of them were thoroughly chastened and came to the manager anxious to learn where their knowledge was inadequate and needed supplementing. According to this manager, it was much easier from this point on to establish a good give-and-take relationship.

It should be noted that the success of such socializing techniques depends upon two factors which are not always under the control of the organization. The first factor is the initial motivation of the entrant to join the organization. If his motivation is high, as in the case of a fraternity pledge, he will tolerate all kinds of uncomfortable socialization experiences, even to extremes of hell week. If his motivation for membership is low, he may well decide to leave the organization rather than tolerate uncomfortable initiation rites. If he leaves, the socialization process has obviously failed.

The second factor is the degree to which the organization can hold the new member captive during the period of socialization. His motivation is obviously one element here, but one finds organizations using other forces as well. In the case of basic training there are legal forces to remain. In the case of many schools one must pay one's tuition in advance, in other words, invest one's self materially so that leaving the system becomes expensive. In the case of religious orders, one must make strong initial psychological commitments in the form of vows and the severing of relationships outside the religious order. The situation is defined as one in

49

which one will lose face or be humiliated if one leaves the organization.

In the case of business organizations, the pressures are more subtle but nevertheless identifiable. New members are encouraged to get financially committed by joining pension plans, stock option plans, and/or house purchasing plans which would mean material loss if the person decided to leave. Even more subtle is the reminder by the boss that it takes a year or so to learn any new business; therefore, if you leave, you will have to start all over again. Why not suffer it out with the hope that things will look more rosy once the initiation period is over?

Several of my panel members told me at the end of one year at work that they were quite dissatisfied, but were not sure they should leave because they had invested a year of learning in that company. Usually their boss encouraged them to think about staying. Whether or not such pressures will work depends, of course, on the labor market and other factors not under the control of the organization.

Let me summarize thus far. Organizations socialize their new members by creating a series of events which serve the function of undoing old values so that the person will be prepared to learn the new values. This process of undoing or unfreezing is often unpleasant and therefore requires either strong motivation to endure it or strong organizational forces to make the person endure it. The formation of a peer group of novices is often a solution to the problem of defense against the powerful organization, and, at the same time, can strongly enhance the socialization process if peer group norms support organizational norms.

Let us look next at the positive side of the socialization process. Given some readiness to learn, how does the novice acquire his new learning? The answer is that he acquires it from multiple sources--the official literature of the organization; the example set by key models in the organization; the instructions given to him directly by his trainer, coach, or boss; the example of peers who have been in the organization longer and thus serve as big brothers; the rewards and

50

punishments which result from his own efforts at problem solving and experimenting with new values and new behavior.

The instructions and guidelines given by senior members of the organization are probably one of the most potent sources. I can illustrate this point best by recalling several incidents from my own socialization into the Sloan School back in 1956. I came here at the invitation of Doug McGregor from a research job. I had no prior teaching experience or knowledge of organizational or managerial matters. Contrary to my expectations, I was told by Doug that knowledge of organizational psychology and management was not important, but that some interest in learning about these matters was.

The first socializing incident occurred in an initial interview with Elting Morison, who was then on our faculty. He said in a completely blunt manner that if I knew what I wanted to do and could go ahead on my own, the Sloan School would be a great place to be. If I wasn't sure and would look to others for guidance, not to bother to come.

The second incident occurred in a conversation with our then Dean, Penn Brooks, a few weeks before the opening of the semester. We were discussing what and how I might teach. Penn said to me that he basically wanted each of his faculty members to find his own approach to management education. I could do whatever I wanted--so long as I did not imitate our sister school up the river. Case discussion leaders need not apply, was the clear message.

The third incident (you see I was a slow learner) occurred a few days later when I was planning my subject in social psychology for our master's students. I was quite nervous about it and unsure of how to decide what to include in the subject. I went to Doug and innocently asked him to lend me outlines of previous versions of the subject, which had been taught by Alex Bavelas, or at least to give me some advice on what to include and exclude. Doug was very nice and very patient, but also quite firm in his refusal to give me either outlines or advice. He thought there was really no need to rely on history, and expressed confidence that I could probably make up my own mind. I suffered that term but learned a good deal about the value system of the Sloan School, as well as how to organize a subject. I was, in fact, so well socialized by these early experiences that nowadays no one can get me to coordinate anything with anybody else.

Similar kinds of lessons can be learned during the course of training programs, in orientation sessions, and through company literature. But the more subtle kinds of values which the organization holds, which indeed may not even be well understood by the senior people, are often communicated through peers operating as helpful big brothers. They can communicate the subtleties of how the boss wants things done, how higher management feels about things, the kinds of things which are considered heroic in the organization, the kinds of things which are taboo.

Of course, sometimes the values of the immediate group into which a new person is hired are partially out of line with the value system of the organization as a whole. If this is the case, the new person will learn the immediate group's values much more quickly than those of the total organization, often to the chagrin of the higher levels of management. This is best exemplified at the level of hourly workers where fellow employees will have much more socializing power than the boss.

An interesting managerial example of this conflict was provided by one recent graduate who was hired into a group whose purpose was to develop cost reduction systems for a large manufacturing operation. His colleagues on the job, however, showed him how to pad his expense account whenever they traveled together. The end result of this kind of conflict was to accept neither the cost reduction values of the company nor the cost inflation values of the peer group. The man left the company in disgust to start up some businesses of his own.

One of the important functions of organizational socialization is to build commitment and loyalty to the organization. How is this accomplished? One mechanism is to invest much greater effort and time in the new member and thereby build up expectations of being repaid by loyalty, hard work, and rapid learning. Another mechanism is to get the new member to make a series of small behavioral commitments which can only be justified by him through the acceptance and incorporation of company values. He then becomes his own agent of socialization. Both mechanisms involve the subtle manipulation of guilt.

To illustrate the first mechanism, one of our graduates went to a public relations firm which made it clear to him that he had sufficient knowledge and skill to advance, but that his values and attitudes would have to be evaluated for a couple of years before he would be fully accepted. During the first several months he was frequently invited to join high-ranking members of the organization at their luncheon meetings in order to learn more about how they thought about things. He was so flattered by the amount of time they spent with him that he worked extra hard to learn their values and became highly committed to the organization. He said that he would have felt guilty at the thought of not learning or of leaving the company. Sending people to expensive training programs, giving them extra perquisites, indeed the whole philosophy of paternalism, is built on the assumption that if you invest in the employee he will repay the company with loyalty and hard work. He would feel guilty if he did not.

The second mechanism, that of getting behavioral commitments, was most beautifully illustrated in Communist techniques of coercive persuasion. The Communists made tremendous efforts to elicit a public confession from a prisoner. One of the key functions of such a public confession, even if the prisoner knew he was making a false confession, was that it committed him publicly. Once he made this commitment, he found himself under strong internal and external pressure to justify why he had confessed. For many people it proved easier to justify the confession by coming to believe in their own crimes than to have to face the fact that they were too weak to withstand the captor's pressure.

In organizations, a similar effect can be achieved by promoting a rebellious person into a position of responsibility. The same values which the new member may have criticized and jeered at from his position at the

53

bottom of the hierarchy suddenly look different when he has subordinates of his own whose commitment he must obtain.

Many of my panel members had very strong moral and ethical standards when they first went to work, and these stood up quite well during their first year at work even in the face of less ethical practices by their peers and superiors. But they reported with considerable shock that some of the practices they had condemned in their bosses were quickly adopted by them once they had themselves been promoted and faced the pressures of the new position. As one man put it very poignantly, "My ethical standards changed so gradually over the first five years of work that I hardly noticed it, but it was a great shock to suddenly realize what my feelings had been five years ago and how much they had changed."

Another version of obtaining commitment is to gain the new member's acceptance of very general ideals like "one must work for the good of the company," or "one must meet the competition." Whenever any counter-organizational behavior occurs one can then point out that the ideal is being violated. The engineer who does not come to work on time is reminded that his behavior indicates lack of concern for the good of the company. The employee who wears the wrong kind of clothes, lives in the wrong neighborhood, or associates with the wrong people can be reminded that he is hurting the company image.

One of my panel members on a product research assignment discovered that an additive which was approved by the Food and Drug Administration might in fact be harmful to consumers. He was strongly encouraged to forget about it. His boss told him that it was the F.D.A.'s problem. If the company worried about things like that it might force prices up and thus make it tough to meet the competition.

Many of the upending experiences which new members of organizations endure are justified to them by the unarguable ideal that they should learn how the company really works before expecting a position of real responsibility. Once the new man accepts this ideal it serves to justify all kinds of training and quantities of menial work which others who have been around longer are unwilling to do themselves. This practice is known as "learning the business from the ground up," or "I had to do it when I first joined the company, now it's someone else's turn." There are clear elements of hazing involved not too different from those associated with fraternity initiations and other rites of passage.

The final mechanism to be noted in a socialization process is the transition to full-fledged member. The purpose of such transitional events is to help the new member incorporate his new values, attitudes, and norms into his identity so that they become part of him, not merely something to which he pays lip service. Initiation rites which involve severe tests of the novice serve to prove to him that he is capable of fulfilling the new role--that he now is a man, no longer merely a boy.

Organizations usually signal this transition by giving the new man some important responsibility or a position of power which, if mishandled or misused, could genuinely hurt the organization. With this transition often come titles, symbols of status, extra rights or prerogatives, sharing of confidential information or other things which in one way or another indicate that the new member has earned the trust of the organization. Although such events may not always be visible to the outside observer, they are felt strongly by the new member. He knows when he has finally "been accepted" and feels it when he becomes "identified with the company."

So much for examples of the process of socialization. Let us now look at some of the dilemmas and conflicts which arise within it.

Failures of Socialization:
Nonconformity and Overconformity

Most organizations attach differing amounts of importance to different norms and values. Some are pivotal. Any member of a business organization who does not believe in the value of getting a job done will not survive long. Other pivotal values in most business organizations might be belief in a reasonable profit, belief in the free enterprise system and competition,

55

belief in a hierarchy of authority as a good way to get things done, and so on.

Other values or norms are what may be called relevant. These are norms which are not absolutely necessary to accept as the price of membership, but which are considered desirable and good to accept. Many of these norms pertain to standards of dress and decorum, not being publicly disloyal to the company, living in the right neighborhood, and belonging to the right political party and clubs. In some organizations some of these norms may be pivotal. Organizations vary in this regard. You all know the stereotype of IBM as a company that requires the wearing of white shirts and hats. In some parts of IBM such values are indeed pivotal; in other parts, they are only relevant, and in some parts they are quite peripheral. The point is that not all norms to which the new member is exposed are equally important for the organization.

The socialization process operates across the whole range of norms, but the amount of reward and punishment for compliance or noncompliance will vary with the importance of the norm. This variation allows the new member some degrees of freedom in terms of how far to conform and allows the organization some degrees of freedom in how much conformity to demand. The new man can accept none of the values, but carefully remain independent on all those areas not seen as pivotal, or he can accept the whole range of values and norms. He can tune in so completely on what he sees to be the way others are handling themselves that he becomes a carbon-copy and sometimes a caricature of them.

These basic responses to socialization can be labeled as follows:

- Type 1: Rebellion
  Rejection of all values and norms.
- Type 2: Creative individualism
  Acceptance only of pivotal values and norms; rejection of all others.
- Type 3: Conformity
  Acceptance of all values and norms.

Most analyses of conformity deal only with the type 1 and 3 cases, failing to note that both can be viewed as socialization failures. The rebellious individual either is expelled from the organization or turns his energies toward defeating its goals. The conforming individual curbs his creativity and thereby moves the organization toward a sterile form of bureaucracy. The trick for most organizations is to create the type 2 response--acceptance of pivotal values and norms, but rejection of all others, a response which I would like to call "creative individualism."

To remain creatively individualistic in an organization is particularly difficult because of the constant resocialization pressures which come with promotion or lateral transfer. Every time the employee learns part of the value system of the particular group to which he is assigned, he may be laying the groundwork for conflict when he is transferred. The engineer has difficulty accepting the values of the sales department, the staff man has difficulty accepting the high pressure ways of the production department, and the line manager has difficulties accepting the service and helping ethic of a staff group. With each transfer, the forces are great toward either conforming or rebelling. It is difficult to keep focused on what is pivotal and retain one's basic individualism.

Professional Socialization and Organizational Socialization

The issue of how to maintain individualism in the face of organizational socialization pressures brings us to the final and most problematical area of concern. In the traditional professions like medicine, law, and teaching, individualism is supported by a set of professional attitudes which serve to immunize the person against some of the forces of the organization. The questions now to be considered are (1) Is management a profession?, (2) If so, do professional attitudes develop in managers?, and (3) If so, do these support or conflict with organizational norms and values?

Professionalism can be defined by a number of characteristics:

57

- Professional decisions are made by means of general principles, theories, or propositions which are independent of the particular case under consideration. For management this would mean that there are certain principles of how to handle people, money, information, etc., independent of any particular company. The fact that we can and do teach general subjects in these areas would support management's claim as a profession.

- Professional decisions imply knowledge in a specific area in which the person is expert, not a generalized body of wisdom. The professional is an expert only in his profession not an expert at everything. He has no license to be a "wise man." Does management fit by this criterion? I will let you decide.

- The professional's relations with his clients are objective and independent of particular sentiments about them. The doctor or lawyer makes his decisions independently of his liking or disliking of his patients or clients. On this criterion we have a real difficulty since, in the first place, it is very difficult to specify an appropriate single client for a manager, and, in the second place, it is not at all clear that decisions can or should be made independently of sentiments. What is objectively best for the stockholder may conflict with what is best for the enterprise, which, in turn, may conflict with what is best for the consumer.

- A professional achieves his status by accomplishment, not by inherent qualities such as birth order, his relationship to people in power, his race, religion, or color. Industry is increasingly moving toward an acceptance of this principle for managerial selection, but in practice the process of organizational socialization may undermine it by rewarding the conformist and rejecting the individualist whose professional orientation may make him look disloyal to the organization.

- A professional's decisions are assumed to be on behalf of the client and to be independent of self-interest. Clearly this principle is at best equivocal in manager-customer relations, though again one senses that industry is moving closer to accepting the idea.

- The professional typically relates to a voluntary association of fellow professionals and accepts only the authority of these colleagues as a sanction on his own behavior. The manager is least like the professional in this regard, in that he is expected to accept a principle of hierarchical authority. The dilemma is best illustrated by the previous example which I gave our Sloan Fellows alumni who, after the program, related themselves more to other Sloans than to their company hierarchy. By this criterion they had become truly professionalized.

- A professional has sometimes been called someone who knows better what is good for his client than the client. The professional's expertness puts the client into a very vulnerable position. This vulnerability has necessitated the development of strong professional codes and ethics which serve to protect the client. Such codes are enforced through the colleague peer group. One sees relatively few attempts to develop codes of ethics for managers or systems of enforcement.

On several bases, then, management is a profession, but on several others it is clearly not yet a profession.

This long description of what is a profession was motivated by the need to make a very crucial point. I believe that management education, particularly in a graduate school like the Sloan School, is increasingly attempting to train professionals, and in this process is socializing the students to a set of professional values which are, in fact, in severe and direct conflict with typical organizational values.

For example, I see us teaching general principles in the behavioral sciences, economics, and quantitative methods. Our applied subjects like marketing, operations management, and finance are also taught as bodies of knowledge governed by general principles which are applicable to a wide variety of situations. Our students are given very broad concepts which apply to the corporation as a whole and are taught to see the relationship between the corporation, the community, and the society. They are taught to value the long-range health and survival of economic institutions, not the short-range profit of a particular company. They come to appreciate the necessary interrelationships between government, labor, and management rather than to define these as mutually warring camps. They are taught to look at organizations from the perspective of high-ranking management, to solve the basic problems of the enterprise rather than the day-to-day practical problems of staff or line management. Finally, they are taught an ethic of pure rationality and emotional neutrality--analyze the problem and make the decisions independently of feelings about people, the product, the company, or the community. All of these are essentially professional values.

Organizations value many of the same things, in principle. But what is valued in principle by the higher-ranking and senior people in the organization often is neither supported by their own behavior, nor even valued lower down in the organization. In fact, the value system which the graduates encounter on their first job is in many respects diametrically opposed to the professional values taught in school. The graduate is immediately expected to develop loyalty and concern for a particular company with all of its particular idiosyncrasies. He is expected to recognize the limitation of his general knowledge and to develop the sort of ad hoc wisdom which the school has taught him to avoid. He is expected to look to his boss for evaluation rather than to some group of colleagues outside the company.

Whereas the professional training tells him that knowledge is power, the graduate now must learn that knowledge by itself is nothing. It is the ability to sell knowledge to other people which is power. Only by being able to sell an application of knowledge to a highly specific, local situation, can the graduate obtain respect for what he knows. Where his education has taught the graduate principles of how to manage others and to take the corporate point of view, his

60

organizational socialization tries to teach him how to be a good subordinate, how to be influenced, and how to sell ideas from a position of low power.

On the one hand, the organization via its recruiters and senior people tells the graduate that it is counting on him to bring fresh points of view and new techniques to bear on its problems. On the other hand, the man's first boss and peers try to socialize him into their traditional mold.

A man is hired to introduce linear programming into a production department, but once he is there he is told to lay off because if he succeeds he will make the old supervisors and engineers look bad. Another man is hired for his financial analysis skills but is not permitted access to data worth analyzing because the company does not trust him to keep them confidential. A third man is hired into a large group responsible for developing cost reduction programs in a large defense industry, and is told to ignore the fact that the group is overstaffed, inefficient, and willing to pad its expense accounts. A fourth man, hired for his energy and capability, put it this way as an explanation of why he quit to go into private consulting: "They were quite pleased with work that required only two hours per day; I wasn't."

In my panel of 1962 graduates, 73 percent have already left their first job and many are on their third or fourth. In the class of 1963, the percentage is 67, and in the class of 1964 the percentage is 50. Apparently, most of our graduates are unwilling to be socialized into organizations whose values are incompatible with the ones we teach. Yet these organizations are precisely the ones who may need creative individualists most.

What seems to happen in the early stages of the managerial career is either a kind of postponement of professional socialization while organizational socialization takes precedence, or a rebelling by the graduate against organizational socialization. The young man who submits must first learn to be a good apprentice, a good staff man, a good junior analyst, and perhaps a good low-level administrator. He must prove his loyalty to the company by accepting this career path with good

61

graces, before he is trusted enough to be given a position of power. If he has not lost his education by then, he can begin to apply some general principles when he achieves such a position of power.

The businessman wants the school to provide both the professional education and the humility which would make organizational socialization smoother. He is not aware that teaching management concepts of the future precludes justifying the practices of today. Some professional schools clearly do set out to train for the needs of the profession as it is designed for today. The Sloan School appears to me to reject this concept. Instead we have a faculty which is looking at the professional manager of five, ten, or twenty years from now, and is training its graduates in management techniques which we believe are coming in the future.

Symptomatic of this approach is the fact that in many of our subjects we are highly critical of the management practices of today, and highly committed to reeducating those managers like Sloan Fellows and Senior Executives who come back to study at MIT. We get across in a dozen different ways the belief that most organizations of today are obsolete, conservative, constipated, and ignorant of their own problems. Furthermore, I believe that this point of view is what society and the business community demands of a good professional school.

It would be no solution to abandon our own vision of the manager of the future, and I doubt that those of you in the audience from business and industry would really want us to do this. What you probably want is to have your cake and eat it too--you want us to teach our students the management concepts of tomorrow, and you want us to teach them how to put these concepts into deep freeze while they learn the business of today. Then when they have proven themselves worthy of advancement and have achieved a position of some influence, they should magically resurrect their education and put it to work.

Unfortunately, socialization processes are usually too powerful to permit that solution. If you succeed in socializing your young graduates to your organizations, you will probably also succeed in proving to them that

62

their education was pretty worthless and might as well be put on a permanent rather than temporary shelf. We have research evidence that many well-educated graduates do learn to be complacent and to play the organizational game. It is not at all clear whether they later ever resurrect their educational arsenal.

What Is to Be Done About This Situation?

I think we need to accept, at the outset, the reality of organizational socialization phenomena. As my colleague, Leo Moore, so aptly put it, organizations like to put their fingerprints on people, and they have every right to do so. By the same token, graduate schools of business have a right and an obligation to pursue professional socialization to the best of their ability. We must find a way to ameliorate the conflicts at the interface, without, however, concluding that either schools or organizations are to blame and should stop what they are doing.

The schools, our school in particular, can do several concrete things which would help the situation. First, we can insert into our total curriculum more apprenticeship experience which would bring the realities of organizational life home to the student earlier. But such apprenticeship experiences will not become educational unless we combine them with a second idea, that of providing a practicum on how to change organizations. Such a practicum should draw on each of the course specialities and should be specifically designed to teach a student how to translate his professional knowledge into viable action programs at whatever level of the organization he is working.

Ten years ago we would not have known how to do this. Today there is no excuse for not doing it. Whether the field is operations research, sophisticated quantitative marketing, industrial dynamics, organizational psychology or whatever, we must give our students experience in trying to implement their new ideas, and we must teach them how to make the implementation effective. In effect, we must teach our students to become change-agents, whatever their disciplinary speciality turns out to be. We must teach

63

them how to influence their organizations from low positions of power without sacrificing their professional values in the process. We must teach them how to remain creative individualists in the face of strong organizational socialization pressures.

Combined with these two things, we need to do a third thing. We need to become more involved in the student's efforts at career planning and we need to coordinate our activities more closely with the company recruiters and the university placement officers. At the present I suspect that most of our faculty is quite indifferent to the student's struggles to find the right kind of job. I suspect that this indifference leaves the door wide open to faulty selection on the part of the student, which can only lead, in the end, to an undermining of the education into which we pour so much effort. We need to work harder to insure that our graduates get jobs in which they can further the values and methods we inculcate.

Companies can do at least two things. First, they can make a genuine effort to become aware of and understand their own organizational socialization practices. I fear very few higher-level executives know what is going on at the bottom of their organization, where all the high-priced talent they call for is actually employed. At the same time, I suspect that it is their own value system which ultimately determines the socialization activities which occur throughout all segments of the organization. Greater awareness and understanding of these practices should make possible more rational choices as to which practices to encourage and which to de-emphasize. The focus should be on pivotal values only, not on peripheral or irrelevant ones.

Second, companies must come to appreciate the delicate problems which exist both for the graduate and for his first boss in the early years of the career when socialization pressures are at the maximum. If more companies appreciated the nature of this dilemma they would recognize the necessity of giving some training to the men who will be the first bosses of the graduates.

I have argued for such training for many years, but still find that most company effort goes into training the graduate rather than his boss. Yet it is the boss who really has the power to create the climate which will lead to rebellion, conformity, or creative individualism. If the companies care whether their new hires use one or the other of these adaptation strategies, they had better start looking at the behavior of the first boss and training him for what the company wants and hopes for. Too many bosses concentrate on teaching too many peripheral values and thus undermine the possibilities for creative individualism and organization improvement.

The essence of management is to understand the forces acting in a situation and to gain control over them. It is high time that some of our managerial knowledge and skill be focused on those forces in the organizational environment which derive from the fact that organizations are social systems that socialize their new members. If we do not learn to analyze and control the forces of organizational socialization, we are abdicating one of our primary managerial responsibilities. Let us not shrink away from a little bit of social engineering and management in this most important area of the human side of the enterprise.

Retrospective Commentary

My article on organizational socialization and the profession of management was written just over twenty years ago, after a decade or so of studying how individuals and organizations come to terms with each other. As I think back to the motivation for writing he paper, some paradoxes and ironies surface.

My original motivation to study this problem stemmed from the discovery that it was possible for organizations to "coercively persuade" their new members to quite an extraordinary degree. Sales and management training programs operating in the 1950's were proudly touted as "indoctrina-tion"; company loyalty was seen as a central value, and learning the corporate point of view was considered an absolute necessity.

I noted in the article that our educational programs in schools of management often taught individualized professional values that could and would run counter to many values taken for granted in business. When I faced senior executives in the classroom, I was often taken to task for either failing to teach our young MBA students the proper "realities" of life in business, or for actually instilling values of autonomy and individualism that were viewed as counterproductive. From the point of view of executives, our job in the university was to teach future leaders how to adjust and conform to business values and practices.

However, in the late 1950's there was a strong reaction in the form of David Riesman's The Lonely Crowd, William Whyte's The Organization Man, Sloan Wilson's The Man in the Gray Flannel Suit, and many other books that indicted corporate indoctrination as stultifying and dangerous. Managers, they argued, would simply clone themselves and stifle all creativity.

In response to this reaction, or perhaps out of some sense of guilt, companies adopted a new line. Indoctrination centers became education centers, IBM tried to collect all of its songbooks in an apparent effort to deny that it had ever advocated group singing as part of its corporate socialization, and companies generally started to worry more about retaining creative talent than about brainwashing such talent into loyal submissiveness. Management schools could now publicly claim to be producing the innovative manager of the future, rather than the clone of today; if this produced too high a rate of turnover, one could always claim that this was the price of creativity and innovation.

Then came the shocking confrontation with Asian companies in the late 1970's and early 1980's. We "discovered," to our seeming horror, that the Japanese, Koreans, and Taiwanese could out-engineer and out-produce us with companies that emphasized indoctrination, company spirit, slogans, group calisthenics, lifetime employment, loyalty, individual subordination to the team, and all the things we had vigorously condemned in the 1950's and 1960's.

"Corporate culture" was not only found to be a useful concept for understanding what went on in organizations, but managers discovered or were told by management gurus that "strong" corporate cultures supported by appropriate socialization practices would lead to much better performance. Suddenly we scholars and consultants found ourselves being asked how companies could create these magical strong cultures; this trend led to a rash of quick-and-dirty culture diagnostic instruments and workshops that would help companies "fix" their cultures. Heavy socialization and indoctrination (though we haven't dared call it that yet) were back in style.

We seem to have come full circle. Is it really better to have strong, stable organizations populated by loyal conformists who believe totally in the company and will work their hearts out for it? Or is it better to have organizations that make it very easy for people to enter and leave, that value diversity and dissent, and whose socialization practices emphasize individual contribution and innovation? (In a sense, these organizations have very weak cultures because the group is not stable enough to form a strong culture.) And better for whom--the company or the individual? Is it better for society to have an effective company that stifles individuality or a company that enhances individuality even though it is less effective? Can we imagine integrative solutions whereby what is best for the company is also best for the individual?

What I have learned from observing these goings-on for several decades is that you get what you pay for--but that most organizations don't know what they are buying. Organizational leaders must learn to first ask themselves what they want, and then what they are willing to pay for it.

From the company's point of view, if you are in an industry in which product and process innovation are strategically critical, you had better avoid a socialization process that creates strong conformity. If you don't, you will get very good at what you are doing, but you will set up strong forces that undermine the person with new ideas. Instead you should emphasize diversity and easy entry into and exit from your organization. Paradoxically, the only thing in the culture that <u>must</u> perpetuate itself is the assumption that change is a good thing--that people are creative and capable of change.

If you are in a more stable situation because technology is not changing rapidly or your market does not want much diversity, than a socialization process that indoctrinates new company members, that builds loyalty and pride in the company, and that perpetuates the things that have worked in the past should build an effective organization.

Paradoxically, both kinds of cultures can be thought of as "strong." Yet they differ dramatically in the underlying assumptions they make about the nature of the world, how important change and innovation are, how creative individuals are, and how much value should be placed on past history. What I have learned from watching this cycle is that there is no right or wrong in organizational socialization independent of a company's particular circumstances.

So long as we have a pluralistic society that itself values some degree of diversity, more individuals may be better able to operate in industries that thrive on innovation. Organizations that are more conformist may have a hard time finding people willing to make the necessary psychological contract. So the larger cultural context also affects the feasibility of maintaining a certain kind of corporate culture.

What this says to me is that it's time we learned to substitute insight for judgment. We should stop comparing ourselves with other societies and companies whose circumstances may be totally different from our own, and instead figure out what we need and are good at in this particular time in our own history.

CONFUCIAN ETHICS AMD JAPANESE
MANAGEMENT PRACTICES

Marc J. Dollinger

There seems to be little doubt that the management practices of Japanese corporations will have, and are having, an important impact on management thinking and practice in the United States and the rest of the world. In the academic arena, papers are being published and research programs launched to determine the nature and efficacy of the phenomenon.   A major portion of the curricula development effort in "International Business" is directed toward the study of, and contact with, Japanese firm and trading company.   Japanese firms and the Japanese government have established academic centers within the university environment to help foster cooperative projects and mutual understanding.

Questions have naturally arisen concerning the adoption of Japanese ways and whether or not non-Japanese firms can successfully implement techniques which have been proved in another culture (e.g., Tsurumi, 1978; Buckley and Mirza, 1985; Dillon, 1983; Sethi _et al_., 1984).   The debate over the issues of convergence and divergence places the question in an academic framework and the evidence is thoroughly mixed (Dunphy, 1987).   It is unclear from both theoretical development and empirical findings whether or not the Japanese (and therefore other East Asian economies) are becoming more like the West or vice versa.

Even though references to culture as a factor in the convergence debate are ubiquitous, a gap exists in our understanding of the ethics of Japanese culture.   Most

Westerners, including business academics, have had little or no exposure to original source materials (in translation). There has been considerable reliance on secondary sources for interpretations and representations of the cultural phenomena. For example, Ouchi (1981) offers a set of managerial prescriptions and concludes that both East and West are converging on a Z form of organization which is not dependent on Japanese culture for its existence. Abegglen and Stalk (1985) briefly summarize the theory that Japanese managerial and industrial practices are embedded in the culture, and then discount the theory's influence. Hamada (1985) rejects Theory Z and attempts to build a model of the corporation which integrates corporate practices, Japanese culture and the economic environment. Jaeger and Baliga (1985) attribute the effectiveness of control systems in Japanese organizations to the shared values and culture. All of these authors, and others (see Dunphy, 1987, for a voluminous review), offer their interpretation of the culture of Japan and their enactment of it. Since most Western readers have no direct experience of Japanese ethics and society, its philosophical and historical roots, the reader is forced to accept reconstructions of Japanese culture rather than the logic-in-use (Kaplan, 1964).

The purposes of this paper are twofold. One design is to offer original material from one of the major sources of Japanese ethical tradition, the Analects of Confucius, and illustrate its contributions in the context of Japanese managerial and industrial practices. The Analects are regarded as the most reliable source of Confucius' writings. In the Analects, Confucius set the tone and introduced the major themes of Chinese philosophy. The most important of these themes is humanism. Confucius wrote of the importance of the individual, the character of human nature and the value of developing oneself through learning. He wrote of the perfectability of human beings and the need for constant renovation of the spirit in order to achieve that perfection.

The second purpose is to offer the hypothesis that much of the contradictory results obtained in researching the convergence-divergence question can be explained by the contradictory nature of Japanese tradition. This

70

approach may be termed an exercise in hermeneutics. Hermeneutical method relies on textual interpretation and emphasizes the historical dimension of research. The researcher interprets first level-constructs found in the text material and translates these into symbolic representations (Steffy and Grimes, 1986). Hermeneutical exegesis is one of a number of methodologies that fall into the general classification of subjective, qualitative research, emphasizing a idiographic perspective (Morey and Luthans, 1984).

Japan is a complex society combining Buddhism, Shintoism and Confucianism with the artifacts of modernization. The contributions of Confucian thought are directed at the ethical aspects of human interaction, leading some to call Japan a Confucian society (Adler et al., 1986; MacFarquhar, 1980). Japanese Confucianism has at its core four distinct, though not mutually exclusive (or consistent) themes. First, in its most essential form, Confucianism is a humanistic philosophy and the human being is regarded with dignity and respect. Second, Confucianism inculcates the values of harmony with its concurrent emphasis on loyalty group and family identification, and the submergence of the individual. Righteousness and the acts of righteous individuals within the framework of loyalty provide a third dimension. Lastly, there is the integrating theme of the morally superior person, the Chun-Tzu, who leads by example and is devoted to the other Confucian values. It is through the Chun-Tzu that the ethical system comes alive and is actuated. The Chun-Tzu is the leader of the Confucian society.

Before the beginning, a note of caution is offered. The purposes here are not to subsume all managerial phenomena under a cultural imperative model. Culture is not the only determinant of managerial behavior. Models which posit culture as the single cause of managerial behavior and practice have been critiqued by Kagono et al. (1985) and these are seen as insufficient to explain all Japanese business phenomena. Indeed the empirical question of whether or not Confucian societies differ more among themselves than with the West has not been settled. There is no suggestion that societies cannot change in some ways while maintaining underlying traditions. This is in fact exactly the Japanese

71

experience, reflected in one of Japan's most famous slogans of the modernization era, "Eastern ethics, Western science" (toyo no do toku, seiyo no gei). However, although causality cannot be proved, two of the three criteria of causality are present; covariance and time precedence (Selltiz et al., 1976). Only the elimination of alternative explanations, e.g., materialism, is missing.

Confucianism in Japan

Confucius was born in 551 or 552 B.C. in the state of Lu in modern Shantung. His career was devoted almost exclusively to teaching and education. He gathered around him a group of scholars as he made his way, serving in minor administrative posts. At the age of 56, finding that his superiors were unwilling to adopt his teachings as policy, he began a 13 year journey pushing for social reforms. He returned to Lu at the age of sixty-eight and for the next five years he wrote and taught. Among the writings thought to be produced during this period are the Analects. He died at age 73 (see Chan, 1963, for a good historical accounting).

Confucianism spread out from China throughout Asia in spite of the fact that Confucianism had no missionaries. The bearers of the message of Confucius were Buddhist monks, who while proselytizing for Buddha, carried the day-to-day values of Confucius with them. Since Confucianism is not native to Japan, having been imported from China, in order to understand the divergent route that Japanese Confucianism has taken, it is necessary to trace the history of Confucian thought in Japan.

The course of Confucian philosophy has changed many times since Confucius wrote and lived. A detailed historical perspective of Confucianism is beyond the scope of this paper. However, due to the influence of Chu Hsi (1130-1200) the philosophy of Confucius was re-established as the fundamental philosophy of Chinese civilization. Chu Hsi's Neo-Confucianism remains a pervasive influence throughout East Asia and has shaped behavior there for hundreds of years (Chan, 1986). It was among Chu Hsi's accomplishments to select the four books that became known as the Classics: the Analects, the Book of Mencius, the Great Learning and the Doctrine of the Mean. These four Classics preserved Confucian thought intact down through to the twentieth century. The Classics and Chu Hsi's commentaries on them were adopted in 1313 as the official texts for the civil service examinations and remained so, unchanged until 1905.

The earliest record of Confucianism in Japan occurs somewhere between the 6th and 7th centuries A.D. (de Bary, 1958). The more important wave of Confucian influence arrived in Japan in the sixteenth century with Zen Buddhist monks. This Confucianism, the Sung Neo-Confucianism of Chu Hsi, was quickly adopted by the early Tokugawa rulers (1600-1868) to help them justify and solidify their reign. The Shogun was the military and political ruler of Japan under Tokugawa rule. Confucianism provided the focus for precisely the problem that the Shogun faced: the creation and maintenance of a stable political and social order on the basis of a firm ethical code (Reischauer and Fairbank, 1960). Conversely, Confucian scholars used the peace and unity created by the Tokugawa's military government as an opportunity to rid themselves of the clerical dominance of Chinese-style mandarins and to unite Confucian thinking with statism.

The Tokugawa Confucianists had a different thrust than the Manchu Chinese although the orthodoxy was, in principle, the same. Jansen (1965) sees the Japanese Confucianist of the time as a forerunner of administrative innovation and experiment. The political organization of the decentralized daimyo (the local clan chief) provided many opportunities for heterodoxy and allowed Confuciansim to interact with local political conditions. (The Manchu thrust was on administrative control of a large central state).

Thus there began a mutual dependency between the state as represented by the Tokugawa Shogunate, the baku-han system (the decentralized political-military network) and the Neo-Confucianists. Much of the Chu Hsi orthodoxy was adopted intact; the natural hierarchy of classes (elite and samurai, farmer, artisan, merchant), the four themes described previously, and the shedding of Buddhist and Taoist philosophical tenets (Hall, 1970).

Basic education in Japan was Chinese Confucian by the
mid-1700's; its purpose was to develop the individual's
moral character both as an absolute human duty and in
order to better fulfill the samurai's function (Dore,
1965).

> In the Japanese setting, Confucian teachings
> served to reinforce values of duty,
> self-discipline, loyalty and achievement--in
> honor to one's name and gratitude and respect
> to one's superiors. . . (Jansen, 1965, p. 96).

Later on in Tokugawa rule, during the late 17th and
early 18th centuries, some distinctly Japanese elements
of Confucianism began to emerge. These Japanese elements
helped to tighten the bonds between the philosophy and
the secular needs of the ruling elite. Two of the more
important aspects of this new heterodoxy were the
development of bushido (the code of ethics and behavior
for the samurai) and the increasing respectability of
commercial activities (Hall, 1970). These two
developments were not unrelated. As a means of
regulating society and controlling the social order, each
class of people was given its own Tao (do), or code of
behavior. The samurai's code was the bushido, the
warrior's way. The merchant's code was chonindo, the
merchant's way. There could be righteousness, humanity
and principle for each class in a Confucian scheme, and
each class could perform its duties according to the
ethical principles of its do without shame.

The elements of bushido were devotion to duty,
cultivation of the martial arts, austerity, temperance,
self-discipline and the readiness to die immediately for
their superiors. The chonin, or merchants, attempted to
imitate the more highly esteemed samurai. Their code
demanded loyalty (to the trading house or firm),
frugality (re-investment of profits, renovation of
equipment and machines) as well as harmony and
righteousness. In fact, the class barriers that
prevented wealthy merchants from changing their status
made them even richer by forcing them to reinvest their
wealth in commercial activities (Reischauer and Fairbank,
1960). Over time class lines began to blur, but were
never completely eliminated. Warriors, deeply in debt
to merchants, commonly had their debts cancelled by the

merchants in exchange for higher status (Borton, 1970). And even though original Confucian thought denigrated money and profit, it was possible for a 17th century Confucian, Moro Kyuso to write,

> To rejoice when one makes a profitable transaction or buys valuable merchandise cheaply is part of a merchant's trade, but it is unpardonable in a samurai . . . (de Bary, 1958, p. 430).

By the 19th century, it was possible to argue from the very Confucian manner of historical reflection that human society rested on the twin pillars of labor and the exchange of merchandise. De Bary quotes Kaiho Seiyo,

> . . . it is a ridiculous thing that the aristocracy and the military class in Japan should disdain profit, or that they should say that they disdain profit. When a man does not disdain profit, he is called a bad person. Such is the perverse practice of the times . . . Rice is li (principle), gold is li, li is the commodity . . . buying, selling and paying interest are all part of li . . . the Law of the Universe . . . (de Bary, 1958, p. 491).

In 1868 the Tokugawa rule of over 150 years came to an end with the restoration of the Emperor Meiji. This was essentially a peaceful revolution designed to begin Japan on the rode to modernization. The lessons drawn from the Chinese experience in the Opium Wars (1842) and the Perry Expedition of 1854 demonstrated to the Japanese that change was needed to preserve their nation's independence. At the time of the Meiji Restoration there were a number of exceptional individuals (like Iwasaki of Mitsubishi) who straddled samurai and merchant traditions and helped lead Japan through this revolutionary time. There even emerged a group of peasant entrepreneurs who possessed capital, skill and technology necessary to form large business organizations (Fairbank et al., 1965). The guiding philosophy of the Restoration, epitomized by Sakuma Shozan's slogan "Eastern ethics, Western science" (Passin, 1965), was characterized by an easy blend of Confucianism, which taught the perfectability of society through the proper ethical/political organization and leadership (Fairbank et al., 1965). Many Japanese recognized that their Confucianism was on the fringe of Chinese Confucianism, however it was clear that this Confucian philosophy contributed to the development of a strong sense of nationalism, and promoted education and ambition as fundamental values in the general population (Jansen, 1965a).

The modernization brought on by the Meiji Restoration and the opening of Japan succeeded in creating a strong military and economic state, capable of resisting Western pressures. However much of the culture of Confucian Japan persisted. Although social classes were formally abolished, strong class distinctions remained. The Confucian concept of superior/ inferior was ingrained. By 1890, as a part of the Meiji Constitution, the Imperial Rescript of Education made Confucian education mandatory and universal (Borton, 1970).

In the late 20th century, Confucianism as a philosophy was been [sic] weakened by emerging patterns of individuation (Maruyama, 1965) but as a moral and ethical code it is still dominant.

Japanese management practices

The survival from feudal times of a sense of personal relationship between employer and employee in industry [is] paralleled by a strong sense of personal or corporate loyalty within management itself (Reischauer and Fairbank, 1960, p. 511).

There is no single homogeneous set of managerial behaviors that can safely be labeled as "Japanese." Within Japan there is a good deal of variance in managerial practice, especially between the larger trading company/financial center firm and the smaller firms. Variation surely exists within these two groups as well. Additionally, as Ouchi (1981) observes, there are a number of American firms that appear to use similar practices (labeled Theory Z) and therefore these managerial behaviors may be deemed accultural. Another interpretation however is that the practices are pan-cultural; that is, there are multiple cultures and ethical systems capable of producing very similar management practices (equifinality). However, a great deal has been written about Japanese management and many authors agree on its major components (Pascale, 1978; Tsurumi, 1978; Munchus, 1983; Nonaka and Johansson, 1985; Kagono et al., 1985).

Keys and Miller (1984) review and attempt to integrate what they refer to as the "Japanese management theory jungle." Their review encompasses Japanese manufacturing practices, human resource policies, and decision-making modes. Through a subjective review of the literature, they reduce a myriad of observable managerial practices to three underlying factors: long run planning horizon, a commitment to lifetime employment, and the Japanese sense of collective responsibility. All three underlying factors have bases in Confucian thought.

The practices which underline the first factor in their integration, the long run planning horizon, include: a commitment to sufficient time to manage, diligence in implementation, discipline in work, and the development and the articulation of an organizational philosophy. These are all consistent with the Confucian goal of the search for perfection and the development of a righteous character.

It is in the fullfilment of these obligations that the Chun-Tzu is expected to make his contribution. Writing on these subjects (all quotes from Chan, 1963),

> Confucius said, 'A ruler who governs his state by virtue is like the north polar star, which remains in place while the others revolve around it.'

> Confucius said, 'Lead the people with governmental measures and regulate then by law and punishment, and they will avoid wrong-doing but have no sense of honor or shame. Lead them by virtue and regulate them by the rules of propriety and they will have a sense of shame, and moreover, set themselves right.'

Confucius said, 'The superior man brings the good things of others to completion and does not bring the bad things of others to completion. The inferior man does just the opposite.'

These three Analects help describe what could be characterized as the "preferred leadership style" in Confucian society. Leaders are constant, steady, and this behavior provides guidance for subordinates. Leaders must act with magnanimity, compassion, vision and wisdom (Sethi et al., 1984). Also, the Confucian leader does not resort to rules and laws to lead, but instead trusts that the shared virtue of propriety will enable the people to accomplish their tasks. The one exception to this in Chinese history was the Legalist School of the Ch'in dynasty (221-206 B.C.) which rejected Confucian doctrine in favor of a legalistic society based upon power. The Legalists succeeded in unifying China but their violence and brutality lead to their overthrow (Chan, 1963). Even now in Japan, there is a decided preference for shared values over legalisms.

Following are four additional Analects commenting on the character of the Chun-Tzu:

Confucius said, 'The superior man does not seek fulfillment of his appetite nor comfort in his lodging. He is diligent in his duties and careful in his speech. He associates with men of moral principles and thereby realizes himself. Such a person may be said to love learning.'

Confucius said, 'The superior man thinks of virtue; the inferior man thinks of possessions. . . .'

Confucius said, 'The superior man wants to be slow in word but diligent in action.'

Confucius was completely free from four things: He had no arbitrariness of opinion, no dogmatism, no obstinacy and no egotism.

The tasks of achieving perfection cannot be accomplished overnight, require a patient attention to detail and encourage Japanese workers to "pursue the last grain of rice in the corner of their lunch box" (Hayes, 1981). The Confucian ideal of renovation and renewal enables the Japanese to renew each day the commitment to the long term goals of the organization, and a search for perfection without the pressure for immediate results. From the book, the Great Learning (Chan, 1963) comes this description:

> The inscription on the bath tub of King T'ang read, 'If you can renovate yourself one day, then you can do so everyday, and keep doing so everyday, and keep doing so day after day.

and

> Confucius said, 'Is it not a pleasure to learn and to repeat or practice from time to time what has been learned?'. . .

> Confucius said, 'A man who reviews the old so as to find out the new is qualified to teach others.'

The second underlying factor identified by Keys and Miller (1984) was the commitment, albeit by a minority of firms, to lifetime employment. This factor manifested itself by high levels of investment in employee development, training and socialization, reduced turnover, non-specialized career paths and the development of internal labor markets. The Confucian emphasis on the family, which has been redirected to the firm, and the groupism that dominates the Confucian ethos serve as a foundation for these practices. Abegglen and Stalk (1985), who also identify career employment as one of the signature characteristics of Japanese corporation, note that new recruits are selected for the general characteristics of their character, as opposed to their skills. The characteristics that are valued are, of course, the Confucian ones of loyalty, diligence, and the submergence of individual
needs. Writing on these subjects, Confucius said,

> . . . The superior man is not an implement.

79

This saying expresses the fundamental view that people are good, they have inherent value, they exist as total organisms, not to be treated as tools.

Originally, the Confucian ethic of group was most often applied to relationships in the family and to government. These are traditionally lifetime relationships. In Japan, the group concept was extended first to the clan, around which agriculture was organized and then, in the industrial era, to the firm.

> Yu Tzu [a student of Confucius] said, 'Few of those who are filial and respectful brothers will show disrespect to superiors, and there has never been a man who is not disrespectful to superiors, yet creates disorder. A superior man is devoted to the fundamentals (roots). When the root is firmly established, the moral law (Tao) will grow. Filial piety and brotherly respect are the root of humanity (jen).'

> Confucius said, '[A good man] does not worry about being known by others but rather worries about not knowing them.'

On loyalty:

> Tseng-Tsu [a student] said, 'Everyday I examine myself on three points; whether in counseling others I have not been loyal; whether in intercourse with my friends I have not been faithful; and whether I have not repeated again and again and practiced the instructions of my teacher.'

When Japanese are offered lifetime employment, they are expected to stay as well. Job hopping is not a positive value in Japan (Browning, 1986). The leaders of the kaisha speak of entry into the company as "being born again into another family" (Abegglen and Stalk, 1985, p. 200).

The third factor that emerges from the Keys and Miller study (1984) is that of collective responsibility. This value and its practice may trace its roots to the necessities of rice cultivation which requires the whole village to cooperate at planting and harvest time. (Since rice cultivation pre-dates Confucianism, a materialist explanation is a plausible alternative.)

This collectivism finds its values in the group centered nature of Confucian thought. Such practices as consensus decision-making (ringi), participative management (nemawashi), and quality circles all use the group as the basis for action. Concomitant with the group values are the personal values that are required to make the group work. Ouchi (1981) describes these in his Theory Z as: trust, subtlety, intimacy and loyalty. These are all components of the current worker's bushido.

Meng I Tzu asked about filial piety. Confucius said, 'Never disobey . . . '

. . . Confucius said, 'A ruler should employ his ministers according to the principles of propriety, and ministers should serve their ruler with loyalty.'

. . . Hold loyalty and faithfulness to be fundamental. Have no friends who are not as good as yourself. When you make mistakes, don't be afraid to correct them.

Meng Wu-po asked about filial piety. Confucius said, 'Especially be anxious lest parents should be sick.'

The quotations above reflect the character of Confucian loyalty, and it is readily apparent that if the dicta are expanded from family to firm, this is a powerful tool of social control (Abegglen and Stalk, 1986). It requires the submergence of the individual to achieve perfection. Self-promotion is more than egotism, it is disloyal and immoral.

Confucius said, 'A man with clever words and an ingratiating appearance is seldom a man of humanity.'

Ethical contradictions in Japanese management

In addition to the positive values and practices detailed above, negative and contradictory aspects of the Confucian tradition have been noted. Contradictions can be classified into two types; internal contradictions of Confucian thought and contractions between Confucian ethics and the realities of modern democratic capitalism. Each of these types helps to explain the disparate results obtained by researchers investigating the convergence/divergence issue.

Internal contradictions

The core themes of humanity and harmony produce major stress for the modern Japanese. The importance of the human being is emphasized throughout, yet for the sake of harmony individuals are to submerge desires and needs. In the West, there is a bias which values the individual above the need for harmony. In the East the bias is generally reversed (Maruyama, 1965). The Japanese have consciously attempted to avoid Westernization as they achieved modernization through "Western science, Eastern ethics". For example, when the Japanese ruling elite after the Meiji Restoration went searching for a constitution on which to model their new one, they chose the German model of Bismarck because it played down individual freedoms. This made it more attractive to the Confucian ethic. However, once the country was opened it was inevitable that Western elements and ideas would seep into the Japanese consciousness.

Another source of internal conflict in the Confucian value system is the need for rigid hierarchy and the full development of humanity (jen). Clearly, the hierarchical barriers prevent each person from reaching full potential. The integration of Confucianism with the Taoist concept of the Way helps alleviate some of the stress by enabling people, within their strata, to develop fully while never leaving that level. However there remains in Japan great resistance to an egalitarian ethic that would allow full personal rights for all. For example, Japanese of Korean ancestry are discriminated against and kept segregated from Japanese of native ancestry, and women are discriminated against in almost all forms of economic life. Irish (1986) describes an experience he had while working in a Japanese firm, in which he is reprimanded for showing sympathy with a woman manager who has been passed over for promotion many times and is treated as the lowest ranking member of the group, even though she is senior to a number of the men. As Confucius said (Chan, 1963),

> . . . Women and servants are most difficult to deal with. If you are familiar with them, they will cease to be humble. If you keep them at a distance they will resent it.

A third internal contradiction concerns the emergence of the superior person as leader. From where is this individual to come from? If individuality is to be suppressed, and self-promotion abhorred how will the superior person be known? The difference between a true Chun-Tzu standing calmly amidst confusion and chaos while his trusty subordinates accomplish superior things, and a do-nothing, know-nothing over-promoted senior official who silently stands by while better educated juniors solve problems can be very difficult to determine by unobtrusive observation. Confucius himself faced a similar problem. As a virtuous but minor administrator he was unable, within his own lifetime, to exert any leadership other than among his disciples.

External contradictions

Confucian ethics and teachings occasionally clash with the realities of the modern and complex business world. For example, the emphasis on renovation and the values of ritualizing behavior seem inconsistent with the need for change and innovation. The Japanese mitigate this contradiction by focusing their rituals on interpersonal behavior and concentrating their efforts in technological innovation.

Similarly, the Confucian distaste for profit and the corresponding suspicion of ill-gotten gain have been reconciled as well. Japanese companies prefer to emphasize growth and their contributions to the national polity instead of profit. And while all are aware that profits are necessary for future investment, they are made to appear a by-product of virtuous behavior. This puts enormous pressure on Japanese executives to be both pure and productive at the same time. When profits are obtained in inferior ways, by inferior people, the consequences for those individuals are severe.

> Confucius said, 'Wealth and honor are what every man desires. But if they have been obtained in violation of moral principles (li), they must not be kept. . .'

> Confucius said, 'If one's acts are motivated by profit, he will have many enemies..'

> Confucius said, 'The superior man understands righteousness, the inferior man understands profit.'

A legitimate question would be, "If Confucius disdained wealth, how do Confucian societies maintain capitalism?" This is not unlike the question Weber asked and answered in his critique of the Chinese mandarin system (Weber, 1951). His point was to show that Protestantism was conducive and supportive of capitalism while Confucianism was not. The answer for Japan is different from the one Weber construed for China. Japanese Confucianism developed differently and the merchant was encouraged to follow his Way (Tao), and the seek perfection in commercial transactions. For example, according to the Mitsui house laws, the chonin (merchants), were inferior to the samurai, yet within the chonin's world, he was master (Hall, 1970).

Chief executive resignations at Kikkoman, Japan Airlines, and most recently Toshiba are significant because the executives surrender authority but no responsibility for corporate mistakes (Passin, cited in the Wall Street Journal, 7/10/1987, p. 19).

> Within Japanese corporate culture and social ethics, the whole notion is that the leader can delegate the authority to anyone he or she wishes, but not the responsibility. In the U.S. (leaders) delegate authority and

responsibility (Yoshi Tsurumi, cited in the <u>Wall Street Journal</u>, 7/10/1987, p. 19).

The potential for unreconciled inconsistency exists between human perfectability, endless renovation and the economic realities of failed policies. What does failure mean to a Japanese Confucian? Failure to a Confucian is shame and dishonor, and is not immediately grasped in economic terms. The executive resignations above were not as an immediate consequence of economic failure. The Kikkoman incident was over tainted wine, the JAL incident over a crash which killed 500 people, the Toshiba scandal concerned selling top-secret American technology to the Soviets. While each case has secondary financial repercussions, the primary cause of the resignations was the reality of imperfectability.

> Confucius said, 'The superior man seeks [room for improvement or occasion to blame] in himself; the inferior man seeks it in others.

The Japanese's dedication to hierarchical systems, following the Confucian model, and to extreme loyalty within the hierarchy, can be seen as dysfunctional. Bresler (1986) blames Japan's group-centered, hierarchical social mores for interfering with the free play of market forces. He claims that loyalty to a firm or a family of related firms is more important than price and quality in many purchasing decisions. He also claims that the special emphasis that Japanese culture places on long term relationships and social harmony results in massive distribution inefficiencies. Layers of middlemen and small stores are protected from the development of more efficient distribution policies because of their long service to larger firms.

Sullivan (1983) has suggested that the Theory Z mentality produces minimally competent managers chosen for their characteristics and not their abilities. He adds that the rigidity of the strict adherence to hierarchical relationships, which emanate from the earlier industrial clan, are stifling and counter-productive. Ouchi (1981) also recognized the negative aspects of a Confucian dominated organizational culture. He noted that xenophobia and racism are by-products of this intense group loyalty as well.

85

Confucian values also have occasional negative consequences for the industrial organization of Japan. Morgan (1985), in his observations of the just-in-time (kanban) inventory practices, calls the relationships between the larger assemblers and the smaller manufacturers "incestuous". Arms length contracting is not common in Japan. The hierarchical structure of industrial organization puts smaller, lower class firms at a severe economic disadvantage. Similarly, lower class workers, women, the retired elderly, and part time workers are often shabbily treated.

Popper, Janow and Wheeler (1958) suggest another consequence of the Confucian tendency to order by hierarchy.

In societies with Confucian traditions . . . concepts of obligation are generally based upon unequal relationships in a vertical hierarchy. Equal rights in a Western sense are not part of the traditional system (p. 10).

Pyle, discussing the status of freedom in Confucian Asia (cited in the <u>Wall Street Journal</u>, 3/27/87, p. 15), illustrates the differences between Western and Eastern conceptions of equality:

. . . In particular there seems to be in Asia greater tolerance for governmental guidance, less value placed on individualism, greater respect for community interests, far less reliance on legal guarantees, and more stress upon the need for morality on the part of the leaders and the masses. Dissent remains suspect in most of the Asian countries . . . (from Freedom at Issue, Jan.- Feb. 1987)

Conclusions

This paper was designed to enable the reader to examine the writings of Confucius and the Confucian tradition, and the managerial practices found in the Japanese corporation. There is abundant evidence that the ethos of the Confucian tradition continues to contribute to interpersonal and organizational practices in Japanese firms.

In terms of the evidence on convergence versus divergence, it seems that the Japanese have adopted and implemented a voluntarist mode (Dunphy, 1987). They have consciously chosen to diverge and maintain their traditions on matters social and interpersonal. On technological issues, they have adopted Western science and practice when it is in their best interests. When the issue has been the adoption or design of a socio-technical system, the Japanese have chosen system harmony over individual rights.

Whether or not this will continue indefinitely in the face of contractions and inconsistencies are conceived of by the Japanese as superficial, no change will be forthcoming. If the problems are serious, dissonance theory predicts that the Japanese will either change their behavior or their attitudes. The historical evidence suggests that, in Japan, Confucian thought was an instrument of political elites who consciously interpreted it to give priority to modernization. A forecaster of trends in Japanese management practices would monitor the proceedings and papers of Confucian scholars and philosophers. A conservative or fundamentalist trend would indicate a call for the Japanese way of management to be maintained. Liberal re-interpretations and trends would portend the legitimizing of new behaviors and practices. The "collective mental programming" known as culture (Hofstede, 1983) is too entrenched to be abandoned but malleable enough to promote continuity during change.

PRIVILEGE AND THE PUBLIC INTEREST
Paul Weaver

The corporation was a tough sell in the nation of Jefferson, Madison, and Jackson, especially at first. What the large majority of Americans believed in--individualism, limited government, free markets--the corporation often scorned and worked against. What corporations wanted--subsidies, industrial policy, protection from competition, governmentally sanctioned monopoly--most Americans hated. Unsurprisingly, the turbulent politics of the late nineteenth century and early twentieth century revolved around the corporation, and for a time the corporation's ability to extract from the political system what it wanted to extract, indeed its very survival, were open questions.

But if the corporation's ideology and business strategy saddled it with a political vulnerability, they also gave the institution's founders the energizing convictions that survival and growth are the only unalterable principles of business life and that no problem should be beyond the ability of scientific managers to solve. So armed, the founders created a strategy of political self-definition of such cunning and power that it not only enabled them to achieve their unpopular policy objectives but reshaped the entire landscape of modern politics.

The founders called their strategy publicity. Today we use the less elegant phrase public relations. By whatever name, the underlying idea was brilliant in its manipulative simplicity. The new corporation committed itself to the language of social policy and social purpose. It defined private property, private profit, private transactions among private parties as sources of trouble and injustice. Thus it created a public-regarding justification for government interference with market processes that it desired for essentially private, self-serving purposes. The corporation cloaked the privileges it sought in the concept of the public interest.

From The Suicidal Corporation. Copyright 1988 by Paul H. Weaver. Reprinted by permission of Simon and Schuster, Inc.

There were three ways to organize relations between the corporation and society, the founders argued. At one extreme was a system of private ownership, private management, limited government, and free markets. That, of course, they considered highly undesirable. To them, competition was the problem, not the solution, and anyway they doubted that Americans would trust markets to control corporations.

At the other extreme was public ownership, public management, and public direction of the economy. The founders dismissed the possibility out of hand. They had shareholders to think of, they had no intention of becoming civil servants, and they were sure that public ownership would quickly self-destruct. "Imagine the Erie and Tammany rings rolled into one and turned loose on the field of politics," scoffed Charles Francis Adams, Jr., "and the result of State ownership would be realized."

The founders meant to steer a middle way between these extremes. There would be private ownership as in the first scenario. There would be broad governmental direction of the economy through industrial and social policy as in the second. The corporation's conduct would be subject to public review and control by virtue of extensive disclosure of corporate information, supervision by government regulators, and potential legislative intervention on any outstanding problems. The corporation, in short, would be private property infused with public purpose, private property sanctified by public approval, private property disciplined by public authority, private property answerable to public scrutiny. Corporations were "taking the public into partnership," said Edward L. Bernays, the early-twentieth-century coinventor of public relations. In Bernays's illuminating oxymoron, the corporation would "make a majority movement of itself."

From the beginning, executives defined the corporation as an institution dedicated mainly to the service of society and the welfare of others. It was not primarily the private property of its owners, and making a profit was not its major motive or purpose--though businessmen readily conceded that it did have to show a reasonable profit to keep the enterprise afloat. "The

great semi-public business corporations of the country
. . . have in our day become not only vast business
enterprises but great trusteeships," said George Perkins.
"The larger the corporation becomes, the greater become
its responsibilities to the entire community."

Perkins and his contemporaries were quick to admit
that the corporation wasn't always and everywhere in
perfect alignment with the public interest. Unbridled
competition could break out; executives in a moment of
weakness might forget their responsibilities and try to
maximize profits. When this happened, Perkins argued,
it was usually the result of attitudes left over from the
precorporate era. Executives who had once been "in
business for themselves," he lamented, found it hard "to
cease looking at questions from the sole standpoint of
personal gain and personal advantage, and to take the
broader view of looking at them from the standpoint of
the community of interest principle."

But for the most part, the founders argued, the
corporation did embody social values--an almost endless
list of them, in fact. Richand McCurdy, president of
Mutual Life Insurance Co. at the turn of the century,
declared that industry "combined business with pleasure,
business with sentiment, business with philanthropy,
business with great and ennobling ideas of humanity."
In the 1920s, U.S. Steel, proud of its worker benefits
and anxious to keep the union out, billed itself as "the
corporation with a soul." To George Perkins, the
corporation "develop[ed] men of a higher order of
business ability." "The larger the corporation, the more
certain is the office boy to ultimately reach the
foremost place if he is made of the right stuff," Perkins
declared. "'Influence,' so called, as an element in
selecting men for responsible posts, has been rapidly on
the wane. Everything is giving way . . . to the one
supreme test of fitness."

        II

As corporations zeroed in on benefits or exemptions
they sought from the political system, their sense of
social responsibility and their enthusiasm for social
policy grew. In the early 1850's, when the Illinois

Central, along with other fledgling railroads, was lobbying for federal land grants, the company became extremely adept at creating reasons why the national government should break with its tradition of nonintervention. The arguments the railroad lobby was up against were tough to answer. What the Illinois Central's executives proposed was a swindle, said the American Railroad Journal. They were offering a plan for "the public to furnish the means necessary to build the road, while they pocket the profits." Asked another opponent: "Where is the power in this Government to make a donation to A in a manner that pressed B into paying double price?"

The Illinois Central's lobbying and public relations team hit upon a brilliant response. At the time, slavery had risen to the top of the national agenda, and fear was growing that the issue would destroy the Union. Cleverly the Illinois Central turned the issue to its advantage. It is important to remember, the railroad said, that we will be running from Chicago in the north to New Orleans in the south. That makes our proposed grant a special case. By giving us a subsidy, Congress will be creating the nation's first major north-south railroad. Our trains will set up a pattern of intercommunication and interdependency binding north and south "together so effectually that the idea even of separation" would become unthinkable.

In other words, by giving the Illinois Central what it wanted, the federal government wouldn't be subsidizing a private business, it would be funding a social policy to save the Union. Surely that goal justified a one-time deviation from the traditional relationship between government and business. Surely Americans weren't going to put absolute adherence to the free-market, limited-government ideal ahead of the nation's survival.

This argument, together with some expensive lobbying, carried the day. The Illinois Central became the first major railroad to receive federal subsidies. The corporation's new concept of business-government relations took a giant step forward.

Half a century later, when AT&T president Theodore Vail launched his campaign for regulated monopoly status as AT&T's share of the telephone market dwindled alarmingly, he committed his company to a bold new social policy:

> It is believed that the telephone system should be universal, interdependent, an intercommunicating, affording opportunity for any subscriber of any exchange to communicate with any other subscriber of any other exchange . . . It is believed that some sort of connection with the telephone system should be within reach of all . . .
>
> It is not believed that this can be accomplished by separately controlled or distinct systems nor that there can be competition in the accepted sense of competition.
>
> It is believed that all this can be accomplished to the reasonable satisfaction of the public and with its acquiescence, under such control and regulation as will afford the public much better service at less cost than any competition or government-owned monopoly could permanently afford and at the same time be self-sustaining.

In short, the American people deserved cheaper, better-integrated, higher-quality phone service than the market was providing. AT&T meant to meet this emerging social need, but voters should be on notice that this would require state governments to make AT&T an official monopoly.

In the campaign for regulated-monopoly status for electric power companies that was led by Chicago utility tycoon Samuel Insull, the pitch was that competition in electricity was unworkable and would lead either to bankruptcy or to inadequate service. This in turn would leave city governments no choice but to step in and take over the electric business--and that would be socialism. Surely, Insull argued, Americans weren't going to embrace that alien ideology when an ideologically superior alternative was available, namely, giving investor-owned utility companies regulated monopoly status.

Today, though competitive electricity is both
profitable for companies selling it and cheaper for
people buying it, most U.S. markets are served by private
monopolies, thanks in no small part to Insull's success
in manipulating Americans into thinking that monopoly was
the realistic alternative to socialism, and that it was
the destiny of monopolistic electric and gas companies
to deflect the nation from a noncapitalist future.

III

To make sure corporations served social purposes and
didn't lapse into self-interest, said George Perkins,
government should "regulate and control" them.

Government regulation of business was a key part of
the concept of publicity, and it enjoyed wide acceptance
among the founders. Perkins explained it this way:

> If the managers of the giant corporations feel
> themselves to be semi-public servants, and
> desire to be so considered, they must of course
> welcome supervision by the public . . . The
> responsibility for the management of a giant
> corporation is so great that the men in control
> should be glad to have it shared by proper
> public officials.

Judge Elbert Gary, the first chairman of U.S. Steel
and a tireless if often frustrated practitioner of
price-fixing, declared in 1911 that he would welcome a
government commission to set steel prices:

> I would be very glad if we had some place we
> could go, to a responsible governmental
> authority, and say to them, "Here are our facts
> and figures, here is our property, here our
> cost of production: now you tell us what we
> have the right to do and what prices we have
> the right to charge."

To the founders, the purpose of government
regulation of business was to free the corporation from
the bondage of the competitive marketplace. Mere private
interests would no longer control an industry's destiny;

now the public interest could be the decisive consideration. Instead of letting prices and product offerings be governed by the innumerable decisions of free buyers and free sellers, experts [sic] about what suits their personal wants, now the decisions of bureaucrats and managers would determine outcomes. Someone would be in control; policy rather than personal preferences would prevail. Regulation represented the extension of the visible hand to the control of the marketplace as a whole.

And whose hand would that be? The founders of the corporation meant it to be their own. Charles Francis Adams, Jr., often cited as the father of regulation, stressed the issue-defining, opinion-leading, initiative-taking functions of the railroad commission he helped create in Massachusetts. It would not set rates but usher in a new phase of representative government. Work hitherto badly done, spasmodically done, superficially done, ignorantly done, and too often corruptly done by temporary and irresponsible legislative committees, is in the future to be reduced to order and science by the labors of permanent bureaus, and placed by them before legislatures for intelligent action.

In other words, despite public representations to the contrary, Adams's commission was not to be a soure [sic] of politically neutral expertise. It was to function as a lever to pry public opinion and public policy away from the Jeffersonian center. The "ignorance" the commission was to curb was actually the legislature's old-fashioned belief in competition, its refusal to bow down before what Adams called the "irresistible law" of economic concentration, its direct link to the electorate, its whole commitment to separation of powers and limited government. A commission, Adams hoped, would be insulated from popular opinion and offer a bully pulpit from which experts could educate their fellow citizens. The more the commissioners knew about railroads, Adams thought, the more they would see things the industry's way, and the more they would push for consolidation of the industry and control of rates and entry.

Any doubts as to Adams's concept of regulation were laid to rest when, after a decade's service as a

Massachusetts railroad commissioner, he resigned in 1879 to head the board of arbitration of the Eastern Trunk Line Association--a pool of major railroads created to cartelize the industry east of the Mississippi. Adams accepted the post, he wrote, in the hope that "the relations of railroads, not only between themselves, but with the community, can be regulated and reduced to a certain degree of order." He looked forward to helping "familiarize the public mind with the justice an economy of the . . . [pool] system." To Adams, a cartel and a regulatory agency were essentially the same thing.

                    IV

    Regulation was risky, of course. The corporation had adversaries, and if regulatory powers were to fall into their hands, the result could be a disaster for business. This was no mere theoretical possibility; antibusiness groups were also big supporters of government regulation, which they meant to turn to their chosen ends. In many of the industries that sought government help in containing competition, executives debated vigorously among themselves what the chances were that regulation, which they intended to be the industry's Trojan horse in government and the marketplace, would become their adversaries' Trojan horse instead.

    But the new corporate executives believed that these dangers could be minimized. They believed that here, too, publicity would save them.

    From the beginning the corporation was a lavishly communicative institution. Many of the first big companies spent large sums and much energy putting out a flood of press interviews and news releases, product advertising, issue advocacy, business reports, promotional events, lobbying, and the like. In the nineteenth century, some corporations owned newspapers, and many distributed canned features and editorials, often without disclosing their source. Bribes and freebies to journalists were commonplace. By 1905 a business group was organizing a program to persuade college students of the evils of socialism and the merits of capitalism.

The purpose of all this corporate communication was to create what Edward Bernays called an "invisible government" that would manage the public opinions that, in turn, shaped everything from consumer demand to the decisions of government regulators. "The conscious and intelligent manipulation of the organized habits and opinions of the masses is an important element in democratic society," Bernays wrote.

Those who manipulate this unseen mechanism of society constitute an invisible government which is the true ruling power of our country . . . It is they who pull the wires which control the public mind, who harness old social forces and contrive new ways to bind and guide the world.

The communications crafted by Bernays and his ilk aimed to "pull the wires which guide . . . the world" by conveying openness and honesty along with corporate propaganda.

Companies routinely disclosed an enormous amount of information to a wide variety of audiences. They cooperated with the press, even on embarrassing stories, and they worked to persuade the public that they had nothing to hide, that they were socially responsible, that they put the public interest above any private interests.

To create trust, particularly among journalists, the new corporate communications were rigorously accurate about matters of fact. Said Ivy Lee, the other coinventor of public relations, "I send out only matter every detail of which I am willing to assist any editor in verifying for himself." Lee explained, "Success in dealing with crowds . . . rests upon the art of getting believed in." He pointed out: "We know that Henry the Eighth by his obsequious deference to the forms of the law was able to get the people to believe in him so completely that he was able to do almost anything with them."

Otherwise, however, the new corporate communicators said whatever it took to persuade the audience, no matter how far-fetched or how inconsistent with what they'd said before. The only test was whether the theme put people in a frame of mind that would lead to the desired outcomes.

Publicity reflected then-fashionable theories of social psychology that stressed the nonrational character of public opinion and the power of leadership. "Universal literacy was supposed to educate the common man to control his environment," wrote Edward Bernays.

> Once he could read and write, he would have a mind fit to rule. So ran the democratic doctrine. But instead of a mind, universal literacy has given him rubber stamps, rubber stamps inked with advertising slogans, with editorials, with . . . the trivialities of the tabloids and the platitudes of history.

An earlier generation of advocates had treated people as rational being responsive to facts and reasons.

> Suppose the old type of salesmanship . . . was seeking to increase the sale of bacon. It would reiterate innumerable times in full page ads: "Eat bacon . . . it is cheap . . . good for you . . . gives you reserve energy."

Scientific psychologists, Bernays argued, had learned that bacon could be sold better by paying doctors to endorse bacon and using their prestige to increase people's appetite for the stuff.

V

But is it really possible that the first corporate executives were so respectful of public opinion and so adroit in managing it? Weren't they the ones who went about saying, "The public be damned"?

One who scans the record of the late nineteenth and early twentieth centuries for examples of executives acting like Attila the Hun scans largely in vain. Even in the nineteenth century--the era, supposedly, of the ruthless robber barons--businessmen sought to downplay the self-interested basis of corporate behavior and

98

aggressively insisted on what they called their social responsibilities to the community, the poor, and other groups and institutions. Not even railroad tycoon William K. Vanderbilt's infamous statement, "The public be damned," turns out to be a good example.

Vanderbilt made the statement in 1882 in an interview with two reporters from The New York Times. Queried about one of his rail lines, Vanderbilt lamented that, though it wasn't profitable, he had to keep it running because competition from another railroad on the same route gave him no choice. "But don't you run it for public benefit?" one of the reporters asked. Vanderbilt took the bait:

> The public be damned. What does the public care for the railroads except to get as much out of them for as small a consideration as possible! I don't take any stock in this silly nonsense about working for anybody's good but our own because we are not. When we make a move we do it because it is in our interest to do so, not because we expect to do someone else some good. Of course we like to do everything possible for the benefit of humanity in general, but when we do we first see that we are benefiting ourselves. Railroads are not run on sentiment, but on business principles and to pay.

Vanderbilt wasn't saying he didn't care about the public. He was saying that self-interest and profit are the main motives in business and that altruistic objectives are secondary. Had an economist or journalist made such a statement, the reporters wouldn't have bothered to write it down in their notebooks. But coming from a big railroad executive, the statement was a bombshell. Ideologically speaking, man was biting the dog. The dominant theory of corporate behavior and corporate legitimacy was being revealed as a fraud by someone who knew.

The next day, when the Times printed the story, Vanderbilt, who was as interested in his public as the next tycoon, was aware that he had blundered. He scrambled to undo the damage. He complained to the

99

editors of the _Times_ that he had been misquoted, that he never said or meant any such thing, that the reporters had made it up. In other words, such was the power of public relations--of deferring to the idea to the public interest in the hope of creating or concealing business privilege--that the one business in U.S. history who is thought to have said, "The public be damned," didn't mean what we imagine he meant and refused to admit he said it.

CHAPTER IV

MORAL PSYCHOLOGY

INTRODUCTION

In the preceding chapters we have assumed that business ethics is a workable idea and have attempted to delineate some of the procedures to make it even more workable. But what if ethical behavior is impossible, because persons are concerned solely to maximize their own profit? Many people believe that humans are selfish and that their values merely reflect personal opinions about how to do the best for oneself.

One psychologist who has challenged these egoistic assumptions is Lawrence Kohlberg. Kohlberg claims that there are universal stages of moral development and that egoism is universally recognized as among the lowest stages. These stages reflect ethical thinking as an increasingly abstract human activity, based upon increasingly abstract human motivations. Motivation is stressed because human conduct is unique in that the point is not what one says or does but why one does what one does.

The Kohlberg stages of moral motivations are:

1. Selfish motives
    a. Avoiding pain to one's self
    b. Seeking pleasure for one's self

2. Limited other-directed motives
    a. Acting for the benefit of friends or to harm enemies, i.e., those to whom one is emotionally attached, either positively or negatively
    b. Acting for the benefit of harm or political friends or enemies, i.e., those with whom one has shared authority relationships, for example citizenship.

3. Universal other-directed motives
   a. Acting for the greatest good for the greatest number.
   b. Acting to promote the rights of individuals.

One argument that some stages are higher than other stages is that persons in the higher stages are capable of considering the interest of others as equally valuable to their own. That is, stage 1 persons are psychologically unable to think about others, other than as a means for their own interest, while stage 4 persons are able to conceptualize other citizens' interests as equally valuable to their own.

One important aspect of a stage theory of moral development, is that it suggest procedures in order to discuss successfully ethical issues with other persons. Suppose that you are involved in a business decision regarding whether drug packages which have been tampered with should be removed from the market. The company gathers together the various decision makers to plan a course of action. Different persons involved in the decision will have different views about how to proceed because they will be at different stages of moral development. If you are a member of such a team, how can you present your arguments most persuasively? Moral development theory suggests that your arguments should be tailored to the moral stage of your audience. For example, if you are at a stage 6, convinced that respect for human life requires pulling the companies packages from the shelves, even though this will be very expensive for the company, how should you persuade another manager who is a stage 2? The answer is certainly not by using stage 6 reasoning but to use stage 2 reasoning.

The usefulness of Kohlberg's theory has been challenged by evidence that women think about ethics differently than men. The Gilligan hypothesis is that women are moved by caring relationships, whereas men are motivated by obligations and duties as described by Kohlberg. One aspect of this argument associates the concept of morality with the concept of individuality. Thus, the claim that women are motivated by caring relationships is tied to the claim that women's sense of self necessarily includes a sense of others. Women's relationships to others are not accidental to who they are but are essential to their individuality. By contrast, the male concept of self is of an atomistic, alienated self for whom relationships with others are instrumental but not essential.

You should consider whether the Kohlberg and Gilligan theories are supported in your experience. Furthermore if the Gilligan hypothesis is correct, will this have an impact on the likelihood of women's advancement in business? Alternatively, assuming that substantial numbers of women rise to top positions in business, will their different style of ethical thinking affect how business is done? If corporations are becoming more loyalty and team oriented, is it arguable that this management style will be more conducive to women's moral thinking and advancement than to men's?

In conclusion, this chapter focused on more specific issues of moral philosophy by considering how moral concepts have been used by moral psychologists. In order to make the concepts of moral philosophy more concrete, you should test the developmental theories of Lawrence Kohlberg and Carol Gilligan in your personal and business experience. In light of your experience, how would you change these theories?

QUESTIONS AND PROJECTS

1.   Using the Kohlberg and Gilligan discussions, describe your ethical position. Be specific in terms of describing your responses to the moral dilemma set out in the text.

2.   Based on the Gilligan studies, do you agree that women exhibit a different style of ethical thinking than men? Do you believe that more women in upper levels of business will affect the ethical thinking of males in business?

3.   Does the ethical thinking of women offer a possible resolution of the individual/loyalty tension described earlier, in that women's sense of self includes caring for others for whom she feels loyalty.

103

4.   If women's ethical thinking is more caring than
     men's, should there be a separate track for women
     in business who devote more time to their family?
     Should women be limited to certain business
     departments which require more human caring, like
     human resources rather than finance or production?

BUSINESS LAW AND MORAL GROWTH

Edward J. Conry
Donald R. Nelson

INTRODUCTION

This article responds to the current national debate about the role of ethics in business education. It draws upon a relatively new discipline called moral psychology, and an experiment rooted in that discipline, to clarify several fundamental issues in the debate. The article describes three debates about "ethics and business education." One debate is in the press, another is among business faculty generally, and the third is by business law faculty. Within these debates, we find substantial disagreement on such basic issues as whether ethics can or should be taught to business students.

Next the article outlines the field of moral psychology. This field describes how individuals grow in their capacity to make moral judgments. A review of the moral psychology literature indicates that, in contrast to other college education experiences, neither traditional business education nor traditional legal education fosters moral growth. The article then describes an experiment based on moral psychology. The experiment tested an approach to integrating ethics and business law that produced an unusually large amount of moral growth.

Lastly, we discuss the implications of the experiment and the field of moral psychology for several of the issues raised in the debates that open the article. We conclude that business law and legal environment courses are distinctly suitable places for the integration of ethics into the business curriculum.

From <u>American Business Law Journal</u> pp.1-39 (1989).
Copyright 1989 by the American Business Law Journal.
Reprinted by permission. Notes omitted.

THE DEBATE ABOUT ETHICS IN BUSINESS EDUCATION

The Media

Recent news stories and magazine articles clearly indicate our nation's increasing concern with ethical conduct. Many reasons have been advanced to explain this resurgence of interest. Some researchers observe that "[p]erhaps public discussion of and media attention paid to such issues as racism, the Vietnam war, Watergate, illegal corporate payoffs, crime and drugs have sensitized people to the moral dimension in society." In recent years, the media concern with ethical conduct has centered on the issue of ethics in business and business education. But media commentators have not been uniform in their conclusions. Some argue for more emphasis on ethics, while others make arguments against such a change.

Business Faculty

The media debate has a parallel among business faculty. Some influential faculty make arguments which may imply that business schools should not emphasize ethics. Thus, Lester Thurow, an economist and dean of the business school at MIT, writes: "Sacrificing self-interest for the common good is not going to be advocated by business schools unless a majority of Americans also support the premise. In the end, business ethics is merely a reflection of American ethics." David Vogel, Editor of the California Management Review, makes an even more clear-cut argument. He is quoted as follows: "Business schools have a lot of other things [beside business ethics] to worry about, such as the survival of the American economy." Moreover, some institutions have indicated by their actions a lack of support for teaching business ethics.

Business faculty arguing on the other side strongly support the integration of ethics with business. This group frequently criticizes the current business curriculum as based on a single style of moral reasoning, a style that emphasizes wealth maximization and market efficiency to the exclusion of other moral viewpoints. Critics sometimes call this the "Orthodox single-set value system."

Business Law Faculty

The community of legal scholars in business schools is currently engaged in a sometimes subtle debate over the relative emphasis it ought to give to black letter law (i.e., legal rules) and to ethics. This ethics debate is not entirely new. It has its roots in a somewhat similar issue argued under the label of "business law and liberal arts" for at least a quarter of a century.

One side of the current debate has argued for including ethics materials along with black letter law. Those on the other side, the traditionalists, argue that ethics has no significant role to play in business law education. Professor Joseph Frascona has made the most forthright arguments in favor of the traditional approach:

> Morals require keeping one's promise, but they do not teach one to make a legal promise or to understand the legal significance of doing so.
> . . It is submitted that courses in business law must give major emphasis to the rules of business law, because society has imposed constructive notice of that law.

The pro-ethics side of this debate has recently made noticeable progress. Both the discipline's recent articles on teaching and its current textbooks reflect a significant ethics shift--a move away from the traditional approach and toward incorporation of some ethics material. But criticism from sources external to the discipline has probably been more influential in promoting the shift than debate within the discipline. The external sources harshly attack the discipline for its traditional, technical, black letter law, ethics-free approach. In a recent book attack, Lester Thurow has written: "Business law courses outline what is legal and imply that firms and individuals should go right up to the line between legality and illegality. Ethics does not consist in asking one's lawyer, 'Is it legal?' The question, 'Is it right?' is not the same as "Is it legal?'"

The Research Agenda

Clearly, the various debates outlined above have raised several important arguments or assertions. These debates then, can be the source of a research agenda--a group of important issues--which can be assessed by traditional methods of modern scholarship. Public statements about ethics in business education generally argue a variety of issues. But there has been little theoretical or empirical progress reported in the business literature. Clearly, an important step toward scholarly progress is to translate the public arguments or assertions into research topics. Accordingly, we offer the following five statements, which summarize important public arguments or assertions and state related research issues.

1. **The Argument:** Ethics is learned in the home or church and people have already formed their moral beliefs by the time they reach college, particularly graduate school. Thus, attempts to teach ethics are ineffectual. The Research Issue: Is ethics education effective with older students?

2. **The Argument:** The connection between ethics education and ethical behavior is insignificant, nonexistent, or not established. The Research Issue: Does ethics education promote ethical behavior?

3. **The Argument:** Business ethics is currently taught the wrong way. It focuses on transitory contemporary issues that students are unlikely to encounter in their future careers. The Research Issue: Is the "issues approach" effective pedagogy in ethics education?

4. **The Argument:** Business education is ethically one-sided, focused on an "orthodox single-set value system." The Research Issue: Is business education ethically deficient?

5. **The Argument:** Business law and/or legal environment courses are appropriate places in which to integrate ethics. The "ethics shift"

in business law is justified. The Research
Issue: Are business law/legal environment
courses good hosts for ethics education?

MORAL PSYCHOLOGY

Our effort to evaluate the issues just framed is
based on the discipline of moral psychology. Moral
psychology is a relatively new and, for business faculty,
a relatively unfamiliar discipline. Psychology is moral
psychology's mother discipline, so naturally moral
psychology's focus is narrower. Moral psychology
describes the rational (cognitive) and emotional
(affective) processes, and the behaviors, of individuals
confronting moral dilemmas. Moral psychology contrasts
with moral philosophy, which seeks by means almost
exclusively rational to determine what is right and
wrong. Moral philosophy is normative, describing what
ought to be, while moral psychology is largely
descriptive, depicting how people facing moral quandaries
think, feel, and act. The broadest perspective on moral
psychology is achieved by examining moral decision
making.

An Overview of Moral Decision Making

Most scholars acknowledge the following four
elements in the moral decision making process: 1) moral
sensitivity--an awareness of the moral content in a
situation; 2) moral judgment--the selection of a standard
of judgment, or framework of analysis, and its
application to a situation to identify morally
appropriate action; 3) moral will--the resolve to act in
conformity with the moral judgment; and 4) moral action--
the implementation of the moral judgment. To date, most
research on moral decision making has focused on step 2,
the moral judgment component. Problems of moral
sensitivity, moral will, and moral action have been given
little attention by moral psychology researchers.

Kohlberg's and Loevinger's Theories of Moral Development

While there are a variety of fields within moral
psychology, the dominant one is Lawrence Kohlberg's
cognitive developmental psychology. This paradigm
focuses on the way individuals utilize a standard of

moral judgment and <u>reason</u> about justice. A second major field of moral psychology is Jane Loevinger's <u>ego development</u> theory. Grounded on the work of Freud, Adler, and Erickson, the ego development school differs from Kohlberg's paradigm mainly in its emphasis on affect. Next to Kohlberg's cognitive developmental theory, ego development is the most empirically based and widely accepted field in moral psychology.

The principal features of Kohlberg's cognitive developmental theory and Loevinger's ego development theory are strikingly similar. Both are <u>developmental</u>. That is, they view individuals as evolving through a small number of stages of moral judgment. Within each of these stages, moral problems are evaluated in a uniform way. Kohlberg and Loevinger also both identify similar causes for growth, for movement through stages.

Kohlberg's Cognitive Developmental Psychology

Although we use a few of the empirical findings from ego development research to supplement Kohlberg's theory, his paradigm is the foundation for this article. In describing Kohlberg's theory, we start with Piaget's determination that children, beginning with infancy and progressing through adolescence, grow through moral stages. Kohlberg extended Piaget's work to adults. Beginning with his dissertation in 1958 and continuing with subsequent work that spans the last three decades, Kohlberg has advanced the <u>stage theory of moral development</u>. Each stage is characterized by a consistent social perspective. People at different stages therefore differ in the way they evaluate, judge, or assess moral problems. And the stages are hierarchial building blocks, with each new stage built upon and incorporating previous stages.

Content and Structure in Moral Judgment

The Kohlberg stages are based, not on <u>content</u>, but rather on the <u>structure</u>, of moral judgments. Content, in the language of cognitive developmental psychology, refers to particular moral conclusions, or beliefs, such as "I should not steal," "I am obligated to obey the law," or "Human life is more important than property." In contrast, structure refers to the underlying <u>reason</u>

110

for the moral conclusion or belief. For example, one person might decide that she should not steal "because I might get caught," while another might reach the same conclusion because "stealing would injure others." Thus, these moral judgments would display the same content but different structures. Kohlberg described this distinction when he wrote:

> Following Piaget, we distinguish between the content of moral judgment and its structure or form. By structure we mean general organizing principles or patterns of thought rather than specific moral beliefs or opinions. . . Our focus is on the form of thinking rather than the content, because it is the form that exhibits developmental regularity and generalizability within and across individuals.

This distinction between content and structure is one of the most powerful insights of moral psychology. Arguably, the distinction frees cognitive developmental psychology from indoctrination. Since Kohlberg's stages are based on the reasons for specific beliefs, they are largely content-neutral. This contrasts with indoctrination, which advocates content--i.e. specific beliefs such as "Aryans are superior and thus ought to dominate inferior races," or "Communism is superior to democratic capitalism." The fact that persons operating at the same stages often display completely opposite beliefs also supports the argument that cognitive developmental psychology is not a form of indoctrination.

The Structure of the Stages

Kohlberg found that people progress through six stages of moral development grounded on structures of increasingly complex thinking and increasingly sophisticated social perspectives. At stage one, for example, a person determines what is right based largely on avoiding punishment. In contrast, a stage five person has a perspective that incorporates such complex conceptions as "the common good" and "respect for individual rights." Figure 1 presents a brief summary of the perspectives of each stage. The Appendix to this article gives a more detailed description of the stages. Although all people progress sequentially through some

111

stages, they do so at differing rates and end at different points. Within the population at large, only a small percentage develop to the highest stages.

Figure 1

Stage	Title	Evaluation Standard
1.	Obedience	"How do I avoid punishment?"
2.	Instrumental	"What helps me now? An Egoism exchange is good if it helps me, even while it injures others."
3.	Interpersonal Concordance	"Being kind will advance my long-term self-interest."
4.	Law and Duty to the Social Order	"Everyone is obligated by and protected by the law."
5.	Societal Consensus	"I am obligated by arrangements created by due process procedures."
6.	Nonarbitrary Social Cooperation	"Is this how rational, impartial people would organize cooperation?"

The Greater Adequacy of the Higher Stages

Two lines of justification have been advanced to support the claim that higher stages are more adequate. One is rooted in the descriptive nature of the psychology. It asserts that because advanced stages are associated with older, more mature, better educated persons, they therefore are more adequate. For example, philosophers have been shown to operate at the highest stages.

The second line of justification has tended to focus on the logical properties of the stages. In a logical sense, higher stages are more adequate because they are more internally consistent. For example, higher stages are, in Kohlberg's language, more reversible. This means

112

thinking in higher stages allows one to articulate decision rules where rational persons can say: "The rule is so fair that it doesn't matter if I am party A or party B." To illustrate, stage one reasoning says: "Mom cuts the cake and whatever the size of my piece, it's O.K." Given the choice, any rational person would prefer being Mom over being the child. Stage six reasoning, however, would say: "One of us should cut the cake in half and the other should get the first choice. Which role do you want to play?" This decision rule is completely reversible. Its internal logic is more consistent, so it is more adequate.

Stage and Moral Action

A relationship between stage of moral development and moral action has been established. This research has typically involved tempting a group of experimental subjects, frequently students, to cheat. Then the stages of those who cheated were compared with the stages those who did not. Those at higher stages were found to cheat at a lower rate. Similarly, the rate of whistle blowing increases with stage, while juvenile delinquency is inversely related to stage.

But since moral judgment is only a part of the moral decision making process, the relationship between stage and moral action is only moderate, with correlations generally in the 0.3 range. The relationship has been established on the group, but not the individual, level.

Moral Growth

Moral growth is the movement from one stage to the next higher stage. The underlying cause common to all moral growth experiences is thought to be cognitive disequilibrium. Disequilibrium occurs when an individual becomes aware that this moral reasoning is inadequate. That realization produces dissonance and stimulates a search for new ways of thinking about moral issues. This search can generate growth toward higher stages. Disequilibrium can be stimulated by a variety of of experiences, but aging through adolescence and education seem to be the most powerful.

People naturally grow in moral maturity as they age during youth. The inadequacy of the youthful moral judgment produces a natural disequilibrium as it interacts with the judgments of more mature parents, teachers, and social systems. But at some point the aging process seems to stop stimulating moral growth. Thus, persons over age twenty tend to remain at the same level or moral maturity, unless they encounter disequilibrium from some other source.

The most likely source of such further disequilibrium is education. Research on the role of both age and education indicates that these factors together account for about thirty-eight percent to forty-nine percent of moral development. Other research finds that education is the more significant variable for adults. Further, higher education appears to be a requisite for growth to stages five and six.

In normal education and aging, moral growth appears to be an incidental, unplanned by-product of these processes. Intervention techniques, in contrast, are attempts to <u>directly</u> promote disequilibrium and the moral growth that flows from it. The pioneering work on intervention techniques was done by Moshi Blatt. He discussed ethical dilemmas with students, challenged their views, and encouraged them to compare their moral views with those of their peers. This process produced statistically significant upward movement in measured stage. Blatt's work has been frequently replicated.

Intervention techniques become more powerful as persons age. Thus, intervention has an effect on junior high students, and a still greater effect on college and adult subjects. The largest amount of upward movement in moral development is achieved in interventions where the students are twenty-four years or older.

Measurement of Stage

The ability to gauge the impact of intervention techniques depends upon high-quality processes for measuring stages. The most widely used measurement instrument is the Defining Issues Test (DIT) developed by James Rest. The DIT is a paper and pencil questionnaire that can be easily administered to groups.

It consists of six separate fact patterns, each posing a moral dilemma. Figure 2 is representative of all the fact patterns.

Each fact pattern presents the test-taker with a dilemma requiring an ethical choice between competing moral values. In Figure 2, for example, test-takers are presented with a conflict between the values of preserving life and protecting property. The basic question below the dilemma--"Should Heinz steal the drug?"--compels an ethical choice between the conflicting values. But this decision is one of content, not structure. Accordingly, this response is not used in computing the test score.

Following the basic question are the twelve "structure statements," or rationales for the content decision. Each statement supports a decision from the perspective of a particular stage. For example, statement 3 expresses a stage two perspective and statement 12 articulates a stage five perspective. Some statements are nonsense items that sound lofty but have no meaning. These are used to identify inaccurate tests caused by a test-taker's inattention and/or faking.

Figure 2

In Europe a woman was near death from a special kind of cancer. There was one drug that doctors thought might save her. It was a form of radium that a druggist in the same town had recently discovered. The drug was expensive to make, but the druggist was charging ten times what the drug cost to make. He paid $200 for the radium and charged $2,000 for a small dose of the drug. The sick woman's husband, Heinz, went to everyone he knew to borrow the money, but he could only get together about $1,000, which is half of what it cost. He told the druggist that his wife was dying, and asked him to sell it cheaper or let him pay later. But the druggist said, "No, I discovered the drug and I'm going to make money from it." So Heinz got desperate and began to think about breaking into the man's store to steal the drug for his wife.

Should Heinz steal the drug?   (Check one)

```
_____ Should steal it
_____ Can't decide
_____ Should not steal it
```

IMPORTANCE:
Great Much Some Little No

					1.	Whether a community's laws are going to be upheld.
					2.	Isn't it only natural for a loving husband to care so much for his wife that he'd steal?

IMPORTANCE:
Great Much Some Little No

					3.	Is Heinz willing to risk getting shot as a burglar or going to jail for the chance that stealing the drug might help?
					4.	Whether Heinz is a professional wrestler, or has considerable influence with professional wrestlers.
					5.	Whether Heinz is stealing for himself or doing this solely to help someone else.

116

6.   Whether the druggist's rights to his invention have to be respected.

7.   Whether the essence of living is more encompassing than the termination of dying, socially and individually.

8.   What values are going to be the basis for governing how people act towards each other.

IMPORTANCE:
Great Much Some Little No

9.   Whether the druggist is going to be allowed to hide behind a worthless law which only protects the rich anyhow.

10.   Whether the law in this case is getting in the way of the most basic claim of any member of society.

11.   Whether the druggist deserves to be robbed for being so greedy and cruel.

12. Would stealing in such a case bring about more total good for the whole society or not.

From the list of questions above, select the four most important:

_____ Most important
_____ Second most important
_____ Third most important
_____ Fourth most important

The subject is required to rank the importance of each of the twelve statements on a scale of importance ranging from "great" importance to "no" importance. Then the subject selects from the twelve statements the four that the subject judges most important in reaching the decision. These the subject ranks from first through fourth. The responses are scored according to a protocol which generates a <u>P% score</u>. The P% score represents the approximate percentage of stage five and six structure statements that the test-taker ranked in the "four most important" category. P% is a continuous variable on a scale from 0 to 95. Figure 3 illustrates the way the P% score changes with age and education.

Criticisms of the Kohlberg Paradigm

The Kohlberg paradigm has been subjected to a variety of challenges. The most publicized occurred in 1977 when Carol Gilligan published an influential article attacking the paradigm. She argued that because Kohlberg's dissertation focused only on males, he failed to account for the way women think about morality. Gilligan asserted that men think about moral issues in terms of justice principles (stages five and six) while women tend to think in terms of care and responsibility along with obligations to family and peers (stage three). As a consequence, Gilligan alleged, women were systematically underscored.

118

While the Gilligan argument has very strong intuitive appeal, the recent empirical evidence tends to undermine it. In a meta analysis involving fifty-five DIT studies and over 6,000 subjects, Thoma determined that gender had only a small effect on the DIT score. Further, women as a group scored slightly higher than men. That study demonstrated that age and education combined produce an effect that is over 150 times more powerful than gender. Recently, Gilligan's conception of care as an alternative to justice-oriented reasoning has also been challenged. While the debate is still unresolved, the most persuasive empirical evidence now supports Kohlberg rather than Gilligan.

Figure 3

Age, Education and P% Scores

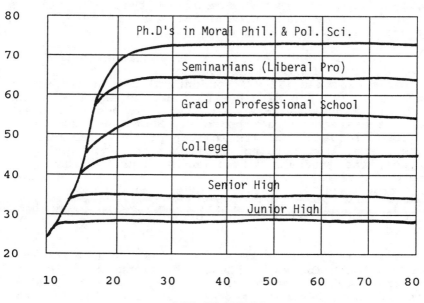

Other, more technical, criticism of Kohlberg's work occurred during the early stages of the paradigm's evolution. Today, however, Kohlberg's model is widely accepted. Its maturity has encouraged a variety of studies, including the assessments of business and legal education discussed below.

Moral Growth and Business Education

Three studies in moral psychology measuring the effects of business education are now available. One is a longitudinal ego development study of 175 undergraduates. In it, Sargent tested students at the beginning of the freshman year and near the end of the senior year. She demonstrated that business students scored lower on the freshman test than any of the other majors—humanities, social science, science, or engineering. Further, the test at the end of the students' senior year demonstrated that non-business majors had undergone significant moral growth, while business majors had not grown.

A second experiment, a cross sectional study, was based on traditional cognitive development theory. In it, Davis examined 152 MBA students at the University of Minnesota. Davis's findings parallel those of Sargent. Thus, the Minnesota MBAs "had lower average P% scores, than the average score reported by Rest . . . for other American graduate students in such professional schools as medicine, law, nursing, liberal arts, and theology." Further, the graduating business students scored lower than the entering business students. Their mean P% score fell from 48.15 to 43.77. This contrasts with, for example, the results for medical students, who entered medical school with a mean score of 53.7 and finished with 58.0.

Taken together these two studies are significant, though not conclusive, evidence of serious deficiencies in current methods of business education. Both studies indicate that business attracts students who use the lower stages of moral reasoning. Further, both studies suggest that business education does not produce the moral growth normally associated with higher education.

120

They lend persuasive empirical support to the argument that business education is based on an "orthodox, single-set, value system."

The third experiment, a longitudinal DIT study by Boyd, involved 262 undergraduate business students who were tested at the beginning and end of the term. The experimental subjects attended a course on Business and Society. Boyd's description of the course is as follows:

> Ethical aspects of the following issues . . . [were] considered in some depth: energy and ecology, business-government relations, equal employment opportunity, occupational safety/product safety, consumerism, union management relations, urban problems, multinational enterprises, socio-economic accounting and environmental forecasting.

A small, but statistically significant, increase in measured stage was produced by the end of the course. The control group for this experiment was a class titled Quantitative Methods and Organizational Behavior. No statistically significant change occurred in the control group. Boyd's research suggests that addressing ethics in the context of business education can facilitate moral development.

Moral Growth and Legal Education

For a variety of reasons, one might conclude that legal education would promote moral growth more than other forms of education. For example, Richards writes:

> [T]he method and substance of professional legal education . . . [lend] . . . themselves to the use of moral philosophy which Kohlberg identifies as one of the organs by which movement upwards in the moral stages of reasoning can be facilitated. Thus Kohlberg indicates that the moral dilemma problems which he has profitably used in facilitating moral development are drawn from moral problems in the law.

The empirical evidence, however, points in the opposite
direction. In a longitudinal study of sixty-one law
students, Willing and Dunn administered the DIT at the
beginning and end of the first year of law school. No
significant change in the average P% score was observed.
Since this was the result of a full year of work,
presumably eight courses, it suggests that modern legal
education does not produce significant moral growth. A
second study by the same researchers focused on a single
course--Legal Ethics and Professional Responsibility.
Here, the pre-intervention and post-intervention
measurements showed no significant increase in the P%
score. The results again suggest that traditional legal
education is not stimulating significant growth. These
researchers summarize their findings as follows:

> The major question in both Study I and Study
> II related to the effects of a particular
> intervention experience on the moral reasoning
> of law students. In Study I this experience
> was a very broad one--that of the first year
> of law school--while in Study II it was a Legal
> Ethics and Professional Responsibility course.
> The major analysis in each of these studies
> indicated that neither experience resulted in
> significant change in moral reasoning.

Other less rigorously developed research suggests
the same conclusion. Tapp and Levin observe the
following:

> In considering the lawyer's role as a
> socializer, we observed that third-year law
> students were just as conventional [in an ego
> development sense] in their perspectives as
> teachers and college students. Professional
> legal education apparently exerts little
> influence in changing the views of the purpose
> of the law. The focus of these graduating
> lawyers was on rules serving to prevent chaos,
> not on their establishing consistency, clarity
> and due process, or guaranteeing personal
> liberties and human rights.

In even stronger language, Tapp and Levin conclude:
"Juxtaposed against other adults, graduating law

122

professionals were apparently somewhat more entrenched in a conventional pattern of reasoning. A 25 year old reasoned that people should obey, 'to achieve the rewards that following the rules brings.'"

Clearly, the empirical evidence suggests that, in general, neither business education nor legal education fosters moral growth. This, then, is the hostile subject matter milieu in which our business law experiment was conducted.

THE BUSINESS LAW EXPERIMENT

The Research Objective

While our experiment had multiple goals, the most fundamental was to determine whether business law/legal environment courses are appropriate places within the business curriculum for integrating ethics. Implicitly then, it also would determine whether the discipline's ethics shift is empirically justified by promoting moral growth.

The Experimental Design

To test the effects of an ethics orientation, five business law/legal environment classes taught by four different instructors were selected for the experiment. All classes were the first law course for the business students in question. Three classes with a total of 71 students were designated as the experimental group and two classes with 31 students were made the control group. The subject students consisted of both undergraduate and MBA students. Of the 62 graduate students, 28 were male and 34 were female. Of the 55 undergraduate students, 26 were male and 29 were female.

The three experimental classes were taught using an ethics intervention designed by the writers to maximize moral growth. The two control classes were taught in the traditional manner; that is, instructors teaching the control did not have an explicit ethical dimension to their teaching. On the first day of the term, all students completed the DIT. Near the last day of the term they were retested. To prevent contamination, no reference was made in any class to any concepts from moral psychology.

The Intervention

The experimental intervention involved a three-step experience for students: 1) learning certain ethical theories, 2) analyzing the law using those ethical theories, and 3) articulating personal views about the ethical content of the law. These steps are described in detail below.

Step One: Learning Ethical Theory

Students were trained to use certain classic forms of ethical reasoning. This involved teaching them teleological and deontological styles of moral reasoning. Teleology is the form of reasoning which focuses on the consequences of an act. If the consequences are good, the act is judged to be morally good. If the consequences are bad, the act is judged morally bad. Deontology, in contrast, rejects the idea that the moral character of an act is determined by its consequences. In deontology, acts have inherent attributes of moral rightness or wrongness. Truth telling presents the classic example of the conflict between teleology and deontology. For the teleologist, lies are only wrong if they generate bad consequences. For the deontologist, they are always wrong, no matter what consequences they generate.

Teleology and deontology were selected as the core of the intervention because they frequently lead to different conclusions about what is morally right. Thus, we theorized that these forms of ethical thought, when used together, would maximize disequilibrium and stimulate a large amount of moral growth.

The two major expressions of teleology--ethical egoism and utilitarianism--were taught to students. While ethical egoism generally focuses on consequences, the particular "good" by which the consequences are measured is the self-interest of the decision maker. In egoism, therefore, an act is good if it advances the self-interest of the decision maker. The other form of teleology we presented was Bentham's utilitarianism. In

124

utilitarianism, the consequence sought--the "good"--is not the self-interest of the decision maker, but the "greatest good for the greatest number." For Bentham, the good was pleasure.

Next students were taught basic deontology. Here, emphasis was placed on the reasoning of Immanuel Kant and of John Rawls. The Kantian viewpoint presented to students can be summarized as follows.

Human beings are unique living creatures since they have the capacity to engage in moral reasoning. Because of this capacity, they are entitled to distinctive treatment. Accordingly, three rules, of increasing complexity, can be articulated for testing ethical alternatives.

1) We cannot use persons exclusively as means to an end;
2) We must act as one who both makes and is bound by laws or rules, i.e., as one who is both subject and sovereign; and
3) acts or rules are not ethical unless they can be made universal--that is, applicable to everyone--without generating a state that is illogical, self-defeating, or inconsistent.

The Rawlsian expression of deontology used by students is captured in the following statement.

Justice is grounded on consent--that is, on social contract. However, in the real world consent to social relations is very difficult to directly identify. Because we don't have direct consent from every individual, we must evaluate rules, laws, and principles of justice by a hypothetical test that would be acceptable to all rational persons. Accordingly, Rawls develops a mental test, one similar to Kant's conception of being both a sovereign and subject, to determine what is just. That test defines an imaginary "original position." In this position everyone acts in his rational self-interest. But in the original position all individuals are behind a "veil of ignorance." This means that they do not know what their <u>status</u> would be on the other side of the veil, in the actual world. Thus they do not know their preferences; their conception of the good; or whether they would be poor or rich, male or female, weak or strong, black or white, young or old, talented or untalented.

From this original position people ask what rules or principles would appear rationally just to everyone. The veil permits them to evaluate social arrangements impartially, without regard to their own particular case.

Rawls concludes that in the original position people would reject Bentham's principle of utility. No one would be willing to accept a loss for herself in return for a net increase in benefits for the whole group. Rawls <u>does</u> conclude that people would agree to two basic principles. <u>First</u>, each person is to have an equal right to the most extensive basic liberty (freedom of thought, speech, assembly, etc.) compatible with similar liberty for others. <u>Second</u>, social and economic inequalities (e.g., social status and wealth) are to be arranged so that they are both: a) reasonably expected to be to everyone's advantage, particularly for the least advantaged members of society; and b) attached to positions and offices open to all under conditions of equal opportunity. The first principle is called the "liberty principle." It must be satisfied before the second principle--called the "difference principle"--can be invoked.

The process of building in students this basic analytic skill--the ability to reason with both teleology and deontology--was completed very early in the courses. Once this was accomplished, the classes were ready to move to the next step in the intervention.

Step Two: Application of Ethical Reasoning to
Business Law

The second step involved giving students ongoing, repeated experience in ethical reasoning <u>about the law</u>. During the course of the term, certain legal concepts were selected for ethical evaluation. The criterion for selection was simply this: does the legal concept yield vividly conflicting results when evaluated deontologically and teleologically? If the answer to this question was yes, the topic was a candidate for ethical evaluation.

The statute of frauds is an example of such a concept. In the experimental classes, it was presented in the traditional manner but also was evaluated using the two styles of moral reasoning. In class discussion, students typically came to the conclusion that, under the utilitarian criterion, the statute of frauds is good. They reasoned that by making certain contracts unenforceable when they were not placed in writing and signed, this rule of law strongly encourages writing and signing. This, they argued, reduces misunderstanding, conflict, litigation, and fraud; and smooths the flow of commerce--results that help the vast majority of persons in society. Thus, the students concluded, the statute of frauds generates the greatest good for the greatest number.

On the other hand, when students analyzed the statute of frauds from a deontological perspective, such as Kant's, they frequently judged it to be morally wrong. Their reasoning typically went along the following lines:

> By not enforcing the oral agreement, the court sacrifices one individual, the party seeking enforcement, in order to benefit many others. The injured party was used exclusively as a means to an end, in this case the end of commercial efficiency. In Kantian deontology, this is wrong; the injury to an innocent party cannot be justified on the basis of good consequences to a majority.

When employing Kantian deontology, students also reasoned that enforcement of promises could be made universal. If promises should be enforced, the written or oral form of the promise was judged to be not significant. If there was an agreement, according to this form of student

127

reasoning, the courts ought to enforce it because promises should be kept no matter what the consequences. According to these students, therefore, this law was morally wrong when evaluated in terms of Kantian deontology.

In a repetitive process, the students were required to employ different styles of moral reasoning to analyze a variety of concepts in business law. They were therefore forced to reason with styles that often led to conflicting conclusions about right and wrong. This, we theorized, would promote disequilibrium and moral growth.

Step Three: Examination of Personal Beliefs

The next step in the intervention involved conducting a dialogue with, and among, students about their personal beliefs concerning the rule of law being discussed. To make this viable, a mutually supportive, collaborative classroom atmosphere was established. Students were encouraged to call into question their own values and to listen carefully to the statements and arguments of others. Students felt free to express their own views, justify them, and challenge the viewpoints (but not the person) of others in the classroom. To illustrate, a student might volunteer that she believed it was acceptable to injure a few individuals under the statute of frauds "if there weren't very many, the injury was small, and there was a great deal of benefit to the rest of society." Another student might respond: "If I were the scapegoat, Sara, I would feel exploited and therefore I can't justify doing that to others. Would you feel exploited? If you would, are you still willing to impose that feeling on others?" Early in some experimental classes, a student would overstep the boundary of mutual respect with a jokingly derogatory comment about another's beliefs. Gently pointing this out to the class, and justifying mutual respect as requisite to meaningful moral discourse, was sufficient to restore the appropriate tone for the balance of the course.

This three-step intervention was an interwoven theme of the experimental classes, occupying perhaps fifteen percent of lecture time. The time allocated to the intervention was distributed rather evenly throughout the

128

term, although it received slightly more emphasis at the beginning as students learned the styles of ethical reasoning.

Data Analysis

The intervention just described was the core of our experiment. Both before and after that intervention, the DIT was administered to assess whether moral growth occurred. Our analysis of these pre-intervention and post-intervention DIT's is presented in three ways. First, the P% scores are presented and compared with the scores of other studies. Second, t-tests are used to determine whether the findings are merely the result of chance or are statistically significant. Third, a particular statistics, called effect size, is used to gauge the power of this intervention in comparison with other interventions.

Change in P% Scores

The control group produced a mean P% score of 37.71 on the first DIT. For this group, the standard deviation of the P% scores was 11.58. By the end of the classes, the mean of the control group on the second DIT had risen to 38.87, for an increase of 1.16. In contrast, the mean beginning P% score of the subjects in the experimental group was 45.33. The standard deviation was 11.24. On the second DIT, the P% score was 50.85, an increase of 5.52.

A movement of approximately eleven P% points normally occurs over a period of four years during the formal education process. The movement by the control group was at the low end of the range normally expected for one term. In contrast, over the course of the term the experimental group achieved results that would be expected over a two-year period of higher education. This suggests the power of the intervention.

Tests of Significance

In the tests of significance, the three experimental classes were collapsed into one group and the two control classes were merged into another group. The data were analyzed to test the following three hypotheses.

I.   No statistically significant gain in measured stage would occur for the control group.

II. Statistically significant gains in measured stage would occur for the experimental group.

III. There would occur a statistically significant difference in gain between the experimental group and the control group.

Analysis of the data strongly supports research hypotheses I, II, and III. The intervention did produce statistically significant moral growth.

Effect Size

Effect size, sometimes called treatment effect, is a widely used statistic which attempts to gauge, on a uniform scale, the relative power of interventions. In general, it does this by dividing the measured change, in this case the change in the mean P% scores, by the standard deviation of the pooled pre-intervention and post-intervention scores.

The effect size for the experimental group was 0.49. For comparison, Rest reports that the average effect size of sixty-eight interventions from 1972 to 1983 was 0.28. Of the nine interventions which, like the one described here, occurred in academic courses, the average effect size was 0.09. As Figure 4 indicates, only one academic intervention produced a larger effect size. That intervention occurred over a two-semester time period. The effect size statistic indicates that our academic intervention was distinctively powerful.

Weaknesses in the Experiment

   The experiment just described was, like most in the social sciences, not perfect. One weakness is that the subjects were not randomly assigned to the control and experimental groups. Since classes were the experimental units, this was not practical. As a result, it is remotely possible that the class selection process used by students may have channeled students into classes of high and low susceptibility to moral growth. For example, higher scoring individuals may have had a preference for early morning classes. The authors think this is unlikely.

   Another weakness is that our hypothesis testing relies on t-tests and accordingly does not correct for the pre-intervention and post-intervention changes in the control group. However, the magnitude of the change in the experimental group suggests that such a correction would not have altered the experimental conclusions. Other criticisms of the experimental design can be made, but the size of the change suggests they are unlikely to cast doubt on the basic findings. All three approaches--change in P% scores, the t-tests, and effect size--indicate that the experimental intervention was quite powerful.

Figure 4

Academic Intervention Studies
(Listed in Order of Effect Size)

Author(s)	Sample	Effect Size
Morrison, Toews, & Rest (1973)	103 Jr. High students	.18
Willing & Dunn (1982)	104 law students	.04
Rest, Ahlgren & Mackey (1972)	61 Jr. High students	.12
Finkler (1980)	99 criminal justice, philosophy, & doctoral students	.17
Boyd (1980)	262 undergraduate business students	.19
Stevenson (1981)	56 college students in social science, humanitites, & English	.25
Conry & Nelson (1989)	101 graduate and undergraduate business students	.49
Redman (1980)	33 students	.63

IMPLICATIONS

Our experimental results and the theory of moral psychology on which they are based speak directly to the research issues identified at the beginning of this article.

On the basis of that experiment and that theory, definite statements can be made about each of the five research issues identified in this article's first section. While our findings do not resolve all five issues, as a group they significantly clarify the controversy surrounding ethics education in business.

1. Research Issue: Is Ethics Education Effective with Older Students?

The argument that college students are too old to be taught ethics is at least partially wrong. When ethics education is defined from the structural perspective--as the capacity to engage in high quality reasoning about moral issues--then it seems clear that the college years are among the best times to teach ethics. On the other hand, if one defines ethics education from the content perspective--as teaching a set of specific beliefs--then moral psychology and this experiment do not contribute to the resolution of the issue.

2. Research Issue: Does Ethics Education Promote Ethical Behavior?

While research in moral psychology has established a significant connection between stage and moral action, no direct evidence of a connection between ethics education and moral action has been presented. Of course, one may persuasively argue that since ethics education has been shown to increase measured stage, and since stage is linked to moral action, ethics education must also influence moral action. But as yet this is just argument.

3. Research Issue: Is the Issues Approach Effective Pedagogy in Ethics Education?

Critics of ethics education argue that the focus on contemporary ethical issues does not equip students to deal with those problems likely to arise later in their careers. This attack on the "issues" approach of current business ethics education appears to be partly valid and partly invalid.

Moral psychology has established the importance of the structure of one's thinking for moral behavior. From the structure perspective, capacity for moral reasoning is not issue-specific. And the experiment demonstrates that addressing a series of business law issues helps build the students' ability to engage in moral reasoning. So again, the criticism is valid from the content perspective, but not from the structural perspective. Accordingly, to the extent that courses build skills in thinking about what is right and wrong, they should be effective in promoting moral growth. To the extent that they are merely descriptive of ethical theories or ethical issues, they are unlikely to foster this type of growth.

4. Research Issue: Is Business Education Ethically Deficient?

The allegation that current business education is doing something wrong, perhaps fostering an "orthodox single-set value system," receives substantial support from other studies in moral psychology. The empirical findings of moral psychology suggest that the business major attracts the least morally mature students, trains them in ways that foster little growth, and thus produces persons who are morally underdeveloped for their level of education. While higher education in general is the principal growth-producing experience, its business component appears to be flawed.

5. Research Issue: Are Business Law/Legal Environment Courses Good Hosts for Ethics Education?

Our experimental findings provide an empirical justification for the discipline's shift toward an ethics orientation. The inclusion of ethics, at least in the form of the intervention described, produces significant moral growth. Clearly, then, this field is an appropriate host for ethics education.

Host Effect

There is a "host effect." Both the theory of moral psychology and its empirical findings indicate that courses vary in their capacity to facilitate moral growth. Theory suggests that courses promote disequilibrium when students' values are challenged by conflicting reasoning about right and wrong. Since courses vary in their capacity to provide this source of disequilibrium, logic indicates they must vary in their ability to foster growth. Empirical findings also

134

support the presence of a host effect. Sargent has found that academic majors influence moral growth. If groups of courses have different effects, it is likely single courses do so as well. Accordingly, both theory and the existing empirical evidence strongly suggest a host effect.

Host Effect and Business Law/Legal Environment Courses

The authors assert that this host effect is distinctively powerful in business law/legal environment courses. Theory suggests that the study of business law has an inherent, if apparently latent, capacity for stimulating disequilibrium. It is the conflict between the nature of business law courses and the balance of the business curriculum that is the source of this disequilibrium. Empirical evidence is equally persuasive. The difference between the effect size of the intervention described here and those in other courses suggests that business law/legal environment courses are, relatively speaking, quite good hosts for ethics education.

CONCLUSION

This new information ought to mobilize the nation's business schools to rethink their educational objectives. Our experiment and the other research reported here indicate a direction for change in portions of the existing business curriculum. Some of these changes can profitably occur within the business law curriculum. Transmitting black letter rules of law to our students is an essential task; but it is not, as the "traditional approach to business law" would have us believe, this discipline's only obligation. If the business law profession can promote moral growth in students, it has a fundamental obligation to do so. We are persuaded that students who know the rules of law, but have no mature personal beliefs about one's duty to obey them, have not been educated.

Appendix

A Detailed Description of the Stages
of Moral Development

Stage 1: Obedience

General Characteristics: At this stage, being moral is
being obedient. An external authority provides rules and
these rules are accepted. The child sees no
justifications for the rules other than obedience and
avoidance of punishment. The rules do not exhibit any
plan, or purpose, or interconnectedness. They are simply
there to be uncritically accepted.

The child extends the rule-giver's rules to other
children and thereby begins to see the idea of generality
of rules. The child's only right is to be free from
punishment when obeying the rules.

Prototypical Views: Right conduct is obedience to fixed
rules. Punishment follows violation of a rule and anyone
punished has acted wrongly.

Response to the Heinz Story: "When you take a drug like
that, it's stealing. Stealing has always been against
the law. That's the way it is, the law is the law."

Stage 2: Instrumental Egoism and Simple Exchange

General Characteristics: At this stage being moral is
acting in one's self-interest. To do this, one must
account for the self-interest of others. Two people may
want to cooperate if each gets something out of the
cooperation. And it's what they get out of the
cooperation that makes it fair. Transactions are
one-time deals, favor for favor, renegotiated with each
new exchange opportunity.

Unlike Stage 1, where morality is blind, Stage 2
morality serves the purpose of broad self-interest. At
this stage, the child begins to sense ideas of equality
and reciprocity.

Prototypical Views: An act is moral if it advances the actor's self-interest. One should obey the law only if it is prudent to do so. Cooperation is based on simple exchange.

Responses to the Heinz Story: "Heinz is running more risk that it's worth unless he's so crazy about her he can't live without her. Neither of them will enjoy life if she's an invalid."

Stage 3: Interpersonal Concordance

General Characteristics: At this stage morality is viewed in terms of creating and nurturing long-term relationships of mutual support. Parties form alliances based on friendships and other personal relationships. Implicit in these relationships is the idea that one understands the other's goals and is obligated, because of the relationship, to support them. Allies anticipate each other's needs, desires, and expectations. The interests of the allies are balanced against each other, but the concerns of third parties are not accounted for in moral decision making. At this stage persons begin to appreciate long-term cooperative equilibrium.

Prototypical Views: An act is good if it is prosocial. Being moral implies concern for the approval of others.

Responses to the Heinz Story: "If you were so heartless as to let your own wife die, you would feel terrible and everybody would really think you were inhuman. It would be terrible to think of what you allowed to happen to your own wife and what they must have thought when she realized you weren't going to save her."

Stage 4: Law and Duty to the Social Order

General Characteristics: This stage judges morality as upholding law and order. Law is seen as a mechanism for coordinating the roles and expectations of others, whether allies or not, in order to avoid chaos. The law is supreme and the source of all other values. But it is vulnerable. Deviations from the legal order threaten the whole system and raise the prospect of actual social chaos. So compliance with the law is paramount. Individuals relate to one another based upon social or legal roles. Thus, one must respect authority. Prototypical Views: Right is defined by rules that are binding on all and fix shared expectations as a basis for the social order. Values are derived from the social order and the maintenance of law. Respect for legitimate authority is part of one's obligation to society.

Responses to the Heinz Story: "It is a natural thing for Heinz to want to save his wife, but it's still always wrong to steal. You have to follow the rules regardless of how you feel or regardless of the special circumstances. Even if his wife is dying, it's still his duty as a citizen to obey the law. No one else is allowed to steal, so why should he be? If everyone starts breaking the law when they get in a jam, there'd be no civilization, just crime and violence."

Stage 5: Social Consensus

General Characteristics: At this stage, morality is seen in terms of processes for rules, laws, or systems of law that win the allegiance of everyone by giving each person a stake in the system. It is an attempt to articulate rational rules that respect both the majority and the minority. Its assumption is that people can agree about laws if the process reflects the general will and provides certain minimal safeguards for everyone.

Prototypical Views: Moral obligation derives from voluntary commitments of society's members to cooperate. Procedures should exist for selecting laws that maximize welfare as discerned by the majority will. Basic rights are preconditions to social obligation.

Responses to the Heinz Story: "Heinz has to respect the general will of his society as it is set down in the law. The law represents the basic terms on which people have agreed to live with each other."

Stage 6: Nonarbitrary Social Cooperation

General Characteristics: At this stage, morality is based on commitment to rational, abstract, self-selected universal principles for governing social cooperation. These principles are derived by trying to imagine what impartial, rational, equal persons would identify as the appropriate standards under which social life should proceed.

<u>Prototypical Views:</u>   Moral judgments are ultimately justified by principles of ideal cooperation. Individuals each have an equal claim to benefit from the governing principles of cooperation.

<u>Responses to the Heinz Story:</u>   "Where the choice must be made between disobeying a law and saving a human life, the higher principle of preserving life makes it morally right--not just understandable--to steal the drug.   If Heinz does not do everything he can to save his wife, then he is putting some value higher than the value of life.   By not acting in accordance with your sense of the value of human life, you would condemn yourself--you would know that you have betrayed your own moral integrity."

TWO PERSPECTIVES:
ON SELF, RELATIONSHIPS, AND MORALITY

Nona Plessner Lyons

Asked in the course of an open-ended interview to respond to the question, "What does morality mean to you?" two adults give different definitions. A man replies:

> Morality is basically having a reason for or a way of knowing what's right, what one ought to do; and, when you are put into a situation where you have to choose from among alternatives, being able to recognize when there is an issue of "ought" at stake and when there is not; and then . . . having some reason for choosing among alternatives.

A woman responds:

> Morality is a type of consciousness, I guess, a sensitivity to humanity, that you can affect someone else's life. You can affect your own life, and you have the responsibility not to endanger other people's lives or to hurt other people. So morality is complex. Morality is realizing that there is a play between self and others and that you are going to have to take responsibility for both of them. It's sort of a consciousness of your influence over what's going on.

In contrast to the man's notion of morality—as "having a reason," "a way of knowing what's right, what one ought to do"—is the woman's sense of morality as a type of "consciousness," "a sensitivity" incorporating an injunction not to endanger or hurt other people. In the first image of an individual alone deciding what

Lyons, Nona Plessner, "Two Perspectives: On Self, Relationships, and Morality," Harvard Educational Review, 53:2, 125-145. Notes and appendices omitted.

ought to be done, morality becomes a discrete moment of rational "choosing." In the second image, of an individual aware, connected, and attending to others, morality becomes a "type of consciousness" which, although rooted in time, is not bound by the single moment. Thus, two distinct ways of making moral choices are revealed.

The representation in psychological theory of these two different images and ideas of making moral choices is the concern of this paper. One view has come to dominate modern moral psychology--the image of the person in a discrete moment of individual choice. The identification of a second image--the individual connected and attending to others--and the systematic description of both views from empirical data are presented in this work. In her critique of moral philosophy, Murdoch, (1970) the British novelist and philosopher, indicates the importance of this investigation. She elaborates two issues raised by this second image of the self which apply as well to moral psychology: the need for a conception of self not limited to that of a rational, choosing agent, and a concern for acknowledging a conception of love as central to people and to moral theory.

Describing present-day moral philosophy as "confused," "discredited," and "regarded as unnecessary," Murdoch focuses on philosophy's idea and image of the self. Believing that modern moral philosophy has been "dismantling the old substantial picture of the self." Murdoch sees the moral agent reduced to an "isolated principle of will or burrowing point of consciousness." The self as moral agent, "thin as a needle, appears only in the quick flash of the choosing will". Murdoch rejects this classic Kantian image of the self as pure, rational agent. For her, moral choice is "as often a mysterious matter, because, what we really are seems much more like an obscure system of energy out of which choices and visible acts of will emerge at intervals in ways that are often unclear and often dependent on the condition of the system in between the moments of choice."

The picture of the self as ever capable of detached objectivity in situations of human choice is thus

142

rejected by Murdoch. Yet this is the image assumed in
Kohlberg's (1969, 1981) model of moral development. That
model, which is a hierarchically ordered sequence of
stages of moral judgment-making based in part on the
pioneering work of Piaget (1932/1966), is the dominant
model of modern moral psychology. In addition, Murdoch's
challenge to philosophy "that we need a moral philosophy
in which the concept of love, so rarely mentioned now .
. . can once again be made central," can also be directed
to moral psychology (1970). Murdoch's assumption is that
love is a central fact of people's everyday lives and
morality. But modern moral psychology, grounded in the
concepts of justice and rights, subsumes any notion of
care or concern for another we might call love. It was
Gilligan (1977) who first revealed this distortion of
moral psychological theory.

Gilligan (1977, 1982), listening to women's
discussions of their own real-life moral conflicts,
recognized a conception of morality not represented in
Kohlberg's work. To her, women's concerns centered on
care and response to others. Noting too that women often
felt caught between caring for themselves and caring for
others, and characterized their failures to care as
failures to be "good" women, Gilligan suggested that
conceptions of self and morality might be intricately
linked. In sum, Gilligan hypothesized (1) that there are
two distinct modes of moral judgment--justice and
care--in the thinking of men and women; (2) that these
are gender-related; and (3) that modes of moral judgment
might be related to modes of self-definition.

The research described here includes the first
systematic, empirical test of these hypotheses. This
paper reports on the identification, exploration, and
description from data of two views of the self and two
ways of making moral choices. The translation of these
ideas into a methodology made possible the testing of
Gilligan's hypotheses.

The empirical data consist of responses of
thirty-six individuals to questions asked in open-ended
interviews designed to draw out an individual's
conception of self and orientation to morality. The data
were analyzed first for descriptions of self, then for
considerations individuals presented from their own

143

real-life moral conflicts, and finally for correlations between the two.

The first part of this article presents interview data on ways that individual males and females--children, adolescents, and adults--describe themselves. These data reveal two characteristic modes of describing the self-in-relation-to-others: a self separate or objective in its relations to others and a self connected or interdependent in its relations to others. Then, from individuals' discussions of their own real-life moral conflicts, two ways of considering moral issues are distinguished: a morality of rights and justice and a morality of response and care. These data are then used to develop two coding schemes, methodologies for systematically and reliably identifying peoples' modes of self-definition and bases of moral choice.
Finally, results of the study designed to test Gilligan's hypotheses and a discussion of the implications of this work for psychological theory and practice are presented. Thus, this article moves between the discursive essay and the research report, to show the evolution of a conceptual framework based on peoples' real-life experiences, and the translation of that framework into a systematic methodology for analyzing data and testing hypotheses.

A social dimension emerges as central in this work: in each of the two images of people making moral choices, there is a distinct way of seeing and being in relation to others. Although Kohlberg has identified a developmental pattern of a morality of justice, he has not elaborated the connection between his conceptualization of moral development and an understanding of relationships. Because this present work assumes that an understanding of relationships is central to a conception of morality, it is not directly parallel to Kohlberg's, yet it does maintain an indebtedness to it. Gilligan and her associates (Gilligan, 1977, 1982; Langdale & Gilligan, Note 1; Lyons, Notes 2, 3) have outlined, but only broadly, the developmental patterns of a morality of justice and of care within a framework or relationships. This present work supports, modifies, and elaborates Gilligan's ideas and confirms Piaget's central insight that "apart from our relations to other people, there can be no moral necessity" (Piaget, 1932/1966, p. 196).

Data

When asked to talk about themselves, individuals differ in how they describe themselves in relation to others. Because these differences become central to the construction of the coding schemes for identifying modes of self-definition and moral choice, it is useful to look closely at the differences in the responses of adolescents, children, and adults. These data reveal two distinct conceptions of relationships, each characterized by a unique perspective toward others.

For two fourteen-year-olds taking part in an open ended interview, the question was the same: "How would you describe yourself to yourself?" Jack begins:

> What I am? (pause) That's a hard one . . .
> Well, I ski--I think I'm a pretty good skier.
> And basket ball, I think I'm a pretty good
> basketball player. I'm a good runner. . . and
> I think I'm pretty smart. My grades are good
> . . . I get along with a lot of people, and
> teachers. And . . . I'm not too fussy, I don't
> think--easy to satisfy, usually--depending on
> what it is.

Presenting ways by which he evaluates himself, Jack comments on how he measures up in terms of some ranking of abilities: good skier, basketball player, runner, pretty smart. Talking about his relations with others, Jack continues to focus on his abilities: "I get along with a lot of people and teachers."

Fourteen-year-old Beth's response begins as Jack's did with the activities that engage her; however, she then tells of the network of relations that connect her to others:

> I like to do a lot of things. I like to do
> activities and ski and stuff. I like people.
> I like little kids and babies. And I like
> older people, too, like grandparents and

145

everything; they're real special and stuff. I don't know, I guess I'd say I like myself. I have a lot of stuff going on. I have a lot of friends in the neighborhood. And I laugh a lot.

The interviewer asks, "Why do you like yourself?" and Beth replies:

I don't know. I think it's the surroundings around me that make my life pretty good. And I have a nice neighborhood and a lot of nice friends and older people . . . We visit new people everywhere we go. And there's my grandmother, and every time I go to my grandmother's, she makes me see all her friends and stuff. And I think that helps me along the line, 'cause you get to know them, and it makes you more friendly.

The contrast between these two responses may not at first glance seem striking, but there is a difference between the images and ideas of each person's relationships to others. Jack connects himself to others through his abilities. Like his ranking of himself as a "pretty good skier" and a "good runner," Jack's way of relating to others is another measure of his abilities: "I get along with a lot of people and teachers." Jack's perspective toward others is in his own terms, through the self's "I." Beth's connection to others is through the people who make up her "surroundings"--nice friends, older people, little kids, and babies. Her connections through others are in turn to others: "My grandmother . . . she makes me see all her friends and stuff." Thus, Beth's perspective towards others is to see them in their own terms. She sees, for example, her grandmother with her own friends, in her own context. Further, Beth seems to see a circle of interdependence in these relationships: "And I think that helps me along the line, 'cause you get to know them, and it makes you more friendly." Although both young people discuss relational topics that sound similar, they reflect different perspectives towards others: seeing others in their own terms, or through the self's perspective.

These different ways of seeing others also emerge
in individuals' considerations when talking about moral
conflict. When asked, "Have you ever been in a situation
where you had to make a decision about what was right but
you weren't sure what to do?" Jack relates an experience
of being with a group of his peers who wanted to wax
windows on Halloween. To an earlier question, "What
makes something a moral problem?" Jack had replied,
"Somewhere I have to decide . . . whether I should do
this or not . . . whether it's right that I should do
something or whether it's wrong." Now, talking about his
conflicts about that Halloween, he echoes the earlier
response: "I knew it wasn't right, but they, the kids,
they would think, 'Oh, he's no fun, he doesn't want to
do it, he's afraid he's going to get in trouble,' stuff
like that." Urged by the interviewer to describe the
consequences he considered when making his decision, Jack
mentions "getting in trouble," "my mother and father
would have been upset by something like that--they
wouldn't like it," and "if I didn't go, some of my
friends would think . . . 'Well, he's no fun'." Jack
also describes his major consideration in making the
decision: "Well, you have to think about what would be
right . . . and then . . . are you gonna stand up for
what's right and wrong to your friends, or are you gonna
let them--get you into going." Revealing that in the end
he didn't go with his friends, he elaborates why: "I
didn't think it was right . . . and if somebody wanted
to wax my windows, I wouldn't like it, so I wasn't going
to do that to someone else."

Through reciprocity Jack resolves this moral
conflict. Asked if he had made the right decision, Jack
replies, "Well . . . my parents would have been pleased
that I had not gone . . . If the kids had gotten into
trouble, I would have known that I made the right
decision, 'cause I wouldn't have wanted to have been in
that group." When challenged, "What if no one knew about
it?" Jack resorts again to his "principle" for choice:
"I don't think you could think that was the right
decision if you were to do that--to wax somebody's
windows and go away thinking that was the right thing to
do."

For Jack, the moral problem hinges on knowing what
is right and acting on that in spite of pressures or

taunts from his friends. Solving the problem, then, becomes a matter of thinking about what would be right and standing up to that. His reciprocity-based justification is derived from the self's perspective: "If somebody wanted to wax my windows, I wouldn't like it, so I wasn't going to do that to someone else." Like the measure of self-in-relation-to-others found in his self-description, Jack sees and resolves moral conflict through the self's perspective.

Beth's moral problem arises from a different set of concerns as well as a different perspective towards others. First she narrates the events surrounding her conflict: "I had a decision to give up my paper route. And I had a decision over two people, like two people wanted it. And I didn't know what was the right decision." Asked to describe the conflicts for her in that situation, she says: "Well, some friends of the person that I said could not have the route were going against me and saying that, you know, 'You did it' and 'What a stupid thing to do, to give it to the other person.' The person got kinda upset, and kinda turned against me."

Reconstructing how she thought through the problem, Beth illuminates her way of thinking in choice:

> [at first] I was trying to think mostly who I thought was going to do better at it. I don't know, it kinda got me all upset because I didn't want to hurt somebody, one person's feelings by telling them they couldn't have it. And going to the other person and saying you can. I think that's mostly what bothered me . . . And then it bothered me more when I thought of what person was mostly gonna get it. I was thinking, well, are they really going to do a good job? . . . I didn't want anybody doing it that was gonna be nasty to anybody. Because I have some older people that I do on the route, and they like to talk to you and everything. And I didn't want to give it to anybody that was gonna walk away. I wanted them to get along . . . I didn't want anybody getting in fights or anything.

As she envisions the elderly people on her paper route, Beth's decision turns on her considerations of their needs. The moral problem at first hinges on seeing the possible fractures between people and trying to avert them. Caught between wanting someone good for the paper route job and not wanting to hurt the person she had to turn down, Beth's concerns for relationships and for the welfare of others conflicts.

Asked, "How did you know that it was the right decision?" Beth tells us how things worked out: "The person that was bad for the job finally realized that the person [chosen] was going to be a good person to do it." She also described how she evaluates the decision: "I told my friends about it and my parents, and they said, 'Yeah.' And I told my paper route people that there was going to be a new person, and they said 'Yeah,' they liked that person. And so I thought, 'Well, I think I did a pretty good job, if everybody's happy'." Beth measures the rightness of her choice by how things worked out. Having told her friends, parents, and "my paper route people," and having their concurrence, she finds in the restoration of relationships the validation of her choice.

Although Jack and Beth both wrestle with issues raised by friendships, two different kinds of moral problems concern them. Through two different perspectives--the perspective of self or the perspective of others--different problems arise and different resolutions are sought. These distinctions are found in data from younger children and adults as well.

Two eight-year-olds are asked, "How would you describe yourself to yourself?" Jeffrey answers in the third person, saying that "he's got blond hair" and "has a hard time going to sleep." He also focuses on abilities: "He learns how to do things; when he thinks they're going to be hard, he learns how to do them." Describing his way of relating to others, Jeffrey says, "He bugs everybody and he fights everybody," concluding with, "That's it. I'm lazy."

To the interviewer's question, eight-year-old Karen replies in the first person. "I don't know, I do a lot of things. I like a lot of things." Adding, "I get mad not too easy," she comments that she has "made a lot of new friends" and concludes, "And, um, I don't know if everyone thinks this, but I think I tell the truth most of the time."

Echoing themes of Jack, the adolescent, Jeffrey presents a measure of himself by abilities: "He learns how to do things; when he thinks they're going to be hard, he learns how to do things." Karen's observation that she has "made a lot of new friends" echoes adolescent Beth's self-description of her connection to the people surrounding her. It is in contrast to Jeffrey's "he bugs everybody and he fights everybody."

Themes in the real-life conflicts which the children report repeat those of the adolescents. Jeffrey talks with the interviewer about a real-life conflict. "Like when I really want to go to my friends and my mother's cleaning the cellar. I don't know what to do." Urged by the interviewer to say why this is a conflict, Jeffrey elaborates:

> 'Cause it's kinda hard to figure it out. Unless I can go get my friends and they can help me and my mother clean the cellar.
>
> Why is it hard to figure it out?
> 'Cause you haven't thought about it that much.
>
> So what do you do in a situation like that?
> Just figure it out, and do the right thing that I should do.
>
> And how do you know what you should do?
> 'Cause when you think about it a lot, then you know the right thing to do first.
>
> How do you know it's the right thing?
> 'Cause you've been thinking about it a lot.
>
> Can you tell me how you think about it?
> It's really simple if you think about it real quick. I think about my friends and then I think about my mother. And then I think about the right thing to do.

150

To the interviewer's question, "But how do you know it's the right thing to do?" Jeffrey concludes, "Because usually different things go before other things. Because your mother--even though she might ask you second--it's in your house."

For Jeffrey, having a rule--"different things go before other things"--allows him to resolve the dilemma of choice. Like Jack's use of the Golden Rule, Jeffrey finds a resolution to his conflict in the rule of "some things go first." For both Jack and Jeffrey it is through the self's perspective--the self's rule or standard--that moral conflict is cast and resolved.

Different issues concern eight-year-old Karen. She describes conflict with friends: "I have a lot of friends and I can't always play with all of them, so I have to take turns. Like, they get mad sometimes when I can't play with them. And then that's how it all starts." Asked what kinds of things she considers when trying to decide with whom to play, Karen replies, "Um, someone all alone, loneliness. Um, even if they are not my friends, not my real friends, I play with them anyways because not too many people do that . . . They never think of the right person."

Describing the "right person" as someone who is "quiet who . . . doesn't talk too much, who doesn't have any brothers or sisters," Karen, like Beth, tries to connect people to one another, "to make them feel more like at home." Asked to elaborate, Karen responds: "If a person's all alone . . . if that person never has anyone to talk to or anything . . . they are never going to have any friends. Like when they get older they are gonna have to talk. And if they never talk or anything, then nobody's going to know them . . . If that person always stays alone, she's not going to have any fun."

For Karen, as for Beth, moral conflicts arise from having to maintain connections between people, not wanting people to be isolated, alone, or hurt. For both, resolutions are found by considering the needs of those involved. Like their adolescent counterparts, these two eight-year-olds reflect different perspectives towards others. They see and attend to different things.

151

These distinguishing characteristics and different ways of seeing others are manifest in adulthood. John, the thirty-six-year-old professional educator quoted at the beginning of this paper, reveals a "logic" consistent with that of Jack and Jeffrey. He describes the decision to fire a colleague as a personal moral conflict. Although believing that the firing breached a prior agreement, he describes his conflict as "lack of confidence in my own judgment . . . feeling like maybe the others were right." His co-workers had decided, after the deadline, to fire the staff member. Describing how he felt in trying to think about what to do, he says: "I felt I had a commitment to live with . . . [we] all had a commitment to honor . . . But for me it was a serious matter of principles."

Later, reflecting on his decision to offer his resignation in protest, he comments on how he thought about the decision:

> Well, I guess I will never know for sure . . . but I am comfortable with it, in the sense that given the pressures, and given the fact I had to decide and I don't feel I perverted any principle I hold now in making that decision. For me it was a test, in a way it became a symbol, because all this had been weighing on me. In a way the principle was commitment to principle, and I had to decide whether I had it or not, and if I let it go by, then maybe I didn't have the right to ever challenge anybody else.

In childhood and adulthood, a line of thinking in moral choice is revealed in the conflicts expressed by Jack, Jeffrey, and John in which issues of morality hinge on "moments of choice" and "knowing how to decide," thus conjuring up Murdoch's image of the self in the "quick flash of the choosing will."

Answering the question, "How would you describe yourself to yourself?" John goes on to talk explicitly about his own perspective towards others. He acknowledges: "I happen to be a person who likes the world of ideas," who can "delight myself for hours on end reading and thinking, puzzling over things . . . I am not

152

the sort of person who has a natural outreaching towards other people. That for me is always sort of an effort . . . an effort that I need to be nudged to do." Suggesting the importance of relationships to him, he continues talking about their difficulties and rewards for him personally:

> I am nudged [towards others] in several ways--by other people . . . but also by my convictions that tell me that I have responsibilities to other people; and, once nudged though, the interesting thing is that it is always rewarding. And I am grateful because most of the personal growth I have gone through has been through these other people and not through thinking about the world of ideas and that sort of stuff. But somehow I always retreat into the corner and want to be off by myself. It is a paradox about me, one that I still haven't fully understood . . . Gregarious people I think can't fully understand sometimes how hard it is for certain people to become involved with people because what they regard as either minor personal risks or non-risks altogether, can strike a person like me sometimes as insurmountable obstacles. So that is one aspect of myself that just happens to come to mind. This is interesting because I had never thought about this much.

John picks up the themes of relating to others from the self's perspective heard earlier in the responses of Jack and Jeffrey. So, too, an adult woman repeats themes found in the concerns of Karen and Beth.

Forty-six-year-old Sarah, a lawyer, who describes herself as "perceptive" and "responsive" to others, tells about a moral dilemma she faced. She discovered in the course of a contested custody case that her client's boyfriend was an illegal alien. Although withholding this information was not technically illegal, she sensed that the information could affect the judge's ruling. She asked herself if telling would really make a difference in the long run and decided that it would not, "that it would resolve itself one way or the other." She concludes, "nobody is getting particularly hurt by this."

153

Talking about her dilemma in a larger context, she describes the conflict her role creates:

> I think that I run into a dilemma in doing domestic relations work in the sense that I am dealing with a legal system that is dealing with something that it doesn't know how to deal with very well and I get very distressed because it is hard for me to put together exactly what my role is supposed to be . . . you are presiding over some pretty emotional moments in people's lives, and I never know whether I should be sort of, here is the lawbook, and not do anything to try to do whatever kind of counseling, whatever kind of support one might provide for people without costing them a fortune . . . On the other hand, I think people need something like this. I end up in a dilemma in dealing with custody decisions, which are very messy. And God knows, there is no right and no wrong. It is a question of how can you work out something that is going to be the least painful alternative for all the people involved . . .

The ultimate principle for resolving moral conflict, for Sarah, seems to be to work out "the least painful alternative for all the people involved."

From these examples, we see that individuals describe different kinds of considerations in moral choice tied to different ways of being with, and seeing, others: to treat others as you would like to be treated or to work out something that is "the least painful alternative for all involved." To treat others as you would be treated demands distance and objectivity. It requires disengaging oneself from a situation to ensure that each person is treated equally. In contrast, to work out the least painful alternative for all those involved means to see the situation in its context, to work within an existential reality and ensure that all persons are understood in their own terms. These two ways of perceiving others and being in relation to them are thus central both to a way of describing the self and to thinking in moral choice.

154

Development of the Coding Schemes

When moving from data to the conceptual constructs on which a coding scheme is based, a circular interaction occurs: the data account for the constructs and are in turn explained by them. Indeed, as Loevinger (1979) argues, such circularity is necessary to validate the coding schemes and to build the theory of which they are a part. This interactive process is described below to illuminate how ideas about human relationships, identified first in the statements of individuals, were translated into systematic categories of a coding scheme, a methodology for analyzing data.

Many researchers (Broverman, Vogel, Broverman, Clarkson, & Rosenkrantz, 1972; Erikson, 1968; Freud, 1925/1961, Piaget, 1932/1966) have commented on the relational bias of women's conceptions of self and morality. But it was Gilligan (1977) who first suggested that this relational bias might represent a unique construction of social reality. The study discussed below, designed by Gilligan, hypothesized that men and women do think differently about themselves in relation to others. That there is such a difference was supported in examinations of data--such as the comments of those quoted above--and then elaborated conceptually on the basis of that data. In that process two different ideas and ways of experiencing human relationships were revealed that seemed tied to two characteristic ways of seeing others. This distinction was then conceptualized as two perspectives towards others. Table 1 presents schematically the two modes of being-in-relation-to-others, separate/objective and connected, and their respective perspective towards others, reciprocity or response.

TABLE 1

Relationships of Reciprocity and Relationships of
Response

The Separate/Objective Self

Relationships are experienced in terms of	mediated through	and grounded in
RECIPROCITY between separate individuals, that is, as a concern for others considering them as one would like to be considered, with objectivity and in fairness;	RULES that maintain fairness and reciprocity in relationships;	ROLES which come from duties of obligation and commitment.

The Connected Self

Relationships are experienced as	mediated through	and grounded in
RESPONSE to OTHERS in THEIR TERMS that is, as a concern for the good of others or for the alleviation of their burdens, hurt, or suffering (physical or psychological);	THE ACTIVITY OF CARE which maintains and sustains caring and connection in relationships;	INDEPENDENCE which comes from recognition of the interconnectedness of people.

Each of these two ideas of relationships with their characteristic perspective towards others implies a set of related ideas. The perspective of the separate/objective self--labeled "reciprocity"--is based on impartiality, objectivity, and the distancing of the self from others. It assumes an ideal relationship of equality. When this is impossible, given the various kinds of obligatory role relationships and the sometimes conflicting claims of individuals in relationships, the best recourse is to fairness as an approximation of equality. This requires the maintenance of distance between oneself and others to allow for the impartial mediation of relationships. To consider others in reciprocity implies considering their situations as if one were in them oneself. Thus, an assumption of this perspective is that others are the same as the self.

The perspective of the connected self--labeled "response"--is based on interdependence and concern for another's well-being. It assumes an ideal relationship of care and responsiveness to others. Relationships can best be maintained and sustained by considering others in their specific contexts and not always invoking strict equality. To be responsive requires seeing others in their own terms, entering into the situations of others in order to know them as the others do, that is, to try to understand how they see their situations. Thus, an assumption of this perspective is that others are different from oneself.

In Table 2 the relationship between these conceptions of self and orientations to morality, as they emerged from the empirical data, are presented schematically. The data revealed that separate/objective individuals tend to use a morality of "justice," while connected individuals use a morality of "care."

The conceptions of morality and the perspectives towards others are constructs, and as such represent ideals containing strengths and weaknesses. Equality is an ideal and a strength of a morality of justice; the consideration of individuals' particular needs--in their own terms--is both an ideal and a strength of a morality of care. On the other hand, an impartial concern for others' rights may not be sufficient to provide for care, and caring for others may tend to leave individuals

157

TABLE 2
The Relationship of Conceptions of Self and of Morality
to Considerations Made in Real-Life Moral Choice: An
Overview

A Morality of Justice

Individuals defined as SEPARATE/OBJECTIVE in RELATION to
OTHERS: see others as one would like to be seen by them,
in objectivity; and tend to use a morality of

Justice as Fairness that rests on an understanding of
RELATIONSHIPS   as   RECIPROCITY   between   separate
individuals, grounded in the duty and obligation of their
roles;

moral problems are generally construed as issues,
especially decisions of conflicting claims between self
and others (including society); resolved by invoking
impartial rules, principles, or standards,

considering: (1) one's role-related obligations, duty,
or commitments; or (2) standards, rules or principles for
self, other or society; including reciprocity, that is
fairness--how one should treat another considering how
one would like to be treated if in their place;

and evaluated considering: (1) how decisions are thought
about and justified; or (2) whether values, principles,
or standards are (were) maintained, especially fairness.

A Morality of Response and Care

Individuals defined as CONNECTED in RELATION to OTHERS:
see others in their own situations and contexts; and

tend to use a morality of Care that rests on an
understanding or RELATIONSHIPS as RESPONSE to ANOTHER in
their terms;

moral problems are generally construed as issues of
relationships or of response, that is, how to respond to
others in their particular terms; resolved through the
activity of care;

considering: (1) maintaining relationships and response, that is, the connections of interdependent individuals to one another, or, (2) promoting the welfare of others or preventing their harm; or relieving the burdens, hurt, or suffering (physical or psychological) of others;

and evaluated considering: (1) what happened/will happen, or how things worked out; or (2) whether relationships were/are maintained or restored.

---

uncaring of their own needs and rights to care for themselves. In addition, the response perspective may suggest an unqualified and overly emotional concern for meeting the needs of others. However, the present research suggests a greater complexity of meaning. Response to another is an interactive process in which a developing and changing individual views others as also changing across the life cycle.

Within most psychological models the ability to see another's perspective is considered a cognitive capacity which gradually becomes more objective and abstract. In contrast, the perspective of response described here emphasizes the particular and the concrete. While it is assumed that this perspective changes over the course of development, the nature of these changes is not yet known. It may be that in "maturity" one generalizes the particular, that is, one always looks at the particular, and this is the general principle. This research suggests that our current unitary models of perspective-taking may need revision. Perspective-taking and a "perspective-towards-others" conceptualized here are separate phenomena.

It is important also that the use of the word "response" or "reciprocity" in subjects' responses not be assumed to indicate automatically the possession of that particular perspective on morality or relationships. For example, an individual using a morality of justice and having a perspective of reciprocity might state, as did fourteen-year-old Jack, "I would not do that because I would not like some one to do that to me." However, an individual using a morality of care and having a perspective of response might use the word "reciprocity"

159

but with a different meaning. "I want to reciprocate because they will need that kind of help and I will be able to do that for them." In a perspective of response, the focus is always on the needs of others; it is the welfare or well-being of others in their terms that is important, not strictly what others might do in return or what the principle of fairness might demand or allow.

What follows from these distinctions is that the language of morality must always be scrutinized for differences in underlying meaning. For example, words like "obligation" or "responsibility" cannot be taken at face value. (The moral imperatives of what one is "obliged" to do, "should" do, or what "responsibilities" one has are, in fact, shaped by one's perspective towards others.)

Research is needed to elaborate the conceptualizations presented here--of two perspectives on self, relationship, and morality--across the life cycle, especially attending to the issues of change and development. Research should also address potential interactions, that is, ways in which one orientation to morality may affect or be affected by the other. In addition, individuals' understanding and awareness of their own perspectives of themselves-in-relation-to-others needs to be elaborated. The work presented here shows the logic of each mode of morality and self-description has been elicited from interview data. The next section will describe how that logic was captured in a methodology, that is, in two coding schemes and used to test a set of hypotheses.

An Empirical Study Testing Gilligan's Hypotheses

In this empirical study, male and female subjects were interviewed in order to ascertain their modes of self-definition and of moral choice, and to explore the connection between self-definition and modes of moral choice. A wider age-range was sampled to help elaborate modes of moral choice and of self-definition previously observed by Gilligan in a narrower age span of women. Both men and women were included to avoid the bias of a single-sex sample and to allow for the exploration of both justice and care orientations across the life-cycle. If--as Gilligan suggested--the absence of women subjects

160

in past research obscured an understanding of the morality of care, the inclusion of men and women within this study may reveal its complexity for both sexes.

A secondary purpose of the study was to explore a suggestion of Kohlberg and Kramer that when women are engaged professionally outside the home and occupy equivalent educational and social positions as do men, they will reach higher stages of moral development than the typical adult women's stage (stage three-- interpersonal mode) of his six stage system of moral judgment making. Therefore, a sample of professional women was essential. It was also expected that such a sample would provide evidence concerning Gilligan's hypothesis that women consistently demonstrate a morality of care regardless of their profession.

Sample. The sample of thirty-six people consisted of two males and two females at each of the following ages: 8, 11, 14-15, 19, 22, 27, 36, 45, and 60-plus years. The sample was identified through personal contact and recommendation, and all subjects referred met the sampling criteria of high levels of intelligence, education, and social class.

Procedure. The data were collected in a five-part, open-ended interview which was conducted in a clinical manner, a method derived from Piaget (1929/1976). The interview proceeds from structured questions to a more unstructured exploration and clarification of each person's response. Interview questions were developed to illuminate how the individual constructs his or her own reality and meaning, in this case, the experience of self and the domain of morality.

Data Analysis. The data were analyzed first for modes of self-definition, then for the subjects' orientations within considerations of real-life moral conflicts. Finally, they were analyzed for correlations between the two.

Considerations of Justice or Care in Moral Conflicts

By examining the considerations individuals present in the construction, resolution, and evaluation of real-life moral dilemmas, the relative predominance of justice or care orientations to morality was determined. Considerations were categorized as either response (care) or rights (justice), and scored by counting the number of considerations each individual presented within either mode. In addition to identifying the presence of justice or care considerations, predominance of mode within this scoring system was determined by the higher frequency of one or the other mode in a subject's responses. Results were also expressed as percentages indicating the relationship of the dominant mode to all considerations the individual gave.

Intercoder reliability was established by two additional coders for both identification of considerations within real-life dilemmas (Step 1) and categorization of considerations as belonging to response or rights modes within the subject's construction, resolution, and evaluation of their moral conflict (Step 2). Agreements for Step 1 were 75 and 76 percent, for Step 2, 84 and 78 percent.

Table 3 summarizes the predominance of response and rights considerations in real-life moral dilemmas for both males and females. The table shows that in real-life conflicts, while women use considerations of response more frequently than rights and men use considerations of rights more frequently than response, in some instances the reverse is true.

Table 3
Predominance of Considerations of Response or Rights in
Real-Life Dilemmas by Females and Males

Sex	Response Predominating	Rights Predominating	Equal Response/ Rights Considerations
	% (N)	% (N)	% (N)
Females (N=16)	75 (12)	25 (4)	0 (0)
Males (N=14)	14 (2)	79 (11)	7 (1)

Table 4 illustrates this pattern in another way,
indicating that all the females in this sample presented
considerations of response, but 37 percent (6) failed to
mention any considerations of rights. Similarly, all
the males presented considerations of rights, but 36
percent (6) failed to mention any considerations of
response. These findings show that, in real-life moral
conflict, individuals in this sample call upon and think
about both care and justice considerations but use
predominantly one mode which is related to but not
defined or confined to an individual by virtue of gender.

Table 4
Absence of Considerations of Response or Rights: by
Females and Males

Sex	No Considerations of Response	No Considerations of Rights
	% (N)	% (N)
Females (N=16)	0 (0)	37 (6)
Males (N=14)	36 (6)	0 (0)

Although this study did not specifically consider developmental changes in moral thinking and self-definition, some results suggest possible developmental issues. It is clear that considerations of both response and rights are found across the life cycle. However, after age 27, women show increased consideration of rights in their conceptualization of moral problems or conflict, although they still use considerations of response more frequently than rights in the resolution of conflict. This may be related to a second finding: the disappearance of the response consideration of "care of the self" at the same age. These findings suggest the possibility of an interaction between the rights and response orientations for women in their late twenties. Another finding with implications for developmental change is the greater persistence of considerations of response among male adolescents. In general, however, across the life cycle men's considerations of rights maintain greater consistency than do women's considerations of response. Taken together, these findings suggest separate developmental shifts for men and women which deserve further study.

Keeping in mind that the sample is small (N=36), the results reported here support the hypothesis that there are two different orientations to morality--an orientation towards rights and justice, and an orientation towards care and response to others in their own terms. Morality is not unitarily justice and rights, nor are these orientations mutually exclusive: individuals use both kinds of considerations in the construction, resolution, and evaluation of real-life moral conflicts, but usually one mode predominantly. This finding of gender-related differences, however, is not absolute since individual men and women use both types of considerations.

Modes of Self-Definition: Separate/Objective or Connected

This study also tested the hypothesis that individuals use two distinct modes of self-definition. Respondents were asked "How would you describe yourself to yourself?" and responses were analyzed to determine

164

the predominance of one of two modes of self-definition--
separate/objective or connected. In a manner similar to
that used for the analysis of the moral conflicts data,
these self-descriptive responses were categorized
according to four components: general and factual;
abilities and agency; psychological; and relational.
Each individual was scored by counting the number of
separate/objective or connected relational
characterizations, and then the predominant mode was
determined.

Intercoder reliability for the self-description
data was established using two independent coders in a
two-step coding process which was more rigorous than most
correlational reliability procedures. Every statement
about self-definition was coded. In Step 1, in which
each idea about the self was identified, intercoder
reliability was 70 and 71 percent. In Step 2, in which
each idea was categorized according to specific aspects
within components, intercoder reliability was 74 and 82
percent.

A summary of male and female modes of self
definition is given in Table 5. As the table indicates,
women more frequently used characterizations of a
connected self, while men more frequently use
characterizations of a separate/ objective self.
Although these different gender-related modalities occur
systematically across the life-cycle, they are not
absolute; some women and men define themselves with
elements of either mode. In addition, and perhaps most
striking, is the finding that both men and women define
themselves in relation to others with equal frequency,
although their characterizations of these relationships
are different.

TABLE 5
Modes of Self-definition: Females and Males

Sex	Predominantly Connected	Predominantly Separate/ Objective	Equally Connected and Separate	No Relational Component Used
	% (N)	% (N)	% (N)	% (N)
Females (N=16)	63 (10)	12 (2)	6 (1)	19 (3)
Males (N=14)	0 (0)	79 (11)	7 (1)	14 (2)

Relationship of Definitions of Self to Considerations in Real-Life Moral Choice

Some of the most important results of this study concern the testing of the hypothesis of the relationship between modes of moral choice and modes of self-definition. Table 6 presents these findings. In this sample, regardless of sex, individuals who characterized themselves predominantly in connected terms more frequently used considerations of response in constructing and resolving real-life moral conflicts; and individuals who characterized themselves predominantly in separate/objective terms more frequently used considerations of rights.

TABLE 6
Modes of Self-definition Related to Modes of Moral
Choice

Predominant Modes of Moral Choice	Modes of Self-definition: Connected	Separate/ Objective	Other (S/C or none)
Response N=13 (1M, 12F)	10 (10F)	0	3 (1M, 2F)
Rights N=16 (12M, 4F)	0	13 (11M, 2F)	3 (1M, 2F)

Although these results do not allow us to claim a causal relationship between modes of self-definition and modes of moral choice, we can say an important relationship exists. Further research is needed to see if these results hold over larger samples of a broader socio-economic status. Furthermore, research is needed to test the possibility that patterns of decision-making in areas other than moral choice may also be related to these modes of self-definition.

Implications

The development of the methodologies presented here--the coding schemes for identifying modes of self-definition and moral judgment--made possible the testing of a set of hypotheses important for theories of ego and moral development and for educational and clinical practice as well. Although all of the implications cannot be addressed fully, some of the most important ones are identified as an invitation to others to join in further clarification.

1.   Psychological theories of moral development should recognize a morality of care as a systematic, lifelong concern of individuals. It should not be identified solely as a temporary stage- or level-specific concern, or as subsumed within a morality of justice, as Kohlberg's work posits.

2.   Psychological theories of ego and identity development need to consider a relational conception--the self-in-relation-to-others--as central to self-definition. This concern for connection to others should not be considered as present only at particular stages or as issues pertaining only to women. Although men and women tend to understand and define relationships in different ways, definition of self in relation to others is found in both sexes at all ages.

3.   Theories of cognitive and social development should recognize that individuals construct, resolve, and evaluate problems in distinctively different ways. These differences are not simply in content, but seem to be related to two different perspectives towards others. Theories of cognitive and social development built on unitary models of social perspective-taking should be reconsidered.

4.   Counselors, teachers, and managers, when dealing with conflicts within relationships, need to take into account that the language of morality in everyday speech has different meanings for people and that these may carry behavioral implications. For example, what people feel obliged to do or what their responsibilities to others are may be defined and understood differently.

5.   Designs for psychological research need to reflect in their subjects of study the centrality of interpersonal interactions. This means research should focus not just on the individual but on both members of an interacting unit--husband and wife, friends,

mother and child, teacher and student, manager and staff, and so forth.

6.   Sex as a variable for study ought to be included in research designs and methodologies as a matter of course. This paper suggests both the difficulty in understanding sex differences and their importance to an improved understanding of theory and practice

To accommodate the problems of modern moral philosophy, Murdoch (1970) has called for psychology and philosophy to join in creating a "new working philosophical psychology." This paper offers to psychologists and philosophers alike some new premises and methodologies by which to explore further the meaning of morality in our lives.

CHAPTER V

MORAL PHILOSOPHY

INTRODUCTION

We have been introduced to some of the basic ethical
principles in the psychological theories of Lawrence
Kohlberg and Carol Gilligan. The readings of this
chapter will develop some of these theories, but first
some preliminary distinctions need to be made. Morality
has two separate components. First, there is the
morality of obligation-of doing what is right and wrong.
This is the primary concern of the Kohlberg stages and
the first three readings of this chapter. Second, there
is the morality of ideals, of virtue or excellence. This
is the focus of the Plato selection. Generally,
questions of obligation are thought to be capable of
rational discussion, while ideals are considered matters
of opinion.

Most moral philosophy since 1600 AD has been
concerned with obligations, with giving reasons for
various proposed standards for a supreme principle to
enable moral agents to decide in a reasonable way about
what they are obligated or ought to do in a particular
case. For example, the principle of utility, or the
greatest happiness principle, tells us to seek the
maximum amount of good or produce the greatest happiness,
in order to do what is morally right. Other philosophers
have argued that there are good moral reasons for acting
which are not dependent on consequences. For example,
we ought not to lie, even when we might produce more
happiness, or we should respect the equality of all
persons, because such conduct is basic to human beings.

The question regarding the supreme moral principle
may seem remote to practical business concerns unless you
think of the problem functionally. In order for any
society to continue to exist, its members must share
certain basic norms. Similarly for a business society
there must be shared business norms. The justification
for such norms becomes problematic in a pluralistic
society where individuals have very different ideals.
In such pluralistic societies the justification for the
supreme moral principle may be compared to the

171

justification of the constitution of a club. If a club
is about to break up because there has been a loss of
agreement about its basic rules, then each individual
will have his or her own ideas about how the club should
be reorganized and the obligations it ought to impose
upon its members. But if the club is to survive then
there will have to be basic rules about which all club
members can come to an agreement.

Presumably one source of the disagreement is that
the club's members disagree about the strength of the
obligations and commitments that the club should require.
Thus, at a minimum, each person will need to agree to a
procedure of how to settle disagreements regarding the
minimum acceptable level of duties and responsibilities.
Key to such a procedure will be respect for the equality
of all the members of the club, because all the members
will have agreed to this basic decision making principle.

The analogy with business is that the basic norms
of a business society also must be forged by democratic
agreement. They cannot be given by an external authority
for not all persons accept such authority; they cannot
be given by the law for the state derives its legitimacy
from the agreement of its members.

In this chapter I have included samples of some of
the modern answers to questions about the basic moral
rules of society. You should evaluate these moral
standards from the democratic perspective of whether all
reasonable persons in society would accept one or more
as basic rules for a society, such as ours which is
predominately business-oriented.

One influential theory has been utilitarianism which
states that the morally right act produces the greatest
good for all persons. This theory is particularly
attractive because it is readily workable and acceptable
to business persons who know how to calculate benefits
and costs. It is also democratic in that each persons'
interest are to be considered.

The Ligget case provides an interesting application
of the utilitarian theory. In the moral principle of the
utility, all consequences are to be considered and
weighted in the moral calculation. The court in the

172

Ligget case had to decide whether all utilities should be applied in a products liability law suit. The Tobacco company argued "yes"; the injured plaintiff argued "no", that certain social benefits, for example, the number of employees hired and the taxes paid by cigarette companies should not be considered by the jury in deciding whether a product was defective under a risk utility standard.

Utilitarianism has been subjected to much criticism; one example is the morality of lying. It has been argued that utilitarianism allows some persons to be used as a means for the happiness of others, e.g., when lies are told. I have included an article by Michael Walzer defending a version of equality of treatment which is non-utilitarian. An important key to the Walzer article is expressed in the sentence, "What equalitarianism requires is that many bells should ring." What does Walzer mean by this phrase and is utilitarianism, or the moral theory you are prepared to defend, consistent with the view of equality that Walzer defends. You should also consider the connection between the principle of equality and free market economy. Is equalitarianism indefensible, because its implementation would cost too much in terms of loss of individual liberty? Which do you value more highly, liberty or equality?

The problems of the interrelationships between business and society are not new. I have included a selection from Plato's Republic in which Socrates, speaking for Plato, tries to persuade an Athenian business man Thrasymachus that justice is better than injustice, that the life of virtue is better than the life of monetary self interest.

In this chapter you have been invited to consider some of the basic materials regarding moral philosophy. You should consider whether the principles expressed in these materials and your moral theory would be agreed to by all reasonable persons in a democratic society. If an ethical theory cannot satisfy this test, then arguably it is unacceptable as a first principle of morality.

QUESTIONS AND PROJECTS

1. Write an editorial to a newspaper justifying placing a particular dollar value on human life. For

173

example, should the state build a highway to a ski area which will cost the lives of five highway workers? What if 50 lives are involved? Should the workers be deceived regarding the dangers of the work in order to decrease labor costs and avoid increasing taxes?

2. Write a dialogue in which two or more persons are placed alone on a desert island and try to agree to the basic moral principles to regulate a new society. Would such persons accept the principle of utility, or the principle of equality, or some other principle, perhaps Plato's, perhaps yours?

3. Write a memo to your supervisor defending an advertisement which she has challenged as deceptive. Explain why you believe that, even if the ad is deceptive, deception in advertising is defensible.

4. How much taxation is justified in order to provide a welfare floor for all citizens in a business society? Is equality of opportunity a sufficient justification for the economic inequalities which exist in modern society?

CIPOLLONE v. LIGGETT GROUP, INC.
644 F.S.283 (D.N.J. 1986)

The court turns, then, to the merits. The basis for plaintiff's motion in limine is that the societal benefits that result from producing and marketing a product are simply irrelevant to risk/utility analysis. Defendants argue to the contrary, claiming that such benefits are as integral to a fair evaluation of a product's value to society as are those attendant to the product's use. While resolution of this issue is largely preordained by the basic theoretical underpinnings of strict liability generally, the court must look to the pronouncements of the New Jersey Supreme Court in order to frame the issue and advance its resolution in this diversity case.

In recent years, the New Jersey Supreme Court has devoted much attention to the issue of strict liability. Drawing on its own substantial precedent, the court stated in Feldman, that, "We commence our strict liability analysis with the now familiar refrain that to establish strict liability a plaintiff must prove that the product was defective, that the defect existed when the product left the defendant's control, and that the defect caused injury to a reasonably foreseeable consumer . . . . The defect may take one of three forms: a manufacturing flaw, a design defect, or an inadequate warning." Proceeding then to define the meaning of "defect" in improper design and warning cases, the court noted that, "The question . . . is whether, assuming that the manufacturer knew of the defect in the product, he acted in a reasonably prudent manner in marketing the product or in providing the warnings given." The court had already discussed this "reasonableness" standard a year earlier in O'Brien, where it explained that it may be based on either "a comparison of the utility of the product with the risk of injury that it poses to the public," or on "the consumer expectations test, which recognizes that the failure of the product to perform safely may be viewed as a violation of the reasonable expectations of the consumer."

Here, plaintiff alleges that defendants' products fail to meet the former, that is, the "risk/utility" standard. This particular aspect of risk/utility theory has itself been given considered attention by the New Jersey Supreme Court. In Cepeda, for example, the court adopted the seven factors outlined by Dean Wade as relevant to the determination of whether a product's risk outweighs its utility. The court further elucidated the standard in O'Brien, where it made clear by the following language that the inquiry is essentially a balancing test in which numerous factors may appropriately be considered in arriving at a conclusion as to a product's utility.

The assessment of the utility of a design involves the consideration of available alternatives. If no alternatives are available, recourse to a unique design is more defensible. The existence of a safer and equally efficacious design, however, diminishes the justification of using a challenged design.

The evaluation of the utility of a product also involves the relative need for that product; some products are essentials, while others are luxuries. A product that fills a critical need and can be designed in only one way should be viewed differently from a luxury item. Still other products, including some for which no alternative exists, are so dangerous and of such little use that under the risk-utility analysis, a manufacturer would bear the cost of liability of harm to others. That cost might dissuade a manufacturer from placing the product on the market, even if the product has been made as safely as possible.

These passages further suggest, however, that although the risk/utility analysis mandated by the New Jersey Supreme Court may be far-reaching, its focus remains solely on the usefulness of, and dangers inherent in, the product. For while it is true that the "reasonableness" of the manufacturer will in the end be relevant to a determination of whether the product should have been placed on the market, such "reasonableness" is determined by looking only to the social benefits of a product, as opposed to its production. Notwithstanding

176

defendants' attempts to extract such meaning by means of selective citation the New Jersey Supreme Court's decisions have never said that a product's utility may be established by looking to whether the defendant "reasonably" believed that its profits would be sufficient to maintain a livelihood, hire employees, or pay taxes by operating the company that placed a product on the market.

The New Jersey Supreme Court's silence in this regard becomes all the more deafening upon an inspection of the principles underlying strict liability theory. Defendants' proposed evidence, when distilled to its essence, aims to establish that their product is profitable, that some of those profits are disseminated to others in society, and that such benefits would be reduced or eliminated if liability were imposed. But strict liability law is, if anything, intended to temper the profit motive by making a manufacturer or marketer aware that it may be less costly in the long run to market a product more safely, or not to market it at all. As noted by Dean Wade, "Manufacturers are frankly in the business of making and selling products for the profit involved." To permit defendants to introduce the evidence that they here propose would undercut the very goals of strict liability law insofar as it suggests that defendants' interest in making a profit could transform an otherwise insufficient evaluation of their product's safety into a reasonable one.

Secondly, a fundamental purpose behind the imposition of strict liability is to require that a product "pay its way" by compensating for the harms it causes. For this purpose to be furthered it is of course necessary to accept that a product's profitability will be reduced as it bears the costs attendant to its use, and indeed that its true costs to society may so outweigh its usefulness that those costs, when reflected in the product's price, will ultimately lead to that product's withdrawal from the market. That some economic dislocation may thereby result in the short run is, inturn, an accepted fact of life in the operation of a free market system in which those entities who profit from the marketing of a product--rather than its individual victims, or the government, or society--are the ones who are expected to bear the risks that such

177

products are not economically viable. Indeed, any avoidance of product liability for reasons unrelated to the inherent value of the product itself would permit the continued marketing of products that do not truly pay their way, thus discouraging the profiting entities from devoting their energies to making their product safer, or to producing products that are more socially beneficial in the long term. To permit a manufacturer or marketer to introduce evidence of a product's profitability, and to suggest that such profitability will be endangered if legal liability is found, would thus undermine these goals of greater overall economic efficiency and product safety. Wholehearted adoption of strict liability theory does not appear to have given the New Jersey Supreme Court any pause whatsoever, nor have defendants identified any opinion by which that court has expressed substantial hesitancy as to these or any other of the theory's broader economics.

Finally, defendants argue that a tort theory which might potentially price cigarettes out of the market would contravene Congress' intention in the Cigarette Labelling and Advertising Act. As this court has noted in its opinion of September 20, 1986, and as has been confirmed by the Third Circuit, Cipollone v. Liggett Group, Inc., the Act does not expressly preempt all state common law claims, but rather only those which directly impinge on the use of warning labels or advertising. Furthermore, while it may be the case that the legislative branch has formulated some policies which favor the cigarette industry, defendants have identified no other provision in the federal law which so favors that industry that it directly prohibits states from enforcing those laws which protect the health and safety of their citizens in any way which might affect the profitability of cigarette sales. This court cannot, therefore, conclude that federal law affords defendants an automatic right to undermine plaintiff's state law claim with evidence that would otherwise constitute an irrelevant defense.

In any event, viewing the matter from a more practical perspective, it is by no means clear that a finding of liability in this case, should it occur, would spell the end of cigarette sales. For it is also possible under an efficient risk-spreading system that

178

the price of defendants' product will rise to a level
that will both be accepted by the many who consume that
commodity, and reflect the costs of compensating those
who are harmed by it. Thus the state's interest in risk
spreading may well coexist quite harmoniously with any
federal policy that may favor the cigarette industry.

IS IT EVER RIGHT TO LIE?

Robert C. Solomon and Kristen R. Hanson

No.

Now, let's get down to business.

It may never be right to tell a lie, but nevertheless it is often prudent, preferable, and--if the way people behave is any indication at all of morals--popular as well.

Consider the familiar dilemma of HGT sales representative John G., who is asked whether his product is in fact as good as a Xerox. One curious fact is that John G. owns a Xerox himself, but another not insignificant fact is that he is employed by the HGT company to sell their line of products, not to express his personal preferences or conduct a neutral survey of product quality. What does he do? What can he do? Of course, he says, "Yes--and better besides." Is he lying? Or just doing his job? He is doing both, of course, but only a moral prig would say that he is thereby doing wrong.

"Truth" and "falsehood" are evasive qualities even in an academic seminar or a scientist's laboratory; they are even more so in the real world. Is a lover lying to himself when he says that his love is the "most wonderful woman in the world"? Is a salesman lying to a customer when he praises an imperfect product? To be sure, there is such a thing as outright deception--the standard case in which a used-car salesman insists that an old convertible is in excellent mechanical condition, knowing full well that the unhappy new owner will be lucky to get the heap off the lot. But one can also argue that shopping at certain used-car lots (the kind advertised by a hand-painted sign that says "Honest Harry Has the Bargains") carries with it the knowledge of risk on the part of the buyer--that risk is a trade-off for the

From It's Good Business, 1985, pp. 92-98. Reprinted by permission of the authors.

bargain.   Of   course,   there   are   outright   lies--
falsification of the odometer reading or the false claim
that the engine was overhauled three thousand miles ago,
but there is a certain latitude in lying that depends on
the context, the customer, and the costs. Not only lying
but giving misleading information is intolerable in the
health-care industry--for example, not mentioning the
side effects of a new drug.   Showing hyperdramatic
demonstrations of "action" toys to kids or giving
technical information to people who cannot possibly
understand it may involve neither false nor misleading
information but nevertheless be morally dubious (given
the huge proportion of the adult population that can be
swayed by mere adjectives such as "scientific" or
natural"). Cost counts, too. Exaggerated claims for the
cleaning powers of an inexpensive soap product or the
convenience of a household gadget advertised on TV for
(inevitably) $19.95 are more easily forgiven than even
mildly bloated praise for the value of a new house or
bulldozer. On the other hand, it is clear that it is not
only self-defeating but cruel to tell a customer
everything horrible that might befall him with his
product.   (Imagine the warnings that would have to
accompany even such a simple household appliance as a
food processor.)

     Lying may always be wrong, but some lies are much
more wrong than others. Truth may always be desirable,
but the "whole truth and nothing but the truth" is just
as likely to be a nightmare.

     To say that it is never right to lie is not the same
as to say that one should never lie. It is rather to say
that a lie is always a later resort, a strategy that is
not first choice. If the salesman could sell his wares
by saying nothing but the truth, he could, should, and
would do so.   But one must always excuse a lie, by
showing that some greater evil would result from telling
the truth or, most often, simply by showing that there
is minimal harm done by lying and that, in this context,
the lie was not wholly inappropriate. The one thing that
a person cannot do is to think that telling a lie--any
lie--is just as good or right as telling the truth, and
so needs no special justification for doing so.

182

Lying has almost always been considered a sin or an immoral act. In a recent best-selling book, Sissela Bok has argued that lying is always wrong because, in a variety of ways, it always has bad consequences--worse, that is, than if the lie had not been told. Common experience indicates otherwise, perhaps, for the general attitude both in business and in society is that lies have a perfectly proper social place. Indeed there are clearly contexts in which it would be wrong not to lie. Lies can prevent family fights and quarrels among couples. They can prevent bad feelings and help avoid misunderstandings. And, often, they can help an employee keep his or her job. ("I was caught in traffic" is a transparent lie but an acceptable excuse for being late; "I hated the idea of coming to work so much that I forgot to set the alarm" is, though true, unacceptable.)

We can all agree, looking only at short-term and immediate benefits, that the harm done by some lies is considerably less than the harm that would be done by telling the "unvarnished truth." An employer forced to fire a mediocre worker is certainly not to be blamed for saying that "financial exigencies" have forced him to lay off several low-seniority personnel, instead of telling the truth, which is that the fellow borders on incompetence and doesn't have either the charm or the imagination of a pocket calculator. An advertiser would be judged an idiot, not honest, if he baldly stated that this pain remedy is no more nor less effective than any other on the market, though its packaging is prettier. Nevertheless, there are reasons for saying that lying is always wrong.

The first reason has to do with the enormous amount of effort involved in telling a lie--any lie. The truth--even the incomplete truth--is an enormously complex network of interlocking facts. Anyone who has found himself caught in the nervous web of fabrications involved in even such a simple lie as "We don't know a thing about what our competitors are doing" ("Then how do you know that . . .?") knows how many seemingly disparate facts can come crashing in when a lie has torn just a small piece out of the truth. As recent national politics has so prominently displayed, the cost of a cover-up is often many times more than the damage done by the lie itself, even if the cover-up is successful.

183

The second reason looks beyond the short-term benefits of lying to the longer-term damage, which may be harder to see. Every lie diminishes trust. A lie discovered is guaranteed to undermine faith in the liar, but, more subtly, <u>telling</u> a lie diminishes one's trust in others. ("If I'm lying to them, they are probably lying to me as well.") Most Americans now look at television advertising as if it were nothing but a tissue of lies--ironically making the more successful ads just those that ignore substantial content and concentrate on memorable associations and effects. A businessman may make many a profit through deception--for a while--but unless one wants to keep on the road for the rest of one's life (sounds good at twenty, not so good at forty), deception almost always catches up and destroys just the business it used to ensure. As long-term investments, lies are usually a bad risk.

The third and strongest reason for thinking that it is never right to lie was suggested by Kant. He asked himself the question "What would happen if lying were generally accepted? For example, what would happen if it were an everyday and unexceptional feature of the business world that one person would borrow money from another with no intention whatever of repaying the loan?" His answer was that telling the truth and, in the example, borrowing money would both become impossible, so that if I were to approach you and ask for a $10,000 loan, which I would promise to repay on the first of the year, you would simply laugh in my face, since everyone by then would know that such promises were not to be taken seriously. Lying, in other words, must always be wrong, since to treat lying as acceptable undermines just that trust that makes telling the truth meaningful.

HOW NOT TO TEACH BUSINESS VALUES

By the age of twelve, many children find it easier to decide that all commercials lie than to try to determine which are telling the truth . . . . They become ready to believe that, like advertising, business and other institutions are riddled with hypocrisy.

Does this mean that one should never lie? Well, no. But it does mean that it is never right to tell a lie, that telling a lie always requires extra thought and some very good reasons to show that this cardinal violation of the truth should be tolerated.

This said, perhaps we should clear up a few common misconceptions about the place of lying in business. It is sometimes suggested that advertising is always a lie, since it tells only one side of the story and that side, needless to say, in the best possible light. But now it is important to distinguish--in facing any such accusation--among the following:

1. telling less than the whole truth;

2. telling a biased truth, with one's own interests in mind;

3. idealizing one's products or services;

4. giving misleading information; that is, true statements that are intended to be misunderstood or misinterpreted;

5. stating obvious falsehoods;

6. stating vicious falsehoods.

An obvious falsehood, for example, is the displayed claim of some toothpaste manufacturers--that use of a certain gel will overnight convert Shy Sam or Plain Jane to Fabulous Fred or Super Sally, the heartthrob of the high-school prom. One might object to other aspects of such advertising, but "It isn't true" seems too silly to say.

Vicious falsehoods, on the other hand, are those that are not at all obvious and are a deliberate and possibly dangerous form of deception. Saying that a product will do such and such when it will not is vicious deception, as is intentionally withholding information--for example, the flammability of children's pajamas or the side effects of a popular over-the-counter drug. Misleading information can be as vicious as false information--indeed it is only a matter of logical nuance that allows us to distinguish between the two.

It is impossible to tell the "whole story," especially in the limited time of a fifteen-second radio or TV slot or in the small space available on a paper package. But advertising isn't supposed to be a scientific study, even if it utilizes some (more or less) scientific evidence on the product's behalf. Of course advertising expresses a bias on the behalf of the product. Of course it idealizes the product in its presentation. But neither bias nor idealization is lying, and it is surely foolish to insist that advertising, unlike almost every other aspect of social life, be restricted to the simple, boring truth--that is, that this product is not much different from its competitors and that people have lived for hundreds of years without any of them.

It is often challenged--these days with Orwellian overtones--that if advertising in general and TV advertising in particular have turned the American consumer into something of a supermarket zombie, without a will of his or her own, without judgment, buying hundreds of innocuous but sometimes tasteless products that no one really needs. But the zombie image contradicts precisely what lies beneath the whole discussion of truth--namely, the confidence that we are, more or less, capable of making value judgments on our own, and that if we buy or even need to buy products that are of no particular cosmic importance, this does not signal either the end of civilization or the disintegration of the human mind. Encouraging someone to buy a product that is only a fad or a mark of status is not deception, and to call it that tends to undermine the ethical distinction that is of enormous importance-- between vicious falsehoods and any number of other "varnishings" of the truth. These may be vulgar. They may encourage us to compete for some pretty silly achievements--the shiniest (and most slippery) floor, a car that can win the grand prix (to be driven in bumper-to-bumper traffic up and down the freeway), a soap that makes one speak in a phony Irish brogue. But to

186

condemn all advertising is to make it impossible to
attack vicious advertising and thus to bring about the
logical conclusion imagined by Kant--an entire world in
which no one believes anything, in which advertising
serves at most as a source of amusement and seduction of
the feebleminded.

AND WHAT ABOUT DETERGENTS AND "ACTION TOYS"?

> Competitive advertising [by lawyers] would
> encourage extravagant, artful, self-laudatory
> brashness in seeking business and thus could
> mislead the layman . . . . It would inevitably
> produce unrealistic expectations . . . and
> bring about distrust of law and lawyers.
>
> From a report of the American Bar Association

Let's end our discussion of lying by commenting once
again on Alfred Carr's suggestion that business is like
poker, that it has its own rules, which are different
from ordinary ethics. One of these rules, supposedly,
is the permissibility of lying. But business (like
poker) forbids lying. Contrary to Carr, a generally
accepted practice of lying would undermine the business
world faster than any external threat that has ever faced
it. Promises and contracts, if not good faith, are the
presuppositions of all business. The exact nature of
truth in advertising may be controversial, but
advertising in general must be not only based on fact but
believable and trustworthy. If it were not, the
commercial world in America would be about as effective
as the provocations of Hari Krishnas in America's
airports--an annoyance to be ignored as we all go on with
the rest of our lives.

Honesty isn't just the best policy in business; it
is, in general, the only possible policy.

187

MEDALS FOR HONESTY?

What is universal about these examples [of lying in business] is that these managers, each functioning on a different corporate level, are concerned with one thing--getting the job done. Most companies give numerous awards for achievement and accomplishment, for sales, for growth, for longevity and loyalty; but there are no medals in the business world for honesty, compassion, or truthfulness.

IN DEFENSE OF EQUALITY

Michael Walzer

I

At the very center of conservative thought lies this idea: that the present division of wealth and power corresponds to some deeper reality of human life. Conservatives don't want to say merely that the present division is what it ought to be, for that would invite a search for some distributive principle--as if it were possible to <u>make</u> a distribution. They want to say that whatever the division of wealth and power is, it naturally is, and that all efforts to change it, temporarily successful in proportion to their bloodiness, must be futile in the end. We are then invited, as in Irving Kristol's recent <u>Commentary</u> article, to reflect upon the perversity of those who would make the attempt. Like a certain sort of leftist thought, conservative argument seems quickly to shape itself around a rhetoric of motives rather than one of reasons. Kristol is especially adept at that rhetoric and strangely unconcerned about the reductionism it involves. He aims to expose egalitarianism as the ideology of envious and resentful intellectuals. No one else cares about it, he says, except the "new class" of college-educated, professional, most importantly, professorial men and women, who hate their bourgeois past (and present) and long for a world of their own making.

I suppose I should have felt, after reading Kristol's piece, that the decent drapery of my socialist convictions has been stripped away, that I was left naked and shivering, small-minded and self-concerned. Perhaps I did feel a little like that, for my first impulse was to respond in kind, exposing anti-egalitarianism as the ideology of those other intellectuals--"that are mostly professors, of course"--whose spiritual path was sketched some years ago by the editor of <u>Commentary</u>. But that would be at best a degrading business, and I doubt that my analysis would be any more accurate than Kristol's.

From <u>Dissent</u>, 1973. Reprinted by permission. Footnotes omitted.

It is better to ignore the motives of these "new men" and focus instead on what they say: that the inequalities we are all familiar with are inherent in our condition, are accepted by ordinary people (like themselves), and are criticized only by the perverse. I think all these assertions are false; I shall try to respond to them in a serious way.

Kristol doesn't argue that we can't possibly have greater equality or greater inequality than we presently have. Both communist and aristocratic societies are possible, he writes, under conditions of political repression or economic under-development and stagnation. But insofar as men and women are set free from the coerciveness of the state and from material necessity, they will distribute themselves in a more natural way, more or less as contemporary Americans have done. The American way is exemplary because it derives from or reflects the real inequalities of mankind. People don't naturally fall into two classes (patrician and plebeians) as conservatives once thought; nor can they plausibly be grouped into a single class (citizens or comrades) as leftists still believe. Instead, "human talents and abilities . . . distribute themselves along a bell-shaped curve, with most people clustered around the middle, and with much smaller percentages at the lower and higher ends." The marvels of social science!--this distribution is a demonstrable fact. And it is another "demonstrable fact that in all modern bourgeois societies, the distribution of income is also along a bell-shaped curve . . . ." The second bell echoes the first. Moreover, once this harmony is established, "the political structure--the distribution of political power--follows along the same way . . . ." At this point, Kristol must add, "however slowly and reluctantly," since he believes that the Soviet economy is moving closer every year to its natural shape, and it is admittedly hard to find evidence that nature is winning out in the political realm. But in the United States, nature is triumphant: we are perfectly bell-shaped.

The first bell is obviously the crucial one. The defense of inequality reduces to these two propositions: that talent is distributed unequally and that talent will out. Clearly, we all want men and women to develop and express their talents, but whenever they are able to do

190

that, Kristol suggests the bell-shaped curve will appear or reappear, first in the economy, then in the political system. It is a neat argument but also a peculiar one, for there is no reason to think that "human talents and abilities" in fact distribute themselves along a single curve, although income necessarily does. Consider the range and variety of human capacities: intelligence, physical strength, agility and grace, artistic creativity, mechanical skill, leadership, endurance, memory, psychological insight, the capacity for hard work--even, moral strength, sensitivity, the ability to express compassion. Let's assume that with respect to all these, most people (but different people in each case) cluster around the middle of whatever scale we can construct, with smaller numbers at the lower and higher ends. Which of these curves is actually echoed by the income bell? Which, if any, ought to be?

There is another talent that we need to consider: the ability to make money, the green thumb of bourgeois society--a secondary talent, no doubt, combining many of the others in ways specified by the immediate environment, but probably also a talent that distributes, if we could graph it, along a bell-shaped curve. Even this curve would not correlate exactly with the income bell because of the intervention of luck, that eternal friend of the untalented, whose most important social expression is the inheritance of property. But the correlation would be close enough, and it might also be morally plausible and satisfying. People who are able to make money ought to make money, in the same way that people who are able to write books ought to write books. Every human talent should be developed and expressed.

The difficulty here is that making money is only rarely a form of self-expression, and the money we make is rarely enjoyed for its intrinsic qualities (at least, economists frown upon that sort of enjoyment). In a capitalist world, money is the universal medium of exchange; it enables the men and women who possess it to purchase virtually every other sort of social good; we collect it for its exchange value. Political power, celebrity, admiration, leisure, works of art, baseball teams, legal advice, sexual pleasure, travel, education, medical care, rare books, sailboats--all these (and much more) are up for sale. The list is as endless as human

191

desire and social invention. Now isn't it odd, and morally implausible and unsatisfying, that all these things should be distributed to people with a talent for making money? And even odder and more unsatisfying that they should be distributed (as they are) to people who have money, whether or not they made it, whether or not they possess any talent at all?

Rich people, of course, always look talented--just as the beautiful people always look beautiful--to the deferential observer. But it is the first task of social science, one would think, to look beyond these appearances. "The properties of money," Marx wrote, "are my own (the possessor's) properties and faculties. What I _am_ and _can_ do is, therefore, not at all determined by my individuality. I _am_ ugly, but I can buy the most beautiful woman for myself. Consequently, I am not ugly, for the effect of ugliness, its power to repel, is annulled by money . . . . I am a detestable, dishonorable, unscrupulous, and stupid man, but money is honored and so also is its possessor."

It would not be any better if we gave people money in direct proportion to their intelligence, their strength, or their moral rectitude. The resulting distributions would each, no doubt, reflect what Kristol calls "the tyranny of the bell-shaped curve," though it is worth noticing again that the populations in the lower, middle, and upper regions of each graph would be radically different. But whether it was the smart, the strong, or the righteous who enjoyed all the things that money can buy, the oddity would remain: why them? Why anybody? In fact, there is no single talent or combination of talents that plausibly entitles a man to every available social good--and there is no single talent or combination of talents that necessarily must win the available goods of a free society. Kristol's bell-shaped curve is tyrannical only in a purely formal sense. Any particular distribution may indeed be bell-shaped, but there are a large number of possible distributions. Nor need there be a single distribution of all social goods, for different goods might well be distributed differently. Nor again need all these distributions follow this or that talent curve, for in the sharing of some social goods, talent does not seem a relevant consideration at all.

Consider the case of medical care: surely it should not be distributed to individuals because they are wealthy, intelligent, or righteous, but only because they are sick. Now, over any given period of time, it may be true that some men and women won't require any medical treatment, a very large number will need some moderate degree of attention, and a few will have to have intensive care. If that is so, then we must hope for the appearance of another bell-shaped curve. Not just any bell will do. It must be the right one, echoing what might be called the susceptibility-to-sickness curve. But in America today, the distribution of medical care actually follows closely the lines of the income graph. It's not how a man feels, but how much money he has that determines how often he visits a doctor. Another demonstrable fact! Does it require envious intellectuals to see that something is wrong?

There are two possible ways of setting things right. We might distribute income in proportion to susceptibility-to-sickness, or we might make sure that medical care is not for sale at all, but is available to those who need it. The second of these is obviously the simpler. Indeed, it is a modest proposal and already has wide support, even among those ordinary men and women who are said to be indifferent to equality. And yet, the distribution of medical care solely for medical reasons would point the way toward an egalitarian society, for it would call the dominance of the income curve dramatically into question.

II

What egalitarianism requires is that many bells should ring. Different goods should be distributed to different people for different reasons. Equality is not a simple notion, and it cannot be satisfied by a single distributive scheme--not even, I hasten to add, by a scheme that emphasizes need. "From each according to his abilities, and to each according to his needs" is a fine slogan with regard to medical care. Tax money collected from all of us in proportion to our resources (these will never correlate exactly with our abilities, but that problem I shall leave aside for now) must pay the doctors who care for those of us who are sick. Other people who deliver similar sort of social goods should probably be

193

paid in the same way--teachers and lawyers, for example.
But Marx's slogan doesn't help at all with regard to the
distribution of political power, honor and fame, leisure
time, rare books, and sailboats. None of these things
can be distributed to individuals in proportion to their
needs, for they are not things that anyone (strictly
speaking) needs. They can't be distributed in equal
amounts or given to whoever wants them, for some of them
are necessarily scarce, and some of them can't be
possessed unless other people agree on the proper name
of the possessor. There is no criterion, I think, that
will fit them all. In the past they have indeed been
distributed on a single principle: men and women have
possessed them or their historical equivalents because
they were strong or well-born or wealthy. But this only
suggests that a society in which any single distributive
principle is dominant cannot be an egalitarian society.
Equality requires a diversity of principles, which
mirrors the diversity both of mankind and of social
goods.

Whenever equality in this sense does not prevail,
we have a kind of tyranny, for it is tyrannical of the
well-born or the strong or the rich to gather to
themselves social goods that have nothing to do with
their personal qualities. This is an idea beautifully
expressed in a passage from Pascal's _Pensees_, which I am
going to quote at some length, since it is the source of
my own argument.

> The nature of tyranny is to desire power over
> the whole world and outside its own sphere.

> There are different companies--the strong, the
> handsome, the intelligent, the devout--and each
> man reigns in his own, not elsewhere. But
> sometimes they meet, and the strong and the
> handsome fight for mastery--foolishly, for
> their mastery is of different kinds. They
> misunderstand one another, and make the mistake
> of each aiming at universal dominion. Nothing
> can win this, not even strength, for it is
> powerless in the kingdom of the wise . . . .

Tyranny. The following statements, therefore, are false and tyrannical: "Because I am handsome, so I should command respect." "I am strong, therefore men should love me . . . ." "I am . . . etc."

Tyranny is the wish to obtain by one means what can only be had by another. We owe different duties to different qualities: love is the proper response to charm, fear to strength, and belief to learning.

Marx makes a very similar argument in one of the early manuscripts; perhaps he had this pensee in mind.

Let us assume man to be man, and his relation to the world to be a human one. Then love can only be exchanged for love, trust for trust, etc. If you wish to enjoy art you must be an artistically cultivated person; if you wish to influence other people, you must be a person who really has a stimulating and encouraging effect upon others . . . . If you love without evoking love in return, i.e., if you are not able, by the manifestation of yourself as a loving person, to make yourself a beloved person, then your love is impotent and a misfortune.

The doctrine suggested by these passages is not an easy one, and I can expound it only in a tentative way. It isn't that every man should get what he deserves--as in the old definition of justice--for desert is relevant only to some of the exchanges that Pascal and Marx have in mind. Charming men and women don't deserve to be loved: I may love this one or that one, but it can't be the case that I ought to do so. Similarly, learned men don't deserve to be believed: they are believed or not depending on the arguments they make. What Pascal and Marx are saying is that love and belief can't rightly be had in any other way--can't be purchased or coerced, for example. It is wrong to seek them in any way that is alien to their intrinsic character. In its extended form, their argument is that for all our personal and collective resources, there are distributive reasons that are somehow right, that are naturally part of our ideas

195

about the things themselves. So nature is re-established as a critical standard, and we are invited to wonder at the strangeness of the existing order.

This new standard is egalitarian, even though it obviously does not require an equal distribution of love and belief. The doctrine of right reasons suggests that we pay equal attention to the "different qualities," and to the "individuality" of every man and woman, that we find ways of sharing our resources that match the variety of their needs, interests, and capacities. The clues that we must follow lie in the conceptions we already have, in the things we already know about love and belief, and also about respect, obedience, education, medical care, legal aid, all the necessities of life--for this is not esoteric doctrine, whatever difficulties it involves. Nor is it a panacea for human misfortune, as Marx's last sentence makes clear: it is only meant to suggest a humane form of social accommodation. There is little we can do, in the best of societies, for the man who isn't loved. But there may be ways to avoid the triumph of the man who doesn't love--who buys love or forces it--or at least of his parallels in the larger social and political world: the leaders, for example, who are obeyed because of their coercive might or their enormous wealth. Our goal should be an end to tyranny, a society in which no human being is master outside his sphere. That is the only society of equals worth having.

But it isn't readily had, for there is no necessity implied by the doctrine of right reasons. Pascal is wrong to say that "strength is powerless in the kingdom of the wise"--or rather, he is talking of an ideal realm and not of the intellectual world as we know it. In fact, wise men and women (at any rate, smart men and women) have often in the past defended the tyranny of the strong, as they still defend the tyranny of the rich. Sometimes, of course, they do this because they are persuaded of the necessity or the utility of tyrannical rule; sometimes for other reasons. Kristol suggests that whenever intellectuals are not persuaded, they are secretly aspiring to a tyranny of their own: they too would like to rule outside their sphere. Again, that's certainly true of some of them, and we all have our own lists. But it's not necessarily true. Surely it is possible, though no doubt difficult, for an intellectual

to pay proper respect to the "different companies." I
want to argue that in our society the only way to do
that, or to begin to do it, is to worry about the tyranny
of money.

III

    Let's start with some things that money cannot buy.
I can't buy the American League pennant: star players
can be hired but victories presumably are not up for
sale. It can't buy the National Book Award: writers
can be subsidized, but the judges presumably can't be
bribed. Nor, it should be added, can the pennant or the
award be won by being strong, charming, or ideologically
correct--at least we hope not. In these sorts of cases,
the right reasons for winning are built into the very
structure of the competition. I am inclined to think
that they are similarly built into a large number of
social practices and institutions. It's worth focusing
again, for example, on the practice of medicine. From
ancient times, doctors were required to take an oath to
help the sick, not the powerful or the wealthy. That
requirement reflects a common understanding about the
very nature of medical care. Many professionals don't
share that understanding, but the opinion of ordinary men
and women, in this case at least, is profoundly
egalitarian.

    The same understanding is reflected in our legal
system. A man accused of a crime is entitled to a fair
trial simply by virtue of being an accused man; nothing
else about him is a relevant consideration. That is why
defendants who cannot afford a lawyer are provided with
legal counsel by the state; otherwise justice would be
up for sale. And that is why defense counsel can
challenge particular jurors thought to be prejudiced:
the fate of the accused must hang on his guilt or
innocence, not on his political opinions, his social
class, or his race. We want different defendants to be
treated differently, but only for the right reasons.

    The case is the same in the political system,
whenever the state is a democracy. Each citizen is
entitled to one vote simply because he is a citizen. Men
and women who are ambitious to exercise greater power
must collect votes, but they can't do that by purchasing

197

them; we don't want votes to be traded in the marketplace, though virtually everything else is traded there, and so we have made it a criminal offense to offer bribes to voters. The only right way to collect votes is to campaign for them, that is, to be persuasive, stimulating, encouraging, and so on. Great inequalities in political power are acceptable only if they result from a political process of a certain kind, open to argument, closed to bribery and coercion. The freely given support of one's fellow citizens is the appropriate criterion for exercising political power and, once again, it is not enough, or it shouldn't be, to be physically powerful, or well-born, or even ideologically correct.

It is often enough, however, to be rich. No one can doubt the mastery of the wealthy in the spheres of medicine, justice, and political power, even though these are not their own spheres. I don't want to say their unchallenged mastery, for in democratic states we have at least made a start toward restricting the tyranny of money. But we have only made a start: think how different America would have to be before these three companies of men and women--the sick, the accused, the politically ambitious--could be treated in strict accordance with their individual qualities. It would be immediately necessary to have a national health service, national legal assistance, the strictest possible control over campaign contributions. Modest proposals, again, but they represent so many moves toward the realization of that old socialist slogan about the abolition of money. I have always been puzzled by that slogan, for socialists have never, to my knowledge, advocated a return to a barter economy. But it makes a great deal of sense if it is interpreted to mean <u>the abolition of the power of money outside its sphere</u>. What socialists want is a society in which wealth is no longer convertible into social goods with which it has no intrinsic connection.

But it is in the very nature of money to be convertible (that's all it is), and I find it hard to imagine the sorts of laws and law enforcement that would be necessary to prevent monied men and women from buying medical care and legal aid over and above whatever social minimum is provided for everyone. In the United States today, people can even buy police protection beyond what the state provides, though one would think that it is the primary purpose of the state to guarantee equal security to all its citizens, and it is by no means the rich, despite the temptations they offer, who stand in greatest need of protection. But this sort of thing could be prevented only by a very considerable restriction of individual liberty--of the freedom to offer services and to purchase them. The case is even harder with respect to politics itself. One can stop overt bribery, limit the size of campaign contributions, require publicity, and so on. But none of these things will be enough to prevent the wealthy from exercising power in all sorts of ways to which their fellow citizens have never consented. Indeed, the ability to hold or spend vast sums of money is itself a form of power, permitting what might be called preemptive strikes against the political system. And this, it seems to me, is the strongest possible argument for a radical redistribution of wealth. So long as money is convertible outside its sphere, it must be widely and more or less equally held so as to minimize its distorting effects upon legitimate distributive processes.

IV

What is the proper sphere of wealth? What sorts of things are rightly had in exchange for money? The obvious answer is also the right one: all those economic goods and services, beyond what is necessary to life itself, that men and women find useful or pleasing. There is nothing degraded about wanting these things; there is nothing unattractive, boring, debased, or philistine about a society organized to provide them for its members. Kristol insists that a snobbish dislike for the sheer productivity of a bourgeois society is a feature of egalitarian argument. I would have thought that a deep appreciation of that productivity has more often marked the work of socialist writers. The question is, how are the products to be distributed? Now, the right way to possess useful and pleasing things is by making them, or growing them, or somehow providing them for others. The medium of exchange is money, and this is the proper function of money and, ideally, its only function.

199

There should be no way of acquiring rare books and sailboats except by working for them. But this is not to say that workers deserve whatever money they can get for the goods and services they provide. In capitalist society, the actual exchange value of the work they do is largely a function of market conditions over which they exercise no control. It has little to do with the intrinsic value of work or with the individual qualities of the worker. There is no reason for socialists to respect it, unless it turns out to be socially useful to do so. There are other values, however, that they must respect, for money isn't the only or necessarily the most important thing for which work can be exchanged. A lawyer is surely entitled to the respect he wins from his colleagues and to the gratitude and praise he wins from his clients. The work he has done may also constitute a good reason for making him director of the local legal aid society; it may even be a good reason for making him a judge. It isn't, on the face of it, a good reason for allowing him an enormous income. Nor is the willingness of his clients to pay his fees a sufficient reason, for most of them almost certainly think they should be paying less. The money they pay is different from the praise they give, in that the first is extrinsically determined, the second freely offered.

In a long and thoughtful discussion of egalitarianism in the Public Interest, Daniel Bell worries that socialists today are aiming at an "equality of results" instead of the "just meritocracy" (the career open to talents) that he believes was once the goal of leftist and even of revolutionary politics. I confess that I am tempted by "equality of results" in the sphere of money, precisely because it is so hard to see how a person can merit the things that money can buy. On the other hand, it is easy to list cases where merit (of one sort or another) is clearly the right distributive criteria, and where socialism would not require the introduction of any other principle.

- Six people speak at a meeting, advocating different policies, seeking to influence the decision of the assembled group.

- Six doctors are known to aspire to a hospital directorship.

200

- Six writers publish novels and anxiously await the reviews of the critics.
- Six men seek the company and love of the same woman.

Now, we all know the right reasons for the sorts of decisions, choices, judgments that are in question here. I have never heard anyone seriously argue that the woman must let herself be shared, or the hospital establish a six-man directorate, or the critics distribute their praise evenly, or the people at the meeting adopt all six proposals. In all these cases, the personal qualities of the individuals involved, or the arguments they make, or the work they do (as these appear to the others) should carry the day.

But what sorts of personal qualities are relevant to owning a $20,000 sailboat? A love for sailing, perhaps, and a willingness to build the boat or do an equivalent amount of work. In America today, it would take a steelworker about two years to earn that money (assuming that he didn't buy anything else during all that time) and it would take a corporation executive a month or two. How can that be right, when the executive also has a rug on the floor, air-conditioning, a deferential secretary, and enormous personal power? He is being paid as he goes, while the steelworker is piling up a kind of moral merit (so we have been taught) by deferring pleasure. Surely there is no meritocratic defense for this sort of difference. It would seem much better to pay the worker and the executive more or less the same weekly wage and let the sailboat be bought by the person who is willing to forgo other goods and services, that is, by the person who really wants it. Is this "equality of result"? In fact, the results will be different, if the people are, and it seems to me that they will be different for the right reasons.

Against this view, there is a conventional but also very strong argument that can be made on behalf of enterprise and inventiveness. If there is a popular defense of inequality, it is this one, but I don't think it can carry us very far toward the inequalities that Kristol wants to defend. Consider the case of the man who builds a better mousetrap, or opens a restaurant and sells delicious blintzes, or does a little teaching on

201

the side. He has no air-conditioning, no secretary, no power; probably his reward has to be monetary. He has to have a chance, at least, to earn a little more money than his less enterprising neighbors. The market doesn't guarantee that he will in fact earn more, but it does make it possible, and until some other way can be found to do that, market relations are probably defensible under the doctrine of right reasons. Here in the world of the petty-bourgeoisie, it seems appropriate that people able to provide goods or services that are novel, timely, or particularly excellent should reap the rewards they presumably had in mind when they went to work. And that they were right to have in mind: no one would want to feed blintzes to strangers, day after day, merely to win their gratitude.

But one might well want to be a corporation executive, day after day, merely to make all those decisions. It is precisely the people who are paid or who pay themselves vast sums of money who reap all sorts of other rewards too. First of all, there are rewards, like the pleasure of exercising power, that are intrinsic to certain jobs. An executive must make decisions-- that's what he is there for--and even decisions seriously affecting other people. It is right that he should do that, however, only if he has been persuasive, stimulating, encouraging, and so on, and won the support of a majority of those same people. That he owns the corporation or has been chosen by the owners isn't enough. Indeed, given the nature of corporate power in contemporary society, the following statement (to paraphrase Pascal) is false and tyrannical: because I am rich, so I should make decisions and command obedience. Even in corporations organized democratically, of course, the personal exercise of power will persist. It is more likely to be seen, however, as it is normally seen in political life--as the chief attraction of executive positions. And this will cast a new light on the other rewards of leadership.

The second of these consists in all the side-effects of power: prestige, status, deference, and so on. Democracy tends to reduce these, or should tend that way when it is working well, without significantly reducing the attractions of decision making. The same is true of the third form of reward, money itself, which is owed to

202

work, but not necessarily to place and power. We pay political leaders much less than corporation executives, precisely because we understand so well the excitement and appeal of political office. Insofar as we recognize the political character of corporations, then, we can pay their executives less too. I doubt that there would be a lack of candidates even if we paid them no more than was paid to any other corporation employee. Perhaps there are reasons for paying them more--but not meritocratic reasons, for we give all the attention that is due to their merit when we make them our leaders.

We do not give all due attention to the restaurant owner, however, merely by eating his blintzes. Him we have to pay, and he can ask, I suppose, whatever the market will bear. That's fair enough, and no real threat to equality so long as he can't amass so much money that he becomes a threat to the integrity of the political system and so long as he does not exercise power, tyrannically, over other men and women. Within his proper sphere, he is as good a citizen as any other. His activities recall Dr. Johnson's remark: "There are few ways in which man can be more innocently employed than in getting money."

V

The most immediate occasion of the conservative attack on equality is the reappearance of the quota system--newly designed, or so it is said, to move us close to egalitarianism rather than to maintain old patterns of religious and racial discrimination. Kristol does not discuss quotas, perhaps because they are not widely supported by professional people (or by professors): the disputes of the last several years do not fit the brazen simplicity of his argument. But almost everyone else talks about them, and Bell worries at some length, and rightly, about the challenge quotas represent to the "just meritocracy" he favors. Indeed, quotas in any form, new or old, establish "wrong reasons" as the basis of important social decisions, perhaps the most important social decisions: who shall be a doctor, who shall be a lawyer, and who shall be a bureaucrat. It is obvious that being black or a woman or having a Spanish surname (any more than being white, male, and Protestant) is no qualification for entering a university

203

or a medical school or joining the civil service. In a
sense, then, the critique of quotas consists almost
entirely of a series of restatements and reiterations of
the argument I have been urging in this essay. One only
wishes that the critics would apply it more generally
than they seem ready to do. There is more to be said,
however, if they consistently refuse to do that.

The positions for which quotas are being urged are,
in America today, key entry points to the good life.
They open the way, that is, to a life marked above all
by a profusion of goods, material and moral:
possessions, conveniences, prestige, and deference. Many
of these goods are not in any plausible sense appropriate
rewards for the work that is being done. They are merely
the rewards that upper classes throughout history have
been able to seize and hold for their members. Quotas,
as they are currently being used, are a way of
redistributing these rewards by redistributing the social
places to which they conventionally pertain. It is a bad
way, because one really wants doctors and (even) civil
servants to have certain sorts of qualifications. To the
people on the receiving end of medical and bureaucratic
services, race and class are a great deal less important
than knowledge, competence, courtesy, and so on. I don't
want to say that race and class are entirely unimportant:
it would be wrong to underestimate the distortions
introduced by an inegalitarian society into these sorts
of human relations. But if the right reason for
receiving medical care is being sick, then the right
reason for giving medical care is being able to help the
sick. And so medical schools should pay attention, first
of all and almost exclusively, to the potential
helpfulness of their applicants.

But they may be able to do that only if the usual
connections between place and reward are decisively
broken. Here is another example of the doctrine of right
reasons. If men and women wanted to be doctors primarily
because they wanted to be helpful, they would have no
reason to object when judgments were made about their
potential helpfulness. But so long as there are
extrinsic reasons for wanting to be a doctor, there will
be pressure to choose doctors (that is, to make medical
school places available) for reasons that are similarly
extrinsic. So long as goods that medical schools

distribute include more than certificates of competence, include, to be precise, certificates of earning power, quotas are not entirely implausible. I don't see that being black is a worse reason for owning a sailboat than being a doctor. They are equally bad reasons.

Quotas today are a means of lower-class aggrandizement, and they are likely to be resolutely opposed, opposed without guilt and worry, only by people who are entirely content with the class structure as it is and with the present distribution of goods and services. For those of us who are not content, anxiety cannot be avoided. We know that quotas are wrong, but we also know that the present distribution of wealth makes no moral sense, that the dominance of the income curve plays havoc with legitimate distributive principles, and that quotas are a form of redress no more irrational than the world within which and because of which they are demanded. In an egalitarian society, however, quotas would be unnecessary and inexcusable.

VI

I have put forward a difficult argument in very brief form, in order to answer Kristol's even briefer argument--for he is chiefly concerned with the motives of those who advocate equality and not with the case they make or try to make. He is also concerned, he says, with the fact that equality has suddenly been discovered and is now for the first time being advocated as the chief virtue of social institutions: as if societies were not complex and values ambiguous. I don't know what discoverers and advocates he has in mind. But it is worth stressing that equality as I have described it does not stand alone, but is closely related to the idea of liberty. The relation is complex, and I cannot say very much about it here. It is a feature of the argument I have made, however, that the right reason for distributing love, belief, and, most important for my immediate purposes, political power is the freely given consent of lovers, believers, and citizens. In these sorts of cases, of course, we all have standards to urge upon our fellows: we say that so and so should not be believed unless he offers evidence or that so and so should not be elected to political office unless he commits himself to civil rights. But clearly credence

and power are not and ought not to be distributed
according to my standards or yours. What is necessary
is that everyone else be able to say yes or no. Without
liberty, then, there could be no rightful distribution
at all. On the other hand, we are not free, not
politically free at least, if his yes, because of his
birth or place or fortune, counts seventeen times more
heavily than my no. Here the case is exactly as
socialists have always claimed it to be: liberty and
equality are the two chief virtues of social
institutions, and they stand best when they stand
together.

THE REPUBLIC, SELECTIONS FROM BOOK I

Plato

All this time Thrasymachus had been trying more than once to break in upon our conversation; but his neighbours had restrained him, wishing to hear the argument to the end. In the pause after my last words he could keep quiet no longer; but gathering himself up like a wild beast he sprang at us as if he would tear us in pieces. Polemarchus and I were frightened out of our wits, when he burst out to the whole company:

What is the matter with you two, Socrates? Why do you go on in this imbecile way, politely deferring to each other's nonsense? If you really want to know what justice means, stop asking questions and scoring off the answers you get. You know very well it is easier to ask questions than to answer them. Answer yourself, and tell us what you think justice means. I won't have you telling us it is the same as what is obligatory or useful or advantageous or profitable or expedient; I want a clear and precise statement; I won't put up with that sort of verbiage.

I was amazed by this onslaught and looked at him in terror. If I had not seen this wolf before he saw me, I really believe I should have been struck dumb; but fortunately I had looked at him earlier, when he was beginning to get exasperated with our argument; so I was able to reply, though rather tremulously:

Don't be hard on us, Thrasymachus. If Polemarchus and I have gone astray in our search, you may be quite sure the mistake was not intentional. If we had been looking for a piece of gold, we should never have deliberately allowed our politeness to spoil our chance of finding it; and now when we are looking for justice, a thing much more precious than gold, you cannot imagine we should defer to each other in that foolish way and not

Reprinted from The Republic of Plato, translated by F. M. Cornford (1941) by permission of Oxford University Press. Editor's comments and notes omitted.

do our best to bring it to light. You must believe we are in earnest, my friend; but I am afraid the task is beyond our powers, and we might expect a man of your ability to pity us instead of being so severe.

Thrasymachus replied with a burst of sardonic laughter.

Good Lord, he said; Socrates at his old trick of shamming ignorance! I knew it; I told the others you would refuse to commit yourself and do anything sooner than answer a question.

Yes, Thrasymachus, I replied; because you are clever enough to know that if you asked someone what are the factors of the number twelve, and at the same time warned him: 'Look here, you are not to tell me that 12 is twice 6, or 3 times 4, or 6 times 2, or 4 times 3; I won't put up with any such nonsense'--you must surely see that no one would answer a question put like that. He would say: 'What do you mean, Thrasymachus? Am I forbidden to give you any of these answers, even if one happens to be right? Do you want me to give a wrong one?' What would you say to that?

Humph! said he. As if that were a fair analogy!

I don't see why it is not, said I; but in any case, do you suppose our barring a certain answer would prevent the man from giving it, if he thought it was the truth?

Do you mean that you are going to give me one of those answers I barred?

I should not be surprised, if it seemed to me true, on reflection.

And what if I give you another definition of justice, better than any of those? What penalty are you prepared to pay?

The penalty deserved by ignorance, which must surely be to receive instruction from the wise. So I would suggest that as a suitable punishment.

I like your notion of a penalty! he said; but you

must pay the costs as well.

I will, when I have any money.

That will be all right, said Glaucon; we will all subscribe for Socrates. So let us have your definition, Thrasymachus.

Oh yes, he said; so that Socrates may play the old game of questioning and refuting someone else, instead of giving an answer himself!

But really, I protested, what can you expect from a man who does not know the answer or profess to know it, and, besides that, has been forbidden by no mean authority to put forward any notions he may have? Surely the definition should naturally come from you, who say you do know the answer and can tell it us. Please do not disappoint us. I should take it as a kindness, and I hope you will not be chary of giving Glaucon and the rest of us the advantage of your instruction.

Glaucon and the others added their entreaties to mine. Thrasymachus was evidently longing to win credit, for he was sure he had an admirable answer ready, though he made a show of insisting that I should be the one to reply. In the end he gave way and exclaimed:

So this is what Socrates' wisdom comes to! He refuses to teach, and goes about learning from others without offering so much as thanks in return.

I do learn from others, Thrasymachus; that is quite true; but you are wrong to call me ungrateful. I give in return all I can--praise; for I have no money. And how ready I am to applaud any idea that seems to me sound, you will see in a moment, when you have stated your own; for I am sure that will be sound.

Listen then, Thrasymachus began. What I say is that 'just' or 'right' means nothing but what is to the interest of the stronger party. Well, where is your applause? You don't mean to give it me.

I will, as soon as I understand, I said. I don't see yet what you mean by right being the interest of the stronger party. For instance, Polydamas, the athlete, is stronger than we are, and it is to his interest to eat beef for the sake of his muscles; but surely you don't mean that the same diet would be good for weaker men and therefore be right for us?

You are trying to be funny, Socrates. It's a low trick to take my words in the sense you think will be most damaging.

No, no, I protested; but you must explain.

Don't you know, then, that a state may be ruled by a despot, or a democracy, or an aristocracy?

Of course.

And that the ruling element is always the strongest?

Yes.

Well then, in every case the laws are made by the ruling party in its own interest; a democracy makes democratic laws, a despot autocratic ones, and so on. By making these laws they define as 'right' for their subjects whatever is for their own interest, and they call anyone who breaks them a 'wrongdoer' and punish him accordingly. This is what I mean: in all states alike 'right' has the same meaning, namely what is for the interest of the party established in power, and that is the strongest. So the sound conclusion is that what is 'right' is the same everywhere: the interest of the stronger party.

Now I see what you mean, said I; whether it is true or not, I must try to make out. When you define in terms of interest, you are yourself giving one of those answers you forbade to me; though, to be sure, you add 'to the stronger party.'

An insignificant addition, perhaps!

Its importance is not clear yet; what is clear is that we must find out whether your definition is true. I agree myself that right is in a sense a matter of interest; but when you add 'to the stronger party,' I don't know about that. I must consider.

Go ahead, then.

I will. Tell me this. No doubt you also think it is right to obey the men in power?

I do.

Are they infallible in every type of state, or can they sometimes make a mistake?

Of course they can make a mistake.

In framing laws, then, they may do their work well or badly?

No doubt.

Well, that is to say, when the laws they make are to their own interest; badly, when they are not?

Yes.

But the subjects are to obey any law they lay down, and they will then be doing right?

Of course.

If so, by your account, it will be right to do what is not to the interest of the stronger party, as well as what is so.

What's that you are saying?

Just what you said, I believe; but let us look again. Haven't you admitted that the rulers, when they enjoin certain acts on their subjects, sometimes mistake their own best interests, and at the same time that it is right for the subjects to obey, whatever they may enjoin?

Yes, I suppose so.

Well, that amounts to admitting that it is right to do what is not to the interest of the rulers or the stronger party. They may unwittingly enjoin what is to their own disadvantage; and you say it is right for the others to do as they are told. In that case, their duty must be the opposite of what you said, because the weaker will have been ordered to do what is against the interest of the stronger. You with your intelligence must see how that follows.

Yes, Socrates, said Polemarchus, that is undeniable.

No doubt, Cleitophon broke in, if you are to be a witness on Socrates' side.

No witness is needed, replied Polemarchus; Thrasymachus himself admits that rulers sometimes ordain acts that are to their own disadvantage, and that it is the subjects' duty to do them.

That is because Thrasymachus said it was right to do what you are told by the men in power.

Yes, but he also said that what is to the interest of the stronger party is right; and, after making both these assertions, he admitted that the stronger sometimes command the weaker subjects to act against their interests. From all which it follows that what is in the stronger's interest is no more right than what is not.

No, said Cleitophon; he meant whatever the stronger believes to be in his own interest. That is what the subject must do, and what Thrasymachus meant to define as right.

That was not what he said, rejoined Polemarchus.

No matter, Polemarchus, said I; if Thrasymachus says so now, let us take him in that sense. Now, Thrasymachus, tell me, was that what you intended to say--that right means what the stronger thinks is to his interest, whether it really is so or not?

212

Most certainly not, he replied. Do you suppose I should speak of a man as 'stronger' or 'superior' at the very moment when he is making a mistake?

I did think you said as much when you admitted that rulers are not always infallible.

That is because you are a quibbler, Socrates. Would you say a man deserves to be called a physician at the moment when he makes a mistake in treating his patient and just in respect of that mistake; or a mathematician, when he does a sum wrong and just in so far as he gets a wrong result? Of course we do commonly speak of a physician or a mathematician or a scholar having made a mistake; but really none of these, I should say, is ever mistaken, in so far as he is worthy of the name we give him. So strictly speaking--and you are all for being precise--no one who practises a craft makes mistakes. A man is mistaken when his knowledge fails him; and at that moment he is no craftsman. And what is true of craftsmanship or any sort of skill is true of the ruler: he is never mistaken so long as he is acting as a ruler; though anyone might speak of a ruler making a mistake, just as he might of a physician. You must understand that I was talking in that loose way when I answered you question just now; but the precise statement is this. The ruler, in so far as he is acting as a ruler, makes no mistakes and consequently enjoins what is best for himself; and that is what the subject is to do. So, as I said at first, 'right' means doing what is to the interest of the stronger.

Very well, Thrasymachus, said I. So you think I am quibbling?

I am sure you are.

You believe my questions were maliciously designed to damage your position?

I know it. But you will gain nothing by that. You cannot outwit me by cunning, and you are not the man to crush me in the open.

Bless your soul, I answered, I should not think of trying. But, to prevent any more misunderstanding, when

213

you speak of that ruler or stronger party whose interest the weaker ought to serve, please make it clear whether you are using the words in the ordinary way or in that strict sense you have just defined.

I mean a ruler in the strictest possible sense. Now quibble away and be as malicious as you can. I want no mercy. But you are no match for me.

Do you think me enough to beard a lion or try to outwit a Thrasymachus?

You did try just now, he retorted, but it wasn't a success.

Enough of this, said I. Now tell me about the physician in that strict sense you spoke of: is it his business to earn money or to treat his patients? Remember, I mean your physician who is worthy of the name.

To treat his patients.

And what of the ship's captain in the true sense? Is he a mere seaman or the commander of the crew?

The commander.

Yes, we shall not speak of him as a seaman just because he is on board a ship. That is not the point. He is called captain because of his skill and authority over the crew.

Quite true.

And each of these people has some special interest?

No doubt.

And the craft in question exists for the very purpose of discovering that interest and providing for it?

Yes.

Can it equally be said of any craft that it has an interest, other than its own greatest possible perfection?

What do you mean by that?

Here is an illustration. If you ask me whether it is sufficient for the human body just to be itself, with no need of help from without, I should say, certainly not; it has weaknesses and defects, and its condition is not all that it might be. That is precisely why the art of medicine was invented: it was designed to help the body and provide for its interests. Would not that be true?

It would.

But now take the art of medicine itself. Has that any defects or weaknesses? Does any art stand in need of some further perfection, as the eye would be imperfect without the power of vision, or the ear without hearing, so that in their case an art is required that will study their interests and provide for their carrying out those functions? Has the art itself any corresponding need of some further art to remedy its defects and look after its interests; and will that further art require yet another, and so on for ever? Or will every art look after its own interests? Or, finally, is it not true that no art needs to have its weaknesses remedied or its interests studied either by another art or by itself, because no art has in itself any weakness or fault, and the only interest it is required to serve is that of its subject-matter? In itself, an art is sound and flawless, so long as it is entirely true to its own nature as an art in the strictest sense--and it is the strict sense that I want you to keep in view. Is not that true?

So it appears.

Then, said I, the art of medicine does not study its own interest, but the needs of the body, just as a groom shows his skill by caring for horses, not for the art of grooming. And so every art seeks, not its own advantage --for it has no deficiencies--but the interest of the subject on which it is exercised.

215

It appears so.

But surely, Thrasymachus, every art has authority and superior power over its subject.

To this he agreed, though very reluctantly.

So far as arts are concerned, then no art ever studies or enjoins the interest of the superior or stronger party, but always that of the weaker over which it has authority.

Thrasymachus assented to this at last, though he tried to put up a fight. I then went on:

So the physician, as such, studies only the patient's interest, not his own. For as we agreed, the business of the physician, in the strict sense, is not to make money for himself, but to exercise his power over the patient's body; and the ship's captain, again, considered strictly as no mere sailor, but in command of the crew, will study and enjoin the interest of his subordinates, not his own.

He agreed reluctantly.

And so with government of any kind: no ruler, in so far as he is acting as ruler, will study or enjoin what is for his own interest. All that he says and does will be said and done with a view to what is good and proper for the subject for whom he practises his art.

At this point, when everyone could see that Thrasymachus' definition of justice had been turned inside out, instead of making any reply, he said:

Socrates, have you a nurse?

Why do you ask such a question as that? I said. Wouldn't it be better to answer mine?

Because she lets you go about sniffling like a child whose nose wants wiping. She hasn't even taught you to know a shepherd when you see one, or his sheep, either.

What makes you say that?

Why, you imagine that a herdsman studies the interests of his flocks or cattle, tending and fattening them up with some other end in view than his master's profit or his own; and so you don't see that, in politics, the genuine ruler regards his subjects exactly like sheep, and thinks of nothing else, night and day, but the good he can get out of them for himself. You are so far out in your notions of right and wrong, justice and injustice, as not to know that 'right' actually means what is good for someone else, and to be 'just' means serving the interest of the stronger who rules, at the cost of the subject who obeys; whereas injustice is just the reverse, asserting its authority over those innocents who are called just, so that they minister solely to their master's advantage and happiness, and not in the least degree to their own. Innocent as you are yourself, Socrates, you must see that a just man always has the worst of it. Take a private business: when a partnership is wound up, you will never find that the more honest of two partners comes off with the larger share; and in their relations to the state, when there are taxes to be paid, the honest man will pay more than the other on the same amount of property; or if there is money to be distributed, the dishonest will get it all. When either of them hold some public office, even if the just man loses in no other way, his private affairs at any rate will suffer from neglect, while his principles will not allow him to help himself from the public funds; not to mention the offence he will give to his friends and relations by refusing to sacrifice those principles to do them a good turn. Injustice has all the opposite advantages. I am speaking of the type I described just now, the man who can get the better of other people on a large scale: you must fix your eye on him, if you want to judge how much it is to one's own interest not to be just. You can see that best in the most consummate form of injustice, which rewards wrong doing with supreme welfare and happiness and reduces its victims, if they won't retaliate in kind, to misery. That form is despotism, which uses force or fraud to plunder the goods of others, public or private, sacred or profane, and to do it in a wholesale way. If you are caught committing any one of these crimes on a small scale, you are punished and disgraced; they call it sacrilege,

217

kidnapping, burglary, theft and brigandage. But if, besides taking their property, you turn all your countrymen into slaves, you will hear no more of those ugly names; you countrymen themselves will call you the happiest of men and bless your name, and so will everyone who hears of such a complete triumph of injustice; for when the people denounce injustice, it is because they are afraid of suffering wrong, not of doing it. So true is it, Socrates, that injustice, on a grand enough scale, is superior to justice in strength and freedom and autocratic power; and 'right,' as I said at first, means simply what serves the interest of the stronger party; 'wrong' means what is for the interest and profit of oneself.

Having deluged our ears with this torrent of words, as the man at the baths might empty a bucket over one's head, Thrasymachus meant to take himself off; but the company obliged him to stay and defend his position. I was specially urgent in my entreaties.

My good Thrasymachus, said I, do you propose to fling a doctrine like that at our heads and then go away without explaining it properly or letting us point out to you whether it is true or not? Is it so small a matter in your eyes to determining the whole course of conduct which every one of us must follow to get the best out of life?

Don't I realize it is a serious matter? he retorted.

Apparently not, said I; or else you have no consideration for us, and do not care whether we shall lead better or worse lives for being ignorant of this truth you profess to know. Do take the trouble to let us into your secret; if you treat us handsomely, you may be sure it will be a good investment; there are so many of us to show our gratitude. I will make no secret of my own conviction, which is that injustice is not more profitable than justice, even when left free to work its will unchecked. No; let your unjust man have full power to do wrong, whether by successful violence or by escaping detection; all the same he will not convince me that he will gain more than he would by being just. There may be others here who feel as I do, and set

218

justice above injustice. It is for you to convince us that we are not well advised.

How can I? he replied. If you are not convinced by what I have just said, what more can I do for you? Do you want to be fed with my ideas out of a spoon?

God forbid! I exclaimed; not that. But I do want you to stand by your own words; or, if you shift your ground, shift it openly and stop trying to hoodwink us as you are doing now. You see, Thrasymachus, to go back to your earlier argument, in speaking of the shepherd you did not think it necessary to keep to that strict sense you laid down when you defined the genuine physician. You represent him, in his character of shepherd, as feeding up his flock, not for their own sake but for the table or the market, as if he were out to make money as a caterer or a cattle-dealer, rather than a shepherd. Surely the sole concern of the shepherd's art is to do the best for the charges put under its care; its own best interest is sufficiently provided for, so long as it does not fall short of all that shepherding should imply. On that principle it followed, I thought, that any kind of authority, in the state or in private life, must, in its character of authority, consider solely what is best for those under its care. Now what is your opinion? Do you think that the men who govern states--I mean rulers in the strict sense--have no reluctance to hold office?

I don't think so, he replied; I know it.

Well, but haven't you noticed, Thrasymachus, that in other positions of authority no one is willing to act unless he is paid wages, which he demands on the assumption that the benefit of his action will go to his charges? Tell me: Don't we always distinguish one form of skill from another by its power to effect some particular result? Do say what you really think, so that we may get on.

Yes, that is the distinction.

And also each brings us some benefit that is peculiar to it: medicine gives health, for example; the art of navigation, safety at sea; and so on.

219

Yes.

And wage-earning brings us wages; that is its distinctive product. Now, speaking with that precision which you proposed, you would not say that the art of navigation is the same as the art of medicine, merely on the ground that a ship's captain regained his health on a voyage, because the sea air was good for him. No more would you identify the practice of medicine with wage-earning because a man may keep his health while earning wages, or a physician attending a case may receive a fee.

No.

And, since we agreed that the benefit obtained by each form of skill is peculiar to it, any common benefit enjoyed alike by all these practitioners must come from some further practice common to them all?

It would seem so.

Yes, we must say that if they all earn wages, they get that benefit in so far as they are engaged in wage-earning as well as in practising their several arts.

He agreed reluctantly.

This benefit, then--the receipt of wages--does not come to a man from his special art. If we are to speak strictly, the physician, as such, produces health; the builder, a house; and then each, in his further capacity of wage-earner, gets his pay. Thus every art has its own function and benefits its proper subject. But suppose the practitioner is not paid; does he then get any benefit from his art?

Clearly not.

And is he doing no good to anyone either, when he works for nothing?

No, I suppose he does some good.

Well then, Thrasymachus, it is now clear that no form of skill or authority provides for its own benefit. As we were saying some time ago, it always studies and prescribes what is good for its subject--the interest of the weaker party, not of the stronger. And that, my friend, is why I said that no one is willing to be in a position of authority and undertake to set straight other men's troubles, without demanding to be paid; because, if he is to do his work well, he will never, in his capacity of ruler, do, or command others to do, what is best for himself, but only what is best for the subject. For that reason, if he is to consent, he must have his recompense, in the shape of money or honour, or of punishment in case of refusal.

What do you mean, Socrates? asked Glaucon. I recognize two of your three kinds of reward; but I don't understand what you mean by speaking of punishment as a recompense.

Then you don't understand the recompense required by the best type of men, or their motive for accepting authority when they do consent. You surely know that a passion for honours or for money is rightly regarded as something to be ashamed of.

Yes, I do.

For that reason, I said, good men are unwilling to rule, either for money's sake or for honour. They have no wish to be called mercenary for demanding to be paid, or thieves for making a secret profit out of their office; nor yet will honours tempt them, for they are not ambitious. So they must be forced to consent under threat of penalty; that may be why a readiness to accept power under no such constraint is thought discreditable. And the heaviest penalty for declining to rule is to be ruled by someone inferior to yourself. That is the fear, I believe, that makes decent people accept power; and when they do so, they face the prospect of authority with no idea that they are coming into the enjoyment of a comfortable berth; it is forced upon them because they can find no one better than themselves, or even as good, to be entrusted with power. If there could ever be a society of perfect men, there might well be as much competition to evade office as there now is to gain it;

221

and it would then be clearly seen that the genuine ruler's nature is to seek only the advantage of the subject, with the consequence that any man of understanding would sooner have another to do the best for him than be at the pains to do the best for that other himself. On this point, then, I entirely disagree with Thrasymachus' doctrine that right means what is to the interest of the stronger.

However, I continued, we may return to that question later. Much more important is the position Thrasymachus is asserting now: that a life of injustice is to be preferred to a life of justice. Which side do you take, Glaucon? Where do you think the truth lies?

I should say that the just life is the better worth having.

You heard Thrasymachus' catalogue of all the good things in store for injustice?

I did, but I am not convinced.

Shall we try to convert him, then, supposing we can find some way to prove him wrong?

By all means.

We might answer Thrasymachus' case in a set speech of our own, drawing up a corresponding list of the advantages of justice; he would then have the right to reply, and we should make our final rejoinder; but after that we should have to count up and measure the advantages on each list, and we should need a jury to decide between us. Whereas, if we go on as before, each securing the agreement of the other side, we can combine the functions of advocate and judge. We will take whichever course you prefer.

I prefer the second, said Glaucon.

Come then, Thrasymachus, said I, let us start afresh with our questions. You say that injustice pays better than justice, when both are carried to the further point?

I do, he replied; and I have told you why.

222

And how would you describe them? I suppose you would call one of them an excellence and the other a defect?

Of course.

Justice an excellence, and injustice a defect?

Now is that likely, when I am telling you that injustice pays, and justice does not?

Then what do you say?

The opposite.

That justice is a defect?

No; rather the mark of a good-natured simpleton.

Injustice, then, implies being ill-natured?

No; I should call it good policy.

Do you think the unjust are positively superior in character and intelligence, Thrasymachus?

Yes, if they are the sort that can carry injustice to perfection and make themselves masters of whole cities and nations. Perhaps you think I was talking of pickpockets. There is profit even in that trade, if you can escape detection; but it doesn't come to much as compared with the gains I was describing.

I understand you now on that point, I replied. What astonished me was that you should class injustice with superior character and intelligence and justice with the reverse.

Well, I do, he rejoined.

That is a much more stubborn position, my friend; and it is not so easy to see how to assail it. If you would admit that injustice, however well it pays, is nevertheless, as some people think, a defect and a discreditable thing, then we could argue on generally accepted principles. But now that you have gone so far as to rank it with superior character and intelligence, obviously you will say it is an admirable thing as well as a source of strength, and has all the other qualities we have attributed to justice.

You read my thoughts like a book, he replied.

However, I went on, it is no good shirking; I must go through with the argument, so long as I can be sure you are really speaking your mind. I do believe you are not playing with us now, Thrasymachus, but stating the truth as you conceive it.

Why not refute the doctrine? he said. What does it matter to you whether I believe it or not?

It does not matter, I replied.

Thrasymachus' assent was dragged out of him with a reluctance of which my account gives no idea. He was sweating at every pore, for the weather was hot; and I saw then what I had never seen before--Thrasymachus blushing. However, now that we had agreed that justice implies superior character and intelligence, injustice a deficiency in both respects, I went on:

Good; let us take that as settled. But we were also saying that injustice was a source of strength. Do you remember, Thrasymachus?

I do remember; only your last argument does not satisfy me, and I could say a good deal about that. But if I did, you would tell me I was haranguing you like a public meeting. So either let me speak my mind at length, or else, if you want to ask questions, ask them, and I will nod or shake my head, and say 'Hm?' as we do to encourage an old woman telling us a story.

No, please, said I; don't give your assent against your real opinion.

Anything to please you, he rejoined, since you won't let me have my say. What more do you want?

Nothing, I replied. If that is what you mean to do, I will go on with my questions.

Go on, then.

Well, to continue where we left off. I will repeat my question: What is the nature and quality of justice as compared with injustice? It was suggested, I believe, that injustice is the stronger and more effective of the two; but now we have seen that justice implies superior character and intelligence, it will not be hard to show that it will also be superior in power to injustice, which implies ignorance and stupidity; that must be obvious to anyone. However, I would rather look deeper into this matter than take it as settled off-hand. Would you agree that a state may be unjust and may try to enslave other states or to hold a number of others in subjection unjustly?

Of course it may, he said; above all if it is the best sort of state, which carries injustice to perfection.

I understand, said I; that was your view. But I am wondering whether a state can do without justice when it is asserting its superior power over another in that way.

Not if you are right, that justice implies intelligence; but if I am right, injustice will be needed.

I am delighted with your answer, Thrasymachus; this is much better than just nodding and shaking your head.

It is all to oblige you.

Thank you. Please add to you kindness by telling me whether any set of men--a state or an army or a band of robbers or thieves--who were acting together for some unjust purpose would be likely to succeed, if they were always trying to injure one another. Wouldn't they do better, if they did not?

Yes, they would.

225

Because, of course, such injuries must set them quarrelling and hating each other. Only fair treatment can make men friendly and of one mind.

Be it so, he said; I don't want to differ from you.

Thank you once more, I replied. But don't you agree that, if injustice has this effect of implanting hatred wherever it exists, it must make any set of people, whether freemen or slaves, split into factions, at feud with one another and incapable of any joint action?

Yes.

And so with any two individuals: injustice will set them at variance and make them enemies to each other as well as to everyone who is just.

It will.

And will it not keep its character and have the same effect, if it exists in a single person?

Let us suppose so.

The effect being, apparently, wherever it occurs--in a state or a family or an army or anywhere else--to make united action impossible because of factions and quarrels, and moreover to set whatever it resides in at enmity with itself as well as with any opponent and with all who are just.

Yes, certainly.

Then I suppose it will produce the same natural results in an individual. He will have a divided mind and be incapable of action, for lack of singleness of purpose; and he will be at enmity with all who are just as well as with himself?

Yes.

And 'all who are just' surely includes the gods?

Let us suppose so.

226

The unjust man, then, will be a god-forsaken creature; the goodwill of heaven will be for the just.

Enjoy your triumph, said Thrasymachus. You need not fear my contradicting you. I have no wish to give offence to the company.

You will make my enjoyment complete, I replied, if you will answer my further questions in the same way. We have made out so far that just men are superior in character and intelligence and more effective in action. Indeed without justice men cannot act together at all; it is not strictly true to speak of such people as ever having effected any strong action in common. Had they been thoroughly unjust, they could not have kept their hands off one another; they must have had some justice in them, enough to keep them from injuring one another at the same time with their victims. This it was that enabled them to achieve what they did achieve: their injustice only partially incapacitated them for their career of wrongdoing; if perfect, it would have disabled them for any action whatsoever. I can see that all this is true, as against your original position. But there is a further question which we postponed: Is the life of justice the better and happier life? What we have said already leaves no doubt in my mind; but we ought to consider more carefully, for this is no light matter: it is the question, what is the right way to live?

Go on, then.

I will, said I. Some things have a function; a horse, for instance, is useful for certain kinds of work. Would you agree to define a thing's function in general as the work for which that thing is the only instrument or the best one?

I don't understand.

Take an example. We can see only with the eyes, hear only with the ears; and seeing and hearing might be called the functions of those organs.

Yes.

Or again, you might cut vine-shoots with a carving-knife or a chisel or many other tools, but with none so well as with a pruning-knife made for the purpose; and we may call that its function.

True.

Now, I expect, you see better what I meant by suggesting that a thing's function is the work that it alone can do, or can do better than anything else.

Yes, I will accept that definition.

Good, said I; and to take the same examples, the eye and the ear, which we said have each its particular function: have they not also a specific excellence or virtue? Is not that always the case with things that have some appointed work to do?

Yes.

Now consider: is the eye likely to do its work well, if you take away its peculiar virtue and substitute the corresponding defect?

Of course not, if you mean substituting blindness for the power of sight.

I mean whatever its virtue may be; I have not come to that yet. I am only asking, whether it is true of things with a function--eyes or ears or anything else-- that there is always some specific virtue which enables them to work well; and if they are deprived of that virtue, they work badly.

I think that is true.

Then the next point is this. Has the soul a function that can be performed by nothing else? Take for example such actions as deliberating or taking charge and exercising control: is not the soul the only thing of which you can say that these are its proper and peculiar work?

That is so.

228

And again, living--is not that above all the function of the soul?

No doubt.

And we also speak of the soul as having a certain specific excellence or virtue?

Yes.

Then, Thrasymachus, if the soul is robbed of its peculiar virtue, it cannot possibly do its work well. It must exercise its power of controlling and taking charge well or ill according as it is itself in a good or a bad state.

That follows.

And did we not agree that the virtue of the soul is justice, and injustice its defect?

We did.

So it follows that a just soul, or in other words a just man, will live well; the unjust will not.

Apparently, according to your argument.

But living well involves well-being and happiness.

Naturally.

Then only the just man is happy; injustice will involve unhappiness.

Be it so.

But you cannot say it pays better to be unhappy.

Of course not.

Injustice then, my dear Thrasymachus, can never pay better than justice.

Well, he replied, this is a feast-day, and you may take all this as your share of the entertainment.

For which I have to thank you, Thrasymachus; you have been so gentle with me since you recovered your temper. It is my own fault if the entertainment has not been satisfactory. I have been behaving like a greedy guest, snatching a taste of every new dish that comes round before he has properly enjoyed the last. We began by looking for a definition of justice; but before we had found one, I dropped that question and hurried on to ask whether or not it involved superior character and intelligence; and then, as soon as another idea cropped up, that injustice pays better, I could not refrain from pursuing that.

So now the whole conversation has left me completely in the dark; for so long as I do not know what justice is, I am hardly likely to know whether or not it is a virtue, or whether it makes a man happy or unhappy.

CHAPTER VI

EMPLOYMENT IN A CONTRACT SOCIETY

INTRODUCTION

It is part of the conventional ideology of business society that ours is a society based upon contract principles. Buyers and sellers meet in the market to exchange goods; the sole moral limit on these exchanges is the contract. If the exchange is voluntary, without fraud or coercion, then the parties are bound by the agreement whether it was a wise agreement or not. This simple model has been subject to recent exceptions in that courts refuse to enforce sales contracts which are unfair to one of the parties whether or nor the contract is voluntary. Also, it maybe questioned whether the contract model should be applicable at all to the exchange of services or human labor. If freedom of contract is the basic value, then why should there be a legal prohibition against prostitution or against selling yourself into slavery? If freedom of contract is not the basic value, then why should not society guarantee life time employment for all of its citizens?

Traditionally in America both employers and employees have had the right to terminate the employment relationship at any time without any reason. Thus during periods of high unemployment an employer could discharge older, highly paid employees and replace them with younger less expensive employees. Similarly during periods of low unemployment an employee could leave employment at any time in order to take a better position. During the last 20 years the United States has sustained fairly high rates of unemployment. One effect is the erosion of the doctrine of employment-at-will, that employers and employees may terminate their employment relationship at any time without any reason.

One exception to employment-at-will, the public policy exception, is a recognition of a general principle that society should not provide a right without a remedy; should not create a duty without affording some protection for those who perform the duty. For example, if an employee is discharged for filing a workers compensation claim and for exercising his rights

231

guaranteed him by a workers compensation statute, then should the doctrine of employment-at-will protect the employer from a law suit over the discharge? Courts have increasingly read protection for the employee into the law, without waiting for action from a democratically elected legislature. Are these questions better answered by a judge or a legislature? One might also ask how far this exception might be extended. Should it extend to employees who blow the whistle on their employers for immoral but not for illegal practices? Should it be extended to general statements of policy in the law, for example regarding the health and safety of all citizens? If the public policy exception is extended, what will be the benefits and costs to society?

A second exception to employment-at-will is the handbook exception. This exception is based upon the general contract principle that a person can create a binding contract by conduct without expressly using the term "contract" or "promise". Thus, if an employer uses employee handbooks in a way to lead reasonable employees to believe that they will be treated fairly, then the employer should be held to its promises. This exception requires employers to be careful and not to mislead employees into believing that there are protection for their employment which in fact do not exist.

A third exception to employment-at-will is potentially the most expansive. It is the good faith and fair dealing exception; it represents a substantial limit to an employer's discretion to fire employees. The basis of this exception is that all contracts contain a legally implied duty of fairness. Thus, courts have held that whenever an employer acts in a way which would be considered unfair according to accepted business practice then an employee has a cause of action for breach of the duty of good faith in the employment context. The basic question is whether the employment relationship is an arm's length business transaction between two parties who are presumed to protect themselves or whether the employment relationship is like the insurance relationship where the inequalities between the parties can create special dependencies on the part of the insured which require special judicial protection.

In light of these exceptions, in particular the good faith exception, legislatures are becoming increasingly involved in this issue and are considering legislation which would limit employees' rights to sue for wrongful discharge. An example of such legislation is the MONTANA WRONGFUL DISCHARGE ACT. What problems would you as an employer have in supporting such a statute? For example, is the statute unconstitutional because it violates uniform access to the courts for all injured persons? Does the Act violate equal protection because employees injured by a discharge have limited remedies in compared to consumers injured by the employer's product? Is it fair to require the parties to arbitrate these disputes; is this a fair compromise between the interest of the employer and the interest of the employee? And in any case, whether there is litigation or arbitration, should there be a presumption in favor of management's decision which the employee would have to rebut with clear and convincing evidence in order to prevail?

It appears increasingly that arbitration is being recognized as a workable solution to these problems as it has worked for so many years for union employees. The last selection in this chapter is from an arbitration decision. It is to give you some idea how arbitrators treat the question of just cause discharge. What objections might an employer have to the implementation of these arbitration rules to all employees? For example, should upper level management be treated differently than semi-skilled workers, who, for economic reasons, should be discharged without just cause.

In conclusion, this chapter has attempted to make students aware of the changes which are occurring in the area of employment law and to raise some questions regarding the arguments for and against these changes. You are encouraged to apply the moral principles of the preceding chapter to your decisions regarding whether these changes are defensible or not. As a successful business person you will be considering ethical questions which are internal to your company and ethical questions which concern the relationship between your business and the society at large.

QUESTIONS AND PROJECTS

1. Assume that you are personnel vice president of a
    large corporation, sketch the outlines of an
    employee handbook for your company with a
    justification for your inclusions and exclusions in
    light of applicable moral and legal principles.

2. As a member of the legislative policy committee of
    a business association, draft a policy statement to
    your legislature which is considering adopting a
    statute for your state which is similar to the
    Montana Act.

3. Using the criteria in the Whirlpool Corporation
    arbitration, describe in detail a fact situation
    involving the use of drugs by an employee where
    management would be justified in discharging that
    employee.

4. Is the implied covenant of good faith in the
    employment setting defensible on utilitarian
    grounds, on equalitarian grounds?

Continental Air Lines v. Keenan: Employee Handbooks as a Modification to Employment at Will

Margaret McNett

I.   Introduction

The employment relationship for approximately two-thirds of the work force in the United States is governed by the common-law rule of employment at will. In the absence of specific statutory restrictions regulating the employment relationship, or express contractual commitments, an employee hired for an indefinite period of time may be discharged at any time for any or no reason without subjecting the employer to legal liability. The origins of the employment-at-will rule in America can be traced back to an 1877 treatise in which Horace G. Wood stated that "a general or indefinite hiring is prima facie a hiring at will." Tennessee was one of the first states to embrace Wood's rule in 1884, New York followed in 1895, and employment at will soon became accepted throughout the country. Today most states have judicially developed exceptions to the at-will doctrine. Under modern law, an employee may bring a wrongful discharge action based on three basic theories: public policy, an implied duty of good faith and fair dealing, and contract principles. Despite the growing acceptance of these exceptions, the presumption of at-will employment remains the starting point for analyzing wrongful discharge claims.

In the 1987 case of Continental Air Lines v. Keenan, the Colorado Supreme Court held that the presumption of at-will employment is rebuttable under certain circumstances. More specifically, the court held that an at-will employee may be able to enforce termination procedures in an employee handbook under one of two alternative theories. First, the employee may be entitled to relief under the contract principle of unilateral offer if the employer manifested his willing-

From University of Colorado Law Review, Vol. 60:169-186, (1988). Reprinted with permission of the University of Colorado Law Review. Footnotes omitted.

ness to enter into a bargain and the employee's initial or continued employment constituted acceptance of and consideration for the termination procedures. Second, under the theory of promissory estoppel, an employee may be able to enforce termination procedures even where the requisites for formation of a contract are not present.

After a discussion of the development of modifications to the at-will doctrine in the areas of public policy and implied duty of good faith, this note focuses on courts' use of contract principles to bind employers to provisions in their employee handbooks or personnel manuals. This note analyzes the soundness of the Keenan decision in light of national trends recognizing employee handbooks as modifications to employment at will. Finally, this note suggests that judicial development of the doctrine of wrongful discharge is an appropriate means of protecting employees from arbitrary termination practices by employers and urges the minority of states still adhering to the employment-at-will rule to modify that rule.

II.   Judicial Exceptions to Employment at Will

A.   Public Policy Exception

Many jurisdictions have recognized an exception to employment at will where an employer's action in discharging an employee violates fundamental principles of public policy. Cases following this exception generally fall into one of three categories: (1) employee discharged for refusing to commit a crime, (2) employee discharged for exercising a statutory right, and (3) employee discharged for fulfilling a statutory duty.

Though the public-policy cause of action may be the most widely recognized exception to the at-will doctrine, it has been rejected by some jurisdictions. For example, New York has declined to adopt this exception on the grounds that the better way to temper the harshness of the employment-at-will rule is through a statutory scheme. Other courts have reasoned that since an at-will employee may be terminated for any reason, termination may be for a "wrong" reason. In other words, allegations as to improper motive are legally irrelevant.

To date, no definitive statement on the public policy exception has been made by the Colorado Supreme Court. In Lampe v. Presbyterian Medical Center the Colorado Court of Appeals declined to adopt the public policy exception on the facts of the case but did not rule out the possibility of adopting the exception in the future. The plaintiff in Lampe claimed she could not comply with her employer's request to reduce the overtime hours worked by the nurses on her staff without jeopardizing the care of the patients. Lampe alleged her discharge for failure to reduce overtime violated the public policy enunciated in the statute creating the State Board of Nursing. The court found that the broad statement of policy in the statute was too general to impute to the legislature an intent to modify the contractual relationships between hospitals and their employees. However, the court did appear to leave open the possibility of a cause of action where an employee is discharged for attempting to exercise a specifically enacted statutory right or duty, such as filing a workers' compensation claim or serving on a jury.

The opening in Lampe was recently addressed by the Colorado Court of Appeals in Cronk v. Intermountain Rural Electric Association. The employees in Cronk alleged, inter alia, that they were discharged for failing to follow the employer's policies and directives that required them to violate several specific public utility statutes. For example, one plaintiff claimed he was discharged because he testified truthfully before the Public Utilities Commission which was investigating irregular practices by the employer. Had the employee falsified his testimony, he would have violated the Public Utilities Law. Furthermore, any public utility employee "'who violates or fails to comply with or who procures, aids, or abets any violation by any public utility' of any public utility statute is guilty of a misdemeanor."

In Cronk the court recognized the public policy exception where the employee can show that he or she was discharged for exercising a specific right or duty. To qualify for this exception, the "plaintiff must prove (1)

237

that he refused to perform an action (2) ordered by his employer (3) which would violate a specific statute (4) whose terms are more than a broad general statement of policy and (5) that his termination resulted from his refusal."

The court's concern with a specific expression of public policy in Lampe and Cronk illustrates an important issue with regard to the public policy exception: What definition of public policy will support a cause of action for wrongful discharge? One advocate of an expansive view criticizes narrow judicial interpretations of public policy, arguing that they offer only limited protection against the harshness of the employment-at-will rule. Under this view, all dismissals without just cause should be actionable as against public policy because "no matter how 'private' their motivation, [unjustified discharges] undermine the community's interest in economic productivity, stable employment, and fairness in the workplace."

An example of an expansive view of what constitutes a breach of public policy can be found in Cloutier v. Great Atlantic & Pacific Tea Co. The employee in Cloutier, contrary to company policy, decided not to make a night deposit because of the dangerous neighborhood in which the store was located. The New Hampshire Supreme Court upheld the employee's theory that his discharge for failing to make the deposit violated the public policy in favor of a safe working environment, as expressed in the Occupational Safety and Health Act of 1970.

Conversely, however, it is argued that an expansive view of public policy will completely swallow the employment-at-will rule by requiring a just-cause standard for all discharges. Some commentators recommend that the exception be limited to those cases in which an employee is discharged in contravention of an express, legislatively mandated public policy. Under this narrower view, the public policy cause of action should not be recognized if only private interests are at stake. For example, the employee in Suchodolski v. Michigan Consolidated Gas Co. alleged that he was discharged in retaliation for reporting poor internal accounting practices. The Michigan Supreme Court held that the plaintiff's discharge was not actionable because it

238

"lack[ed] the kind of violation of a clearly mandated public policy that would support an action for retaliatory discharge."

B.   Implied Duty of Good Faith and Fair Dealing Exception

Some courts have restricted an employer's right to terminate an at-will employee where the discharge was fundamentally unfair and occurred under egregious circumstances. These courts have held that all employment contracts contain an implied duty of good faith and fair dealing. This exception to employment at will is based upon traditional contract doctrines emphasizing fairness and prohibiting conduct involving bad faith which violates "community standards of decency, fairness or reasonableness." For example, the implied duty of good faith and fair dealing has been used to sustain an employee's cause of action for wrongful discharge where the employee was terminated for refusing sexual advances by a supervisor, where the employer discharged the employee to avoid paying commissions, and where the employee was terminated to avoid vesting of pension benefits.

The New Hampshire Supreme Court was the first to apply this exception in Monge v. Beebe Rubber Co. The plaintiff in Monge was discharged when she refused to date her supervisor. Upholding the plaintiff's breach of contract action, the court held that "termination by the employer of a contract of employment at will which is motivated by bad faith or malice or based on retaliation is not in the best interest of the economic system or the public good and constitutes a breach of the employment contract." Subsequent New Hampshire decisions, however, indicate a narrowing of this exception.

The most dramatic expansions of the covenant of good faith and fair dealing have occurred in California and Montana. In Cleary v. American Airlines a California appellate court looked at the longevity of the employee's service, eighteen years, together with the employer's expressed policy of job security, and held that the implied duty of good faith and fair dealing precluded any discharge without cause.

239

In *Gates v. Life of Montana Insurance Co.* the
Montana Supreme Court held that although an employee
handbook did not become part of the employment contract,
the employer could be bound by the handbook's termination
procedures based on the implied covenant of good faith
and fair dealing. By promulgating uniform procedures for
dismissal, the employer sought an orderly and cooperative
workforce. The court reasoned that the procedures gave
employees peace of mind about their job security. If the
employer fails to "follow its own policies," the court
concluded, "the peace of mind of its employees is
shattered and an injustice is done."

Those jurisdictions that have recognized the implied
covenant of good faith exception to employment at will
do not agree as to whether an action for breach of the
covenant lies in contract or tort. California, New
Hampshire and Massachusetts, for example, seem to favor
a contract action for which only standard contract
remedies, lost wages and benefits, are recoverable. On
the other hand, Montana has held that breach of the
covenant is a tort for which compensatory damages are
available. Moreover, in extreme circumstances, Montana
also will award punitive damages.

Colorado has rejected the implied duty of good faith
exception to employment at will. In *Corporon v. Safeway
Stores*, the Colorado Court of Appeals held that an
allegation of breach of a duty of fair dealing in a
termination of an at-will contract "does not state a
claim for which relief can be granted under Colorado
law." Furthermore, in *Pittman v. Larson Distributing Co.*
the Colorado Court of Appeals again refused to extend to
employment contracts the implied covenant of good faith
and fair dealing found in some commercial contracts.

A Colorado employee's claim for breach of an implied
covenant of good faith and fair dealing survived the
employer's summary judgment motion in federal district
court, however, in *Price v. Federal Express Corp.* The
employee in *Price* alleged that the employer repeatedly
stated that it would treat employees fairly and would not
lay off employees except under extreme circumstances.
The court stated that "[e]mployers must realize that if
they are going to reap the profits and rewards of
employee loyalty and enhanced workmanship which are

coaxed by implied promises made to the workforce, then such employers must be held to their word."

Colorado has not gone as far as other states in protecting at-will employees. Of the three commonly recognized exceptions to an employer's absolute right to discharge at-will employees, Colorado has recently adopted the public policy exception in narrow circumstances, but has refused to imply any duty of good faith and fair dealing in employment contracts. Colorado courts have, however, recognized that statements in employee handbooks may provide protection to at-will employees.

III The Keenan Decision and Exceptions to Employment at Will Based on Contract Theories

A.   Keenan Facts and Holding

In Continental Air Lines v. Keenan the Colorado Supreme Court joined what one commentator has termed the "progressive courts" by holding that termination procedures in employee handbooks may contractually bind employers and restrict their right to terminate at-will employees.

The facts of Keenan are fairly typical of the cases in this area. Continental published and distributed an employee handbook which contained, among other things, a corporate hearing procedure for management personnel who wished to challenge a disciplinary, discharge, or other job action taken by the company. Continental published the handbook before Keenan was hired in 1974 and revised the hearing procedure in 1979 before Keenan had assumed a management position. There was no evidence that Keenan participated in the revision or negotiated for the terms of the handbook either at the time he accepted his initial position or when he was promoted.

Keenan was discharged in 1981 and his request for a hearing pursuant to the handbook procedure was denied. He then filed suit for wrongful discharge based on Continental's failure to comply with the termination procedures in its handbook. The trial court granted summary judgment for Continental; the Colorado Court of

Appeals reversed and remanded the case for trial. The Colorado Supreme Court reversed in part and remanded the case for reconsideration of Continental's motion for summary judgment in light of its holding that "[a]n employee originally hired under a contract terminable at will may be able to enforce the termination procedures in an employee manual under . . . [two] alternative theories." The court held that an employee may be entitled to relief under ordinary contract principles or under the theory of promissory estoppel.

The Keenan decision does not change the long-established employment-at-will rule in Colorado, that is, that "[a]n employee who is hired in Colorado for an indefinite period of time is an 'at will employee,' whose employment may be terminated by either party without cause and without notice, and whose termination does not give rise to a cause of action." The Colorado Supreme Court made it clear that it was not adopting an absolute rule that employee handbooks automatically become part of an employment contract. On the other hand, the court declined to find that employee handbooks are merely unilateral expressions of general company policy.

Instead, the court's decision in Keenan makes employment at will a rebuttable presumption. In order to overcome the presumption of employment at will, an employee wishing to sustain a wrongful discharge suit must come forward with a preliminary factual showing under one of Keenan's two alternative theories. If the employee claims he is entitled to relief under contract principles, he must demonstrate that the employer was making an offer to the employee by promulgating termination procedures, and that he (the employee) accepted these terms and provided consideration for them by initial or continued employment. Alternatively, under the promissory estoppel theory, the employee must show there was reasonable and detrimental reliance on the termination procedures and that enforcement of the procedures is necessary to avoid in-justice. If the employee cannot come forward with facts sufficient to establish one of these two theories, his claim for relief should fail.

242

B. Promissory Estoppel Theory

Prior to <u>Keenan</u>, Colorado had adopted the principles of promissory estoppel, as set forth in section 90 of the <u>Restatement (Second) of Contracts</u>, to provide a remedy, under certain circumstances, to those who detrimentally rely upon promises that the promisor should have reasonably expected to induce such reliance. The doctrine of promissory estoppel is designed to discourage conduct that unreasonably causes foreseeable economic loss due to action or inaction induced by specific promises.

In the employment context, promissory estoppel has been used to limit an employer's right to terminate an at-will employee. For example, in <u>Thompson v. St. Regis Paper Co.</u> the Supreme Court of Washington held that an employer's act in issuing employee handbook [sic] can lead to obligations that govern the employment relationship, absent a specific contractual agreement to the contrary. An employer may create an atmosphere of job security and fair treatment by promising specific treatment in specific situations. If an employee is "induced thereby to remain on the job and not actively seek other employment, those promises are enforceable components of the employment relationship."

In <u>Keenan</u> the Colorado Supreme Court held that an employee may be entitle to enforce procedures in an employee handbook, even if the requisites for formation of a contract are not present, under the theory of promissory estoppel. An employer expects to benefit, the court reasoned, by adopting certain policies such as termination procedures. Similarly, these policies are likely to create an expectation of benefits on the part of the employee. If an employee can demonstrate that the employer reasonably should have expected the employee to consider the employee manual as a commitment from the employer to follow the termination procedures, and that the employee reasonably relied on those termination procedures to his detriment, the manual procedures may be enforceable if necessary to avoid an injustice.

C. Unilateral Contract Theory

By recognizing that employee handbooks are more than "unilateral expressions of general company policies which have no bearing on the employee's contractual rights," Colorado joined the majority of courts in rejecting the arguments that written employment policies cannot contractually bind the employer.

The minority of courts that still adhere to the view that statements in employee handbooks do not limit an employer's power to terminate an at-will employee base their decision on three common arguments. First, they argue that statements in employee handbooks are unilateral declarations of policy or mere gratuities subject to unilateral amendment or even complete abandonment by the employer. Since the terms of the handbook were not bargained for, the handbook cannot contractually bind either party. Second, some courts reason that no contract exists because there is no "mutuality of obligation." Under this rationale an employee handbook "does not create an obligation on the part of the employer to continue the employment of the employee for life, subject only to the conditions set forth in the manual, while leaving the employee free to terminate his employment at any time and for any or no reason." Finally, absence of consideration has been used by certain courts as an additional justification for rejecting contract analysis. Because an employee's services are consideration for the wages paid by the employer, they hold, separate, additional consideration would be necessary to bind the employer to any other promises, such as job security.

In rejecting these traditional arguments, Colorado now follows the better reasoned approach and recognizes that the earlier arguments do not stand up under unilateral contract analysis. In a unilateral contract only one party makes a promise, which is conditioned upon performance of an act and is not legally binding until the act occurs. In the typical illustration of an offer for a unilateral contract--"If you walk across the Brooklyn Bridge, I will pay you $10."--the offeree is not bound to do anything. However, if he should walk across the Brooklyn Bridge, a contract will be formed, despite the lack of "mutuality of obligation" and despite the

244

fact that the offeror could unilaterally modify or revoke the offer prior to performance. Furthermore, performance by the offeree is the bargained-for consideration making the offeror's promise enforceable.

In the at-will employment context, the employment may be viewed as a series of unilateral offers by the employer similar to the Brooklyn Bridge hypothetical. For example, the employer offers: "If you work today, I will pay your salary." The employer has promised to pay for services, thus creating a binding unilateral contract when accepted by the employee through performance. In addition to the promise to pay for services rendered, the employer exercises substantial control over the employment relationship and may promulgate policies that further define this relationship. In the above example, the employer may decide to adopt termination procedures that modify the offer to include the following promise: "If I want to discharge you, I will follow a certain procedure." The employee's act of continued employment constitutes both acceptance of the employer's unilateral offer through performance as well as consideration for the employer's promise. Thus, the employer becomes contractually bound to follow the termination procedures.

The Michigan Supreme Court in <u>Toussaint v. Blue Cross & Blue Shield</u> was one of the first courts to adopt unilateral contract analysis in the context of employee handbooks. The handbook in <u>Toussaint</u> provided that, once employees completed their probationary period, they could be discharged only for just cause, in accordance with certain disciplinary procedures. By choosing to establish such policies, the employer presumably secures an orderly and cooperative workforce. In addition, employees secure the peace of mind associated with job security and the expectation that they will be treated fairly. Thus, the employer has "created a situation 'instinct with an obligation.'" This analysis led the court to hold that employer statements of policy can give rise to contractual rights in employees, even though they may be unilaterally amended by the employer.

245

In _Pine River State Bank v. Mettille_ the Minnesota Supreme Court followed the _Toussaint_ reasoning that portions of an employee handbook may become part of an employment contract under unilateral contract theory. The handbook provisions at issue in _Mettille_ concerned job security and discipline. In order to constitute a unilateral offer, the court held that the handbook language must be definite in form and communicated to the employee. Moreover, to create an enforceable contract the employee must furnish consideration.

In regard to the job security provision, the court in _Mettille_ held the language was not sufficiently definite to constitute an offer and was no more than a general statement of policy. The disciplinary procedure, on the other hand, did set out in definite language an offer of a unilateral contract for procedures to be followed in job terminations. This offer, the court found, was communicated to the employee by dissemination of the handbook. Continued employment by the plaintiff in _Mettille_ constituted acceptance of this offer and also provided the necessary consideration. Accordingly, the court held that the employer was contractually bound to follow the termination procedures.

The _Keenan_ decision was concerned only with termination procedures and did not address whether other provisions in an employee handbook could become legally enforceable. Though the employee alleged in his complaint that he had been given assurances of job security, the court limited its holding to enforcement of the termination procedures. The law concerning other provisions often contained in employee handbooks, such as those pertaining to job security, is not yet settled in Colorado.

Under the unilateral contract analysis, the interests of both employers and employees are protected. The harshness of the at-will doctrine is somewhat softened because employees receive a measure of protection from arbitrary discharge practices. Moreover, the employer can secure a loyal workforce and possibly avoid unionization by treating employees fairly. In addition, as the _Mettille_ court recognized, applying the unilateral contract theory to employee handbooks does not unduly invade the employer's discretion. An employer still may reserve discretion to modify or amend handbook provisions, or may avoid contract claims altogether by a conspicuous disclaimer.

In the Keenan decision Colorado follows the more reasoned approach by holding that termination procedures published by the employer and distributed to employees in employee handbooks may form binding unilateral contracts. This is true where the language is sufficiently specific that the employee understands that the employer has manifested his willingness to enter into a bargain, and that initial or continued employment constitutes acceptance of, and consideration for, those procedures.

IV.   Role of the Courts in Wrongful Discharge

A few states still adhere to the traditional rule of employment at will on the grounds that any change should be made by the legislature. For example, in Murphy v. American Home Products an employee alleged that he was discharged in retaliation for reporting illegal account manipulations and for refusing to participate in the accounting improprieties. The New York Court of Appeals acknowledged the trend in other jurisdictions to allow causes of action for discharges that violate public policy, but refused to follow that trend. In the court's opinion, "such a significant change in our law is best left to the Legislature."

Similarly, in Kelly v. Mississippi Valley Gas the Mississippi Supreme Court refused to make any exceptions to employment at will even where the plaintiff alleges that he was discharged for filing a workers' compensation claim. The court based its decision on the separation of powers in the state constitution, reasoning that the modern trend of "turn[ing] to the judicial department for a solution to all of the real or imagined ills of our society has increased sometime to the point of requesting the courts to usurp the legislative power of the legislative department."

These cases ignore the fact that the philosophical basis of the employment-at-will rule has become outdated. The rule became popular in the United States early in the twentieth century when freedom of contract was a

247

constitutionally protected property right. However, this philosophy has been discredited and can no longer justify adherence to the traditional rule. The changes in American society brought about by the industrial revolution "made an anachronism of the absolute right of discharge by destroying the classical ideal of complete freedom of contract upon which it is based."

Society has long recognized that employees are in unequal bargaining positions when it comes to dealing with their employers. The union movement was a response to the imbalance between employers and employees and has partially alleviated the inequality in bargaining power. Moreover, there are strong societal interests in protecting employees from coercion and unjust discharges; the numerous state and federal statutes regulating the employment relationship are evidence of this interest. The courts have also recognized their legitimate role in protecting employee rights. As the majority of employees in the American workforce, at-will employees often have no recourse except the courts when faced with arbitrary discharge practices by an employer. The at-will rule is a common-law rule. It is appropriate, therefore, that the courts play an active part in modifying the rule as social and economic conditions dictate. The strength of the common-law court always has been its ability to adapt and respond to such changes. When faced with a wrongful discharge claim, whether based on public policy, implied duty of good faith, or contract principles, state courts should not rely unquestioningly on the outdated notion of employment at will. Rather, they should build on past decisions, draw on new experience, and respond to changing conditions.

V.   Conclusion

The employment-at-will rule is a nineteenth-century notion based on laissez-faire principles and ideas of freedom of contract: If an employee wants more job security, she can bargain for it with her employer. It is only the extremely valuable or unique employee, however, who has this kind of bargaining power. The majority of employees are dependent upon employers for economic stability and hold weaker bargaining positions.

Foley v. Interactive Data Corp.
765 P2d. 337 (Ca, 1988)

After Interactive Data Corporation (defendant) fired plaintiff Daniel D. Foley, an executive employee, he filed this action seeking compensatory and punitive damages for wrongful discharge. In his second amended complaint, plaintiff asserted three distinct theories: (1) a tort cause of action alleging a discharge in violation of public policy (Tameny v. Atlantic Richfield Co.), (2) a contract cause of action for breach of an implied-in-fact promise to discharge for good cause only (Pugh v. See's Candies, Inc.), and (3) a cause of action alleging a tortious breach of the implied covenant of good faith and fair dealing (Cleary v. American Airlines, Inc.). The trial court sustained a demurrer without leave to amend, and entered judgment for defendant.

The Court of Appeal affirmed on the grounds (1) plaintiff alleged no statutorily based breach of public policy sufficient to state a cause of action pursuant to Tameny; (2) plaintiff's claim for breach of the covenant to discharge only for good cause was barred by the statute of frauds; and (3) plaintiff's cause of action based on breach of the covenant of good faith and fair dealing failed because it did not allege necessary longevity of employment or express formal procedures for termination of employees. We granted review to consider each of the Court of Appeal's conclusions.

We will hold that the Court of Appeals properly found that plaintiff's particular Tameny cause of action could not proceed; plaintiff failed to alleged acts showing a violation of a fundamental public policy. We will also conclude, however, that plaintiff has sufficiently alleged a breach of an "oral" or "implied-in-fact" contract, and that the statute of frauds does not bar his claim so that he may pursue his action in this regard. Finally, we will hold that the covenant of good faith and fair dealing applies to employment contracts and that breach of the covenant may give rise to contract but not tort damages.

FACTS

Because this appeal arose from a judgment entered after the trial court sustained defendant's demurrer, "we must, under established principles, assume the truth of all properly pleaded material allegations of the complaint in evaluating the validity" of the decision below (Tameny v. Atlantic Richfield Co.; Alcorn v. Anbro Engineering, Inc.).

According to the complaint, plaintiff is a former employee of defendant, a wholly owned subsidiary of Chase Manhattan Bank that markets computer-based decision-support services. Defendant hired plaintiff in June 1976 as an assistant product manager at a starting salary of $18,500. As a condition of employment defendant required plaintiff to sign a "Confidential and Proprietary Information Agreement" whereby he promised not to engage in certain competition with defendant for one year after the termination of his employment for any reason. The agreement also contained a "Disclosure and Assignment of Information" provision that obliged plaintiff to disclose to defendant all computer-related information known to him, including any innovations, inventions or developments pertaining to the computer field for a period of one year following his termination. Finally, the agreement imposed on plaintiff a continuing obligation to assign to defendant all rights to his computer-related inventions or innovations for one year following termination. It did not state any limitation on the grounds for which plaintiff's employment could be terminated.

Over the next six years and nine months, plaintiff received a steady series of salary increases, promotions, bonuses, awards and superior performance evaluations. In 1979 defendant named him consultant manager of the year and in 1981 promoted him to branch manager of its Los Angeles office. His annual salary rose to $56,164 and he received an additional $6,762 merit bonus two days before his discharge in March 1983. He alleges defendant's officers made repeated oral assurances of job security so long as his performance remained adequate.

Plaintiff also alleged that during his employment, defendant maintained written "Termination Guidelines"

250

that set forth express grounds for discharge and a
mandatory seven-step pre-termination procedure.
Plaintiff understood that these guidelines applied not
only to employees under plaintiff's supervision, but to
him as well. On the basis of these representations,
plaintiff alleged that he reasonably believed defendant
would not discharge him except for good cause, and
therefore he refrained from accepting or pursuing other
job opportunities.

The event that led to plaintiff's discharge was a
private conversation in January 1983 with his former
supervisor, vice president Richard Earnest. During the
previous year defendant had hired Robert Kuhne and
subsequently named Kuhne to replace Earnest as
plaintiff's immediate supervisor. Plaintiff learned that
Kuhne was currently under investigation by the Federal
Bureau of Investigation for embezzlement from his former
employer, Bank of America. Plaintiff reported what he
knew about Kuhne to Earnest, because he was "worried
about working for Kuhne and having him in a supervisory
position. . . , in view of Kuhne's suspected criminal
conduct." Plaintiff asserted he "made this disclosure
in the interest and for the benefit of his employer,"
allegedly because he believed that because defendant and
its parent do business with the financial community on
a confidential basis, the company would have a legitimate
interest in knowing about a high executive's alleged
prior criminal conduct.

In response, Earnest allegedly told plaintiff not
to discuss "rumors" and to "forget what he heard" about
Kuhne's past. In early March, Kuhne informed plaintiff
that defendant had decided to replace him for
"performance reasons" and that he could transfer to a
position in another division in Waltham, Massachusetts.
Plaintiff was told that if he did not accept a transfer,
he might be demoted but not fired. One week later, in
Waltham, Earnest informed plaintiff he was not doing a
good job, and six days later, he notified plaintiff he
could continue as branch manager if he "agreed to go on
a 'performance plan.' Plaintiff asserts he agreed to
consider such an arrangement." The next day, when Kuhne
met with plaintiff, purportedly to present him with a
written "performance plan" proposal, Kuhne instead
informed plaintiff he had the choice of resigning or

251

being fired. Kuhne offered neither a performance plan
nor an option to transfer to another position.

. . . .

We turn now to plaintiff's cause of action for
tortious breach of the implied covenant of good faith and
fair dealing. Relying on Cleary, and subsequent Court
of Appeal cases, plaintiff asserts we should recognize
tort remedies for such a breach in the context of
employment termination.

The distinction between tort and contract is well
grounded in common law, and divergent objectives underlie
the remedies created in the two areas. Whereas contract
actions are created to enforce the intentions of the
parties to the agreement, tort law is primarily designed
to vindicate "social policy." The covenant of good faith
and fair dealing was developed in the contract arena and
is aimed at making effective the agreement's promises.
Plaintiff asks that we find that the breach of the
implied covenant in employment contracts also gives rise
to an action seeking an award of tort damages.

In this instance, where an extension of tort
remedies is sought for a duty whose breach previously has
been compensable by contractual remedies, it is helpful
to consider certain principles relevant to contract law.
First, predictability about the cost of contractual
relationships plays an important role in our commercial
system. Moreover, "Courts traditionally have awarded
damages for breach of contract to compensate the
aggrieved party rather than to punish the breaching
party." "With these concepts in mind, we turn to analyze
the role of the implied covenant of good faith and fair
dealing and the propriety of the extension of remedies
urged by plaintiff.

"Every contract imposes upon each party a duty of
good faith dealing in its performance and its
enforcement." This duty has been recognized in the
majority of American jurisdictions, the Restatement, and
the Uniform Commercial Code. Because the covenant is a

252

contract term, however, compensation for its breach has almost always been limited to contract rather than tort remedies. As to the scope of the covenant, "[t]he precise nature and extent of the duty imposed by such an implied promise will depend on the contractual purposes." Initially, the concept of a duty of good faith developed in contract law as "a kind of 'safety valve' to which judges may turn to fill gaps and qualify or limit rights and duties otherwise arising under rules of law and specific contract language." (94 Harv.L.Rev.369, 371 ["the courts employ the good faith doctrine to effectuate the intentions of parties, or to protect their reasonable expectations"].) As a contract concept, breach of the duty led to imposition of contract damages determined by the nature of the breach and standard contract principles.

An exception to this general rule has developed in the context of insurance contracts where, for a variety of policy reasons, courts have held that breach of the implied covenant will provide the basis for an action in tort. California has a well-developed judicial history addressing this exception. In Comunale v. Traders & General Ins. Co. we stated, "There is an implied covenant of good faith and fair dealing in every contract that neither party will do anything which will injure the right of the other to receive the benefits of the agreement." (See also Egan v. Mutual of Omaha Ins. Co.,) Thereafter, in Crisci v. Security Ins. Co. for the first time we permitted an insured to recover in tort for emotional damages caused by the insurer's breach of the implied covenant. We explained in Gruenberg v. Aetna Ins. Co. that "[t]he duty [to comport with the implied covenant of good faith and fair dealing] is imminent in the contract whether the company is attending [on the insured's behalf] to the claims of third persons against the insured or the claims of the insured itself. Accordingly, when the insurer unreasonably and in bad faith withholds payments of the claim of its insured, it is subject to liability in tort."

In Egan v. Mutual of Omaha Ins. Co., we described some of the bases for permitting tort recovery for breach of the implied covenant in the insurance context. "The insured in a contract like the one before us does not seek to obtain a commercial advantage by purchasing the

policy - rather, he seeks protection against calamity."
Thus, "As one commentary has noted, 'The insurers'
obligations are...rooted in their status as purveyors of
a vital service labeled quasi-public in nature.
Suppliers of services affected with a public interest
must take the public's interest seriously, where
necessary placing it before their interest in maximizing
gains and limiting disbursements... [A]s a supplier of
a public service rather than a manufactured product, the
obligations of insurers go beyond meeting reasonable
expectations of coverage. The obligations of good faith
and fair dealing encompass qualities of decency and
humanity inherent in the responsibilities of a
fiduciary."'

In addition, the Egan court emphasized that "the
relationship of insurer and insured is inherently
unbalanced; the adhesive nature of insurance contracts
places the insurer in a superior bargaining position."
This emphasis on the "special relationship of insurer and
insured has been echoed in arguments and analysis in
subsequent scholarly commentary and cases which urge the
availability of tort remedies in the employment context.

. . . .

In our view, the underlying problem in the line of
cases relied on by plaintiff lies in the decisions'
uncritical incorporation of the insurance model into the
employment context, without careful consideration of the
fundamental policies underlying the development of tort
and contract law in general or of significant differences
between the insurer/insured and employer/employee
relationships. When a court enforces the implied
covenant it is in essence acting to protect "the interest
in having promises performed" the traditional realm of
a contract action - rather than to protect some general
duty to society which the law places on an employer
without regard to the substance of its contractual
obligations to its employee. Thus, in Tameny as we have
explained, the court was careful to draw a distinction
between "ex delicto" and "ex contractu" obligations. An

254

allegation of breach of the implied covenant of good faith and fair dealing is an allegation of breach of an "ex contractu" obligation, namely one arising out of the contract itself. The covenant of good faith is read into contracts in order to protect the express covenants or promises of the contract, not to protect some general public policy interest not directly tied to the contract's purposes. The insurance cases thus were a major departure from traditional principles of contract law. We must, therefore, consider with great care claims that extension of the exceptional approach taken in those cases is automatically appropriate if certain hallmarks and similarities can be adduced in another contract setting. With this emphasis on the historical purposes of the covenant of good faith and fair dealing in mind, we turn to consider the bases upon which extension of the insurance model to the employment sphere has been urged.

The "special relationship" test gleaned from the insurance context has been suggested as a model for determining the appropriateness of permitting tort remedies for breach of the implied covenant of the employment context. One commentary has observed. "[j]ust as the law of contracts fails to provide adequate principles for construing the terms of an insurance policy, the substantial body of law uniquely applicable to insurance contracts is practically irrelevant to commercially oriented contracts...These [unique] features characteristic of the insurance contract make it particularly susceptible to public policy considerations." These commentators assert that tort remedies for breach of the covenant should not be extended across the board in the commercial context, but that, nonetheless, public policy considerations suggest extending the tort remedy if certain salient factors are present. "The tort of bad faith should be applied to commercial contracts only if four of the features characteristic of insurance bad faith actions are present. The features are: (1) one of the parties to the contract enjoys a superior bargaining position to the extent that it is able to dictate the terms of the contract; (2) the purpose of the weaker party in entering into the contract is not primarily to profit but rather to secure an essential service or product, financial security or peace of mind; (3) the relationship of the

255

parties is such that the weaker party places its trust
and confidence in the larger entity; and (4) there is
conduct on the part of the defendant indicating an intent
to frustrate the weaker party's enjoyment of the contract
rights." The discussion of these elements includes an
assumption that a tort remedy should be recognized in
employment relationships within the stated limitations.

Others argue that the employment context is not
sufficiently analogous to that of insurance to warrant
recognition of the right to tort recovery. They contend
that (1) inequality in bargaining power is not a
universal characteristic of employment contracts,
standardized forms are often not used, and there is often
room for bargaining as to special conditions; (2)
employers do not owe similar fiduciary duties to
employees, who are themselves agents of the employer and
obligated to act in the employer's interests; and (3)
unlike insurance companies, employers are not
"quasi-public entities" and they "seldom have
government-like functions, and do not serve primarily,
if at all, to spread losses across society."

In contrast to those concentrating on the match
between insurance and employment relationships, yet
another article suggests, "The fundamental flaw in the
'special relationship' test is that it is illusory. It
provides a label to hang on a result but not a principled
basis for decision . . . . The qualifying contracts
cannot be identified until the issue has been litigated,
which is too late." The authors assert that "public
interest, adhesion and fiduciary responsibility, are not
sufficiently precise to provide a basis for reliable
prediction." Instead, they assert that, "While the
'special relationship' test purports to be only a modest
extension of the tort of bad faith beyond insurance and
employment, it opens the way for pleading a tort cause
of action in nearly every contract case, leaving it
ultimately to a jury to decide whether or not the parties
had a 'special relationship.' Extension of the test to
employment cases would similarly leave the door open to
such a claim in every termination case, and readers are
cautioned not to infer "that the authors support
extension of tort liability beyond insurance through use
of the 'special relationship' test."

256

Similarly, another commentary argues that the special relationship model fails because (1) it does not explain why it "justifies tort liability" for otherwise legal conduct, or for conduct which may give rise to contract remedies, (2) use of the concept "is inadequate to define the scope and application of a tort duty of good faith and fair dealing", (3) use of the model "fails to distinguish between breach of the implied covenant of good faith and fair dealing and 'bad faith breach of contract'" and (4) the model does not provide justification for imposition of punitive damages and thus "might serve to unfairly chill legitimate conduct."

After review of the various commentators, and independent consideration of the similarities between the two areas, we are not convinced that a "special relationship" analogous to that between insurer and insured should be deemed to exist in the usual employment relationship which would warrant recognition of a tort action for breach of the implied covenant. Even if we were to assume that the special relationship model is an appropriate one to follow in determining whether to expand tort recovery, a breach in the employment context does not place the employee in the same economic dilemma that an insured faces when an insurer in bad faith refuses to pay a claim or to accept a settlement offer within policy limits. When an insurer takes such actions, the insured cannot turn to the marketplace to find another insurance company willing to pay for the loss already incurred. The wrongfully terminated employee, on the other hand, can (and must, in order to mitigate damages) make reasonable efforts to seek alternative employment. Moreover, the role of the employer differs from that of the "quasi-public" insurance company with whom individuals contract specifically in order to obtain protection from potential specified economic harm. The employer does not similarly "sell" protection to its employees; it is not providing a public service. Nor do we find convincing the idea that the employee is necessarily seeking a different kind of financial security than those entering a typical commercial contract. If a small dealer contracts for goods from a large supplier, and those goods are vital to the small dealer's business, a breach by the supplier may have financial significance for individuals employed by the dealer or the dealer himself. Permitting only

257

contract damages in such a situation has ramifications no different from a similar limitation in the direct employer-employee relationship.

Finally, there is a fundamental difference between insurance and employment relationships. In the insurance relationship, the insurer's and insured's interest are financially at odds. If the insurer pays a claim, it diminishes its fiscal resources. The insured of course has paid for protection and expects to have its losses recompensed. When a claim is paid, money shifts from insurer to insured, or, if appropriate, to a third party claimant.

Putting aside already specifically barred improper motives for termination which may be based on both economic and noneconomic considerations, as a general rule it is to the employer's economic benefit to retain good employees. The interests of employer and employee are most frequently in alignment. If there is a job to be done, the employer must still pay someone to do it. This is not to say that there may never be a "bad motive" for discharge not otherwise covered by law. Nevertheless, in terms of abstract employment relationships as contrasted with abstract insurance relationships, there is less inherent relevant tension between the interests of employers and employees than exists between that of insurers and insureds. Thus the need to place disincentives on an employer's conduct in addition to those already imposed by law simply does not rise to the same level as that created by the conflicting interests at stake in the insurance context. Nor is this to say that the legislature would have no basis for affording employees additional protections. It is, however, to say that the need to extend the special relationship model in the form of judicially created relief of the kind sought here is less compelling.

We therefore conclude that the employment relationship is not sufficiently similar to that of insurer and insured to warrant judicial extension of the proposed additional tort remedies in view of the countervailing concerns about economic policy and stability, the traditional separation of tort and contract law, and finally, the numerous protections against improper terminations already afforded employees.

258

Our inquiry, however, does not end here. The potential effects on an individual caused by termination of employment arguably justify additional remedies for certain improper discharges. The large body of employment law restricting an employer's right to discharge based on discriminatory reasons or on the employee's exercise of legislatively conferred employee rights, indicates that the Legislature and Congress have recognized the importance of the employment relationship and the necessity for vindication of certain legislatively and constitutionally established public policies in the employment context. The Tameny cause of action likewise is responsive to similar public concerns. In the quest for expansion of remedies for discharged workers which we consider here, however, the policies sought to be vindicated have a different origin. The most frequently cited reason for the move to extend tort remedies in this context is the perception that traditional contract remedies are inadequate to compensate for certain breaches. Others argue that the quest for additional remedies specifically for terminated workers also has it genesis in (1) comparisons drawn between the protections afforded nonunion employees and those covered by collective bargaining agreements, (2) changes in the economy which have led to displacement of middle-level management employees in "unprecedented numbers," and (3) the effect of antidiscrimination awareness and legislation that has "raised expectations and created challenges to employer decision making."

The issue is how far courts can or should go in responding to these concerns regarding the sufficiency of compensation by departing from long established principles of contract law. Significant policy judgments affecting social policies and commercial relationships are implicated in the resolution of this question in the employment termination context. Such a determination, which has the potential to alter profoundly the nature of employment, the cost of products and services, and the availability of jobs, arguably is better suited for legislative decision making. Moreover, as we discuss, the extension of the availability of tort remedies is but one among many solutions posited to remedy the problem of adequately compensating employees for certain forms of "wrongful" termination while balancing the interests of employers in their freedom to make economically based decisions about their work force.

It cannot be disputed that legislation at both the state and national level has profoundly affected the scope of at-will terminations. As noted, regulation of employment ranging from workers' compensation laws to antidiscrimination enactments, fair labor standards, minimum compensation, regulation of hours, etc., all have significantly impinged on the laissez faire underpinnings of the at-will rule. Moreover, unionization of a portion of the domestic workforce has substantial implications for the judicial development of employment termination law because the rights of such workers, when terminated are often governed exclusively by the terms of applicable collective bargaining agreements. The slate we write on thus is far from clean.

Professor Gould asserts, "[t]he new common law of wrongful discharge has provided employer and employee with the worst of all possible worlds...[E]mployers are subject to volatile and unpredictable juries that frequently act without regard to legal instructions. Moreover, the employees who benefit are few and far between, first, because of the difficulties involved in staying the course of a lengthy and expensive judicial process, and second, because of limitations inherent in the legal doctrines adopted by the courts." Gould advocates exploring arbitration as an alternative, and his emphasis on the sporadic effectiveness of the tort cause of action to remedy perceived inadequacies in employee protection is important to our consideration of the effectiveness of the remedy sought here.

Professor Putz and co-author Klippen also suggest "tort liability is not the answer to bad faith defense in commercial contract disputes. A more appropriate response is to make contract damages adequate by permitting a prevailing plaintiff to recover attorney fees where the breaching party is found to have denied liability unreasonably. Yet another commentator advocates expansion of recoverable contract damages. Others would permit tort damages but would limit their application. These various approaches on the one hand suggest a widespread perception that present compensation is inadequate, but on the other hand vividly demonstrate substantial disagreement about the propriety or even the potential form of tort remedies for breaches of contractual duties of covenants. The multiplicity of solutions advanced underscores the caution with which any attempts to extend such relief must be viewed.

As we have reiterated, the employment relationship is fundamentally contractual, and several factors combine to persuade us that in the absence of legislative direction to the contrary contractual remedies should remain the sole available relief for breaches of the implied covenant of good faith and fair dealing in the employment context. Initially, predictability of the consequences of actions related to employment contracts is important to commercial stability. In order to achieve such stability, it is also important that employers not be unduly deprived of discretion to dismiss an employee by the fear that doing so will give rise to potential tort recovery in every case.

Moreover, it would be difficult if not impossible to formulate a rule that would assure that only "deserving" cases give rise to tort relief. Professor Summers, in his seminal article, described the term "good faith" as used in the duty of good faith imposed in contract law and the Uniform Commercial Code, as an "excluder" phrase which is "without general meaning (or meanings) of its own and serves to exclude a wide range of heterogeneous forms of bad faith. In a particular context the phrase takes on specific meaning, but usually this is only by way of contrast with the specific form of bad faith actually or hypothetically ruled out." In a tort action based on an employee's discharge, it is highly likely that each case would involve a dispute as to material facts regarding the subjective intentions of the employer. As a result, these actions could rarely be disposed of at the demurrer or summary judgement stage.

The formulation advanced in Koehrer, affords no real restriction on the employee's ability to bring an action after termination. Nor did the Khanna court's approach provide such necessary delineation. The court provided simply: "A breach of the implied covenant of good faith and fair dealing in employment contracts is established whenever the employer engages in 'bad faith action

261

extraneous to the contract, combined with the obligor's intent to frustrate the [employee's] enjoyment of contract rights.' The facts in <u>Cleary</u> establish only one manner among many by which an employer might violate this covenant." (See also <u>Huber</u>, [discussing necessary showing for a prima facie case: employee need only show "unjust termination" but need not show bad or hidden motivation on employer's part.])

Review of the <u>Koehrer</u>, <u>Khanna</u> and <u>Huber</u> formulations reveals that ultimately they require nothing "unusual" about the breach: under the approaches of those courts, an ordinary contract breach might give rise to a bad faith action. Resolution of the ensuing inquiry into the employer's motives has been difficult to predict and demonstrates the imprecision of the standards thus far formulated. This situation undermines the statutory mandate that neither compensatory tort damages nor exemplary damages are available in an action arising from the breach of a contract obligation. Adoption of tests such as those formulated by the Court of Appeals would result in the anomalous result that henceforth the implied covenant in an employment contract would enjoy protection far greater than that afforded to express and implied-in-fact promises, the breach of which gives rise to an action for contract damages only.

The <u>Koehrer</u> court recognized the problem of distinguishing between breaches of the contract and breaches of obligations imposed by law. It failed, however, to recognize that in traditional contract law, the motive of the breaching party generally has no bearing on the scope of damages that the injured party may recover for the breach of the implied covenant; the remedies are limited to contract damages. Thus, recitation of the parameters of the implied covenant alone is unsatisfactory. If the covenant is implied in every contract, but its breach does not in every contract give rise to tort damages, attempts to define when tort damages are appropriate simply by interjecting a requirement of "bad faith" do nothing to limit the potential reach of tort remedies or to differentiate between those cases properly and traditionally compensable by contract damages and those in which tort damages should flow. Virtually any firing (indeed any breach of a contract term in any context) could provide the basis for a pleading alleging the discharge was in bad faith under the cited standards.

Finally, and of primary significance, we believe that focus on available contract remedies offers the most appropriate method of expanding available relief for wrongful terminations. The expansion of tort remedies in the employment context has potentially enormous consequences for the stability of the business community.

We are not unmindful of the legitimate concerns of employees who fear arbitrary and improper discharges that may have a devastating effect on their economic and social status. Nor are we unaware of or unsympathetic to claims that contract remedies for breaches of contract are insufficient because they do not fully compensate due to their failure to include attorney fees and their restrictions on foreseeable damages. These defects, however, exist generally in contract situations. As discussed above, the variety of possible courses to remedy the problem is well demonstrated in the literature and include increased contract damages, provision for award of attorney fees, establishment of arbitration or other speedier and less expensive dispute resolution, or the tort remedies (the scope of which is also subject to dispute) sought by plaintiff here.

The diversity of possible solutions demonstrates the confusion that occurs when we look outside the realm of contract law in attempting to fashion remedies for a breach of a contract provision. As noted, numerous legislative provisions have imposed obligations on parties to contracts which vindicate significant social policies extraneous to the contract itself. As Justice Kaus observed in his concurring and dissenting opinion in White v. Western Title Ins. Co., "our experience in Seaman's surely tells us that there are real problems in applying the substitute remedy of a tort recovery---with or without punitive damages---outside the insurance area. In other words, I believe that under all the circumstances, the problem is one for Legislature.

. . . .

Broussard, Justice: I concur in part I of the majority opinion, which holds that plaintiff has not stated a cause of action for discharge in violation of public policy.   I join fully in part II of the majority opinion, which upholds plaintiff's cause of action for breach of contract, but add a note exploring the question of the damages recoverable in such an action.   I respectfully dissent to part III of the majority opinion. Although written in conservative tones of deference to legislative action, it is in fact a radical attempt to rewrite California law in a manner which, as the majority themselves acknowledge, will leave the wrongfully discharged worker without an adequate remedy.

. . . .

The majority opinion does not preserve the status quo, leaving it to the Legislature to adopt innovative solutions.   It uproots the status quo, leaving it to the Legislature to remedy the problems the opinion creates.

. . . .

The majority deride the prior cases for their uncritical incorporation of the insurance model into the employment context without considering the significant differences between the insurer-insured and employer-employee relationships.   But when we consider the differences noted by the majority, we find that they are not significant at all.

The majority find one fundamental difference between insurance and employment relationships: "[i]f an insurer pays a claim, it diminishes its fiscal resources . . . [while]as a general rule it is to the employer's economic benefit to retain good employees."   But their comparison is not between insurers and employers, but between short-sighted insurers and far-sighted employers.   In the short run, the insurer saves money by not paying claims, and the employer by not paying wages.   (If the work cannot be deferred, he can hire less experienced but cheaper help.)   In the long run, an insurer that never paid

264

claims would be out of business, and an employer that always fired experienced help would not be much better off. Thus if we examine insurers and employers with the same lens, the difference the majority find fundamental simply disappears.

But the majority's analysis leaves a lingering trace, for it betrays their misunderstanding of the problem. We need not be concerned about insurers that never pay claims or employers that fire all experienced help -- the marketplace will take care of them. The concern is with the insurer or employer that acts arbitrarily some of the time -- and can get away with it unless threatened with damages that, unlike traditional contract damages, exceed the short-term profit.

The majority also point to some nonfundamental distinctions between the insurer-insured and the employer-employee relationships. They argue that the discharged employee may be able to mitigate damages while the insured generally cannot. But as we all know, in many cases the discharged worker cannot mitigate damages. As Justice Kaufman asks, "What market is there for the factory worker laid-off after 25 years of labor in the same plant, or for the middle-aged executive fired after 25 years with the same firm?" The ability of some persons to mitigate damages is no reason to deny a cause of action to those unable to mitigate them.

It is next suggested that the employer, unlike the insurer, is not performing a "public service." I fail to understand the significance of the statement. Employment is even more important to the community than insurance; most people value their jobs more than their insurance policies. The public interest in deterring arbitrary breach of employment contracts is, I suggest, at least equal to that in deterring arbitrary breach of insurance contracts.

Finally, the majority reject the idea that an employee is like an insured because both contract for financial security. A business, they point out, may also seek financial security. They put the case of a business contracting to secure a reliable source of supply. But what emerges from the majority's analysis is three propositions: a) that insureds generally buy insurance

265

policies for financial security; (b) that employees generally seek financial security in their employment; (c) that businesses occasionally contract for financial security. These propositions should lead the majority to conclude that the employment contract is more analogous to an insurance contract than to a commercial contract.

The majority are focusing upon the exceptions, not upon the general rule. If we must argue analogies, the question is not whether the employment contract differs from an insurance contract in one particular respect, or resembles a commercial contract in another. It is whether, as a whole, the contract of employment more closely resembles an insurance contract or an ordinary commercial contract. The answer is clear. The principal reason we permit tort damages for breach of the covenant of good faith and fair dealing in an insurance contract is that persons do not generally purchase insurance to obtain a commercial advantage, but to secure the peace of mind and security it will provide in protecting against accidental loss. That reason applies equally to the employer-employee relationship. A man or a woman usually does not enter into employment solely for the money; a job is status, reputation, a way of defining one's self-worth and worth in the community. It is also essential to financial security, offering assurance of future income needed to repay present debts and meet future obligations. Without a secure job a worker frequently cannot obtain a retirement pension, and often lacks access to affordable medical insurance. In short, "in a modern industrialized economy employment is central to one's existence and dignity."

Because workers value their jobs as more than merely a source of money, contract damages, if limited to loss of income, are inadequate. Again the analogy to the insurance cases is close. Explaining the basis for tort damages in insurance cases, Wallis v. Superior Court, said that "[m]oney damages paid pursuant to a judgement years after . . . do not remedy the harm suffered . . . , namely the immediate inability to support oneself and its attendant horrors"--language which applies equally to a suit for wrongful discharge. As summarized in Recent Judicial Limitations On the Right to Discharge: A California Trilogy, insureds and employees both depend

266

on the contracts "for their security, well-being, and peace of mind. If insurance companies or employers act in bad faith, the consequences can be very severe, indeed much greater than those that result from a breach of contract."

In contrast, commercial contracts, generally speaking, are negotiated between parties of more nearly equal bargaining strength, and are entered into for purpose of profit. Breach entails only lost profits, and often a market exists in which the damaged party can cover its loss. I conclude that past decisions were justified in analogizing the relationship between employer and employee to that between insurer and insured, and in distinguishing both from commercial contracts for the sale of goods and services.

. . . .

Justice Kaufman, concurring and dissenting: First, the majority asserts that a breach in the employment context "does not place the employee in the same economic dilemma that an insured faces" because the insured "cannot turn to the marketplace," while an employee presumably may "seek alternative employment." Next, the majority argues that an employer, unlike an insurance company, does not sell economic "protection." The majority also rejects the insurance analogy because an employee, unlike an insured, allegedly does not seek a "different kind of financial security than those entering a typical commercial contract." Finally, the majority asserts that insurance and employment contracts differ "fundamental[ly]" because the insured's and insurer's interests are "financially at odds," while the employer's and employee's interests allegedly are "most frequently in alignment."

Such conclusions, in my view, expose an unrealistic if not mythical conception of the employment relationship. They also reveal a misplaced reluctance to define the minimal standards of decency required to govern that relationship. The delineation of such

267

standards is not, as the majority strongly implies, judicial legislation, but rather constitutes this court's fundamental obligation.

It is, at best, naive to believe that the availability of the "marketplace," or that a supposed "alignment of interests," renders the employment relationship less special or less subject to abuse than the relationship between insurer and insured. Indeed, I can think of no relationship in which one party, the employee, places more reliance upon the other, is more dependent upon the other, or is more vulnerable to abuse by the other, than the relationship between employer and employee. And, ironically, the relative imbalance of economic power between employer and employee tends to increase rather than diminish the longer that relationship continues. Whatever bargaining strength and marketability the employee may have at the moment of hiring, diminishes rapidly thereafter. Marketplace? What market is there for the factory worker laid-off after 25 years of labor in the same plant, or the middle-aged executive fired after 25 years with the same firm?

Financial security? Can anyone seriously dispute that employment is generally sought, at least in part, for financial security and all that that implies: food on the table, shelter, clothing, medical care, education for one's children. Clearly, no action for breach of the covenant of good faith and fair dealing will lie unless it has first been proved that, expressly or by implication, the employer has given the employee a reasonable expectation of continued employment so long as the employee performs satisfactorily. And that expectation constitutes a far greater and graver security interest than any which inheres in the insurance context. Most of us can live without insurance. Few of us could live without a job.

Peace of mind? One's work obviously involves more than just earning a living. It defines for many people their identity, their sense of self-worth, their sense of belonging. The wrongful and malicious destruction of ones' employment is far more certain to result in serious emotional distress than any wrongful denial of an insurance claim.

If everything this court has written concerning the relation between insurer and insured has any deeper meaning; if we have created a living principle based upon justice, reason and common sense and not merely a fixed, narrow and idiosyncratic rule of law, then we must acknowledge the irresistible logic and equity of extending that principle to the employment relationship. We can reasonably do no less.

MONTANA WRONGFUL DISCHARGE FROM EMPLOYMENT ACT (1987)

Wrongful Discharge from Employment

39-2-901   Short title.   This part may be cited as the "Wrongful Discharge From Employment Act".

39-2-902.   Purpose.   This part sets forth certain rights and remedies with respect to wrongful discharge. Except as limited in this part, employment having no specified term may be terminated at the will of either the employer or the employee on notice to the other for any reason considered sufficient by the terminating party.   Except as provided in 39-2-912, this part provides the exclusive remedy for a wrongful discharge from employment.

39-2-903.   Definitions.   In this part, the following definitions apply:

(1)   "Constructive discharge" means the voluntary termination of employment by an employee because of a situation created by an act or omission of the employer which an objective, reasonable person would find so intolerable that voluntary termination is the only reasonable alternative.   Constructive discharge does not mean voluntary termination because of an employer's refusal to promote the employee or improve wages, responsibilities, or other terms and conditions of employment.

(2)   "Discharge" includes a constructive discharge as defined in subsection (1) and any other termination of employment, including resignation, elimination of the job, layoff for lack of work, failure to recall or rehire, and any other cutback in the number of employees for a legitimate business reason.

(3)   "Employee" means a person who works for another for hire.   The term does not include a person who is an independent contractor.

(4) "Fringe benefits" means the value of any employer-paid vacation leave, sick leave, medical insurance plan, disability insurance plan, life insurance plan and pension benefit plan in force on the date of the termination.

(5) "Good cause" means reasonable job-related grounds for dismissal based on a failure to satisfactorily perform job duties, disruption of the employer's operation, or other legitimate business reason.

(6) "Lost wages" means the gross amount of wages that would have been reported to the internal revenue service as gross income on form W-2 and includes additional compensation deferred at the option of the employee.

(7) "Public policy" means a policy in effect at the time of the discharge concerning the public health, safety, or welfare established by constitutional provision, statute, or administrative rule.

39-2-904. Elements of wrongful discharge. A discharge is wrongful only if:

(1) it was in retaliation for the employee's refusal to violate public policy or for reporting a violation of public policy;

(2) the discharge was not for good cause and the employee had completed the employer's probationary period of employment; or

(3) the employer violated the express provisions of its own written personnel policy.

39-2-905 Remedies.

(1) If an employer has committed a wrongful discharge, the employee may be awarded lost wages and fringe benefits for a period not to exceed 4 years from the date of discharge, together with interest thereon. Interim earnings, including amounts the employee could have earned with reasonable diligence, must be deducted from the amount awarded for lost wages.

(2) The employee may recover punitive damages
otherwise allowed by law if it is established by clear
and convincing evidence that the employer engaged in
actual fraud or actual malice in the discharge of the
employee in violation of 39-2-904(1).

(3) There is no right under any legal theory to
damages for wrongful discharge under this part for pain
and suffering, motional distress, compensatory damages,
punitive damages, or any other form of damages, except
as provided for in subsections (1) and (2).

39-2-906 through 39-2-910 reserved.

39-2-911. Limitation of actions.

(1) An action under this part must be filed within
1 year after the date of discharge.

(2) If an employer maintains written internal
procedures, other than those specified in 39-2-912, under
which an employee may appeal a discharge within the
organizational structure of the employer, the employee
shall first exhaust those procedures prior to filing an
action under this part. The employee's failure to
initiate or exhaust available internal procedures is a
defense to an action brought under this part. If the
employer's internal procedures are not completed within
90 days from the date the employee initiates the internal
procedures, the employee may file an action under this
part and for purposes of this subsection the employer's
internal procedures are considered exhausted. The
limitation period in subsection (1) is tolled until the
procedures are exhausted. In no case may the provisions
of the employer's internal procedures extend the
limitation period in subsection (1) more than 120 days.

(3) If the employer maintains written internal
procedures under which an employee may appeal a discharge
within the organizational structure of the employer, the
employer shall within 7 days of the date of the discharge
notify the discharged employee of the existence of such
procedures and shall supply the discharged employee with
a copy of them. If the employer fails to comply with

273

this subsection, the discharged employee need not comply with subsection (2).

39-2-912.   Exemptions.   This part does not apply to a discharge:

(1)   that is subject to any other state or federal statute that provides a procedure or remedy for contesting the dispute. Such statutes include those that prohibit discharge for filing complaints, charges, or claims with administrative bodies or that prohibit unlawful discrimination based on race, national origin, sex, age, handicap, creed, religion, political belief, color, martial status, and other similar grounds.

(2)   of an employee covered by a written collective bargaining agreement or a written contract of employment for a specific term.

39-2-913.   Preemption of common-law remedies. Except as provided in this part, no claim for discharge may arise from tort or express or implied contract.

39-2-914.   Arbitration.

(1)   Under a written agreement of the parties, a dispute that otherwise could be adjudicated under this part may be resolved by final and binding arbitration as provided in this section.

(2)   An offer to arbitrate must be in writing and contain the following provisions:

(a)   A neutral arbitrator must be selected by mutual agreement or, in the absence of agreement, as provided in 27-5-211. (b)   The arbitration must be governed by the Uniform Arbitration Act, Title 27, chapter 5.   If there is a conflict between the Uniform Arbitration Act and this part, this part applies.   (c)   The arbitrator is bound by this part.

(3)   If a complaint is filed under this part, the offer to arbitrate must be made within 60 days after service of the complaint and must be accepted in writing within 30 days after the date the offer is made.

(4)   A party who makes a valid offer to arbitrate that is not accepted by the other party and who prevails in an action under this part is entitled as an element of costs to reasonable attorney fees incurred subsequent to the date of the offer.

(5)   A discharged employee who makes a valid offer to arbitrate that is accepted by the employer and who prevails in such arbitration is entitled to have the arbitrator's fee and all costs of arbitration paid by the employer.

(6)   If a valid offer to arbitrate is made and accepted, arbitration is the exclusive remedy for the wrongful discharge dispute and there is no right to bring or continue a lawsuit under this part. The arbitrator's award is final and binding, subject to review of the arbitrator's decision under the provisions of the Uniform Arbitration Act.

Appendix

Tests applicable for learning whether employer had just
cause for disciplining an employee

Few if any union-management agreements contain a
definition of "just cause." Nevertheless, over the years
the opinions of arbitrators in innumerable discipline
cases have developed a sort of "common law" definition
thereof. This definition consists of a set of guide lines
or criteria that are to be applied to the facts of any
one case and said criteria are set forth below in the
form of seven Questions, with accompanying Notes of
explanation.

A "no" answer to any one or more of said Questions
normally signifies that just and proper cause did not
exist.   In other words, such "no" means that the
employer's disciplinary decision contained one or more
elements of arbitrary, capricious, unreasonable or
discriminatory action to such an extent that said
decision constituted an abuse of managerial discretion
warranting the arbitrator to substitute his judgment for
that of the employer.

The answers to the Questions in any particular case
are to be found in the evidence presented to the
arbitrator at the hearing thereon.   Frequently, of
course, the facts are such that the guide lines cannot
be applied with precision.   Moreover, occasionally in
some particular case an arbitrator may find one or more
"no" answers so weak and the other, "yes" answers so
strong that he may properly, without any "political" or
spineless intent to "split the difference" between the

Reprinted with permission from <u>Labor Arbitration Reports</u>.
58LA428-430.   Published by the Bureau of National
Affairs, Inc.

opposing positions of the parties, find that the correct decision is to "chastise" both the company and the disciplined employee by decreasing but not nullifying the degree of discipline imposed by the company e.g., by reinstating a discharged employee without back pay.

It should be understood that, under the statement of issue as to whether an employer had just cause for discipline in a case of this sort before an arbitrator, it is the employer and not the disciplined employee who is "on trial" before the arbitrator. The arbitrator's hearing is an appeals proceeding designed to learn whether the employer in the first instance had forewarned the employee against the sort of conduct for which discipline was considered; whether the forewarning was reasonable; whether the employer, as a sort of trial court, had conducted, before making his decision, a full and fair inquiry into the employee's alleged "crime"; whether from the inquiry said trial court had obtained substantial evidence of the employee's guilt; whether the employer, in reaching his verdict and in deciding on the degree of discipline to be imposed, had acted in an even-handed, non-discriminatory manner; and whether the degree of discipline imposed by the employer was reasonable related to the seriousness of the proven offense and to the employee's previous record. In short, an arbitrator "tries" the employer to discover whether the latter's own "trial" and treatment of the employee was proper. The arbitrator rarely has the means for conducting, at a time long after the alleged offense was committed, a brand new trial of the employee.

It should be clearly understood also that the criteria set forth below are to be applied to the employer's conduct in making his disciplinary decision before same has been processed through the grievance procedure to arbitration. Any question as to whether the employer has properly fulfilled the contractual requirements of said procedure is entirely separate from the question of whether he fulfilled the "common law" requirements of just cause before the discipline was "grieved."

Sometimes, although very rarely, a union-management agreement contains a provision limiting the scope of the arbitrator's inquiry into the question of just cause.

For example, one such provision seen by this arbitrator says that "the only question the arbitrator is to determine shall be whether the employee is or is not guilty of the act or acts resulting in his discharge." Under the latter contractual statement an arbitrator might well have to confine his attention to Question No. 5 below or at most to Questions Nos. 3, 4, and 5. But absent any such restriction in an agreement, a consideration of the evidence on all seven Questions (and their accompanying Notes) is not only proper but necessary.

The above-mentioned Questions and Notes do not represent an effort to compress all the facts in a discharge case into a "formula." Labor and human relations circumstances vary widely from case to case, and no formula can be developed where-under the facts can be fed into a "computer" that spews out the inevitably correct answer on a sheet of paper. There is no substitute for sound human judgment. The Questions and Notes do represent an effort to minimize an arbitrator's consideration of irrelevant facts and his possible human tendency to let himself be blown by the variable winds of sentiment on to an uncharted and unchartable sea of "equity."

The Questions

1. Did the company give to the employee forewarning or foreknowledge of the possible or probable disciplinary consequences of the employee's conduct?

Note 1: Said forewarning or foreknowledge may properly have been given orally by management or in writing through the medium of typed sheets or booklets of shop rules and of penalties for violation thereof.

Note 2: There must have been actual oral or written communication of the rules and penalties to the employee.

Note 3: A finding of lack of such communication does not in all cases require a "no" answer to Question No. 1. This is because certain offenses such as insubordination, coming to work intoxicated, drinking intoxicating beverages on the job, or theft of the property of the company or of fellow employees are so serious that any employee in the industrial society may properly be expected to know already that such conduct is offensive and heavily punishable.

Note 4:   Absent any contractual prohibition or restriction, the company has the right unilaterally to promulgate reasonable rules and give reasonable orders; and same need not have been negotiated with the union.

2.   Was the company's rule or managerial orders reasonably related to (a) the orderly, efficient, and safe operation of the company's business and (b) the performance that the company might properly expect of the employee?

Note 1:   Because considerable thought and judgment have usually been given to the development and promulgation of written company rules, the rules must almost always be held reasonable in terms of the employer's business needs and usually in terms of the employee's performance capacities. But managerial orders often given on the spur of the moment, may be another matter. They may be reasonable in terms of the company's business needs, at least in the short run, but reasonable in terms of their employee's capacity to obey. Example: A foreman orders an employee to operate a high-speed band saw known to be unsafe and dangerous.

Note 2:   If an employee believes that a company rule or order is unreasonable, he must nevertheless obey same (in which case he may file a grievance thereover) unless he sincerely feels that to obey the rule or order would seriously and immediately jeopardize his personal safety and/or integrity. Given a firm finding to the latter effect, the employee may properly be said to have had justification for his disobedience.

3.   Did the company before administering discipline to an employee, make an effort to discover whether the employee did in fact violate or disobey a rule or order of management?

Note 1:   This Question (and No. 4)) constitutes the employee's "day in court" principle. An employee has the right to know with reasonable precision the offense with which he is being charged and to defend his

280

behavior.

Note 2: The company's investigation must normally be made before its disciplinary decision is made. If the company fails to do so, its failure may not normally be excused on the ground that the employee will get his day in court through the grievance procedure after the exaction of discipline. By that time there has usually been too much hardening of positions. In a very real sense the company is obligated to conduct itself like a trial court.

Note 3: There may of course be circumstances under which management must react immediately to the employee's behavior. In such cases the normally proper action is to suspend the employee pending investigation, with the understanding that (a) the final disciplinary decision will be made after the investigation and (b) if the employee is found innocent after the investigation, he will be restored to his job with full pay for time lost.

4. Was the company's investigation conducted fairly and objectively?

Note 1: At said investigation the management official may be both "prosecutor" and "judge", but he may not also be a witness against the employee.

Note 2: It is essential for some higher, detached management official to assume and conscientiously perform the judicial role, giving the commonly accepted meaning to that term in his attitude and conduct.

Note 3: In some disputes between an employee and a management person there are not witnesses to an incident other than the two immediate participants. In such cases it is particularly important that the management "judge" question the management participant rigorously and thoroughly, just as an actual third party would.

Note 4: The company's investigation should include an inquiry into possible justification for the employee's alleged rule violation.

Note 5: At his hearing the management "judge"

should actively search out witnesses and evidence, not just passively take what participants or "volunteer" witnesses tell him.

5. At the investigation did the company "judge" obtain substantial and compelling evidence or proof that the employee was guilty as charged?

Note 1: It is not required that the evidence be fully conclusive or "beyond all reasonable doubt." But the evidence must be truly weighty and substantial and not flimsy or superficial.

Note 2. When the testimony of opposing witnesses at the arbitration appeals hearing is irreconcilably in conflict, an arbitrator seldom has any means for resolving the contradictions. His task is then to determine whether the management "judge" originally had reasonable grounds for believing the evidence presented to him by his own people instead of that given by the accused employee and his witnesses. Such grounds may include a decision as to which side had the weightier reasons for falsification.

6. Has the company applied its rules, orders, and penalties evenhandedly and without discrimination to all employees?

Note 1: A "no" answer to this question requires a finding of discrimination and warrants negation or modification of the discipline imposed.

Note 2: If the company has been lax in enforcing its rules and orders and decides henceforth to apply them rigorously, the company may avoid a finding of discrimination by telling all employees beforehand of its intent to enforce hereafter all rules as written.

Note 3: For an arbitral finding of discrimination against a particular grievant to be justified, he and other employees found guilty of the same offense must have been in reasonably comparable circumstances.

Note 4: The comparability standard considers three main items - the degree of seriousness in the offense, the nature of the employees' employment records and the kind of offense.

(a) Many industrial offenses, e.g., in-plant
drinking and insubordination, are found in varying
degree. Thus, taking a single nip of gin from some other
employee's bottle inside the plant is not so serious an
offense as bringing in the bottle and repeatedly tipping
from it in the locker room. Again, making a small, snide
remark to and against a foreman is considerably less
offensive than cussing him out with foul language,
followed by a fist in the face. (b) Even if two or more
employees have been found guilty of identical degrees of
a particular offense the employer may properly impose
different degrees of discipline on them, provided their
records have been significantly different.   The man
having a poor record in terms of previous discipline for
a given offense may rightly, i.e., without true
discrimination, be given a considerably heavier
punishment than the man whose record has been relatively
unblemished in respect to the same kind of violation. (c)
The words "same kind of violation" just above, have
importance.   It is difficult to find discrimination
between two employees found guilty of totally different
sorts (not degrees) of offenses. For example, poor work
performance or failure to call in absences have little
comparability with insubordination or theft.

7.   Was the degree of discipline administered by
the company in a particular case reasonably related to
(a) the seriousness of the employee's proven offense and
(b) the record of the employee in his service with the
company?

Note 1:   A trivial proven offense as such does not
merit harsh discipline unless the employee has properly
been found guilty of the same or other offenses a number
of times in the past. (There is no rule as to what
number of previous offenses constitutes a "good," a
"fair," or a "bad," record. Reasonable judgment thereon
must be used.)

Note 2:   An employee's record of previous offenses
may never be used to discover whether he was guilty of
the immediate or latest one. The only proper use of his
record is to help determine the severity of discipline
once he has properly been found guilty of the immediate

283

offense.

Note 3: Given the same proven offense for two or more employees, their respective records provide the only proper basis for "discriminating" among them in the administration of discipline for said offense. Thus, if employee A's record is significantly better than those of employees B, C, and D, the company may properly give A a lighter punishment than it gives the others for the same offense; and this does not constitute true discrimination.

Note 4: Suppose that the record of the arbitration hearing establishes firm "Yes" answers to all the first six questions. Suppose further that the proven offense of the accused employee was a very serious one, such as drunkenness on the job; but the employee's record had been previously unblemished over a long, continuous period of employment with the company. Should the company be held arbitrary and unreasonable if it decided to discharge such an employee? The answer depends of course on all the circumstances. But, as one of the country's oldest arbitration agencies, the National Railroad Adjustment Board, has pointed out repeatedly in innumerable decisions on discharge cases, leniency is the prerogative of the employer rather than of the arbitrator; and the latter is not supposed to substitute his judgment in this area for that of the company unless there is compelling evidence that the company abused its discretion. This is the rule, even though the arbitrator, if he had been the original "trial judge," might have imposed a lesser penalty. In general, the penalty of dismissal for a really serious first offense does not in itself warrant a finding of company unreasonableness.

CHAPTER VII

EMPLOYMENT PRIVACY

INTRODUCTION

With this chapter we continue to examine the employment relationship. The emphasis, however, is on recent United States Supreme Court decisions in the area of privacy in order to show how moral principles are embedded in the legal decisions of the Court.

Before examining the substance of these decisions, I wish to offer some suggestions regarding how to read judicial opinions. This subject will have more lasting importance than discussions of the specific privacy rights. Specific controversies are resolved and disappear; but the skill to read judicial opinions will enhance your understanding of the law and your ability to reason for your self.

The key to reasoning, and in particular legal reasoning, is to begin with an understanding of the problem or controversy which requires the use of reasons. You should first identify the parties to the controversy and what interests each party is trying to defend. The reasoning of each can be set out in a deductive format, in which the first premise of the reasoning states a general principle supporting those interests, the second premise states the facts which fall under that general principle, and then a conclusion is inferred. For example,

Premise 1:   All murders are immoral.

Premise 2:   This act deliberately causes the death of another human being.

Conclusion: Thus, this act is immoral.

The facts of Supreme Court cases have already been determined by lower courts so that the issue before the Court is to justify which general principles to use to decide a particular case. For example,

Premise 1:   All acts which violate individual
               rights are immoral.

Premise 2:   Murder violates the individual rights
               to life.

Conclusion: Thus, murder is immoral.

To make this discussion more concrete, let us
consider one recent Supreme Court decision involving
employee privacy rights.

In NTEU v. Von Raab the Court in its first paragraph
describes its problem, the question it will be answering.
It then presents the relatively non-controversial facts,
including the summary of the decisions of the lower
court. It is here when one begins to sense the differing
answers to the Court's question and the problem the Court
will have in selecting the appropriate general principle
for resolving this case.

In section two, the Court first describes the
constitutional standard against which public employer
drug testing programs will be measured, namely, the
reasonableness standard. This standard is justified by
the Court, because two alternative standards, the warrant
standard, and the individualized suspicion standard are
too costly in cases such as the present one where there
are special governmental needs. Thus, the Court adopts
utilitarian reasoning in order to justify the
reasonableness standard which is to be applied in this
case. In conclusion, the Court reasons as follows:

Premise 1:   The general standard for privacy case
               is the warrant requirement or the
               individualized suspicion requirement
               or the reasonableness requirement.

Premise 2:   The first two standards sometimes
               interfere with special government
               needs.

Conclusion: Thus, the reasonableness standard
               should be used in such cases.

286

To evaluate the Supreme Court's decision to use the reasonableness standard, consider whether that standard should be used in similar cases. Do you agree that a warrant and individualized suspicion are not required when an employer searches an employee's desk or briefcase. Suppose that the search was based upon an anonymous tip which proved to be false, would not the warrant requirement prevent such intrusions?

Do you agree with the public interest which the Court discusses in justifying its position? Do you agree with the way that it weighs these interests in order to balance employer and employee interests in these cases? Why does the court reject the Union's arguments that the drug testing program is unreasonable?

If you are inclined to agree with the reasoning of the Court on these questions, you should examine the reasoning of Justice Scalia's dissent. Why do you reject the dissent's reasoning in favor of the majority's position?

Finally, if you accept a balancing or reasonableness approach to employee privacy, then can any utilities, even symbolic ones, be ruled out of the calculation? Can it be argued that the purpose of the Bill of Rights requires a presumption in favor of individual rights which can only rarely be outweighed by majority interests?

As was discussed above, the Bill of Rights does not apply to private employers. However, when you consider the Supreme Court's privacy decisions, you should consider the impact that they will have on the private sector. In so far as the Supreme Court is increasingly using a reasonableness test for these questions, is there much of a gap between constitutional rights and common law rights against unreasonable searches and seizures. In considering these common law rights do you agree with the authors of the privacy article that, in general, if certain guidelines are followed, the employer's interest in testing outweighs the employees privacy interest? Would you be willing to listen for the normal sound of urination to insure that samples are not tampered with?

In conclusion in this chapter we have continued to examine the interface between the law and ethics. We have noticed again that the law looks to ethical reasoning in order to resolve legal questions. In the privacy cases courts are increasingly using a utilitarian analysis which balances the rights of employers and employees in coming to the conclusion that employers have the right to interfere with privacy rights.

QUESTIONS AND PROJECTS

1. Reevaluate your answer to the question in Chapter I regarding whether the Bill of Rights should be applied to private sector employees in light of the NTEU case.

2. Assume that you are a personnel vice president responsible for authorizing a search of the office of an employee who is accused of stealing from the company. Write a memorandum to the head of security outlining the conditions of the search.

3. Write a justification for a collective bargaining proposal for your company to negotiate with its union which will allow the company to control workplace searches. What do you believe would be a reasonable compromise with the union which is simultaneously seeking greater employee privacy protections?

NATIONAL TREASURY EMPLOYEES UNION V. VON RAAB, 109 S.Ct. 1384(1989)

Justice Kennedy: We granted certiorari to decide whether it violates the Fourth Amendment for the United States Customs Service to require a urinalysis test from employees who seek transfer or promotion to certain positions.

I

A

The United States Customs Service, a bureau of the Department of the Treasury, is the federal agency responsible for processing persons, carriers, cargo, and mail into the United States, collecting revenue from imports and enforcing customs and related laws. An important responsibility of the Service is the interdiction and seizure of contraband, including illegal drugs.

In the routine discharge of their duties, many Customs employees have direct contact with those who traffic in drugs for profit. Drug import, operations, often directed by sophisticated criminal syndicates, may be effected by violence or its threat. As a necessary response, may Customs operatives carry and use firearms in connection with their official duties.

In December 1985, respondent, the Commissioner of Customs, established a Drug Screening Task Force to explore the possibility of implementing a drug screening program within the Service. After extensive research and consultation with experts in the field, the Task Force concluded "that drug screening through urinalysis is technologically reliable, valid and accurate." Citing this conclusion the Commissioner announced his intention to require drug tests of employees who applied for, or occupied, certain positions within the Service. The Commissioner stated his belief that "Customs is largely drug-free," but noted also that "unfortunately no segment of society is immune from the threat of illegal drug use." Drug interdiction has become the agency's primary enforcement mission, and the Commissioner stressed that "there is no room in the Customs Service for those who break the laws prohibiting the possession and use of illegal drugs."

In May 1986, the Commissioner announced implementation of the drug-testing program. Drug tests were made a condition of placement or employment for positions that meet one or more of three criteria. The first is direct involvement in drug interdiction or enforcement of related laws, an activity the Commissioner deemed fraught with obvious dangers to the mission of the agency and the lives of customs agents. The second criterion is a requirement that the incumbent carry firearms, as the Commissioner concluded that "[p]ublic safety demands that employees who carry deadly arms and are prepared to make instant life or death decisions be drug free." The third criterion is a requirement for the incumbent to handle "classified" material, which the Commissioner determined might fall into the hands of smugglers if accessible to employees who, by reason of their own illegal drug use, are susceptible to bribery or blackmail.

After an employee qualifies for a position covered by the Customs testing program, the Service advises him by letter that his final selection is contingent upon successful completion of drug screening. An independent contractor contacts the employee to fix the time and place for collecting the sample. On reporting for the test, the employee must produce photographic identification and remove any outer garments, such as a coat or a jacket, and personal belongings. The employee may produce the sample behind a partition, or in the privacy of a bathroom stall if he so chooses. To ensure against adulteration of the specimen, or substitution of a sample from another person, a monitor of the same sex as the employee remains close at hand to listen for the normal sounds of urination. Dye is added to the toilet water to prevent the employee from using the water to adulterate the sample.

Upon receiving the specimen, the monitor inspects it to ensure its proper temperature and color, places a tamper-proof custody seal over the container, and affixes an identification label indicating the date and the individual's specimen number. The employee signs a

290

chain-of-custody form, which is initialed by the monitor, and the urine sample is placed in a plastic bag, sealed, and submitted to a laboratory.

The laboratory tests the sample for the presence of marijuana, cocaine, opiates, amphetamines, and phencyclidine. Two tests are used. An initial screening test uses the enzyme-multiplied-immunoassay technique (EMIT). Any specimen that is identified as positive on this initial test must then be confirmed using gas chromatography/mass spectrometry (GC/MS). Confirmed positive results are reported to a "Medical Review Officer," "[a] licensed physician . . . who has knowledge of substance abuse disorders and has appropriate medical training to interpret and evaluate the individual's positive test result together with his or her medical history and any other relevant biomedical information." After verifying the positive result, the Medical Review Officer transmits it to the agency.

Customs employees who test positive for drugs and who can offer no satisfactory explanation are subject to dismissal from the Service. Test results may not, however, be turned over to any other agency, including criminal prosecutors, without the employee's written consent.

B

Petitioners, a union of federal employees and a union official, commenced this suit in the United States District Court for the Eastern District of Louisiana on behalf of current Customs Service employees who seek covered positions. Petitioners alleged that the Custom Service drug-testing program violated, inter alia, the Fourth Amendment. The District Court agreed. The court acknowledged "the legitimate governmental interest in a drug-free work place and work force," but concluded that "the drug testing plan constitutes an overly intrusive policy of searches and seizures without probable cause or reasonable suspicion, in violation of legitimate expectations of privacy." The court enjoined the drug testing program, and ordered the Customs Service not to require drug tests of any applicants for covered positions.

A divided panel of the United States Court of Appeals for the Fifth Circuit, vacated the injunction. The court agreed with petitioners that the drug screening program, by requiring an employee to produce a urine sample for chemical testing, effects a search within the meaning of the Fourth Amendment. The court held further that the searches required by the Commissioner's directive are reasonable under the Fourth Amendment. It first noted that the "[t]he Service has attempted to minimize the intrusiveness of the search" by not requiring visual observation of the act of urination and by affording notice to the employee that he will be tested. The court also considered it significant that the program limits discretion in determining which employees are to be tested, and noted that the tests are an aspect of the employment relationship.

The court further found that the Government has a strong interest in detecting drug use among employees who meet the criteria of the Customs program. It reasoned that drug use by covered employees casts substantial doubt on their ability to discharge their duties honestly and vigorously, undermining public confidence in the integrity of the Service and concomitantly impairing the Service's efforts to enforce the drug laws. Illicit drug users, the court found, are susceptible to bribery and blackmail, may be tempted to divert for their own use portions of any drug shipments they interdict, and may, if required to carry firearms, "endanger the safety of their fellow agents, as well as their own, when their performance is impaired by drug use." Considering the nature and responsibilities of the jobs for which applicants are being considered at Customs and the limited scope of the search," the court stated, "the exaction of consent as a condition of assignment to the new job is not unreasonable."

The dissenting judge concluded that the Customs program is not an effective method for achieving the Service's goals. He argued principally than an employee "given a five day notification of a test date need only abstain from drug use to prevent being identified as a user." He noted also that persons already employed in sensitive positions are not subject to the test. Because he did not believe the Customs program can achieve its purposes the dissenting judge found it unreasonable under the Fourth Amendment.

We granted certiorari. We now affirm so much of the judgment of the court of appeals as upheld the testing of employees directly involved in drug interdiction or required to carry firearms. We vacate the judgment to the extent it upheld the testing of applicants for positions requiring the incumbent to handle classified materials, and remand for further proceedings.

II

In Skinner v. Railway Labor Executives Assn. decided today, we hold that federal regulations requiring employees of private railroads to produce urine samples for chemical testing implicate the Fourth Amendment, as those tests invade reasonable expectations of privacy. Our earlier cases have settled that the Fourth Amendment protects individuals from unreasonable searches conducted by the Government, even when the Government acts as an employer, O'Connor v. Ortega, and in view of our holding in Railway Labor Executives that urine tests are searches, it follows that the Customs Service's drug testing program must meet the reasonableness requirement of the Fourth Amendment.

While we have often emphasized, and reiterate today, that a search must be supported as a general matter, by a warrant issued upon probable cause, our decision in Railway Labor Executives reaffirms the longstanding principle that neither a warrant nor probable cause, nor, indeed, any measure of individualized suspicion, is an indispensable component of reasonableness in every circumstance. As we note in Railway Labor Executives, our cases establish that where a Fourth Amendment intrusion serves special governmental needs, beyond the normal need for law enforcement, it is necessary to balance the individual's privacy expectations against the Government's's interests to determine whether it is impractical to require a warrant or some level of individualized suspicion in the particular context.

It is clear that the Customs Service's drug testing program is not designed to serve the ordinary needs of

293

law enforcement. Test results may not be used in a criminal prosecution of the employee without the employee's consent. The purposes of the program are to deter drug use among those eligible for promotion to sensitive positions within the Service and to prevent the promotion of drug users to those positions. These substantial interests, no less than the Government's concern for safe rail transportation at issue in Railway Labor Executives, present a special need that may justify departure from the ordinary warrant and probable cause requirements.

A

Petitioners do not contend that a warrant is required by the balance of privacy and governmental interests in this context, nor could any such contention withstand scrutiny. We have recognized before that requiring the Government to procure a warrant for every work-related intrusion "would conflict with the common-sense realization that government offices could not function if every employment decision became a constitutional matter." New Jersey v. T.L.O. (Noting that "[t]he warrant requirement . . . is unsuited to the school environment: requiring a teacher to obtain a warrant before searching a child suspected of an infraction of school rules (or of the criminal law) would unduly interfere with the maintenance of the swift and informal disciplinary procedures needed in the schools"). Even if Customs Service employees are more likely to be familiar with the procedures required to obtain a warrant than most other Government workers, requiring a warrant in this context would serve only to divert valuable agency resources from the Service's primary mission. The Customs Service has been entrusted with pressing responsibilities, and its mission would be compromised if it were required to seek search warrants in connection with routine, yet sensitive, employment decisions.

Furthermore, a warrant would provide little or nothing in the way of additional protection of personal privacy. A warrant serves primarily to advise the citizen that an intrusion is authorized by law and limited in its permissible scope and to interpose a neutral magistrate between the citizen and the law enforcement officer "engaged in the often competitive

294

enterprise of ferreting out crime." But in the present context, "the circumstances justifying toxicological testing and the permissible limits of such intrusions are defined narrowly and specifically . . . , and doubtless are well known to covered employees." Under the Customs program, every employee who seeks a transfer to a covered position knows that he must take a drug test, and is likewise aware of the procedures the Service must follow in administering the test. A covered employee is simply not subject "to the discretion of the official in the field." The process becomes automatic when the employee elects to apply for, and thereafter pursue, a covered position. Because the Service does not make a discretionary determination to search based on a judgment that certain conditions are present, there are simply "no special facts for a neutral magistrate to evaluate."

B

Even where it is reasonable to dispense with the warrant requirement in the particular circumstances, a search ordinarily must be based on probable cause. Our cases teach, however, that the probable-cause standard "is peculiarly related to criminal investigations." In particular, the traditional probable-cause standard may be unhelpful in analyzing the reasonableness of routine administrative functions, especially where the Government seeks to prevent the development of hazardous conditions or to detect violations that rarely generate articulable grounds for searching any particular place or person. Cf. Camara v. Municipal Court, (noting that building code inspections, unlike searches conducted pursuant to a criminal investigation, are designed "to prevent even the unintentional development of conditions which are hazardous to public health and safety"); United States v. Martinez-Fuerte, (noting that requiring particularized suspicion before routine stops on major highways near the Mexican border "would be impractical because the flow of traffic tends to be too heavy to allow the particularized study of a given car that would enable it to be identified as a possible carrier of illegal aliens"). Our precedents have settled that, in certain limited circumstances, the Government's need to discover such latent or hidden conditions, or to prevent their development, is sufficiently compelling to justify the intrusion on privacy entailed by conducting such searches

295

without any measure of individualized suspicion. We think the Government's need to conduct the suspicionless searches required by the Customs program outweighs the privacy interests of employees engaged directly in drug interdiction, and of those who otherwise are required to carry firearms.

The Customs Service is our Nation's first line of defense against one of the greatest problems affecting the health and welfare of our population. We have adverted before to "the veritable national crisis in law enforcement caused by smuggling of illicit narcotics." Our cases also reflect the traffickers' seemingly inexhaustible repertoire of deceptive practices and elaborate schemes for importing narcotics. The record in this case confirms that, through the adroit selection of source locations, smuggling routes, and increasingly elaborate methods of concealment, drug traffickers have managed to bring into this country increasingly large quantities of illegal drugs. The record also indicates, and it is well known, that drug smugglers do not hesitate to use violence to protect their lucrative trade and avoid apprehension.

Many of the Service's employees are often exposed to this criminal element and to the controlled substances they seek to smuggle into the country. The physical safety of these employees may be threatened, and many may be tempted not only by bribes from the traffickers with whom they deal, but also by their own access to vast sources of valuable contraband seized and controlled by the Service. The Commissioner indicated below that "Customs [o]fficers have been shot, stabbed, run over, dragged by automobiles, and assaulted with blunt objects while performing their duties." At least nine officers have died in the line of duty since 1974. He also noted that Custom's officers have been the targets of bribery by drug smugglers on numerous occasions, and several have been removed from the Service for accepting bribes and other integrity violations. See also Customs USA, Fiscal Year 1987, (reporting internal investigations that resulted in the arrest of 24 employees and 54 civilians); Customs USA, Fiscal Year 1986, (reporting that 334 criminal and serious integrity investigations were conducted during the fiscal year, resulting in the arrest of 37 employees and 17 civilians); Customs USA, Fiscal

296

Year 1985, (reporting that 284 criminal and serious integrity investigations were conducted during the 1985 fiscal year, resulting in the arrest of 15 employees and 51 civilians).

It is readily apparent that the Government has a compelling interest in ensuring that front-line interdiction personnel are physically fit, and have unimpeachable integrity and judgment. Indeed, the Government's interest here is at least as important as its interest in searching travelers entering the country. We have long held that travelers seeking to enter the country may be stopped and required to submit to a routine search without probable cause, or even founded suspicion, "because of national self protection reasonably requiring one entering the country to identify himself as entitled to come in, and his belongings as effects which may be lawfully brought in." This national interest in self protection could be irreparably damaged if those charged with safeguarding it were, because of their own drug use, unsympathetic to their mission of interdicting narcotics. A drug user's indifference to the Service's basic mission or, even worse, his active complicity with the malefactors, can facilitate importation of sizable drug shipments or block apprehension of dangerous criminals. The public interest demands effective measures to bar drug users from positions directly involving the interdiction of illegal drugs.

The public interest likewise demands effective measures to prevent the promotion of drug users to positions that require the incumbent to carry a firearm, even if the incumbent is not engaged directly in the interdiction of drugs. Customs employees who may use deadly force plainly "discharge duties fraught with such risks of injury to others that even a momentary lapse of attention can have disastrous consequences." We agree with the Government that the public should not bear the risk that employees who may suffer from impaired perception and judgment will be promoted to positions where they may need to employ deadly force. Indeed, ensuring against the creation of this dangerous risk will itself further Fourth Amendment values, as the use of deadly force may violate the Fourth Amendment in certain circumstances.

297

Against these valid public interests we must weigh the interferences with individual liberty that results from requiring these classes of employees to undergo a urine test. The interference with individual privacy that results from the collection of a urine sample for subsequent chemical analysis could be substantial in some circumstances. We have recognized, however, that the "operational realities of the workplace" may render entirely reasonable certain work-related intrusions by supervisors and co-workers that might be viewed as unreasonable in other contexts. While these operational realities will rarely affect an employee's expectations of privacy with respect to searches of his person, or of personal effects that the employee may bring to the workplace, it is plain that certain forms of public employment may diminish privacy expectations even with respect to such personal searches. Employees of the United States Mint, for example, should expect to be subject to certain routine personal searches when they leave the workplace every day. Similarly, those who join our military or intelligence services may not only be required to give what in other contexts might be viewed as extraordinary assurances of trustworthiness and probity, but also may expect intrusive inquiries into their physical fitness for those special positions.

We think Customs employees who are directly involved in the interdiction of illegal drugs or who are required to carry firearms in the line of duty likewise have a diminished expectation of privacy in respect to the intrusions occasioned by a urine test. Unlike most private citizens or government employees in general, employees involved in drug interdiction reasonably should expect effective inquiry into their fitness and probity. Much the same is true of employees who are required to carry firearms. Because successful performance of their duties depends uniquely on their judgment and dexterity, these employees cannot reasonably expect to keep from the Service personal information that bears directly on their fitness. While reasonable tests designed to elicit this information doubtless infringe some privacy expectations, we do not believe these expectations outweigh the Government's compelling interests in safety and in the integrity of our borders.

Without disparaging the importance of the governmental interests that support the suspicionless searches of these employees, petitioners nevertheless contend that the Service's drug testing program is unreasonable in two particulars. First, petitioners argue that the program is unjustified because it is not based on a belief that testing will reveal any drug use by covered employees. In pressing this argument, petitioners point out that the Service's testing scheme was not implemented in response to any perceived drug problem among Customs employees, and that the program actually has not led to the discovery of a significant number of drug users. Counsel for petitioners informed us at oral argument that no more than 5 employees out of 3,600 have tested positive for drugs. Second, petitioners contend that the Service's scheme is not a "sufficiently productive mechanism to justify [its] intrusion upon Fourth Amendment interests," because illegal drug users can avoid detection with ease by temporary abstinence or by surreptitious adulteration of their urine specimens. These contentions are persuasive.

Petitioners' first contention evinces an unduly narrow view of the context in which the Service's testing program was implemented. Petitioners do not dispute, nor can there be doubt, that drug abuse is one of the most serious problems confronting our society today. There is little reason to believe that American workplaces are immune from this pervasive social problem, as is amply illustrated by our decision in Railway Labor Executives. See also, Masino v. United States (describing marijuana use by two Customs Inspectors). Detecting drug impairment on the part of employees can be a difficult task, especially where, as here, it is not feasible to subject employees and their work-product to the kind of day-to-day scrutiny that is the norm in more traditional office environments. Indeed the almost unique mission of the Service gives the Government a compelling interest in ensuring that many of these covered employees do not use drugs even off-duty, for such use creates risks of bribery and blackmail against which the Government is entitled to guard. In light of the extraordinary safety and national security hazards that would attend the promotion of drug users to positions that require the carrying of firearms or the interdiction of controlled substances, the Service's policy of deterring drug users

299

from seeking such promotions cannot be deemed unreasonable.

The mere circumstance that all but a few of the employees tested are entirely innocent of wrongdoing does not impugn the program's validity. The same is likely to be true of householders who are required to submit to suspicionless housing code inspections, and of motorists who are stopped at the checkpoints we approved in United States v. Martinez-Fuerte. The Service's program is designed to prevent the promotion of drug users to sensitive positions as much as it is designed to detect those employees who use drugs. Where, as here, the possible harm against which the Government seeks to guard is substantial, the need to prevent its occurrence furnishes an ample justification for reasonable searches calculated to advance the Government's goal.

We think petitioners' second argument-that the Service's testing program is ineffective because employees may attempt to deceive the test by a brief abstention before the test date, or by adulterating their urine specimens - overstates the case. As the Court of Appeals noted, addicts may be unable to abstain even for a limited period of time, or may be unaware of the "fade-away effect" of certain drugs. More importantly, the avoidance techniques suggested by petitioners are fraught with uncertainty and risks for those employees who venture to attempt them. A particular employee's pattern of elimination for a given drug cannot be predicted with perfect accuracy, and in any event, this information is not likely to be known or available to the employee. Petitioners' own expert indicated below that the time it takes for particular drugs to become undetectable in urine can vary widely depending on the individual, and may extend for as long as 22 days. See also ante, (noting Court of Appeals' reliance on certain academic literature that indicates that the testing of urine can discover drug use "for . . . weeks after the ingestion of the drug"). Thus, contrary to petitioners' suggestion, no employee reasonably can expect to deceive the test by the simple expedient of abstaining after the test is assigned. Nor can he expect attempts at adulteration to succeed, in view of the precautions taken by the sample collector to ensure the integrity of the sample. In all the circumstances, we are persuaded that the program bears a close and substantial relation to the Service's goal of deterring drug users from seeking promotion to sensitive positions.

In sum, we believe the Government has demonstrated that its compelling interests in safeguarding our borders and the public safety outweigh the privacy expectations of employees who seek to be promoted to positions that directly involve the interdiction of illegal drugs or that require the incumbent to carry a firearm. We hold that the testing of these employees is reasonable under the Fourth Amendment.

C

We are unable, on the present record, to assess the reasonableness of the Government's testing program insofar as it covers employees who are required "to handle classified material." We readily agree that the Government has a compelling interest in protecting truly sensitive information from those who, "under compulsion of circumstances or for other reasons, . . . might compromise [such] information." Department of the Navy v. Egan, see also United States v. Robel. ("We have recognized that, while the Constitution protects against invasions of individual rights, it does not withdraw from the Government the power to safeguard its vital interests . . . The Government can deny access to its secrets to those who would use such information to harm the Nation"). We also agree that employees who seek promotions to positions where they would handle sensitive information can be required to submit to a urine test under the Service's screening program, especially if the positions covered under this category require background investigations, medical examinations, or other intrusions that may be expected to diminish their expectations of privacy in respect of a urinalysis test. Cf. Department of the Navy v. Egan, (noting that the Executive branch generally subjects those desiring a security clearance to "a background investigation that varies according to the degree of adverse effect the applicant could have on the national security").

It is not clear, however, whether the category defined by the Service's testing directive encompasses

301

only those Customs employees likely to gain access to sensitive information. Employees who are tested under the Service's scheme include those holding such diverse positions as "Accountant," "Accounting Technician," "Animal Caretaker," "Attorney (All)," "Baggage Clerk," "Co-op Student (All)," "Electric Equipment repairer," "Mail Clerk/Assistant," and "Messenger." We assume these positions were selected for coverage under the Service's testing program by reason of the incumbent's access to "classified" information, as it is not clear that they would fall under either of the two categories we have already considered. Yet it is not evident that those occupying these positions are likely to gain access to sensitive information, and this apparent discrepancy raises in our minds the question whether the Service has defined this category of employees more broadly than necessary to meet the purposes of the Commissioner's directive.

We cannot resolve this ambiguity on the basis of the record before us, and we think it is appropriate to remand the case to the court of appeals for such proceedings as may be necessary to clarify the scope of this category of employees subject to testing. Upon remand the court of appeals should examine the criteria used by the Service in determining what materials are classified and in deciding whom to test under this rubric. In assessing the reasonableness of requiring tests of these employees, the court should also consider pertinent information bearing upon the employees' privacy expectations, as well as the supervision to which these employees are already subject.

III

Where the Government requires its employees to produce urine samples to be analyzed for evidence of illegal drug use, the collection and subsequent chemical analysis of such samples are searches that must meet the reasonableness requirement of the Fourth Amendment. Because the testing program adopted by the Customs Service is not designed to serve the ordinary needs of law enforcement, we have balanced the public interest in the Service's testing program against the privacy concerns implicated by the tests, without reference to

302

our usual presumption in favor of the procedures specified in the Warrant Clause, to assess whether the tests required by Customs are reasonable.

We hold that the suspicionless testing of employees who apply for promotion to positions directly involving the interdiction of illegal drugs, or to positions which require the incumbent to carry a firearm, is reasonable. The Government's compelling interests in preventing the promotion of drug users to positions where they might endanger the integrity of our Nation's borders or the life of the citizenry outweigh the privacy interests of those who seek promotion to these positions, who enjoy a diminished expectation of privacy by virtue of the special, and obvious, physical and ethical demands of those positions. We do not decide whether testing those who apply for promotion to positions where they would handle "classified" information is reasonable because we find the record inadequate for this purpose.

The judgment of the Court of Appeals for the Fifth Circuit is affirmed in part and vacated in part, and the case is remanded for further proceedings consistent with this opinion.

It is so ordered.

JUSTICE MARSHALL, with whom JUSTICE BRENNAN joins:

For the reasons stated in my dissenting opinion in Skinner v. Railway Labor Executives Association, I also dissent from the Court's decision in this case. Here, as in Skinner, the Court's abandonment of the Fourth Amendment's express requirement that searches of the person rest on probable cause is unprincipled and unjustifiable. But even if I believed that balancing analysis was appropriate under the Fourth Amendment, I would still dissent from today's judgment, for the reasons stated by JUSTICE SCALIA in his dissenting opinion, and for the reasons noted by the dissenting judge below relating to the inadequate tailoring of the Customs Service's drug-testing plan.

JUSTICE SCALIA, with whom JUSTICE STEVENS joins:

The issue in this case is not whether Customs Service employees can constitutionally be denied promotion, or even dismissed, for a single instance of unlawful drug use, at home or at work. They assuredly can. The issue here is what steps can constitutionally be taken to detect such drug use. The Government asserts it can demand that employees perform "an excretory function traditionally shielded by great privacy," while "a monitor of the same sex . . . remains close at hand to listen for the normal sounds," and that the excretion thus produced be turned over to the Government for chemical analysis. The Court agrees that this constitutes a search for purposes of the Fourth Amendment and I think it obvious that it is a type of search particularly destructive of privacy and offensive to personal dignity.

Until today this Court had upheld a bodily search separate from arrest and without individualized suspicion of wrong-doing only with respect to prison inmates, relying upon the uniquely dangerous nature of that environment. Today, in Skinner, we allow a less intrusive bodily search of railroad employees involved in train accidents. I joined the Court's opinion there because the demonstrated frequency of drug and alcohol use by the targeted class of employees, and the demonstrated connection between such use and grave harm, rendered the search a reasonable means of protecting society. I decline to join the Court's opinion in the present case because neither frequency of use nor connection to harm is demonstrated or even likely. In my view the Customs Service rules are a kind of immolation of privacy and human dignity in symbolic opposition to drug use.

The Fourth Amendment protects the "right of the people to be secure in their persons, houses, papers, and effects, against unreasonable searches and seizures." While there are some absolutes in Fourth Amendment law, as soon as those have been left behind and the question comes down to whether a particular search has been "reasonable," the answer depends largely upon the social necessity that prompts the search. Thus, in upholding the administrative search of a student's purse in a school, we began with the observation (documented by an agency report to Congress) that "[m]aintaining order in the classroom has never been easy, but in recent years, school disorder has often taken particularly ugly forms: drug use and violent crime in the schools have become major social problems." When we approved fixed checkpoints near the Mexican border to stop and search cars for illegal aliens, we observed at the outset that "the Immigration and Naturalization Service now suggests there may be as many as 10 or 12 million aliens illegally in the country," and that "[i]nterdicting the flow of illegal entrants from Mexico poses formidable law enforcement problems." And the substantive analysis of our opinion today in <u>Skinner</u> begins, "[t]he problem of alcohol use on American railroads is as old as the industry itself," and goes on to cite statistics concerning that problem and the accidents it causes, including a 1979 study finding that "23% of the operating personnel were 'problem drinkers.'"

The Court's opinion in the present case, however, will be searched in vain for real evidence of a real problem that will be solved by urine testing of Customs Service employees. Instead, there are assurances that "[t]he Customs Service is our Nation's first line of defense against one of the greatest problems affecting the health and welfare of our population,"; that "[m]any of the Service's employees are often exposed to [drug smugglers] and to the controlled substances they seek to smuggle into the country,"; that "Customs officers have been the targets of bribery by drug smugglers on numerous occasions, and several have been removed from the Service for accepting bribes and other integrity violations,"; that "the Government has a compelling interest in ensuring that front-line interdiction personnel are physically fit, and have unimpeachable integrity and judgment,"; that the "national interest in self protection could be irreparably damaged if those charged with safeguarding it were, because of their own drug use, unsympathetic to their mission of interdicting narcotics," and that "the public should not bear the risk that employees who may suffer from impaired perception and judgment will be promoted to positions where they may need to employ deadly force." To paraphrase Churchill, all this contains much that is obviously true, and much that is relevant; unfortunately, what is obviously true

305

is not relevant, and what is relevant is not obviously true. The only pertinent points, it seems to me, are supported by nothing but speculation, and not very plausible speculation at that. It is not apparent to me that a Customs Service employee who uses drugs is significantly more likely to be bribed by a drug smuggler, any more than a Customs Service employee who wears diamonds is significantly more likely to be bribed by a diamond smuggler-unless, perhaps, the addiction to drugs is so severe, and requires so much money to maintain, that it would be detectable even without benefit of a urine test. Nor is it apparent to me that Customs officers who use drugs will be appreciably less "sympathetic" to their drug interdiction mission, any more than police officers who exceed the speed limit in their private cars are appreciably less sympathetic to their mission of enforcing the traffic laws. (The only difference is that the Customs officer's individual efforts, if they are irreplaceable, can theoretically affect the availability of his own drug supply - a prospect so remote as to be an absurd basis of motivation.) Nor, finally, is it apparent to me that urine tests will be even marginally more effective in preventing gun-carrying agents from risking "impaired perception and judgment" than is their current knowledge that, if impaired, they may be shot dead in unequal combat with unimpaired smugglers - unless, again, their addiction is so severe that no urine test is needed for detection.

What is absent in the Government's justifications - notably absent, revealingly absent, and as far as I am concerned dispositively absent - is the recitation of even a single instance in which any of the speculated horribles actually occurred: an instance, that is, in which the cause of bribe-taking, or of poor aim, or of unsympathetic law enforcement, or of compromise of classified information, was drug use. Although the Court points out that several employees have in the past been removed from the Service for accepting bribes and other integrity violations, and that at least nine officers have died in the line of duty since 1974, there is no indication whatever that these incidents were related to drug use by Service employees. Perhaps concrete evidence of the severity of a problem is unnecessary when it is so well known that courts can almost take judicial notice

306

of it; but that is surely not the case here. The Commissioner of Customs himself has stated that he "believe[s] that Customs is largely drug-free," that "[t]he extent of illegal drug use by Customs employees was not the reason for establishing this program," and that he "hope[s] and expect[s] to receive reports of very few positive findings through drug screening." The test results have fulfilled those hopes and expectations. According to the Service's counsel, out of 3,600 employees tested, no more than 5 tested positive for drugs.

The Court's response to this lack of evidence is that "[t]here is little reason to believe than American workplaces are immune from [the] pervasive social problem" of drug abuse. Perhaps such a generalization would suffice if the workplace at issue could produce such catastrophic social harm that no risk whatever is tolerable - the secured areas of a nuclear power plant. But if such a generalization suffices to justify demeaning bodily searches, without particularized suspicion, to guard against the bribing or blackmailing of a law enforcement agent, or the careless use of a firearm, then the Fourth Amendment has become frail protection indeed. In Skinner, Bell, T.L.O., and Martinez-Fuerte, we took pains to establish the existence of special need for the search or seizure - a need based not upon the existence of a "pervasive social problem" combined with speculation as to the effect of that problem in the field at issue, but rather upon well known or well demonstrated evils in that field, with well known or well demonstrated consequences. In Skinner, for example, we pointed to a long history of alcohol abuse in the railroad industry, and noted that in an eight-year period 45 train accidents and incidents had occurred because of alcohol and drug-impaired railroad employees, killing 34 people, injuring 66, and causing more than $28 million in property damage.

In the present case, by contrast, not only is the Customs Service thought to be "largely drug-free," but the connection between whatever drug use may exist and serious social harm is entirely speculative. Except for the fact that the search of a person is much more intrusive than the stop of a car, the present case resembles, Delaware v. Prouse, where we held that the

307

Fourth Amendment prohibited random stops to check drivers' licenses and motor vehicle registration. The contribution of this practice to highway safety, we concluded, was "marginal at best" since the number of licensed drivers that must be stopped in order to find one unlicensed one "will be large indeed."

Today's decision would be wrong, but at least of more limited effect, if its approval of drug testing were confined to that category of employees assigned specifically to drug interdiction duties. Relatively few public employees fit that description. But in extending approval of drug testing to that category consisting of employees who carry firearms, the Court exposes vast numbers of public employees to this needless indignity. Logically, of course, if those who carry guns can be treated in this fashion, so can all others whose work, if performed under the influence of drugs, may endanger others - automobile drivers, operators of other potentially dangerous equipment, construction workers, school crossing guards. A similarly broad scope attaches to the Court's approval of drug testing for those with access to "sensitive information." Since this category is not limited to Service employees with drug interdiction duties, nor to "sensitive information" specifically relating to drug traffic, today's holding apparently approves drug testing for all federal employees with security clearances - or, indeed, for all federal employees with valuable confidential information to impart. Since drug use is not a particular problem in the Customs Service, employees throughout the government are no less likely to violate the public trust by taking bribes to feed their drug habit, or by yielding to blackmail. Moreover, there is no reason why this super-protection against harms arising from drug use must be limited to public employees; a law requiring similar testing of private citizens who use dangerous instruments such as guns or cars, or who have access to classified information would also be constitutional.

There is only one apparent basis that sets the testing at issue here apart from all these other situations - but it is not a basis upon which the Court is willing to rely. I do not believe for a minute that the driving force behind these drug-testing rules was any of the feeble justifications put forward by counsel here

308

and accepted by the Court. The only plausible explanation, in my view, is what the Commissioner himself offered in the concluding sentence of his memorandum to Customs Service employees announcing the program: "Implementation of the drug screening program would set an important example in our country's struggle with this most serious threat to our national health and security." Or as respondent's brief to this Court asserted: "if a law enforcement agency and its employees do not take the law seriously, neither will the public on which the agency's effectiveness depends." What better way to show that the Government is serious about its "war on drugs" than to subject its employees on the front line of that war to this invasion of their privacy and affront to their dignity? To be sure, there is only a slight chance that it will prevent some serious public harm resulting from Service employee drug use, but it will show to the world that the Service is "clean," and - most important of all - will demonstrate the determination of the Government to eliminate this scourge of our society! I think it obvious that this justification is unacceptable; that the impairment of individual liberties cannot be the means of making a point; that symbolism, even symbolism for so worthy a cause as the abolition of unlawful drugs, cannot validate an otherwise unreasonable search.

There is irony in the Government's citation, in support of its position, of Justice Brandeis's statement in <u>Olmstead v. United States</u>, that "[f]or good or for ill, [our Government] teaches the whole people by its example." Brandeis was there dissenting from the Court's admission of evidence obtained through an unlawful Government wiretap. He was not praising the Government's example of vigor and enthusiasm in combatting crime, but condemning its example that "the end justifies the means." An even more apt quotation from that famous Brandeis dissent would have been the following:

> "[I]t is... immaterial that the intrusion was in aid of law enforcement. Experience should teach us to be most, on our guard to protect liberty when the Government's purposes are beneficent. Men born to freedom are naturally alert to repel invasion of their liberty by evil-minded rulers. The greatest dangers to liberty lurk in insidious encroachment by men

of zeal, well-meaning but without understanding."

Those who lose because of the lack of understanding that begot the present exercise in symbolism are not just the Customs Service employees, whose dignity is thus offended, but all of us - who suffer a coarsening of our national manners that ultimately give the Fourth Amendment its content, and who become subject to the administration of federal officials whose respect for our privacy can hardly be greater than the small respect they have been taught to have for their own.

FARMERS, FOXES, CHICKENS, AND HEN HOUSES:
A CASE FOR LIMITED MANDATORY RANDOM DRUG TESTING
OF EMPLOYEES IN THE PRIVATE SECTOR

ERIC E. HOBBS--THOMAS W. SCRIVNER

In carefully opening the hen house door, the farmer
realizes immediately what has transpired. Once again a
fox has raided his hen house and foiled his profits. Oh,
how the farmer wishes to catch the fox and end his folly.

I. INTRODUCTION

Despite the Reagan Administration's vigorous war
against drugs in the 1980's, abuse in the United States
is taking an increasing financial toll on American
business. In 1982, the annual business loss attributable
to drug abuse was estimated at seventy million dollars,
by 1986, that annual figure was believed to have grown
to at least one billion dollars. Moreover, neither of
those estimates included the nearly six billion dollar
loss attributable to long-term unemployment traceable to
drug abuse.

Illegal drug use has reached alarming proportions.
Government surveys released in 1986 indicated that 5.8
million Americans used cocaine, and nineteen percent of
persons twelve and older---36.8 million Americans---had
tried marijuana, cocaine, or other drugs within the
previous year. Those surveys, also indicated that
between ten and twenty-three percent of American workers
had used illicit drugs on the job.

From Saint Louis University Law Journal, Vol. 32:605-637
1988. Reprinted by permission. Footnotes omitted.

In 1985, a Cocaine National Help Line study of 227 substance abusers reported that twenty-five percent of the study group had used drugs on a daily basis and that forty-five percent had used drugs weekly. The study also confirmed the impact of that drug abuse on the workplace. Seventy-five percent of the participants had used drugs at work; ninety-two percent had performed their jobs under the influence of drugs; and sixty-four percent conceded that their on-the-job drug use had hindered their job performance and adversely affected the quality of their employers' products; eighteen percent had suffered drug-related, on-the-job accidents; eighteen percent admitted they had stolen from their employers to support their drug habits; and thirty-nine percent stated that a promotion or raise would have increased their use of drugs.

Employee drug use burdens employers with decreased productivity, increased absences and increased numbers of accidents. Compared to the employee who does not use drugs, the average abuser is three times as likely to be late to work and 2.2 times as likely to request early dismissal or time off. The abuser has twenty-five times as many absences of eight days or more and uses three times the normal level of sick benefits. Moreover, the abuser is 3.6 times as likely to have an in-plant accident and five times as likely to file a worker's compensation claim. It is no wonder that the Acting Director of the National Institute on Drug Abuse, speaking before the U.S. House Labor Subcommittee on Health and Safety in December of 1985, said that drug abuse "may well be . . . the most common health hazard in the American workplace today."

In response to that hazard and to the financial burdens that drug abuse imposes on business, many companies have turned to workplace drug testing. In 1982, few of the Fortune 500 companies screened their employees for drug use. By 1985, however, thirty percent of the 500 were screening job applicants or employees--a tenfold increase in testing. And recent figures indicate that forty-eight percent now test employees for drug use.

Even some labor unions have conceded that drug testing can help decrease the costs and risks of drug abuse in the workplace. As early as August of 1984, for

312

example, the Teamsters agreed to allow any Teamsters employer to test an employee upon reasonable belief that the employee was intoxicated. The Oil, Chemical and Atomic Workers Union (OCAW) has adopted a similar policy on drug testing that explicitly recognizes the employer's right to test OCAW-represented employees if there exists "reasonable, objective, 'probable cause' evidence based on job performance."

The Teamsters and OCAW policies allow drug testing based only on individualized suspicion. Some employers, however, believe random testing to be the most effective way to deter drug abuse, and they claim to have not only the right, but also the obligation, to use those methods that will most effectively help to insure a workplace free from such abuse. Critics rejoin that random testing violates employees' rights to privacy, freedom from unreasonable search and seizure, due process, and freedom against self-incrimination. The critics contend that random testing is constitutionally and, in some instances, statutorily infirm, regardless of how effective it may be in combatting drug abuse in the workplace.

The thesis of this Article is that programs providing for the random drug testing of present employees in the private sector can withstand scrutiny under applicable constitutional principles if the programs are promulgated carefully and implemented properly. Case precedent, principles of jurisprudence and common sense support this conclusion. Section II, below, provides a descriptive definition of random testing programs and overview of the relevant court decisions issued as of this writing and involving primarily drug testing in the public sector. Section III then considers the applicability to the private sector of those principles considered by the courts that have addressed drug testing in the public sector and applies the principles, to the extent justified, in making a case for limited mandatory random drug testing by private employers.

313

II. RANDOM DRUG TESTING IN THE PUBLIC SECTOR

A.   Types of Drug Testing Programs

Drug testing programs are of three basic types. "Suspicion-based" programs provide for drug testing only upon a reasonable suspicion of drug use by a particular employee.   Testing is usually conducted only after observation of an employee's erratic or unusual behavior or after his or her involvement in a suspicious on-the-job accident.   "Periodic" programs provide for scheduled testing at particular times, typically at annual physical examinations, upon returns from leaves of absence or upon returns from vacations. And "random" programs provide for testing based not on any particular suspicion or on the occurrence of any particular event, but rather on the systematic selection of test subjects based on neutral criteria.   Of the three types, suspicion-based programs most frequently have been upheld as constitutional.   Periodic programs, which have been treated as quasi-random by a least one court, have proven more   controversial,   but   have   been   upheld   as constitutional if reasonable. Random programs, finally, have been held in the majority (but now shrinking majority) of cases to be unconstitutional in the public sector.

B.   The Case Law

Courts have analyzed the constitutionality of drug testing programs under the fourth, fifth, ninth, and fourteenth amendments to the United States Constitution and   under   similar   provisions   of   various   state constitutions. This section reviews those decisions that consider the federal constitutionality of drug testing programs, with a few references to cases dealing with state   constitutionality   issues.   Most   state constitutional provisions bearing on such programs parallel   those   of   the   federal   Constitution. Consideration of the state provisions' application, therefore, would be largely redundant.

1.   The Fourth Amendment Right To Be Free From Unreasonable Search and Seizure.

314

Where courts have found random and other drug testing unconstitutional, they have done so most often under the fourth amendment, which prohibits unreasonable searches and seizures. Within the meaning of the amendment, "[a] 'search' occurs when an expectation of privacy that society is prepared to consider reasonable is infringed. A 'seizure' of property occurs when there is some meaningful interference with an individual's possessory interest in that property." The search also must be conducted by the state or under color of state authority in order to fall within the amendment's reach.

Courts considering the fourth amendment issue have found that drug testing by a government entity constitutes a fourth amendment search because the process of urinalysis infringes on an employee's reasonable expectation of privacy. As the Fifth Circuit observed in National Treasury Employees Union v. Von Raab.

> There are few activities in our society more personal or private than in the passing of urine. Most people describe it by euphemisms if they talk about it at all. It is a function traditionally performed without public observation; indeed, its performance in public is generally prohibited by law as well as social custom. While individuals may choose not to urinate in private but instead to use public toilet facilities, they make this choice themselves.

In short, drug testing by urinalysis meets the three requirements for implication of the fourth amendment's protection: The tested employee has an expectation of privacy; the expectation is recognized by society as legitimate or reasonable; and the privacy is invaded by the testing process.

However, a privacy invasion by the state violates the fourth amendment only when the invasion is "unreasonable or constitute[s] a meaningful interference." The test for evaluating the reasonableness of a search is a case-by-case balancing of "the need for the particular search against the invasion of personal rights that the search entails." Expounding on that principal, the District Court for the

Eastern District of Virginia noted in a recent drug testing case:

> Determination of Fourth Amendment reasonableness necessitates consideration of the totality of circumstances in each case, weighing all of the factors indicating constitutional violation against all others showing validity. The scope and manner, location, availability of less intrusive measures, justification and effectiveness must be considered as to the obtrusiveness of the search.

It is in making that "subjective analysis of objective factors" that courts considering the constitutionality of random testing have differed. As one judge has observed, "courts are extremely sensitive to the factual context surrounding the testing."

In determining the extent of the need for testing on the first side of the balance, courts have focused on two elements:

> First, whether "reasonable grounds" exist for suspecting that the urinalysis will turn up evidence of "work-related drug use." This is another way of saying that the search must be justified "at its inception" . . . [And, second,] whether the search as it is actually conducted is "reasonably related in scope to the circumstances which justified the interference in the first place." This means that "the measures adopted [must be] reasonably related to the objectives of the search and not excessively intrusive.'"

Both elements must be satisfied in order to justify the alleged need for testing.

316

Courts have often been willing to find "reasonable grounds" for random testing in the employer's interest in the efficient operation of its business and in the pervasiveness of workplace drug abuse. However, the majority of courts also have found that random drug testing programs are not "reasonably related" or are "excessively intrusive."

> The collection of urine sample has little in common with stomach pumping or body cavity searches (or even with the blood sample, which requires the infliction of an injury, albeit a small one). It is even less intrusive than a fingerprint which requires that one's fingers be smeared with black grease and pressed against a paper. A urine sample calls for nothing more than a natural function performed by everyone several times a day--the only difference being the collection of the sample in a jar. Measured against the vital national interest of assuring that FBI agents are not involved in drugs, the claim that such a search is unreasonable is a mockery.

One of the few principles that emerges clearly from the various fourth amendment analysis of random drug testing is that the more regulated the government employer and the more safety- or security-sensitive the tested employees' jobs, the more likely a court is to uphold the employer's random testing program. Individuals in highly-regulated employment or in safety- or security-sensitive positions have diminished legitimate expectation of privacy. As an employee's legitimate expectation of privacy diminishes, the government's intrusion into that privacy is more easily justified.

2.   The Fifth and Fourteenth Amendment Right to Procedural Due Process.

A public-sector employee has a protected property interest in employment if he or she has an expectation of continued employment guaranteed by statue, contract, or policy. For example, federal Civil Service employees have protected property interests in employment because they are statutorily protected from discharge except "for

317

such cause as will promote the efficiency of the service." In addition, government employees have libertyinterests, protected by public policy, in their reputations and in the honor and integrity of their good names. A number of courts consequently have found that random drug testing that might lead to discipline or public humiliation implicates public-sector employees' fifth and fourteenth amendment rights of procedural due process.

Procedural due process in the drug testing context requires notice to the employee of the details of the employer's testing program and requires the provision of adequate safeguards to protect test accuracy. Public employees subject to testing must be given notice of when and how such testing will be conducted, including the means by which test subjects will be selected. Employers must warn employees in advance of what disciplinary measures may be taken upon detection of drug use. Where drug use has been indicated by positive test results, due process requires that the tested employees be afforded the opportunity to confront and rebut the evidence. At least one court has held that employees must be provided the opportunity to have their samples tested independently.

Courts likewise have required that testing programs include safeguards assuring accuracy, to the extent possible, and minimizing the likelihood of specimen contamination or subject misidentification. Some courts and commentators have found the general unreliability of urinalysis methods to constitute a sufficient basis for upholding a due process challenge, particularly when the result of an initial test has not been confirmed by a second one. However, other courts have explicitly recognized the accuracy and reliability of the EMIT initial test when followed up with the GC/MS confirmatory test. The use by employers of those two tests in conjunction with one another, therefore, is likely to increase.

Finally, because of employees' interests in their reputations, employers should safeguard the confidentiality of all test results. The circulation of a test result, or even passive inattention to confidentiality, almost surely will prompt a finding of due process violation.

Some courts have found random testing to constitute a per se violation of due process because the selection of test subjects is "arbitrary" and because employees receive insufficient notice as to when they will be tested. However, systematic random testing based on objective criteria, as opposed to suspicion-based testing, neutralizes the selection process by depriving the testing employer of the opportunity to exercise any discretion. Suspicion-based programs provide the opportunity for supervisors or co-employees to carry out vendettas against other workers or otherwise abuse the "reasonable" suspicion process, whereas such abuse is unlikely under a systematic random program.

Another due process objection raised against drug testing programs of all three types is that the tests can detect only the presence of drug metabolites and not a drug impairment or the amount of time elapsed since drug consumption. Therefore, it is argued, a positive test does not necessarily indicate that the tested employee used drugs or was impaired while at work. The employee may have used the drugs over the previous weekend or on other off-duty time.

Even those courts that have struck down testing programs as unconstitutional, however, have explicitly recognized that employees in safety or security-sensitive jobs have no "fundamental constitutional right to use illegal drugs off-duty." Moreover, one study has indicated that impairment at least by marijuana continues long after the drug's observable symptoms have worn off. Researchers at Stanford University compared the abilities of ten licensed pilots to complete a flight simulator landing task before and after the pilots used marijuana. In attempting the task twenty-four hours after having smoked one marijuana cigarette, the pilots exhibited great difficulty in landing the plane, and one missed the runway altogether. The pilots also reported "no significant subjective awareness" of their deficiencies,

319

indicating that the marijuana consumption twenty-four hours earlier had impaired their judgement.

At least one court has suggested that due process objections to drug testing might be viewed as eased or eliminated where the motivation of the employer in conducting such testing is purely rehabilitative. In Allen v. City of Marietta, the district court upheld the constitutionality of the City's suspicion-based testing program, emphasizing that "the tests were administered in a purely employment context as part of the government's legitimate inquiry into the use of drugs by employees engaged in extremely hazardous work" and were not conducted "in connection with any criminal investigation or procedure." Where an employer's goals in testing are detection and rehabilitation, rather than discipline or criminal prosecution, drug testing arguably does not present a due process problem (unless arbitrary and capricious) because it does not deprive an employee of his or her property or the integrity or honor of his or her name.

3.   The Fifth Amendment Right Against Self-Incrimination

No court has found involuntary urinalysis to constitute compelled self-incrimination in violation of the fifth amendment. Those courts considering the issue have concluded instead that "urinalysis results in 'physical' evidence that is outside the scope of the Fifth Amendment. The privilege against self-incrimination applies only to testimonial evidence. And urine samples, like blood samples, voice exemplars, and criminal line-ups, reveal only physical characteristics, rather than knowledge that the tested individual possesses.

4.   The Right to Privacy

The United States Supreme Court has recognized that a "right of personal privacy, or a guarantee of certain areas or zones of privacy, does exist under the Constitution." In Griswold v. Connecticut, Justice Goldberg, in his concurring opinion, found that right to spring from the ninth amendment, a conclusion apparently accepted by at least one lower federal court in a drug testing case.

Although plaintiffs have argued that urinalysis unconstitutionally tests for off-duty use and requires employees to reveal otherwise confidential information unrelated to on-duty consumption, no court has found mandatory drug testing to violate the ninth amendment right to privacy. However, the Nebraska district court in Rushton v. Nebraska Public Power District, has found the right applicable in the drug testing context. The Rushton court nevertheless denied the plaintiff's ninth amendment claim because the tested employee had not been compelled to urinate under observation and because the employer had not released any medical information gleaned from the urinalysis without authorization. The primary constitutional privacy concern in the drug testing context is the confidentiality of test results and other test-related medical information. Where the act of urination has not been compelled under observation, and where confidentiality has been provided for and secured, a tested individual has no ground for a ninth amendment right-to-privacy challenge.

III. RANDOM DRUG TESTING IN THE PRIVATE SECTOR

Very few employers presently use random testing to identify substance-abusing employees. A major reason likely is concern about potential civil liability given the uncertainty of the law surrounding drug screening. It is the authors' view, however, that except in those jurisdictions that specifically prohibit such testing, random drug testing may be conducted in the private sector consistent with applicable constitutional and statutory principles. As the district court in Mullholland v. Department of the Army noted: "[I]t is not only acceptable but imperative that this random urine testing conducted under proper procedures be required for certain sensitive positioned employees . . .

A.   The Application of Constitutional Principles to the Private Sector.

As observed by the arbitrator in Amoco Oil Co.

321

It has long been held by courts and arbitrators that the Bill of Rights to the Constitution of the United States . . . [protects] individual citizens against government bodies . . . [T]hese rights do not necessarily accrue in the workplace. That is, an employee voluntarily accepts a job and continues to work for an employer with knowledge that the employer has chosen to restrict certain individual rights. The employer often has a need to restrict certain individual rights...in order to protect the employees, its customers or its property. For these reasons the Bill of Rights . . . does not apply in the work place.

Both federal and state courts, however, recently have begun to recognize constitutional, "public policy" exceptions to the general doctrine that a private-sector, at-will employee may be terminated, or may leave his or her employment, for any reason and at any time. Thus, private employers now may be held liable for damages sustained by employees as a consequence of the employers'implementations of drug testing programs that violate the employees' constitutional rights.

Additionally, rights to privacy and against search and seizure are often incorporated in employment policies and labor agreements and are recognized in the jurisprudence of industrial relations. In <u>Rulon-Miller v. IBM</u>, the court held that the discharge of a worker for having dated the employee of a competitor constituted wrongful discharge and intentional infliction of emotional distress where the employer had promulgated a written policy assuring its employees their rights to privacy. Similarly, the arbitrator in Day & Zimmerman observed, "Arbitrators have always considered the just cause protection of collective bargaining agreements to include basic notions of due process as to individual employee rights and protection against unreasonable employer action." Therefore, private-sector employers are well advised to develop and implement only random drug testing programs that are consistent with constitutional principles.

B.   Development of Random Drug Testing Policy that
       is Consistent with Constitutional Principles

       1.   The Fourth Amendment Right Against Unreasonable
Search and Seizure

As explained above, a determination as to whether
an employer's random drug testing constitutes an
unreasonable search under the fourth amendment requires
a careful balancing of the employer and employees'
interests in testing and not being tested, respectively.

       a)   The Employer's Interest in Random Testing

The "general duty clause" of the Occupational Safety
and Health Act of 1970 requires that every private-sector
employer maintain a safe workplace. Each employer must
"furnish to each of his employees employment and a place
of employment which are free from recognized hazards that
are causing or likely to cause death or serious physical
harm." A "recognized hazard" is one that is generally
acknowledged among members of the employer's industry,
a particular one of which the employer is aware or one
detectable either by the senses or by instrumentation.
In addition to its statutory obligation, an employer may
also have a contractual responsibility to provide a
workplace free from recognized hazards.

The authors are of the view that drug abusing
employees in safety-sensitive positions constitute
recognized hazards from which employers must protect
their employees. The dangers posed by employees
performing safety sensitive jobs under the influence of
drugs are widely recognized in many industries, as
evidenced by widespread, interindustry testing and the
often stringent requirements employers impose on
individuals seeking appointment to such positions. Even
off-duty consumption by employees who perform
safety-sensitive jobs can contribute to risks in the
workplace. Therefore, employers may well have a legal
duty to take appropriate action to protect their
employees from drug abusers on the payroll whose drug use
could result in serious or fatal injury to coworkers.

Drug-abusing employees may pose a threat to the
public welfare as well. Those abusers who operate

323

vehicles under the influence of drugs may injure members of the public. And those involved in manufacturing may produce defective, unsafe products.

Drug abusing employees in security-sensitive jobs similarly can endanger the welfare of their employers, their coworkers and even their country. They are more likely than nonabusing co-employees to compromise the security of the workplace, negligently while impaired or even intentionally for a price. In addition, they might reveal trade secret information, having been blackmailed with evidence of their drug use or having sold the secret information to support their drug habits.

Employers incur substantial financial and nonquantifiable losses because of the effect of employee drug abuse. That abuse has been linked to excessive absenteeism, increased rates of accidents, increased rates of accidents, increased numbers of worker's compensation claims filed, and defective goods. Application of the principles of respondeat superior and products liability, furthermore, can result in the imposition of liability on employers for damages sustained by others as a consequence of employee drug use.

b)   The Employee's Interest in Being Free From Random Testing

Although drug testing by urinalysis invades the tested individual's privacy, it is not so obtrusive as to be unconscionable or unconstitutional per se. Unlike blood testing, urinalysis does not require an actual bodily invasion; it requires merely the performance of a bodily function which, while usually performed privately, nonetheless is performed frequently. Additionally, it is worth noting that less intrusive means of drug testing are being developed, and may soon be available for widespread, economical use. If any of these new, less intrusive testing methods are accepted by the scientific community as reliable and then used by employers, many of the emotional and analytical privacy objections to drug testing in the workplace will be rendered moot.

However, employees, courts, and arbitrators have

324

also objected to the observation of the urination process by employer-representatives as violative of test subject privacy. An employer can soften the impact of that objection by requiring that an employer-representative or neutral individual only be present in the room where the sample is provided, rather than observe the provision of samples directly. The representative can insure that specimens are not polluted or substituted by checking any potential hiding places in the room for spare samples or sources of water that could be used to dilute a sample, possibly patting down test subjects, listening for the normal sound of urination, and insuring that the specimen is promptly sealed and labeled. If the representative suspects that the test subject is tampering with the specimen, the representative can stop the process and consult with those in charge of the testing program to determine whether observation is necessary in the subject's case. While this method of supervision arguably invades employee privacy to some extent, the intrusion is not nearly as objectionable as a blanket requirement of direct observation. In light of the employer's interest in testing, this method could and should survive constitutional analysis.

The objection that mandatory testing requires the involuntary disclosure of confidential information is insignificant on balance with the intergrity of security-sensitive positions. In particular, an individual who seeks or accepts a safety- or security-sensitive job retains a diminished expectation of privacy. In order to have been approved for his or her position initially, the employee may well have been required to provide highly confidential information on an employment application or for a security background check. Such information typically includes arrest and conviction record data, the details of diseases or medical conditions that might inhibit the individual's performance of certain work, and other facts. While employees do not waive all rights to confidentiality or privacy by such prior revelations, they certainly thereby recognize that their job choices limit those rights.

Moreover, the scope of the information disclosure stemming from a drug test need not be broad. Although urinalysis can reveal information other than illegal drug use, the laboratory need not in fact test for that

325

additional information, nor need the employer become privy to it. Additionally, laboratories usually test samples anonymously, and they can be requested to do so by client-employers when blind testing is not the normal procedure. The information they collect from urine specimens, therefore, has no nexus with particular donors.

In order to survive muster under constitutional analysis, a drug testing program also must provide for strict maintenance of the confidentiality of all information gleaned from urinalysis. If that confidentiality is breached by reason of employer negligence or intention, an affected employee may hold the employer liable in tort. An employee also might be able to hold his or her employer liable for torts committed by its testing laboratory.

c)   The Balance

A random drug testing program that provides for systematic test-subject selection, discrete specimen-collection procedures, anonymous urinalysis, the limitation of information gleaned to that indicating use or nonuse of drugs, and test-result confidentiality should survive judicial scrutiny in the cases of employees holding safety- and security-sensitive positions. On balance, the employer's interests in testing such employees outweighs the employees' interests in privacy, if those program guidelines are followed. Because an employer's interests in testing nonsafety- or nonsecurity-sensitive employees without reasonable, individualized suspicion are much less weighty, however, it is unlikely that all employees, irrespective of their job safety and sensitivity, could successfully be included in a random program.

A limited random testing program meeting the above guidelines likely would satisfy the Taylor v. O'Grady requirements: that the program be capable of disclosing "evidence of 'work-related drug use'" and that the program be "'justified at its inception,'" that is, that the test measures adopted be "'reasonably related to the objectives of the search and not excessively intrusive.'" Even those courts that have found random testing programs unlawful have agreed that the programs are likely to turn

326

up evidence of work-related drug use. Likewise, the courts have found the programs "justified at [their] inception[s]]" when the programs have served important interests, such as safety or security. The courts have differed, however, over whether the random method adopted is reasonably related to the programs' objectives and is not overly intrusive.

Statistics indicate clearly that drug use affects job performance. Even off-duty drug consumption can impair an employee's judgment and ability to work. Additionally, various sources report that random testing has, in studied cases, deterred substance abuse on and off duty. One court, in fact, noted that limited uniform and random testing is "the only way" safety and security threats can be controlled and that urinalysis is the least intrusive, effective method of testing. Unlike the suspicion-based method, the random method eliminates the exercise of any discretion by the employer in choosing test subjects. No supervisor or co-employee, therefore, can target a certain employee for "suspicion-based" testing. Hence, properly implemented uniform and random drug testing is carefully tailored to its objective and is not excessively intrusive.

2. The Right to Due Process

If an individual is represented by a union that is party to a collective bargaining agreement with his or her employer, the employee is almost certainly entitled to due process in the form of "progressive discipline." And if the individual is an at-will employee or a contractual employee whose employment agreement does not require just cause for termination, the employee may be entitled to a least minimal due process under one or more public policy exceptions to the employment-at-will doctrine. Therefore, a prudent employer should incorporate into any implemented random drug testing program guidelines safeguarding employees' due process rights. Inclusion of the safeguards is in the employer's best interest because they insure the integrity and effectiveness of a testing program.

An employer who adopts a random drug testing program should first promulgate and distribute to all covered employees a written policy describing the program to be

327

implemented, including its effective date. General notice that random testing will be conducted after the effective date, coupled with an explanation of the systematic process by which the employees will be randomly selected, should be sufficient to meet due process notice requirements. The employees' due process rights to notice are not violated merely because the employees are not told exactly when they will be tested.

The criteria for random selection must be neutral and systematically applied, preferably by a computer or neutral third party rather than by the employer. The less the involvement of management, the more persuasive the argument that random testing is less discretionary, and therefore less constitutionally sensitive under due process principles, than is suspicion-based testing.

The written policy also should articulate clearly the need for and purpose(s) of the testing program. If the employer can show statistically that its business has been impacted negatively by drug abuse, it should do so. However, statistics from the employer's industry or even inter-industry statistics should be sufficient to establish the employer's interest in fighting employee drug abuse.

The written policy should make clear, in addition, that those employees discovered to be drug abusers will be referred for rehabilitation, and will not be targeted for immediate discipline or criminal prosecution. While discipline legitimately may be imposed upon evidence of continued abuse or failure to complete rehabilitation, for confidentiality reasons, criminal prosecution should not be a purpose of a testing program. Rehabilitation provided by an employee assistance program at no or reduced cost to employees will lend credence to the employer's contention that rehabilitation is the policy's foremost purpose. As one commentator has noted, "If a company gets into drug screening without any kind of [employee] assistance program, it is asking for trouble. The employer should recognize that rehabilitation is likely to be in its best interest, reducing the long-run costs of doing business and maintaining employees on the payroll.

Notice of the specific discipline that might be

imposed based upon positive test results also should be provided in the written policy. Employees should be afforded the opportunity to rebut test results and to appeal disciplinary decisions. That opportunity should include the chance to have the same urine sample tested by an independent laboratory. Discipline should be imposed only after repeated offenses, a refusal to be tested, a refusal of an offer of rehabilitation, or failure at rehabilitation.

The policy also should note that the chain-of-custody of specimens will be insured and documented. Urine samples should be marked and placed in secure containers at the times they are taken. And the employer should choose a reputable laboratory and has both a proven record of accuracy and stringent chain-of-custody procedures. For confidentiality reasons, those procedures should insure chain-of-custody without the use of test subjects' names.

Finally, the program should provide for the confirmatory testing of all positive initial test results before rehabilitation is required or discipline is imposed. The relative accuracy of easily available confirmatory tests likely would be viewed by a court as a prudent, if not essential, safeguard.

Random testing programs that base the systematic choice of test subjects on neutral criteria safeguard employee due process rights better than suspicion-based programs. Therefore, if a random program incorporates all of the limitations and safeguards outlined above, it should be found by either a court or an arbitrator to comport with due process. Those limitations and safeguards not only rebut the due process objections raised by courts and arbitrators thus far, but also remedy other problems, such as the potential for abuse of discretion permitted by suspicion-based testing.

3.   The Right Against Self-Incrimination

Courts that have considered the issue of self-incrimination in the drug testing context having unanimously held that compelled urinalysis does not implicate the right against self-incrimination. Although one arbitrator has implied that the "self-incrimination"

329

resulting from compelled urinalysis which leads to a positive result is "objectionable," the analyses and conclusion of the unanimous courts are far more persuasive and reasonable. The authors conclude, therefore, that the right against self-incrimination does not limit the use of random drug testing programs.

4.   The Right to Privacy

Implicit in the analysis of an individual's fourth amendment right against search and seizure in the drug testing context is the principle that a person's right to privacy in the American workplace is not inviolable. Both arbitrators and courts, as noted above, have recognized that private-sector employers are not limited in their rights to restrict employees' constitutional rights in the workplace.

Confidentiality, however, is an important issue in the drug testing debate that raises both constitutional and nonconstitutional privacy issues. Even assuming that an employer's random testing program does not, per se, violate employees' rights to privacy under fourth and ninth amendment analyses, the employer still needs to be aware that it might be held liable if it fails to keep test results and other test related information confidential. In those jurisdictions that recognize a private-sector right to privacy under constitutional, statutory or common law, a breach of confidentiality can trigger civil liability. The Restatement (Second) of Torts provides: "One who intentionally intrudes, physically or otherwise, upon the solitude or seclusion of another or his private affairs or concerns, is subject to liability to the other for invasion of his privacy, if the intrusion would be highly offensive to a reasonable person."

A number of states has explicitly applied the Restatement test, but none has done so in the workplace drug testing context. The court in Satterfield v. Lockheed Missiles & Space Co., however, implied that an employer's publication of an employee's drug test results may violate that employee's right to privacy, but found that the plaintiff had failed to establish that the defendant had in fact published any confidential information. The decision is nonetheless notable because it is the only one thus far involving a private employer and applying a nonconstitutional right-to-privacy analysis in the drug testing context.

Other courts have found violations of privacy where employers have intentionally released employees' confidential information. Still others have recognized that employers can be held liable for negligent, rather than intentional, disclosure of confidential personnel information. And a number of courts have found defamation where confidential information published by the employer was false.

All of these cases warn employers to guard carefully the confidentiality of their employees' drug test results and related information. The employer first should not provide its testing laboratory with the names of the individuals whose specimens the laboratory is analyzing. Then, upon employer receipt of the test results, only employees necessarily involved in the rehabilitative or disciplinary processes should be permitted access to the results. No information regarding rehabilitation or disciplinary decisions based on those results should be published, inside or outside the workplace.

If confidentiality is protected, the employer should escape statutory and common law liability for invasion of privacy, negligent release of personnel information and defamation. Furthermore, if the employer's random testing program survives scrutiny under search and seizure principles, the program also should survive scrutiny under other constitutional privacy-guarantee provisions applicable to private-sector employers, because determinations as to whether an individual's privacy has been unreasonably violated inherently require the balancing of the same interests as under search and seizure analysis.

IV. Conclusion

There is no question that employee drug testing---suspicion-based, periodic or random---infringes upon employee rights. Yet an employer's right to promulgate work rules and the rules themselves are not challengeable unless the promulgation or application is unreasonable. Whether promulgation or application is unreasonable is determined by balancing the employer's interest in promulgating and implementing the rules against the employee's interest in being free of the rules promulgated and implemented.

This Article demonstrates that an employer's interest in adopting random drug testing for its employees in safety- and security-sensitive positions outweighs the interests of those employees in not being tested. The employer should not be required to produce either specific evidence of drug abuse or of reasonable suspicion that specific employees are abusers. As the Fifth Circuit so eloquently noted in National Treasury Employees Union v. Von Raab. "It is not unreasonable to set traps to keep foxes from entering hen houses even in the absence of evidence of prior vulpine intrusion or individualized suspicion that a particular fox has an appetite for chickens."

If a private employer develops a limited mandatory random drug testing program consistent with the guidelines outlined in this Article, courts and arbitrators should recognize the program as lawful under applicable constitutional, statutory and jurisprudential principles. If drug abuse by employees in safety and security-sensitive positions is to be combatted effectively, the legitimacy and legality of random testing must be recognized. Legal principles permit such recognition, and the effective and safe operation of American business requires it.

CHAPTER VIII

EMPLOYMENT DISCRIMINATION

INTRODUCTION

Employment discrimination is another area, like privacy, where Supreme Court decisions are an important source of legal conclusions and moral arguments. Initially it may seem that this area should be no problem for the Court, because Congress in 1964 forbade discrimination in employment. However, discrimination may take subtle forms which are difficult to prove and to eradicate.

Courts in interpreting employment discrimination laws have described two ways a plaintiff may prove discrimination. In a disparate treatment case the plaintiff is required to prove that he/she is a member of a protected class. (For purposes of this short introduction, race will be treated as the example of a protected class.) Furthermore, the employee must show that he/she was treated less favorably than another employee who was similarly situated. An employer may defend itself against a discrimination charge by asserting a credible, non-pretexual reason for the difference in treatment.

A disparate impact case involves subtler forms of discrimination. The employer may have a factually neutral policy which does not appear to treat employees differently and yet the effect of the policy is that members of one race become increasingly disadvantaged. For example, a college degree requirement for a particular promotion may not appear discriminatory. Yet because of the policy otherwise qualified persons who are members of one race and who lack college degrees in disproportionately large numbers may be denied promotions. Such a policy may be held to have an adverse impact on these employees. Courts have required that in its defense the employer must show that the neutral policy is manifestly necessary for the operations of its business.

Recently, however, the Supreme Court has lowered the defense requirements for an employer who must only present persuasive reasons that there is a substantial justification for its policies. Why would the Court wish to make it easier for an employer to defend himself against adverse impact discrimination? Is it because discrimination laws unduly interfere with the discretion of business persons to run their own businesses and the court wishes discrimination to be resolved by the free market and not by the courts. However, if the goal of equal opportunity is an essential one for this society, then is a showing of business necessity necessary to eradicate discrimination so that the free market can operate fairly?.

How would you interpret the phrase "substantial justification". Would an opinion by a corporate manager that a practice, such as nepotism or word-of-mouth hiring, was inexpensive, even though it had a disparate impact, be sufficient to meet the Court's new test of substantial justification?   Would a good faith justification without objective evidence be sufficient?

Another problem involves mixed motive discrimination. That is, what if an employer refuses a promotion for reasons some of which are discriminatory and some are not. Should the simple rules of adverse treatment apply. If not, do you agree with the district court in Price Waterhouse which required the employer to defend itself with clear and convincing evidence? Why would the court place such a heavy burden on the employer? Does the Supreme Court's position represent a fair compromise between the employers' and employees' interests in this case?

If the preceding cases create difficult employment decisions, they are nevertheless less controversial than the issue of affirmative action. The basic question is whether affirmative action is justified as consistent with society's objective of breaking down discriminatory patterns, or whether affirmative action is itself a form of discrimination. One line of argument in favor of affirmative action is that it is essential to bring about equality of opportunity for all citizens. However, if affirmative action may be used to create a equal society, should other forms of discrimination be used to create an unequal society, if the inequality had a utilitarian justification?

The court in Johnson discusses the standards a plan must meet in order to be a justified affirmative action plan.   One question not considered in that case is whether an employer should be able to use affirmative action for symbolic purposes in order to eradicate discrimination in society at large, even if a particular employer has never discriminated.

In thinking about affirmative action you should consider the extent to which discrimination legislation has unduly limited the rights of private property owners to make personnel decisions. Is employment discrimination law merely an attempt to require businesses to make their decisions based upon relevant criteria? How far should the government go to force businesses to make decisions solely on relevant grounds; should the state pass discrimination laws to protect gay men and lesbian women from discrimination?

The last selection concerns sexual harassment as a form of sexual discrimination. It presents the answers of the Equal Employment Opportunity Commission to questions regarding illegal sexual harassment. On this issue the details of the law may seem complex but the basic rule is simple: Don't. Don't do anything that even remotely suggests that you are making work easier-or harder-for others because of your sexual preferences. Though this advice is simple, sexual harassment persists and the underlying question remains: why is there sexual harassment? Are some men so uncomfortable working with women that they have to harass them?

Is harassment a result of sexual motives or political needs to compensate for lack of real leadership?

QUESTIONS AND PROJECTS

1.   Draft a justification for your Board of Directors for an affirmation action plan which is similar to that described in Johnson.

2.   Do you think that job discrimination against minorities can ever be ended without legislation? Do you think the free market can eradicate discrimination?

3.   Write a short play or story which illustrates how seemingly innocent conduct may constitute sexual harassment. Utilize role reversal so that, if you are male, consider what it would be like for you to be subject to sexual harassment.

Justice Brennan: Respondent, Transportation Agency of Santa Clara County, California, unilaterally promulgated an Affirmative Action Plan applicable, inter alia, to promotions of employees. In selecting applicants for the promotional position of road dispatcher the Agency, pursuant to the Plan, passed over petitioner Paul Johnson, a male employee and promoted a female employee applicant, Diane Joyce. The question for decision is whether in making the promotion the Agency impermissibly took into account the sex of the applicants in violation of Title VII of the Civil Rights Act of 1964. The District Court for the Northern District of California, in an action filed by petitioner following receipt of a right-to-sue letter from the Equal Employment Opportunity Commission (EEOC), held that respondent had violated Title VII. The Court of Appeals for the Ninth Circuit reversed. We granted certiorari. We affirm.'. . .

As a preliminary matter, we note that petitioner bears the burden of establishing the invalidity of the Agency's Plan. Only last tern in <u>Wygant v. Jackson Board of Education</u>, we held that "[t]he ultimate burden remains with the employees to demonstrate the unconstitutionality of an affirmative-action program," and we see no basis for a different rule regarding a plan's alleged violation of Title VII. This case also fits readily within the analytical framework set forth in <u>Mc Donnell Douglas Corp. v. Green</u>. Once a plaintiff establishes a prima facie case that race or sex has been taken into account in an employer's employment decision, the burden shifts to the employer to articulate a nondiscriminatory rationale for its decision. The existence of an affirmative action plan provides such a rationale. If such a plan is articulated as the basis for the employer's decision, the burden shifts to the plaintiff to prove that the employer's justification is pretextual and the plan is invalid. As a practical matter, of course, an employer will generally seek to avoid a charge of pretext by presenting evidence in support of its plan. That does not mean, however, as petitioner suggests, that reliance on an affirmative action plan is to be treated as an affirmative defense requiring the employer to carry the burden of proving the validity of the plan. The burden of proving its invalidity remains on the plaintiff.

The assessment of the legality of the Agency Plan must be guided by our decision in <u>Weber</u>. In that case, the Court addressed the question whether the employer violated Title VII by adopting a voluntary affirmative action plan designed to "eliminate manifest racial imbalances in traditionally segregated job categories." The respondent employee in that case challenged the employer's denial of his application for a position in a newly established craft training program, contending that the employer's selection process impermissibly took into account the race of the applicants. The selection process was guided by an affirmative action plan, which provided that 50% of the new trainees were to be black until the percentage of black skilled craftworkers in the employer's plant approximated the percentage of blacks in the local labor force. Adoption of the plan had been prompted by the fact that only 5 of 273, or 1.83%, of skilled craftworkers at the plant were black, even though the work force in the area was approximately 39% black. Because of the historical exclusion of blacks from craft positions, the employer regarded its former policy of hiring trained outsiders as inadequate to redress the imbalance in its work force.

We upheld the employer's decision to select less senior black applicants over the white respondent, for we found that taking race into account was consistent with Title VII's objective of "break{ing} down old patterns of racial segregation and hierarchy." As we stated:

"It would be ironic indeed if a law triggered by a Nation's concern over centuries of racial injustice and intended to improve the lot of those who had 'been excluded from the American dream for so long' constituted the first legislative prohibition of all voluntary, private, race-conscious efforts to abolish traditional patterns of racial segregation and hierarchy."

We noted that the plan did not "unnecessarily trammel the interests of its white employees," since it did not require "the discharge of white workers and their replacement with new black hirees." Nor did the plan create "an absolute bar to the advancement of white employees," since half of those trained in the new program were to be white. Finally, we observed that the plan was a temporary measure, not designed to maintain racial balance, but to "eliminate a manifest racial imbalance." As Justice Blackmun's concurrence made clear, Weber held that an employer seeking to justify the adoption of a plan need not point to its own prior discriminatory practices, nor even to evidence of an

338

"arguable violation" on its part. Rather, it need point only to a "conspicuous...imbalance in traditionally segregated job categories." Our decision was grounded in the recognition that voluntary employer action can play a crucial role in furthering Title VII's purpose of eliminating the effects of discrimination in the workplace, and that Title VII should not be read to thwart such efforts.

In reviewing the employment decision at issue in this case, we must first examine whether that decision was made pursuant to a plan prompted by concerns similar to those of the employer in Weber. Next, we must determine whether the effect of the plan on males and non-minorities is comparable to the effect of the plan in that case.

The first issue is therefore whether consideration of the sex of applicants for skilled craft jobs was justified by the existence of a "manifest imbalance" that reflected underrepresentation of women in "traditionally segregated job categories." In determining whether an imbalance exists that would justify taking sex or race into account, a comparison of the percentage of minorities or women in the employer's work force with the percent in the area labor market or general population is appropriate in analyzing jobs that require no special expertise, see Teamsters v. United States, (comparison between percentage of blacks in employer's work force and in general population proper in determining extent of imbalance in truck driving positions), or training programs designed to provide expertise, see Weber (comparison between proportion of blacks working at plant and proportion of blacks in area labor force appropriate in calculating imbalance for purpose of establishing preferential admission to craft training program). Where a job requires special training, however, the comparison should be with those in the labor force who possess the relevant qualifications. See Hazelwood School District v. United States. (Must compare percentage of blacks in employer's work ranks with percentage of qualified black teachers in area labor force in determining under representation in teaching positions). The requirement that the "manifest imbalance" relate to a "traditionally segregated job category" provides assurance both that sex or race will be taken into account in a manner consistent with Title VII's purpose of eliminating the effects of employment discrimination, and that the interest of those employees not benefitting from the plan will not be unduly infringed.

A manifest imbalance need not be such that it would

support a prima facie case against the employer as suggested in Justice O'Connor's concurrence, since we do not regard as identical the constraints of Title VII and the federal constitution on voluntarily adopted affirmative action plans. Application of the "prima facie" standard in Title VII cases would be inconsistent with Weber's focus on statistical imbalance, and could inappropriately create a significant disincentive for employers to adopt an affirmative action plan. See Weber, (Title VII intended as a "catalyst" for employer efforts to eliminate vestiges of discrimination). A corporation concerned with maximizing return on investment, for instance, is hardly likely to adopt a plan if in order to do so it must compile evidence that could be used to subject it to a colorable Title VII suit.

It is clear that the decision to hire Joyce was made pursuant to an Agency plan that directed that sex or race be taken into account for the purpose of remedying under representation. The Agency Plan acknowledged the "limited opportunities that have existed in the past," for women to find employment in certain job classifications "where women have not been traditionally employed in significant numbers." As a result, observed the Plan, women were concentrated in traditionally female jobs in the Agency, and represented a lower percentage in other job classifications than would be expected if such traditional segregation had not occurred. Specifically, 9 of the 10 Para-Professional and 110 of the 145 Office and Clerical Workers were women. By contrast, women were only 2 of the 28 Officials and Administrators, 5 of the 58 Professionals, 12 of the 124 Technicians, none of the Skilled Craft Workers, and 1 --- who was Joyce --- of the 110 Road Maintenance Workers. The Plan sought to remedy these imbalances through "hiring, training and promotion of ... women throughout the Agency in all major job classifications where they are under represented."

As an initial matter, the Agency adopted as a benchmark for measuring progress in eliminating under representation the long-term goal of a work force that mirrored in its major job classifications the percentage of women in the area labor market. Even as it did so, however, the Agency acknowledged that such a figure could not by itself necessarily justify taking into account the sex of applicants for positions in all job categories. For positions requiring specialized training and experience, the Plan observed that the number of minorities and women "who possess the qualifications required for entry into such job classifications is limited." The Plan therefore directed that annual short-term goals be formulated that would provide a more realistic indication of the degree to which sex should be taken into account in filling particular positions. The Plan stressed that such goals "should not be construed as 'quotas' that must be met," but as reasonable aspirations in correcting the imbalance in the Agency's work force. These goals were to take into account factors such as "turnover, layoffs, lateral transfers, new job openings, retirements and availability of minorities, women and handicapped persons in the area work force who possess the desired qualifications or potential for placement." The Plan specifically directed that, in establishing such goals, the Agency work with the County Planning Department and other sources in attempting to compile data on the percentage of minorities and women in the local labor force that were actually working in the job classifications comprising the Agency work force. From the outset, therefor, the Plan sought annually to develop even more refined measures of the under representation in each job category that required attention.

As the Agency Plan recognized, women were most egregiously under represented in the Skilled Craft job category, since none of the 238 positions was occupied by a woman. In mid-1980, when Joyce was selected for the road dispatcher position, the Agency was still in the process of refining its short-term goals for Skilled Craft Workers in accordance with the directive of the Plan. This process did not reach fruition until 1982, when the Agency established a short-term goal for that year of three women for the 55 expected openings in that job category---a modest goal of about 6% for that category.

We reject petitioner's argument that, since only the long-term goal was in place for Skilled Craft positions at the time of Joyce's promotion, it was inappropriate for the Director to take into account affirmative action considerations in filling the road dispatcher position. The Agency's Plan emphasized that the long-term goals were not to be taken as guides for actual hiring decisions, but that supervisors were to consider a host of practical factors in seeking to meet affirmative action objectives, including the fact that in some job categories women were not qualified in numbers comparable to their representation in the labor force.

By contrast, had the Plan simply calculated imbalances in all categories according to the proportion of women in the area labor pool, and then directed that hiring be governed solely by those figures, its validity fairly could be called into question. This is because analysis of a more specialized labor pool normally is necessary in determining under representation in some positions. If a plan failed to take distinctions in qualifications into account in providing guidance for actual employment decisions, it would dictate mere blind hiring by the numbers, for it would hold supervisors to "achievement of a particular percentage of minority employment or membership...regardless of circumstances such as economic conditions or the number of qualified minority applicants..."

The Agency's Plan emphatically did not authorize such blind hiring. It expressly directed that numerous factors be taken into account in making hiring decisions, including specifically the qualifications of female applicants for particular jobs. Thus, despite the fact that no precise short-term goal was yet in place for the Skilled Craft category in mid-1980, the Agency's management nevertheless had been clearly instructed that they were not to hire solely by reference to statistics. The fact that only the long-term goal had been established for this category posed no danger that personnel decisions would be made by reflexive adherence to a numerical standard.

Furthermore, in considering the candidates for the road dispatcher position in 1980, the Agency hardly needed to rely on a refined short-term goal to realize that it had a significant problem of under representation that required attention. Given the obvious imbalance in the Skilled Craft category, and given the Agency's commitment to eliminating such imbalances, it was plainly not unreasonable for the Agency to determine that it was appropriate to consider as one factor the sex of Ms. Joyce in making its decision. The promotion of Joyce thus satisfies the first requirement enunciated in <u>Weber</u>, since it was undertaken to further an affirmative action plan designed to eliminate Agency work force imbalances in traditionally segregated job categories.

We next consider whether the Agency Plan unnecessarily trammeled the rights of male employees or created an absolute bar to their advancement. In contrast to the plan in <u>Weber</u>, which provided that 50% of the positions in the craft training program were exclusively for blacks, and to the consent decree upheld last term in <u>Firefighters v. Cleveland</u>, which required the promotion of specific numbers of minorities, the Plan sets aside no positions for women. The Plan expressly states that "[t]he 'goals' established for each Division

342

should not be construed as 'quotas' that must be met."
Rather, the Plan merely authorizes that consideration be
given to affirmative action concerns when evaluating
qualified applicants. As the Agency Director factors he
took into account in arriving at his decision. The Plan
thus resembles the "Harvard Plan" approvingly noted by
Justice Powell in University of California Regents v.
Bakke, which considers race along with other criteria in
determining admission to the college. As Justice Powell
observed, "In such an admissions program, race or ethnic
background may be deemed a 'plus' in a particular
applicant's file, yet it does not insulate the individual
from comparison with all other candidates for the
available seats." Similarly, the Agency Plan requires
women to compete with all other qualified applicants.
No persons are automatically excluded from consideration;
all are able to have their qualifications weighed against
those of other applicants.

In addition, petitioner had no absolute entitlement
to the road dispatcher position. Seven of the applicants
were classified as qualified and eligible, and the Agency
Director was authorized to promote any of the seven.
Thus, denial of the promotion unsettled no legitimate
firmly rooted expectation on the part of the petitioner.
Furthermore, while the petitioner in this case was denied
a promotion, he retained his employment with the Agency,
at the same salary and with the same seniority, and
remained eligible for other promotions.

Finally, the Agency's Plan was intended to attain
a balanced work force, not to maintain one. The Plan
contains ten references to the Agency's desire to
"attain" such a balance, but no reference whatsoever to
a goal of maintaining it. The Director testified that,
while the "broader goal" of affirmative action, defined
as "the desire to hire, to promote, to give opportunity
and training on an equitable, non-discriminatory basis,"
is something that is "a permanent part" of "the Agency's
operating philosophy," that broader goal "is divorced,
if you will, from specific numbers or percentages."

The Agency acknowledged the difficulties that it
would confront in remedying the imbalance in its work
force, and it anticipated only gradual increases in the
representation of minorities and women. It is thus
unsurprising that the Plan contains no explicit end date,
for the Agency's flexible, case-by-case approach was not
expected to yield success in a brief period of time.
Express assurance that a program is only temporary may
be necessary if the program actually sets aside positions
according to specific numbers. Firefighters, (four year

343

duration for consent decree providing for promotion of particular number of minorities); <u>Weber</u>, (plan requiring that blacks constitute 50% of new trainees in effect until percentage of employer work force equal to percentage in local force). This is necessary both to minimize the effect of the program on other employees, and to ensure that the plan's goals "{are} not being used simply to achieve and maintain...balance, but rather as a benchmark against which" the employer may measure its progress in eliminating the under representation of minorities and women. <u>Sheet Metal Workers</u>. In this case, however, substantial evidence shows that the Agency has sought to take a moderate, gradual approach to eliminating the imbalance in its work force, one which establishes realistic guidance for employment decisions, and which visits minimal intrusion on the legitimate expectations of other employees. Given this fact, as well as the Agency's express commitment to "attain" a balanced work force, there is ample assurance that the Agency does not seek to use its Plan to maintain a permanent racial and sexual balance.

In evaluating the compliance of an affirmative action plan with Title VII's prohibition on discrimination, we must be mindful of "this Court's and Congress' consistent emphasis on 'the value of voluntary efforts to further the objectives of the law.'" <u>Wygant</u>. The Agency in the case before us has undertaken such a voluntary effort, and has done so in full recognition of both the difficulties and the potential for intrusion on males and non-minorities. The Agency has identified a conspicuous imbalance in job categories traditionally segregated by race and sex. It has made clear from the outset, however, that employment decisions may not be justified solely by reference to this imbalance, but must rest on a multitude of practical, realistic factors. It has therefore committed itself to annual adjustment of goals so as to provide a reasonable guide for actual hiring and promotion decisions. The Agency earmarks no positions for anyone; sex is but one of several factors that may be taken into account in evaluating qualified applicants for a position. As both the Plan's language and its manner of operation attest, the Agency has no intention of establishing a work force whose permanent composition is dictated by rigid numerical standards.

We therefore hold that the Agency appropriately took into account as one factor the sex of Diane Joyce in determining that she should be promoted to the road dispatcher position. The decision to do so was made pursuant to an affirmative action plan that represents a moderate, flexible, case-by-case approach to effecting

344

a gradual improvement in the representation of minorities and women in the Agency's work force. Such a plan is fully consistent with Title VII, for it embodies the contribution that voluntary employer action can make in eliminating the vestiges of discrimination in the workplace. Accordingly, the judgment of the Court of Appeals is affirmed.

CLARA WATSON v. FORT WORTH BANK AND TRUST, 108 S. Ct.
2771(1988)

Justice O'Connor: Petitioner Clara Watson, who is
black, was hired by respondent Fort Worth Bank and Trust
(the Bank) as a proof operator in August 1973.   In
January 1976, Watson was promoted to a position as teller
in the Bank's drive-in facility.   In February 1980, she
sought to become supervisor of the tellers in the main
lobby; a white male, however, was selected for this job.
Watson then sought a position as supervisor of the
drive-in bank, but this position was given to a white
female.   In February 1981, after Watson had served for
about a year as a commercial teller in the Bank's main
lobby, and informally as assistant to the supervisor of
tellers, the man holding that position was promoted.
Watson applied for the vacancy, but the white female who
was the supervisor of the drive-in bank was selected
instead.   Watson then applied for the vacancy created at
the drive-in; a white male was selected for that job.
The Bank, which has about 80 employees, had not developed
precise and formal criteria for evaluating candidates
for the positions for which Watson unsuccessfully
applied.   It relied instead on the subjective judgment
of supervisors who were acquainted with the candidates
and with the nature of the jobs to be filled.   All the
supervisors involved in denying Watson the four
promotions at issue were white.

The District Court addressed Watson's individual
claims under the evidentiary standards that apply in a
discriminatory treatment case.   See Mc Donnell Douglas
Corp. v. Green.   It concluded, on the evidence presented
at trail, that Watson had established a prima facie case
of employment discrimination, but that the Bank had met
its rebuttal burden by presenting legitimate and
nondiscriminatory reasons for each of the challenged
promotion decisions.   The court also concluded that
Watson had failed to show that these reasons were
pretexts for racial discrimination.   Accordingly, the
action was dismissed.

A divided panel of the United States Court of
Appeals for the Fifth Circuit affirmed in part.   The
majority affirmed the District Court's conclusion that
Watson had failed to prove her claim of racial
discrimination under the standards set out in Mc Donnell
Douglas and Burdine.

Watson argued that the District Court had erred in
failing to apply "disparate impact" analysis to her
claims of discrimination in promotion.   Relying on Fifth

347

Circuit precedent, the majority of the Court of Appeals panel held that "a Title VII challenge to an allegedly discretionary promotion system is properly analyzed under the disparate treatment model rather than the disparate impact model." Other Courts of Appeals have held that disparate impact analysis may be applied to hiring or promotion systems that involve the use of "discretionary" or "subjective" criteria. We granted certiorari to resolve the conflict.

Section 703 of the Civil Rights Act of 1964 provides:
"(a) It shall be an unlawful employment practice for an employer--

"(1) to fail or refuse to hire or to discharge any individual, or otherwise to discriminate against any individual with respect to his compensation, terms, conditions, or privileges of employment, because of such individual's race, color, religion, sex or national origin; or
"(2) to limit, segregate, or classify his employees or applicants for employment in any way which would deprive or tend to deprive any individual of employment opportunities or otherwise adversely affect his status as an employee, because of such individual's race, color, religion, sex, or national origin.
"(h) Notwithstanding any other provision of this subchapter, it shall not be an unlawful employment practice for an employer...to give and to act upon the results of any professionally developed ability test provided that such test, its administration or action upon the results is not designed, intended or used to discriminate because of race, color, religion, sex or national origin..."

Several of our decisions have dealt with the evidentiary standards that apply when an individual alleges that an employer has treated that particular person less favorably than others because of the plaintiff's race, color, religion, sex, or national origin. In such "disparate treatment" cases, which involve "the most easily understood type of discrimination," the plaintiff is required to prove that the defendant had a discriminatory intent or motive. In order to facilitate the orderly consideration of relevant evidence, we have devised a series of shifting evidentiary burdens that are "intended progressively to sharpen the inquiry into the elusive factual question of intentional discrimination." Under that scheme, a prima facie case is ordinarily established by proof that the employer, after having rejected the plaintiff's application for a job or promotion, continued to seek applicants with qualifications similar to the plaintiff's. The burden of proving a prima facie case is "not onerous," and the employer in turn may rebut it simply by producing some evidence that it had legitimate, nondiscriminatory reasons for the decision. If the defendant carries this burden of production, the plaintiff must prove by a preponderance of all the evidence in the case that the legitimate reasons offered by the defendant were a pretext for discrimination. We have cautioned that these shifting burdens are meant only to aid courts and litigants in arranging the presentation of evidence: "The ultimate burden of persuading the trier of fact that the defendant intentionally discriminated against the plaintiff remains at all times with the plaintiff.

In <u>Griggs v. Duke Power Co.</u>, this Court held that a plaintiff need not necessarily prove intentional discrimination in order to establish that an employer has violated section 703. In certain cases, facially neutral employment practices that have significant adverse effects on protected groups have been held to violate the Act without proof that the employer adopted those practices with a discriminatory intent. The factual issues and the character of the evidence are inevitably somewhat different when the plaintiff is exempted from the need to prove intentional discrimination. The evidence in these "disparate impact" cases usually focused on statistical disparities, rather than specific incidents, and on competing explanations for those disparities.

The distinguishing features of the factual issues that typically dominate in disparate impact cases do not imply that the ultimate legal issue is different than in cases where disparate treatment analysis is used. Nor do we think it is appropriate to hold a defendant liable for unintentional discrimination on the basis of less evidence than is required to prove intentional discrimination. Rather, the necessary premise of the disparate impact approach is that some employment practices, adopted without a deliberately discriminatory motive, may in operation be functionally equivalent to intentional discrimination.

Perhaps the most obvious examples of such functional equivalence have been found where facially neutral job requirements necessarily operated to perpetuate the effects of intentional discrimination that occurred before Title VII was enacted. In <u>Griggs</u> itself, for example, the employer had a history of overt racial discrimination that predated the enactment of the Civil Rights Act of 1964. Such conduct had apparently ceased thereafter, but the employer continued to follow employment policies that had "a markedly dispropor- tionate" adverse effect on blacks. The <u>Griggs</u> Court found that these policies, which involved the use of general aptitude tests and a high school diploma requirement, were not demonstrably related to the jobs for which they were used. Believing that diplomas and tests could become "masters of reality," which would perpetuate the effects of pre-Act discrimination, the Court concluded that such practices could not be defended simply on the basis of their facial neutrality or on the basis of the employer's lack of discriminatory intent.

This Court has repeatedly reaffirmed the principle that some facially neutral employment practices may violate Title VII even in the absence of a demonstrated discriminatory intent. We have not limited this principle to cases in which the challenged practice served to perpetuate the effects of pre-Act intentional discrimination. Each of our subsequent decisions, however, like <u>Griggs</u> itself, involved standardized employment tests or criteria. <u>Albernarle Paper Co. v. Moody</u>, (written aptitude tests); <u>Washington v. Davis</u>, (written test of verbal skills); <u>Dothard v. Rawlinson</u>, (height and weight requirements); <u>New York City Transit Authority v. Beazer</u>, (rule against employing drug addicts); <u>Connecticut v. Teal</u>, (written examination). In contrast, we have consistently used conventional disparate-treatment theory, in which proof of intent to discriminate is required, to review hiring and promotion decisions that were based on the exercise of personal or the application of inherently subjective criteria. See, e.g., <u>McDonnell Douglas Corp. v. Green</u>, (discretionary decision not to rehire individual who engaged in criminal acts against employer while laid off); <u>Furnco Construction Corp. v. Waters</u>, hiring decisions based on personal knowledge of candidates and recommendations); <u>Texas Dept. of Community Affairs v. Burdine</u>, (discretionary decision to fire individual who was said not to get along with co-workers); <u>United States Postal Service Bd. of Governors v. Aikens</u>, (discretionary promotion decision).

Our decisions have not addressed the question whether disparate impact analysis may be applied to cases in which subjective criteria are used to make employment decisions. As noted above, the Courts of Appeals are in conflict on the issue. In order to resolve this conflict, we must determine whether the reasons that support the use of disparate impact analysis apply to subjective employment practices, and whether such analysis can be applied in this new context under workable evidentiary standards.

B

The parties present us with stark and uninviting alternatives. Petitioner contends that subjective selection methods are at least as likely to have discriminatory effects as are the kind of objective tests at issue in Griggs and our other disparate impact cases. Furthermore, she argues, if disparate impact analysis is confined to objective tests, employers will be able to substitute subjective criteria having substantially identical effects, and Griggs will become a dead letter. Respondent and the United States (appearing as amicus curia) argue that conventional disparate treatment analysis is adequate to accomplish Congress' purpose in enacting Title VII. They also argue that subjective selection practices would be so impossibly difficult to defend under disparate impact analysis that employers would be forced to adopt numerical quotas in order to avoid liability.

We are persuaded that our decisions in Griggs and succeeding cases could largely be nullified if disparate impact analysis were applied only to standardized selection practices. However one might distinguish "subjective" from "objective" criteria, it is apparent that selection systems that combine both types would generally have to be considered subjective in nature. Thus, for example, if the employer in Griggs had consistently preferred applicants who had a high school diploma and who passed the company's general aptitude test, its selection system could nonetheless have been considered "subjective" if it also included brief interviews with the candidates. So long as an employer refrained from making standardized criteria absolutely determinative, it would remain free to give such tests almost as much weight as it chose without risking a disparate impact challenge. If we announced a rule that allowed employers so easily to insulate themselves from liability under Griggs, disparate impact analysis might effectively be abolished.

We are also persuaded that disparate impact analysis is in principle no less applicable to subjective employment criteria than to objective or standardized tests. In either case, a facially neutral practice,

351

adopted without discriminatory intent, may have effects that are indistinguishable from intentionally discriminatory practices. It is true, to be sure, that an employer's policy of leaving promotion decisions to the unchecked discretion of lower level supervisors should itself raise no inference of discriminatory conduct. Especially in relatively small businesses like respondent's, it may be customary and quite reasonable simply to delegate employment decisions to those employees who are most familiar with the jobs to be filled and with the candidates for those jobs. It does not follow, however, that the particular supervisors to whom this discretion is delegated always act without discriminatory intent. Furthermore, even if one assumed that any such discrimination can be adequately policed through disparate treatment analysis, the problem of subconscious stereotypes and prejudices would remain. In this case, for example, petitioner was apparently told at one point that the teller position was a big responsibility with "a lot of money...for blacks to have to count." Such remarks may not prove discriminatory intent, but they do suggest a lingering form of the problem that Title VII was enacted to combat. If an employer's undisciplined system of subjective decision making has precisely the same effects as a system pervaded by impermissible intentional discrimination, it is difficult to see why Title VII's proscription against discriminatory actions should not apply. In both circumstances, the employer's practices may be said to "adversely affect [an individual's] status as an employee, because of such individual's race, color, religion, sex, or national origin." We conclude, accordingly, that subjective or discretionary employment practices may be analyzed under the disparate impact approach in appropriate cases.

Having decided that disparate impact analysis may in principle be applied to subjective as well as to objective practices, we turn to the evidentiary standards that should apply in such cases. It is here that the concerns raised by respondent have their greatest force. Respondent contends that a plaintiff may establish a prima facie case of disparate impact through the use of bare statistics, and that the defendant can rebut this statistical showing only by justifying the challenged practice in terms of "business necessity," or "job relatedness." Standardized tests and criteria, like those at issue in our previous disparate impact cases, can often be justified through formal "validation studies," which seek to determine whether discrete selection criteria predict actual on-the-job performance. Respondent warns, however, that "validating" subjective

352

selection criteria in this way is impracticable. Some qualities--for example, common sense, good judgment, originality, ambition, loyalty, and tact--cannot be measured accurately through standardized testing techniques. Moreover, success at many jobs in which such qualities are crucial cannot itself be measured directly. Opinions often differ when managers and supervisors are evaluated, and the same can be said for many jobs that involve close cooperation with one's co-workers or complex and subtle tasks like the provision of professional services or personal counseling. Because of these difficulties, we are told, employers will find it impossible to eliminate subjective selection criteria and impossibly expensive to defend such practices in litigation. Respondent insists, and the United States agrees, that employers' only alternative will be to adopt surreptitious quota systems in order to ensure that no plaintiff can establish a statistical prima facie case.

We agree that the inevitable focus on statistics in disparate impact cases could put undue pressure on employers to adopt inappropriate prophylactic measures. It is completely unrealistic to assume that unlawful discrimination is the sole cause of people failing to gravitate to jobs and employers in accord with the laws of chance. It would be equally unrealistic to suppose that employers can eliminate, or discover and explain, the myriad of innocent causes that may lead to statistical imbalances in the composition of their work forces. Congress has specifically provided that employers are not required to avoid "disparate impact" as such:

"Nothing contained in [Title VII] shall be interpreted to require any employer ... to grant preferential treatment to any individual or to any group because of the race, color, religion, sex, or national origin of such individual or group on account of an imbalance which may exist with respect to the total number or percentage of persons of any race, color, religion, sex, or national origin employed by any employer ... in comparison with the total number or percentage of persons of such race, color, religion, sex, or national origin in any community, State, section, or other area, or in the available work force in any community. State, section, or other area."

Preferential treatment and the use of quotas by public employers subject to Title VII can violate the Constitution and it has long been recognized that legal

353

rules leaving any class of employers with "little choice" but to adopt such measures would be "far from the intent of Title VII. Respondent and the United States are thus correct when they argue that extending disparate impact analysis to subjective employment practices has the potential to create a Hobson's choice for employers and thus to lead in practice to perverse results. If quotas and preferential treatment become the only cost-effective means of avoiding expensive litigation and potentially catastrophic liability such measures will be widely adopted. The prudent employer will be careful to ensure that its programs are discussed in euphemistic terms, but will be equally careful to ensure that the quotas are met. Allowing the evolution of disparate impact analysis to lead to this result would be contrary to Congress' clearly expressed intent, and it should not be the effect of our decision today.

We do not believe that disparate impact theory need have any chilling effect on legitimate business practices. We recognize, however, that today's extension of that theory into the context of subjective selection practices could increase the risk that employers will be given incentives to adopt quotas or to engage in preferential treatment. Because Congress has so clearly and emphatically expressed its intent that Title VII not lead to this result, we think it imperative to explain in some detail why the evidentiary standards that apply in these cases should serve as adequate safeguards against the danger that Congress recognized. Our previous decisions offer guidance, but today's extension of disparate impact analysis calls for a fresh and somewhat closer examination of the constraints that operate to keep that analysis within its proper bounds.

First, we note that the plaintiff's burden in establishing a prima facie case goes beyond the need to show that there are statistical disparities in the employer's work force. The plaintiff must begin by identifying the specific employment practice that is challenged. Although this has been relatively easy to do in challenges to standardized tests, it may sometimes be more difficult when subjective selection criteria are at issue. Especially in cases where an employer combines subjective criteria with the use of more rigid standardized rules or tests, the plaintiff is in our view responsible for isolating and identifying the specific employment practices that are allegedly responsible for any observed statistical disparities.

Once the employment practice at issue has been identified, causation must be proved; that is, the plaintiff must offer statistical evidence of a kind and degree sufficient to show that the practice in question has caused the exclusion of applicants for jobs or promotions because of their membership in a protected group. Our formulations, which have never been framed in terms of any rigid mathematical formula, have consistently stressed that statistical disparities must be sufficiently substantial that they raise such a inference of causation. In Griggs, for example we examined "requirements [that] operate[d] to disqualify Negroes at a substantially higher rate than white applicants." Similarly, we said in Albemarle Paper Co. that plaintiffs are required to show "that the tests in question select applicants for hire or promotion in a racial pattern significantly different from that of the pool of applicants." Later cases have framed the test in similar terms. See, e.g., Washington v. Davis, ("hiring and promotion practices disqualifying substantially disproportionate numbers of blacks"); Dothard, (employment standards that "select applicants for hire in a significantly discriminatory pattern"); Beazer ("statistical evidence showing that an employment practice has the effect of denying the members of one race equal access to employment opportunities"); Teal ("significantly discriminatory impact").

Nor are courts or defendants obliged to assume that plaintiffs' statistical evidence is reliable. "If the employer discerns fallacies or deficiencies in the data offered by the plaintiff, he is free to adduce countervailing evidence of his own." Dothard, see also id., (Rehnquist, J., concurring in result and concurring in part) ("If the defendants in a Title VII suit believe there to be any reason to discredit plaintiffs' statistics that does not appear on their face, the opportunity to challenge them is available to the defendants just as in any other lawsuit. They may endeavor to impeach the reliability of the statistical evidence, they may offer rebutting evidence, or they may disparage in arguments or in briefs the probative weight which the plaintiffs' evidence should be accorded"). Without attempting to catalogue all the weaknesses that may be found in such evidence, we may note that typical examples include small or incomplete data sets and inadequate statistical techniques. Similarly, statistics based on an applicant pool containing individuals lacking minimal qualifications for the job would be of little probative value. See, e.g. Hazlewood School Dist. v. United States ("proper comparison was between the racial composition of [the employer's] teaching staff and the

355

racial composition of the qualified public school teacher population in the relevant labor market"). Other kinds of deficiencies in facially plausible statistical evidence may emerge from the facts of particular cases. See, e.g., Carroll v. Sears, Roebuck & Co., ("The flaw in the plaintiffs' proof was its failure to establish the required causal connection between the challenged employment practices (testing) and discrimination in the work force. Because the test does not have a cut-off and is only one of many factors in decisions to hire or promote, the fact that blacks score lower does not automatically result in disqualification of disproportionate numbers of blacks as in cases involving cut-offs"), Contreras v. Los Angeles, (probative value of statistics impeached by evidence that plaintiffs failed a written examination at a disproportionately high rate because they did not study seriously for it).

A second constraint on the application of disparate impact theory lies in the nature of the "business necessity" or "job relatedness" defense. Although we have said that an employer has "the burden of showing that any given requirement must have a manifest relationship to the employment in question," such a formulation should not be interpreted as implying that the ultimate burden of proof can be shifted to the defendant. On the contrary, the ultimate burden of proving that discrimination against a protected group has been caused by a specific employment practice remains with the plaintiff at all times. Thus, when a plaintiff has made out a prima facie case of disparate impact, and when the defendant has met its burden of producing evidence that its employment practices are based on legitimate business reasons, the plaintiff must "show that other tests or selection devices, without a similarly undesirable racial effect, would also serve the employer's legitimate interest in efficient and trustworthy workmanship." Factors such as the cost or other burdens of proposed alternative selection devices are relevant in determining whether they would be equally as effective as the challenged practice in serving the employer's legitimate business goals. The same factors would also be relevant in determing whether the challenged practice has operated as the functional equivalent of a pretext for discriminatory treatment. Our cases make it clear that employers are not required, even when defending standardized or objective tests, to introduce formal "validation studies' showing that particular criteria predict actual on-the-job performance. In Beazer, for example, the Court considered it obvious that "legitimate employment goals of safety and efficiency" permitted the exclusion of methadone users from employment with the New York City Transit Authority; the Court indicated that the "manifest relationship" test was satisfied even with respect to non-safety-sensitive jobs because those legitimate goals were "significantly served by" the exclusionary rule at issue in that case even though the rule was not required by those goals. Similarly, in Washington v. Davis, the Court held that the "job relatedness" requirement was satisfied when the employer demonstrated that a written test was related to success at a police training academy "wholly aside from [the test's] possible relationship to actual performance as a police officer." See also id., (Stevens, J., concurring) ("[A]s a matter of law, it is permissible for the police department to use a test for the purpose of predicting ability to master a training program even if the test does not otherwise predict ability to perform on the job").

In the context of subjective or discretionary employment decisions, the employer will often find it easier than in the case of standardized tests to produce evidence of a "manifest relationship to the employment in question." It is self-evident that many jobs, for example those involving managerial responsibilities, require personal qualities that have never been considered amenable to standardized testing. In evaluating claims that discretionary employment practices are insufficiently related to legitimate business purposes, it must be borne in mind that "[c]ourts are generally less competent than employers to restructure business practices and unless mandated to do so by Congress they should not attempt it." Furnco Construction Corp. v. Waters. See also Zahorik v. Cornell University, "([The] criteria [used by a university to award tenure], however difficult to apply and however much disagreement they generate in particular cases, are job related....It would be a most radical interpretation of Title VII for a court to enjoin use of an historically settled process and plainly relevant criteria largely because they lead to decisions which are difficult for a court to review"). In sum, the high standards of proof in disparate impact cases are sufficient in our view to avoid giving employers incentives to modify any normal and legitimate practices by introducing quotas or preferential treatment.

We granted certiorari to determine whether the court below properly held disparate impact analysis inapplicable to a subjective or discretionary promotion system, and we now hold that such analysis may be applied. We express no opinion as to the other rulings of the Court of Appeals.

Neither the District Court nor the Court of Appeals has evaluated the statistical evidence to determine whether petitioner made out a prima facie case of discriminatory promotion practices under disparate impact theory. It may be that the relevant data base is too small to permit any meaningful statistical analysis, but we leave the Court of Appeals to decide in the first instance, on the basis of the record and the principles announced today, whether this case can be resolved without further proceedings in the District Court. The judgment of the Court of Appeals is vacated, and the case is remanded for further proceedings consistent with this opinion.

PRICE WATERHOUSE, v. HOPKINS 109S.CT. 1177 (1989)

Justice Brennan: Ann Hopkins was a senior manager
in an office of Price Waterhouse when she was proposed
for partnership in 1982.   She was neither offered nor
denied admission to the partnership; instead, her
candidacy was held for reconsideration the following
year. When the partners in her office later refused to
repropose her for partnership, she sued Price Waterhouse
under Title VII of the Civil Rights Act of 1964 charging
that the firm had discriminated against her on the basis
of sex in its decisions regarding partnership.   Judge
Gesell in the District Court of District of Columbia
ruled in her favor on the question of liability, and the
Court of Appeals for the District of Columbia Circuit
affirmed. We granted certiorari to resolve a conflict
among the Courts of Appeals concerning the respective
burdens of proof of a defendant and plaintiff in a suit
under Title VII when it has been shown that an employment
decision resulted from a mixture of legitimate and
illegitimate motives.

At Price Waterhouse, a nationwide professional
accounting partnership, a senior manager becomes a
candidate for partnership when the partners in her local
office submit her name as a candidate. All of the other
partners in the firm are then invited to submit written
comments on each candidate - either on a "long" or a
"short" form, depending on the partner's degree of
exposure to the candidate. Not every partner in the firm
submits comments on every candidate. After reviewing the
comments and interviewing the partners who submitted
them, the firm's Admissions Committee makes a
recommendation to the Policy Board. This recommendation
will be either that the firm accept the candidate for
partnership, put her application on "hold," or deny her
the promotion outright. The Policy Board then decides
whether to submit the candidate's name to the entire
partnership for a vote, to "hold" her candidacy, or to
reject her.   The recommendation of the Admissions
Committee, and the decision of the Policy Board, are not
controlled by fixed guidelines: a certain number of
positive comments from partners will not guarantee a
candidate's admission to the partnership, nor will a
specific quantity of negative comments necessarily defeat
her application. Price Waterhouse places no limit on the
number of persons whom it will admit to the partnership
in any given year.

Ann Hopkins had worked at Price Waterhouse's Office
of Government Services in Washington, D.C., for five
years when the partners in that office proposed her as

a candidate for partnership. Of the 662 partners at the firm at that time, 7 were women. Of the 88 persons proposed for partnership that year, only 1 - Hopkins - was a woman. Forty-seven of these candidates were admitted to the partnership, 21 were rejected, and 20 - including Hopkins - were "held" for re-consideration the following year. Thirteen of the 32 partners who had submitted comments on Hopkins supported her bid for partnership. Three partners recommended that her candidacy be placed on hold, eight stated that they did not have an informed opinion about her, and eight recommended that she be denied partnership.

In a jointly prepared statement supporting her candidacy, the partners in Hopkins' office showcased her successful 2 year effort to secure a $25 million contract with the Department of State, labeling it "an outstanding performance" and one that Hopkins carried out "virtually at the partner level." Despite Price Waterhouse's attempt at trial to minimize her contribution to this project, Judge Gesell specifically found that Hopkins had "played a key role in Price Waterhouse's successful effort to win a multi-million dollar contract with the Department of State." Indeed, he went on "[n]one of the other partnership candidates at Price Waterhouse that year had a comparable record in terms of successfully securing major contracts for the partnership."

The partners in Hopkins' office praised her character as well as her accomplishments, describing her in their joint statement as "an outstanding professional" who had a "deft touch," a "strong character, independence and integrity." Clients appear to have agreed with these assessments. At trial, one official from the State Department described her as "extremely competent, intelligent," "strong and forthright, very productive, energetic and creative." Another high-ranking official praised Hopkins' decisiveness, broadmindedness, and "intellectual clarity"; she was, in his words, "a stimulating conversationalist." Evaluations such as these led Judge Gesell to conclude that Hopkins "had no difficulty dealing with clients and her clients appear to have been very pleased with her work" and that she "was generally viewed as a highly competent project leader who worked long hours, pushed vigorously to meet deadlines and demanded much from the multidisciplinary staffs with which she worked."

On too many occasions, however, Hopkins' aggressiveness apparently spilled over into abrasiveness. Staff members seem to have borne the brunt of Hopkins brusqueness. Long before her bid for partnership, partners evaluating her work had counseled her to improve her relations with staff members. Although later evaluations indicate an improvement, Hopkins perceived shortcomings in this important area eventually doomed her bid for partnership. Virtually all of the partners' negative remarks about Hopkins - even those of partners supporting her - had to do with her "inter-personal skills." Both "[s]upporters and opponents of her candidacy," stressed Judge Gesell, "indicted that she was sometimes overly aggressive, unduly harsh, difficult to work with and impatient with staff."

There were clear signs, though, that some of the partners reacted negatively to Hopkins' personality because she was a woman. One partner described her as "macho", another suggested that she "overcompensated for being a woman"; a third advised her to take "a course at charm school". Several partners criticized her use of profanity; in response, one partner suggested that those partners objected to her swearing only "because it[']s a lady using foul language." Another supporter explained that Hopkins "ha[d] matured from a tough-talking somewhat masculine hard-nosed mgr to an authoritative, formidable, but much more appealing lady ptr candidate." But it was the man who, as Judge Gesell found, bore responsibility for explaining to Hopkins the reasons for the Policy Board's decision to place her candidacy on hold who delivered the coup de grace: in order to improve her chances for partnership, Thomas Beyer advised, Hopkins should "walk more femininely, talk more femininely, dress more femininely, wear make-up, have her hair styled, and wear jewelry."

Dr. Susan Fiske, a social psychologist and Associate Professor of Psychology at Carnegie-Mellon University, testified at trial that the partnership selection process at Price Waterhouse was likely influenced by sex stereotyping. Her testimony focused not only on the overtly sex-based comments of partners but also on gender-neutral remarks, made by partners who knew Hopkins only slightly, that were intensely critical of her. One partner, for example, baldly stated that Hopkins was "universally disliked" by staff and another described her as "consistently annoying and irritating"; yet these were people who had very little contact with Hopkins. According to Fiske, Hopkins' uniqueness (as the only woman in the pool of candidates) and the subjectivity of the evaluations made it likely that sharply critical remarks such as these were the product of sex stereotyping - although Fiske admitted that she could not say with certainty whether any particular comment was the result of stereotyping. Fiske based her opinion on a review of the submitted comments, explaining that it was commonly accepted practice for social psychologists to reach this kind of conclusion without having met any of the people involved in the decision making process.

In previous years, other female candidates for partnership also had been evaluated in sex-based terms. As a general matter, Judge Gesell concluded, "[c}andidates were viewed favorably if partners believed they maintained their femin[in]ity while becoming effective professional managers"; in this environment, "[t]o be identified as a 'women's lib[b]er' was regarded as [a] negative comment." In fact, the judge found that in previous years "[o]ne partner repeatedly commented that he could not consider any woman seriously as a partnership candidate and believed that women were not even capable of functioning as senior managers - yet the firm took no action to discourage his comments and recorded his vote in the overall summary of the evaluations."

Judge Gesell found that Price Waterhouse legitimately emphasized interpersonal skills in its partnership decisions, and also found that the firm had not fabricated its complaints about Hopkins' interpersonal skills as a pretext for discrimination. Moreover, he concluded, the firm did not give decisive emphasis to such traits only because Hopkins was a woman; although there were male candidates who lacked these skills but who were admitted to partnership, the judge found that these candidates possessed other, positive traits that Hopkins lacked.

The judge went on to decide, however, that some of the partners' remarks about Hopkins stemmed from an impermissibly cabined view of the proper behavior of women, and that Price Waterhouse had done nothing to disavow reliance on such comments. He held that Price Waterhouse had unlawfully discriminated against Hopkins on the basis of sex by consciously giving credence and effect to partners' comments that resulted from sex stereotyping. Noting that Price Waterhouse could avoid equitable relief by proving by clear and convincing evidence that it would have placed Hopkins candidacy on hold even absent this discrimination, the judge decided that the firm had not carried this heavy burden.

The Court of Appeals affirmed the District court's ultimate conclusion, but departed from its analysis in one particular: it held that even if a plaintiff proves that discrimination played a role in an employment decision, the defendant will not be found liable if it

362

proves, by clear and convincing evidence, that it would have made the same decision in the absence of discrimination. Under this approach, an employer is not deemed to have violated Title VII if it proves that it would have made the same decision in the absence of an impermissible motive, whereas under the District Court's approach, the employer's proof in that respect only avoids equitable relief. We decide today that the Court of Appeals had the better approach, but that both courts erred in requiring the employer to make its proof by clear and convincing evidence.

....

In passing Title VII, Congress made the simple but momentous announcement that sex, race, religion, and national origin are not relevant to the selection, evaluation, or compensation of employees. Yet, the statute does not purport to limit the other qualities and characteristics that employers may take into account in making employment decisions. The converse, therefore, of "for cause" legislation, Title VII eliminates certain bases for distinguishing among employees while otherwise preserving employers' freedom of choice. This balance between employees rights and employer prerogatives turns out to be decisive in the case before us.

Congress' intent to forbid employers to take gender into account in making employment decisions appears on the face of the statute. In now-familiar language, the statute forbids an employer to "fail or refuse to hire or to discharge any individual, or otherwise to discriminate with respect to his compensation, terms, conditions, or privileges of employment," or to "limit, segregate, or classify his employes or applicants for employment in any way which would deprive or tend to deprive any individual of employment opportunities or otherwise adversely affect his status as an employee, because of such individual's ...sex." We take these words to mean that gender must be irrelevant to employment decisions. To construe the words "because of" as colloquial shorthand for "but-for causation," as does Price Waterhouse, is to misunderstand them.

But-for causation is a hypothetical construct. In determining whether a particular factor was a but-for cause of a given event, we begin by assuming that that factor was present at the time of the event, and then ask whether, even if that factor had been absent, the event nevertheless would have transpired in the same way. The present, active tense of the operative verbs of 703(a)(1) ("to fail or refuse"), in contrast, turns our attention to the actual moment of the event in question, the adverse employment decision. The critical inquiry, the one commanded by the words of 703(a)(1), is whether gender was a factor in the employment decision at the moment it was made. Moreover, since we know that the words "because of" do not mean "solely because of," we also know that Title VII meant to condemn even those decisions based on a mixture of legitimate and illegitimate considerations. When, therefore, an employer considers both gender and legitimate factors at the time of making a decision, that decision was "because of" sex and the other, legitimate considerations - even if we may say later, in the context of litigation, that the decision would have been the same if gender had not been taken into account.

To attribute this meaning to the words "because of" does not, as the dissent asserts, divest them of casual significance. A simple example illustrates the point. Suppose two physical forces act upon and move an object, and suppose that either force acting alone would have moved the object. As the dissent would have it, neither physical force was a "cause" of the motion unless we can show that but for one or both of them, the object would not have moved; to use the dissent's terminology, both forces were simply "in the air" unless we can identify at least one of them as a but-for cause of the object's movement. Events that are casually overdetermined, in other words, may not have any "cause" at all. This cannot be so.

We need not leave our common sense at the doorstep when we interpret a statute. It is difficult for us to imagine that, in the simple words "because of," Congress meant to obligate a plaintiff to identify the precise casual role played by legitimate and illegitimate motivations in the employment decision she challenges. We conclude, instead that Congress meant to obligate her to prove that the employer relied upon sex-based considerations in coming to its decision.

Our interpretation of the words "because of" also is supported by the fact that Title VII does identify one circumstance in which an employer may take gender into account in making an employment decision, namely, when gender is a "bona fide occupational qualification [(BFOQ)] reasonably necessary to the normal operation of th[e] particular business or enterprise." The only plausible inference to draw from this provision is that, in all other circumstances, a person's gender may not be considered in making decisions that affect her. Indeed, Title VII even forbids employers to make gender an indirect stumbling block to employment opportunities. An employer may not, we have held, condition employment opportunities on the satisfaction of facially neutral tests or qualifications that have a disproportionate, adverse impact on members of protected groups when those tests or qualifications are not required for performance of the job. See <u>Watson v. Fort Worth Bank & Trust</u>, <u>Griggs v. Duke Power Co</u>.

To say that an employer may not take gender into account is not, however, the end of the matter, for that describes only one aspect of Title VII. The other important aspect of the statute is its preservation of an employer's remaining freedom of choice. We conclude that the preservation of this freedom means that an employer shall not be liable if it can prove that, even if it had not taken gender into account, it would have come to the same decision regarding a particular person. The statute's maintenance of employer prerogatives is evident from the statute itself and from its history, both in Congress and in this Court.

To begin with, the existence of the BFOQ exception shows Congress' unwillingness to require employers to change the very nature of their operations in response to the statute. And our emphasis on "business necessity" in disparate-impact cases, see <u>Watson and Griggs</u>, and on "legitimate, nondiscriminatory reason[s]" in disparate-treatment cases, see <u>McDonnell Douglas Corp. v. Green</u>, <u>Texas Dept. of Community Affairs v. Burdine</u>, results from our awareness of Title VII's balance between employee rights and employer prerogatives. In <u>McDonnell Douglas</u>, we described as follows Title VII's goal to eradicate discrimination while preserving workplace efficiency: "The broad, overriding interest, shared by employer, employee, and consumer, is efficient and trustworthy workmanship assured through fair and racially neutral employment and personnel decisions. In the implementation of such decisions, it is abundantly clear that Title VII tolerates no racial discrimination, subtle or otherwise."

When an employer ignored the attributes enumerated in the statute, Congress hoped, it naturally would focus on the qualifications of the applicant or employee. The intent to drive employers to focus on qualifications rather than on race, religion, sex, or national origin is the theme of a good deal of the statute's legislative history. An interpretive memorandum entered into the Congressional Record by Senators Case and Clark, comanagers of the bill in the Senate, is representative of this general theme. According to their memorandum, Title VII "expressly protects the employer's right to insist that any prospective applicant, Negro or white,

365

must meet the applicable job qualifications. Indeed, the very purpose of title VII is to promote hiring on the basis of job qualifications, rather than on the basis of race or color." The memorandum went on; "To discriminate is to make a distinction, to make a difference in treatment or favor, and those distinctions or differences in treatment or favor which are prohibited by section 704 are those which are based on any five of the forbidden criteria: race, color, religion, sex, and national origin. Any other criterion or qualification for employment is not affected by this title."

Many other legislators made statements to a similar effect; we see no need to set out each remark in full here. The central point is this: while an employer may not take gender into account in making an employment decision (except in those very narrow circumstances in which gender is BFOQ), it is free to decide against a woman for other reasons. We think these principles require that, once a plaintiff in a Title VII case shows that gender played a motivating part in an employment decision, the defendant may avoid a finding of liability only by proving that it would have made the same decision even if it had not allowed gender to play such a role. This balance of burdens is the direct result of Title VII's balance of rights. Our holding casts no shadow on Burdine, in which we decided that, even after a plaintiff has made out a prima facie case of discrimination under Title VII, the burden of persuasion does not shift to the employer to show that its stated legitimate reason for the employment decision was the true reason. We stress first, that neither court below shifted the burden of persuasion to Price Waterhouse on this question, and in fact, the District Court found that Hopkins had not shown that the firm's stated reason for its decision was pretextual. Moreover, since we hold that the plaintiff retains the burden of persuasion on the issue whether gender played a part in the employment decision, the situation before us is not the one of "shifting burdens" that we addressed in Burdine. Instead, the employers' burden is most appropriately deemed an affirmative defense; the plaintiff must persuade the factfinder on one point, and then the employer, if it wishes to prevail, must persuade it on another. See NLRB v. Transportation Management Corp.

Price Waterhouse's claim that the employer does not bear any burden of proof (if it bears one at all) until the plaintiff has shown "substantial evidence that Price Waterhouse's explanation for failing to promote Hopkins was not the 'true reason' for its action" merely restates its argument that the plaintiff in a mixed-motives case must squeeze her proof into _Burdine's_ framework. Where a decision was the product of a mixture of legitimate and illegitimate motives, however, it simply makes no sense to ask whether the legitimate reason was "the 'true reason'" for the decision - which is the question asked by _Burdine_. See _Transportation Management_. Oblivious to this last point, the dissent would insist that _Burdine's_ framework perform work that it was never intended to perform. It would require a plaintiff who challenges an adverse employment decision in which both legitimate and illegitimate consideration played a part to pretend that the decision, in fact, stemmed from a single source - for the premise of _Burdine_ is that either a legitimate or an illegitimate set of considerations led to the challenged decision. To say that _Burdine's_ evidentiary scheme will not help us decide a case admittedly involving both kinds of considerations is not to cast aspersions on the utility of that scheme in the circumstances for which it was designed.

In deciding as we do today we do not traverse new ground. We have in the past confronted Title VII cases in which an employer has used an illegitimate criterion to distinguish among employees, and have held that it is the employer's burden to justify decisions resulting from that practice. When an employer has asserted that gender is a bona fide occupational qualification within the meaning of 703(e), for example, we have assumed that it is the employer who must show why it must use gender as a criterion in employment. See _Dothard v. Rawlinson_. In a related context, although the Equal Pay Act expressly permits employers to pay different wages to women where disparate pay is the result of a "factor other than sex," we have decided that it is the employer, not the employee, who must prove that the actual disparity is not sex-linked. See _Corning Glass Works v. Brennan_. Finally, some courts have held that under Title VII as amended by the Pregnancy Discrimination Act, it is the employer who has the burden of showing that its limitations on the work that it allows a pregnant woman to perform are necessary in light of her pregnancy. See, e. g. _Hayes v. Shelby Memorial Hospital_, _Wright v. Olin Corp_. As these examples demonstrate, our assumption always has been that if an employer allows gender to affect its decision making process, then it must carry the burden of justifying its ultimate decision. We have not in the past required women whose gender has proved relevant to an employment decision to establish the negative proposition that they would not have been subject to that decision had they been men, and we do not do so today.

We have reached a similar conclusion in other contexts where the law announces that a certain characteristic is irrelevant to the allocation of burdens and benefits. In Mt. Healthy City School Dist. Board of Education v. Doyle, the plaintiff claimed that he had been discharged as a public school teacher for exercising his free-speech rights under the First Amendment. Because we did not wish to "place an employee in a better position as a result of the exercise of constitutionally protected conduct than he would have occupied had he done nothing," we concluded that such an employee "ought not to be able, by engaging in such conduct, to prevent his employer form assessing his performance record and reaching a decision not to rehire on the basis of that record." We therefore held that once the plaintiff had shown that his constitutionally protected speech was a "substantial" or motivating factor" in the adverse treatment of him by his employer, the employer was obligated to prove "by a preponderance of the evidence that it would have reached the same decision as to [the plantiff] even in the absence of the protected conduct." A court that finds for a plaintiff under this standard has effectively concluded that an illegitimate motive was a "but-for" cause of the employment decision. See Givhan v. Western Line Consolidated School District. See also Arlington Heights v. Metropolitan Housing Corp., (applying Mt. Healthy standard where plaintiff alleged that unconstitutional motive had contributed to enactment of legislation); Hunter v. Underwood, (same).

In Transportation Management, we upheld the NLRB's interpretation of 10(c) of the National Labor Relations Act, which forbids a court to order affirmative relief for discriminatory conduct against a union member "if such individual was suspended or discharged for cause." The Board had decided that this provision meant that once an employee had shown that his suspension or discharge was based in part on hostility to unions, it was up to the employer to prove by a preponderance of the evidence that it would have made the same decision in the absence of this impermissible motive. In such a situation we emphasized, "[t]he employer is a wrongdoer, he has acted out of a motive that is declared illegitimate by the statute. It is fair that he bear the risk that the influence of legal and illegal motives cannot be separated, because he knowingly created the risk and because the risk was created not by innocent activity but by his own wrongdoing."

We have, in short, been here before. Each time we have concluded that the plaintiff who shows that an impermissible motive played a motivating part in an

368

adverse employment decision has thereby placed upon the defendant the burden to show that it would have made the same decision in the absence of the unlawful motive. Our decision today treads this well-worn path.

In saying that gender played a motivating part in an employment decision, we mean that, if we asked the employer at the moment of the decision what its reasons were and if we received a truthful response, one of those reasons would be that the applicant or employee was a woman. In the specific context of sex stereotyping, an employer who acts on the basis of a belief that a woman cannot be aggressive, or that she must not be, has acted on the basis of gender.

Although the parties do not overtly dispute this last proposition, the placement by Price Waterhouse of "sex stereotyping" in quotation marks throughout its brief seems to us an insinuation either that such stereotyping was not present in this case or that it lacks legal relevance. We reject both possibilities. As to the existence of sex stereotyping in this case, we are not inclined to quarrel with the District Court's conclusion that a number of the partners' comments showed sex stereotyping at work. As for the legal relevance of sex stereotyping, we are beyond the day when an employer could evaluate employees by assuming or insisting that they matched the stereotype associated with their group, for "[i]n forbidding employers to discriminate against individuals because of their sex, Congress intended to strike at the entire spectrum of disparate treatment of men and women resulting from sex stereotypes." Los Angeles Dept. of Water & Power v. Manhart, Sprogis v. United Air Lines,Inc.. An employer who objects to aggressiveness in women but whose positions require this trait places women in an intolerable and impermissible Catch-22: out of a job if they behave aggressively and out of a job if they don't. Title VII lifts women of this bind.

Remarks at work that are based on sex stereotypes do not inevitably prove that gender played a part in a particular employment decision. The plaintiff mush show that the employer actually relied on her gender in making its decision. In making this showing, stereotyped remarks can certainly be evidence that gender played a part. In any event, the stereotyping in this case did not simply consist of stray remarks. On the contrary, Hopkins proved that Price Waterhouse invited partners to submit comments; that some of the comments stemmed from sex stereotypes; that an important part of the Policy Board's decision on Hopkins was an assessment of the

369

submitted comments; and that Price Waterhouse in no way disclaimed reliance on the sex-linked evaluations. This is not, as Price Waterhouse suggests, "discrimination in the air"; rather, it is, as Hopkins puts it, "discrimination brought to ground and visited upon" an employee. By focusing on Hopkins' specific proof, however, we do not suggest a limitation on the possible ways of proving that stereotyping played a motivating role in an employment decision, and we refrain from deciding here which specific facts, "standing alone," would or would not establish a plaintiff's case, since such a decision is unnecessary in this case.

As to the employer's proof, in most cases, the employer should be able to present some objective evidence as to its probable decision in the absence of an impermissible motive. Moreover, proving "that the same decision would have been justified...is not the same as proving that the same decision would have been made." Givhan, quoting <u>Ayers v. Western Line Consolidated School District</u>. An employer may not, in other words, prevail in a mixed-motives case by offering a legitimate and sufficient reason for its decision if that reason did not motivate it at the time of the decision. Finally, an employer may not meet its burden in such a case by merely showing that at the time of the decision it was motivated only in part by a legitimate reason. The very premise of a mixed-motive case is that legitimate reason was present, and indeed, in this case, Price Waterhouse already has made this showing by convincing Judge Gesell that Hopkins' interpersonal problems were a legitimate concern. The employer instead must show that its legitimate reason, standing alone, would have induced it to make the same decision.

The courts below held that an employer who has allowed a discriminatory impulse to play a motivating part in an employment decision must prove by clear and convincing evidence that it would have made the same decision in the absence of discrimination. We are persuaded that the better rule is that the employer must make this showing by a preponderance of the evidence.

Conventional rules of civil litigation generally apply in Title VII cases, see, e.g., <u>United States Postal Service Bd. of Governors v. Aikens</u>, (discrimination not to be "treat[ed] . . . differently from other ultimate questions of fact"), and one of these rules is that parties to civil litigation need only prove their case by a preponderance of the evidence. See, e.g., <u>Herman & McLean v. Huddleston</u>. Exceptions to this standard are uncommon, and in fact are ordinarily recognized only when

the government seeks to take unusual coercive action -
action more dramatic than entering an award of money
damages or other conventional relied - against an
individual. See <u>Santosky v. Kramer</u>, (termination of
parental rights); <u>Addington v. Texas</u>, (involuntary
commitment); <u>Woodby v. INA</u>, (deportation); <u>Schneiderman
v. United States</u> (denaturalization). Only rarely have
we required clear and convincing proof where the action
defended against seeks only conventional relief, see,
e.g., <u>Gertz v. Robert Welch, Inc.</u>, (defamation), and we
find it significant that in such cases it was the
defendant rather than the plaintiff who sought the
elevated standard of proof - suggesting that this
standard ordinarily serves as a shield rather than, as
Hopkins seeks to use it, as a sword.

It is true, as Hopkins emphasizes, that we have
noted the "clear distinction between the measure of proof
necessary to establish the fact that petitioner had
sustained some damage and the measure of proof necessary
to enable the jury to fix the amount." <u>Story Parchment
Co. v. Patterson Parchment Paper Co.</u> Likewise, an EEOC
regulation does require federal agencies proved to have
violated Title VII to show by clear and convincing
evidence that an individual employee is not entitled to
relief. And finally, it is true, that we have emphasized
the importance of make-whole relief for victims of
discrimination. See <u>Albemarle Paper Co. v. Moody</u>. Yet
each of these sources deals with the proper determination
of relief rather than with the initial finding of
liability. This is seen most easily in the EEOC's
regulation, which operates only after an agency or the
EEOC has found that "an employee of the agency was
discriminated against." Because we have held that, by
proving that it would have made the same decision in the
absence of discrimination, the employer may avoid a
finding of liability altogether and not simply avoid
certain equitable relief, these authorities do not help
Hopkins to show why we should elevate the standard of
proof for an employer in this position.

Significantly, the cases from this Court that most
resemble this one, <u>Mt. Healthy</u> and <u>Transportation
Management</u>, did not require clear and convincing proof.
We are not inclined to say that the public policy against
firing employees because they spoke out on issues of
public concern or because they affiliated with a union
is less important than the policy against discharging
employees on the basis of their gender. Each of these
policies is vitally important, and each is adequately
served by requiring proof by a preponderance of the
evidence.

Although Price Waterhouse does not concretely tell us how it proof was preponderant, even if it was not clear and convincing, this general claim is implicit in its request for the less stringent standard. Since the lower courts required Price Waterhouse to make its proof by clear and convincing evidence, they did not determine whether Price Waterhouse had proved by a preponderance of the evidence that it would have placed Hopkins' candidacy on hold even if it had not permitted sex-linked evaluations to play a part in the decision making process. Thus, we shall remand this case so that determination can be made.

The District Court found that sex stereotyping "was permitted to play a part" in the evaluation of Hopkins as a candidate for partnership. Price Waterhouse disputes both that stereotyping occurred and that it played any part in the decision to place Hopkins' candidacy on hold. In the firm's view, in other words, the District Court's factual conclusions are clearly erroneous. We do not agree.

In finding that some of the partners' comments reflected sex stereotyping, the District Court relied in part on Dr. Fiske's expert testimony. Without directly impugning Dr. Fiske's credentials or qualifications, Price Waterhouse insinuates that a social psychologist is unable to identify sex stereotyping in evaluations without investigating whether those evaluations have a basis in reality. This argument comes too late. At trial, counsel for Price Waterhouse twice assured the court that he did not question Dr. Fiske's expertise and failed to challenge the legitimacy of her discipline. Without contradiction from Price Waterhouse, Fiske testified that she discerned sex stereotyping in the partners' evaluations of Hopkins and she further explained that it was part of her business to identify stereotyping in written documents. We are not inclined to accept petitioner's belated and unsubstantiated characterization of Dr. Fiske's testimony as "gossamer evidence" based only on "intuitive hunches" and of her detection of sex stereotyping as "intuitively divined". Nor are we disposed to adopt the dissent's dismissive attitude toward Dr. Fiske's field of study and toward her own professional integrity.

Indeed, we are tempted to say that Dr. Fiske's expert testimony was merely icing on Hopkins' cake. It takes no special training to discern sex stereotyping in a description of an aggressive female employee as requiring "a course at charm school." Nor, turning to

372

Thomas Bever's memorable advice to Hopkins, does it require expertise in psychology to know that, if an employee's flawed "interpersonal skills" can be corrected by a soft-hued suit or a new shade of lipstick, perhaps it is the employee' sex and not her interpersonal skills that has drawn this criticism.

Price Waterhouse also charges that Hopkins produced no evidence that sex stereotyping played a role in the decision to place her candidacy on hold. As we have stressed. however, Hopkins showed that the partnership solicited evaluations from all of the firm's partners; that it generally relied very heavily on such evaluations in making its decision; that some of the partners' comments were the product of stereotyping; and that the firm in no way disclaimed reliance on those particular comments, either in Hopkins' case or in the past. Certainly a plausible - and, one might say, inevitable - conclusion to draw from this set of circumstances is that the Policy Board in making its decision did in fact take into account all of the partners' comments, including the comments that were motivated by stereotypical notions about women's proper deportment.

Price Waterhouse concedes that the proof in Transportation Management, adequately showed that the employer there had relied on an impermissible motivation in firing the plaintiff. But the only evidence in that case that a discriminatory motive contributed to the plaintiff's discharge was that the employer harbored a grudge toward the plaintiff on account of his union activity; there was, contrary to Price Waterhouse's suggestion, no direct evidence that grudge had played a role in the decision, and in fact, the employer had given other reasons in explaining the plaintiff's discharge. If the partnership considers that proof sufficient, we do not know why it takes such vehement issue with Hopkins' proof.

Nor is the finding that sex stereotyping played a part in the Policy Board's decision undermined by the fact that many of the suspect comments are made by supporters rather than detractors of Hopkins. A negative comment, even when made in the context of a generally favorable review, nevertheless may influence the decisionmaker to think less highly of the candidate; the Policy Board, in fact, did not simply tally the "yes's" and "no's" regarding a candidate, but carefully reviewed the content of the submitted comments. The additional suggestion that the comments were made by "persons outside the decision making chain" - and therefore could not have harmed Hopkins - simply ignores the critical role that partners' comments played in the Policy Board's partnership decisions.

Price Waterhouse appears to think that we cannot affirm the factual findings of the trial court without deciding that, instead of being overbearing and aggressive and curt, Hopkins is in fact kind and considerate and patient. If this is indeed its impression, petitioner misunderstands the theory on which Hopkins prevailed. The District Judge acknowledged that Hopkins' conduct justified complaints about her behavior as a senior manager. But he also concluded that the reactions of at least some of the partners were reactions to her as a woman manager. Where an evaluation is based on a subjective assessment of a person's strengths and weaknesses, it is simply not true that each evaluator will focus on, or even mention, the same weaknesses. Thus, even if we knew that Hopkins had "personality problems," this would not tell us that the partners who cast their evaluations of Hopkins in sex-based terms would have criticized her as sharply (or criticized her at all) if she had been a man. It is not our job to review the evidence and decide that the negative reactions to Hopkins were based on reality; our perception of Hopkins' character is irrelevant. We sit not to determine whether Ms. Hopkins is nice, but to decide whether the partners reacted negatively to her personality because she is a woman.

We hold that when a plaintiff in a Title VII case proves that her gender played a motivating part in an employment decision, the defendant may avoid a finding of liability only by proving by a preponderance of the evidence that it would have made the same decision even if it had not taken the plaintiff's gender into account. Because the courts below erred by deciding that the defendant must make this proof by clear and convincing evidence, we reverse the Court of Appeals' judgment against Price Waterhouse on liability and remand the case to that court for further proceedings.

EQUAL EMPLOYMENT OPPORTUNITY COMMISSION
MARCH 19, 1990
POLICY GUIDANCE ON CURRENT ISSUES OF SEXUAL HARASSMENT

This document provides guidance on defining sexual harassment and establishing employer liability in light of recent cases.

Section 703(a)(1) of Title VII, 42, U.S.C. 2000e-2(a) provides:

It shall be an unlawful employment practice for an employer -- . . . . to fail or refuse to hire or to discharge any individual, or otherwise to discriminate against any individual with respect to his compensation, terms, conditions, or privileges of employment, because of such individual's race, color, religion, sex, or national origin[.]

In 1980 the Commission issued guidelines declaring sexual harassment a violation of Title VII, establishing criteria for determining when unwelcome conduct of a sexual nature constitutes sexual harassment, defining the circumstances under which an employer may be held liable, and suggesting affirmative steps an employer should take to prevent sexual harassment. See Section 1604.11 of the Guidelines on Discrimination Because of Sex. The Commission has applied the Guidelines in its enforcement litigation, and many lower courts have relied on the Guidelines.

The issue of whether sexual harassment violates Title VII reached the Supreme Court in 1986 in Meritor Savings Bank v. Vinson. The Court affirmed the basic premises of the Guidelines as well as the Commission's definition. The purpose of this document is to provide guidance on the following issues in light of the developing law after Vinson:

--determining whether sexual conduct is "unwelcome";
--evaluating evidence of harassment;
--determining whether a work environment is sexually "hostile;
--holding employers liable for sexual harassment by supervisors; and
--evaluating preventive and remedial action taken in response to claims of sexual harassment.

A.   Definition

     Title VII does not proscribe all conduct of a sexual
nature in the workplace.   Thus it is crucial to clearly
define sexual harassment: only unwelcome sexual conduct
that is a term or condition of employment constitutes a
violation.   The EEOC's Guidelines define two types of
sexual harassment: "quid pro quo" and "environmental."
The Guidelines provide that "unwelcome" sexual conduct
constitutes sexual harassment when "submission to such
conduct is made either explicitly or implicitly a term
or condition of an individual's employment." "Quid pro
quo harassment" occurs when "submission to or rejection
of such conduct by an individual is used as the basis for
employment decisions affecting such individual."   The
EEOC's Guidelines also recognize that unwelcome sexual
conduct that "unreasonably interfer[es] with an
individual's job performance" or creates an
"intimidating, hostile, or offensive working environment"
can constitute sex discrimination, even if it leads to
no tangible or economic job consequences.   The Supreme
Court's decision in Vinson established that both types
of sexual harassment are actionable under section 703 of
Title VII of the Civil Rights Act of 1964, as forms of
sex discrimination.

     Although "quid pro quo" and "environmental"
harassment are theoretically distinct claims, the line
between the two is not always clear and the two forms of
harassment often occur together.   For example, an
employee's tangible job conditions are affected when a
sexually hostile work environment results in her
constructive discharge.   Similarly, a supervisor who
makes sexual advances toward a subordinate employee may
communicate an implicit threat to adversely affect her
job status if she does not comply. "Hostile environment"
harassment may acquire characteristics of "quid pro quo"
harassment if the offending supervisor abuses his
authority over employment decisions to force the victim
to endure or participate in the sexual conduct.   Sexual
harassment may culminate in a retaliatory discharge if
a victim tells the harasser or her employer she will no
longer submit to the harassment, and is then fired in
retaliation for this protest.   Under these circumstances
it would be appropriate to conclude that both harassment
and retaliation in violation of section 704(a) of Title
VII occurred.

     Distinguishing between the two types of harassment
is necessary when determining the employer's liability

(see infra Section D). But while categorizing sexual harassment as "quid pro quo," "hostile environment," or both is useful analytically, these distinctions should not limit the Commission's investigations, which generally should consider all available evidence and testimony under all possibly applicable theories.

B.   Supreme Court's Decision in Vinson
     Meritor Savings Bank v. Vinson posed three questions for the Supreme Court.
       (1) Does unwelcome sexual behavior that creates a hostile working environment, constitute employment discrimination on the basis of sex;
       (2) Can a Title VII violation be shown when the district court found that any sexual relationship that existed between the plaintiff and her supervisor was a "voluntary one"; and
       (3) Is an employer strictly liable for an offensive working environment created by a supervisor's sexual advances when the employer does not know of, and could not reasonably have known of, the supervisor's misconduct.

1) Facts --- The plaintiff had alleged that her supervisor constantly subjected her to sexual harassment both during and after business hours, on and off the employer's premises; she alleged that he forced her to have sexual intercourse with him on numerous occasions, fondled her in front of other employees, followed her into the women's restroom and exposed himself to her, and even raped her on several occasions. She alleged that she submitted for fear of jeopardizing her employment. She testified, however, that this conduct had ceased almost a year before she first complained in any way, by filing a Title VII suit; her EEOC charge was filed later. The supervisor and the employer denied all of her allegations and claimed they were fabricated in response to a work dispute.

2) Lower Courts' Decisions --- After trial, the district court found the plaintiff was not the victim of sexual harassment and was not required to grant sexual favors as a condition of employment or promotion. Without resolving the conflicting testimony, the district court found that if a sexual relationship had existed between plaintiff and her supervisor, it was "a voluntary one...having nothing to do with her continued employment." The district court nonetheless went on to hold that the employer was not liable for its supervisor's actions because it had no notice of the alleged sexual harassment; although the employer had a

policy against discrimination, and an internal grievance procedure, the plaintiff had never lodged a complaint.

The court of appeals reversed and remanded, holding the lower court should have considered whether the evidence established a violation under the "hostile environment' theory. The court ruled that a victim's "voluntary" submission to sexual advances has "no materiality whatsoever" to the proper inquiry; whether "toleration of sexual harassment [was] a condition of her employment." The court further held that an employer is absolutely liable for sexual harassment committed by a supervisory employee, regardless of whether the employer actually knew or reasonably could have known of the misconduct, or would have disapproved of and stopped the misconduct if aware of it.

3) Supreme Court's Opinion --- The Supreme Court agreed that the case should be remanded for consideration under the "hostile environment" theory and held that the proper inquiry focuses on the "unwelcomeness" of the conduct rather than the "voluntariness" of the victim's participation. But the Court held that the court of appeals erred in concluding that employers are always automatically liable for sexual harassment by their supervisory employees.

a) "Hostile Environment" Violates Title VII --- The Court rejected the employer's contention that Title VII prohibits only discrimination that causes "economic" or "tangible" injury: "Title VII affords employees the right to work in an environment free from discriminatory intimidation, ridicule and insult" whether based on sex, race, religion, or national origin. Relying on the EEOC's Guidelines' definition of harassment, the Court held that a plaintiff may establish a violation of Title VII "by proving that discrimination based on sex has created a hostile or abusive work environment." The Court quoted the Eleventh Circuit's decision in Henson v. City of Dundee:

> Sexual harassment which creates a hostile or offensive environment for members of one sex is every bit the arbitrary barrier to sexual equality at the workplace that racial harassment is to racial equality. Surely, a requirement that a man or woman run a gauntlet of sexual abuse in return for the privilege of being allowed to work and make a living can be as demeaning and disconcerting as the harshest of racial epithets.

The Court further held that for harassment to

378

violate Title VII, it must be "sufficiently severe or pervasive 'to alter the conditions of [the victim's] employment and create an abusive working environment."

b) Conduct Must Be "Unwelcome" --- Citing the EEOC's Guidelines, the Court said the gravamen of a sexual harassment claim is that the alleged sexual advances were "unwelcome." Therefore, "the fact that sex-related conduct was 'voluntary,' in the sense that the complainant was not forced to participate against her will, is not a defense to a sexual harassment suit brought under Title VII...The correct inquiry is whether [the victim] by her conduct indicated that the alleged sexual advances were unwelcome, not whether her actual participation in sexual intercourse was voluntary." Evidence of a complainant's sexually provocative speech or dress may be relevant in determining whether she found particular advances unwelcome, but should be admitted with caution in light of the potential for unfair prejudice, the Court held.

c) Employer Liability Established Under Agency Principles --- On the question of employer liability in "hostile environment" cases, the Court agreed with EEOC's position that agency principles should be used for guidance. While declining to issue a "definitive rule on employer liability," the Court did reject both the court of appeals' rule of automatic liability for the actions of supervisors and the employer's position that notice is always required.

The following sections of this document provide guidance on the issues addressed in <u>Vinson</u> and subsequent cases.

GUIDANCE

A.   Determining Whether Sexual Conduct Is Unwelcome
Sexual harassment is "unwelcome...verbal or physical conduct of a sexual nature..." Because sexual attraction may often play a role in the day-to-day social exchange between employees, "the distinction between invited, uninvited-but-welcome, offensive-but-tolerated, and flatly rejected" sexual advances may well be difficult to discern. <u>Barnes v. Costle</u> (Mac Kinnon J., concurring). But this distinction is essential because sexual conduct becomes unlawful only when it is unwelcome. The Eleventh Circuit provided a general definition of "unwelcome conduct" in <u>Henson v. City of Dundee</u>; the challenged conduct must be unwelcome "in the sense that the employee did not solicit or incite it, and

379

in the sense that the employee regarded the conduct as undesirable or offensive."

When confronted with conflicting evidence as to welcomeness, the Commission looks "at the record as a whole and at the totality of circumstances....", evaluating each situation on a case-by-case basis. When there is some indication of welcomeness or when the credibility of the parties is at issue, the charging party's claim will be considerably strengthened if she made a contemporaneous complaint or protest. Particularly when the alleged harasser may have some reason (e.g., a prior consensual relationship) to believe that the advances will be welcomed, it is important for the victim to communicate that the conduct is unwelcome. Generally, victims are well-advised to assert their right to a workplace free from sexual harassment. This may stop the harassment before it becomes more serious. A contemporaneous complaint or protest may also provide persuasive evidence that the sexual harassment in fact occurred as alleged (see infra Section B). Thus, in investigating sexual harassment charges, it is important to develop detailed evidence of the circumstances and nature of any such complaints or protests, whether to the alleged harasser, higher management, co-workers or others.

While a complaint or protest is helpful to charging party's case, it is not a necessary element of the claim. Indeed, the Commission recognizes that victims may fear repercussions from complaining about the harassment and that such fear may explain a delay in opposing the conduct. If the victim failed to complain or delayed in complaining, the investigation must ascertain why. The relevance of whether the victim has complained varies depending upon "the nature of the sexual advances and the context in which the alleged incidents occurred."

> Example --- Charging party (CP) alleges that her supervisor subjected her to unwelcome sexual advances that created a hostile work environment. The investigation into her charge discloses that her supervisor began making intermittent sexual advances to her in June, 1987, but she did not complain to management about the harassment. After the harassment continued and worsened, she filed a charge with EEOC in June, 1988. There is no evidence CP welcomed the advances. CP states that she feared that complaining about the harassment would cause her to lose her job. She also states that she initially believed she could

resolve the situation herself, but as the harassment became more frequent and severe, she said she realized that intervention by EEOC was necessary. The investigator determines CP is credible and concludes that the delay in complaining does not undercut CP's claim.

When welcomeness is at issue, the investigation should determine whether the victim's conduct is consistent, or inconsistent, with her assertion that the sexual conduct is unwelcome.

In Vinson, the Supreme Court made clear that voluntary submission to sexual conduct will not necessarily defeat a claim of sexual harassment. The correct inquiry "is whether (the employee) by her conduct indicated that the alleged sexual advances were unwelcome, not whether her actual participation in sexual intercourse was voluntary." See also Commission Decision No. 84-1 ("acquiescence in sexual conduct at the workplace may not mean that the conduct is welcome to the individual").

In some cases the courts and the Commission have considered whether the complaintant welcomed the sexual conduct by acting in a sexually aggressive manner, using sexually oriented language, or soliciting the sexual conduct. Thus, in Gan v. Kepro Circuit Systems, the plaintiff regularly used vulgar language, initiated sexually oriented conversations with her co-workers, asked male employees about their marital sex lives and whether they engaged in extramarital affairs, and discussed her own sexual encounters. In rejecting the plaintiff's claim of "hostile environment" harassment, the court found that any propositions or sexual remarks by co-workers were "prompted by her own sexual aggressiveness and her own sexually-explicit conversations." And in Vinson, the Supreme Court held that testimony about the plaintiff's provocative dress and publicly expressed sexual fantasies is not per se inadmissible but the trial court should carefully weight its relevance against the potential for unfair prejudice.

Conversely, occasional use of sexually explicit language does not necessarily negate a claim that sexual conduct was unwelcome. Although a charging party's use of sexual terms or off-color jokes may suggest that sexual comments by others in that situation were not unwelcome, more extreme and abusive or persistent comments or a physical assault will not be excused, nor would "quid pro quo" harassment be allowed.

Any past conduct of the charging party that is offered to show "welcomeness" must relate to the alleged harasser. In <u>Swentek v. US Air, Inc.</u>, the Fourth circuit held the district court wrongly concluded that the plaintiff's own past conduct and use of foul language showed that "she was the kind of person who could not be offended by such comments and therefore welcomed them generally, "even though she had told the harasser to leave her alone. Emphasizing that the proper inquiry is "whether plaintiff welcomed the particular conduct in question from the alleged harasser," the court of appeals held that "Plaintiff's use of foul language or sexual innuendo in a consensual setting does not waive 'her legal protections against unwelcome harassment.'" Thus, evidence concerning a charging party's general character and past behavior toward others has limited, if any, probative value and does not substitute for a careful examination of her behavior toward the alleged harasser.

A more difficult situation occurs when an employee first willingly participates in conduct of a sexual nature but then ceases to participate and claims that any continued sexual conduct has created a hostile work environment. Here the employee has the burden of showing that any further sexual conduct is unwelcome, work-related harassment. The employee must clearly notify the alleged harasser that his conduct is no longer welcome. If the conduct still continues, her failure to bring the matter to the attention of higher management or the EEOC is evidence, though not dispositive, that any continued conduct is, in fact, welcome or unrelated to work. In any case, however, her refusal to submit to the sexual conduct cannot be the basis for denying her an employment benefit or opportunity; that would constitute a "quid pro quo" violation.

B.   Evaluating Evidence of Harassment
The Commission recognizes that sexual conduct may be private and unacknowledged, with no eyewitnesses. Even sexual conduct that occurs openly in the workplace may appear to be consensual. Thus the resolution of a sexual harassment claim often depends on the credibility of the parties. The investigator should question the charging party and the alleged harasser in detail. The Commission's investigation also should search thoroughly for corroborative evidence of any nature. Supervisory and managerial employees, as well as co-workers, should be asked about their knowledge of the alleged harassment.

In appropriate cases, the Commission may make a finding of harassment based solely on the credibility of the victim's allegation. As with any other charge of

382

discrimination, a victim's account must be sufficiently detailed and internally consistent so as to be plausible, and lack of corroborative evidence where such evidence logically should exist would undermine the allegation. By the same token, a general denial by the alleged harasser will carry little weight when it is contradicted by other evidence.

Of course, the Commission recognizes that a charging party may not be able to identify witnesses to the alleged conduct itself. But testimony may be obtained from persons who observed the charging party's demeanor immediately after an alleged incident of harassment. Persons with whom she discussed the incident --- such as co-workers, a doctor or a counselor --- should be interviewed. Other employees should be asked if they noticed changes in charging party's behavior at work or in the alleged harasser's treatment of charging party. As stated earlier, a contemporaneous complaint by the victim would be persuasive evidence both that the conduct occurred and that it was unwelcome (see supra Section A). So too is evidence that other employees were sexualy harassed by the same person.

The investigator should determine whether the employer was aware of any other instances of harassment and if so what was the response. Where appropriate the Commission will expand the case to include class claims.

> Example --- Charging Party (CP) alleges that her supervisor made unwelcome sexual advances toward her on frequent occasions while they were alone in his office. The supervisor denies this allegation. No one witnessed the alleged advances. CP's inability to produce eyewitnesses to the harassment does not defeat her claim. The resolution will depend on the credibility of her allegations versus that of her supervisor's. Corroborating, credible evidence will establish her claim. For example, three coworkers state that CP looked distraught on several occasions after leaving the supervisor's office, and that she informed them on those occasions that he had sexually propositioned and touched her. In addition, the evidence shows that CP had complained to the general manager of the office about the incidents soon after they occurred. The corroborating witness testimony and her complaint to higher management would be sufficient to establish her claim. Her allegations would be further buttressed if

other employees testified that the supervisor propositioned them as well.

If the investigation exhausts all possibilities for obtaining corroborative evidence, but finds none, the Commission may make a cause finding based solely on a reasoned decision to credit the charging party's testimony.

In a "quid pro quo" case, a finding that the employer's asserted reasons for its adverse action against the charging party are pretextual will usually establish a violation. The investigation should determine the validity of the employer's reasons for the charging party's termination. If they are pretextual and if the sexual harassment occurred, then it should be inferred that the charging party was terminated for rejecting the employer's sexual advances, as she claims. Moreover, if the termination occurred because the victim complained, it would be appropriate to find, in addition, a violation of section 704(a).

C.   Determining Whether A Work Environment Is "Hostile"
     The Supreme Court said in Vinson that for sexual harassment to violate Title VII, it must be "sufficiently severe or pervasive 'to alter the conditions of (the victim's) employment and create an abusive working environment.'" Since "hostile environment harassment takes a variety of forms, many factors may affect this determination, including: (1) whether the conduct was verbal or physical, or both; (2) how frequently it was repeated; (3) whether the conduct was hostile and patently offensive; (4) whether the alleged harasser was a co-worker or a supervisor; (5) whether others joined in perpetrating the harassment; and (6) whether the harassment was directed at more than one individual.

In determining whether unwelcome sexual conduct rises to the level of a "hostile environment" in violation of Title VII, the central inquiry is whether the conduct "unreasonably interfer[es] . with an individual's work performance" or creates "an intimidating, hostile, or offensive working environment." Thus, sexual flirtation or innuendo, even vulgar language that is trivial or merely annoying, would probably not establish a hostile environment.

1)   Standard for Evaluating Harassment---In determining whether harassment is sufficiently severe or pervasive to create a hostile environment, the harasser's conduct should be evaluated from the objective standpoint of a "reasonable person." Title VII does not serve "as

384

a vehicle for vindicating the petty slights suffered by the hypersensitive." Thus, if the challenged conduct would not substantially affect the work environment of a reasonable person, no violation should be found.

> Example---Charging Party alleges that her co-worker made repeated unwelcome sexual advances toward her. An investigation discloses that the alleged "advances" consisted of invitations to join a group of employees who regularly socialized at dinner after work. The co-worker's invitations, viewed in that context and from the perspective of a reasonable person, would not have created a hostile environment and therefore did not constitute sexual harassment.

A "reasonable person" standard also should be applied to the more basic determination of whether challenged conduct is of a sexual nature. Thus, in the above example, a reasonable person would not consider the co-worker's invitations sexual in nature, and on that basis as well no violation would be found.

This objective standard should not be applied in a vacuum, however. Consideration should be given to the context in which the alleged harassment took place. As the Sixth circuit has stated, the trier of fact must "adopt the perspective of a reasonable person's reaction to a similar environment under similar or like circumstances."

The reasonable person standard should consider the victims perspective and not stereotyped notions of acceptable behavior. For example, the Commission believes that a workplace in which sexual slurs, displays of "girlie" pictures, and other offensive conduct abound can constitute a hostile work environment even if many people deem it to be harmless or insignificant.

2) Isolated Instances of Harassment---Unless the conduct is quite severe, a single incident or isolated incidents of offensive sexual conduct or remarks generally do not create an abusive environment. As the Court noted in Vinson, "mere utterance of an ethnic or racial epithet which engenders offensive feelings in an employee would not affect the conditions of employment to a sufficiently significant degree to violate Title VII." A "hostile environment" claim generally requires a showing of a pattern of offensive conduct. In contrast, in "quid pro quo" cases a single sexual advance may constitute

harassment if it is linked to the granting or denial of employment benefits.

But a single, unusually severe incident of harassment may be sufficient to constitute a Title VII violation; the more severe the harassment, the less need to show a repetitive series of incidents. This is particularly true when the harassment is physical. Thus in Barrett v. Omaha National Bank, one incident constituted actionable sexual harassment. The harasser talked to the plaintiff about sexual activities and touched her in an offensive manner while they were inside a vehicle from which she could not escape.

The Commission will presume that the unwelcome, intentional touching of a charging party's intimate body areas is sufficiently offensive to alter the conditions of her working environment and constitute a violation of Title VII. More so than in the case of verbal advances or remarks, a single unwelcome physical advance can seriously poison the victim's working environment. If a supervisor sexually touches an employee, the Commission normally would find a violation. In such situations, it is the employer's burden to demonstrate that the unwelcome conduct was not sufficiently severe to create a hostile work environment.

When the victim is the target of both verbal and nonintimate physical conduct, the hostility of the environment is exacerbated and a violation is more likely to be found. Similarly, incidents of sexual harassment directed at other employees in addition to the charging party are relevant to a showing of hostile work environment.

3) Non-physical Harassment---When the alleged harassment consists of verbal conduct, the investigation should ascertain the nature, frequency, context, and intended target of the remarks, Questions to be explored might include:

> Did the alleged harasser single out the charging party?
> Did the charging party participate?
> What was the relationship between the charging party and the alleged harasser(s)?
> Were the remarks hostile and derogatory?

No one factor alone determines whether particular conduct violates Title VII. As the Guidelines emphasize, the Commission will evaluate the totality of the circumstances. In general, a woman does not forfeit her right to be free from sexual harassment by choosing to work in an atmosphere that has traditionally included vulgar, anti-female language. However, in Rabidue v. Osceola Refining Co., the Sixth Circuit rejected the plaintiff's claim of harassment in such a situation. One of the factors the court found relevant was "the lexicon of obscenity that pervaded the environment of the workplace both before and after the plaintiff's introduction into its environs, coupled with the reasonable expectations of the plaintiff upon voluntarily entering that environment." Quoting the district court, the majority noted that in some work environments, "'humor and language are rough hewn and vulgar. Sexual jokes, sexual conversations, and girlie magazines may abound. Title VII was not meant to --- or can --- change this.'" The court also considered the sexual remarks and poster at issue to have a "de minimis effect on the plaintiff's work environment when considered in the context of a society that condones and publicly features and commercially exploits open displays of written and pictorial erotica at the newsstands, on prime-time television, at the cinema, and in other public places."

The Commission believes these factors rarely will be relevant and agrees with the dissent in Rabidue that a woman does not assume the risk of harassment by voluntarily entering an abusive, anti-female environment. "Title VII's precise purpose is to prevent such behavior and attitudes from poisoning the work environment of classes protected under the Act." Thus, in a decision disagreeing with Rabidue, a district court found that a hostile environment was established by the presence of pornographic magazines in the workplace and vulgar employee comments concerning them; offensive sexual comments made to and about plaintiff and other female employees by her supervisor; sexually oriented pictures in a company-sponsored movie and slide presentation; sexually oriented pictures and calendars in the workplace; and offensive touching of plaintiff by a co-worker. The court held that the proliferation of pornography and demeaning comments, if sufficiently continuous and pervasive, "may be found to create an atmosphere in which women are viewed as men's sexual playthings rather than as their equal co-workers." The Commission agrees that, depending on the totality of circumstances, such as atmosphere may violate Title VII. See also Waltman v. International Paper Co., (Commission's position in its amicus brief that evidence of ongoing sexual graffiti in the workplace, not all of which was directed at the plaintiff, was relevant to her claim of harassment); Bennett v. Corroon & Black Corp., (the posting of obscene cartoons in an office men's room

387

bearing the plaintiff's name and depicting her engaged in crude and deviant sexual activities could create a hostile work environment).

4)   Sex-based Harassment---Although the Guidelines specifically address conduct that is sexual in nature, the Commission notes that sex-based harassment --- that is, harassment not involving sexual activity or language --- may also give rise to Title VII liability (just as in the case of harassment based on race, national origin or religion) if it is "sufficiently patterned or pervasive" and directed at employees because of their sex.

Act of physical aggression, intimidation, hostility or unequal treatment based on sex may be combined with incidents of sexual harassment to establish the existence of discriminatory terms and conditions of employment.

5)   Constructive Discharge -- Claims of "hostile environment" sexual harassment often are coupled with claims of constructive discharge.   If constructive discharge due to a hostile environment is proven, the claim will also become one of "quid pro quo" harassment. It is the position of the Commission and a majority of courts that an employer is liable for constructive discharge when it imposes intolerable working conditions in violation of the Title VII when those conditions foreseeably would compel a reasonable employee to quit, whether or not the employer specifically intended to force the victim's resignation.   However, the Fourth Circuit requires proof that the employer imposed the intolerable conditions with the intent of forcing the victim to leave.   But this case is not a sexual harassment case and the Commission believes it is distinguishable because specific intent is not as likely to be present in "hostile environment" cases.

An important factor to consider is whether the employer had an effective internal grievance procedure. (See Section E, Preventive and Remedial Action).   The Commission argued in its <u>Vinson</u> brief that if an employee knows that effective avenues of complaint and redress are available, then the availability of such avenues itself becomes a part of the work environment and overcomes, to the degree it is effective, the hostility of the work environment.   As Justice Marshall noted in his opinion in <u>Vinson</u>, "Where a complaintant without good reason bypassed an internal complaint procedure she knew to be effective, a court may be reluctant to find constructive termination..."   Similarly, the court of appeals in <u>Dornhecker v. Malibu Grand Prix Corp.</u>, held the plaintiff

was not constructively discharged after an incident of
harassment by a co-worker because she quit immediately,
even though the employer told her she would not have to
work with him again, and she did not give the employer
a fair opportunity to demonstrate it could curb the
harasser's conduct.

D.   Employer Liability for Harassment by Supervisors

In _Vinson_, the Supreme Court agreed with the
Commission's position that "Congress wanted courts to
look to agency principles for guidance" in determining
an employer's liability for sexual conduct by a
supervisor:

> While such common-law principles may not be
> transferable in all their particulars to Title
> VII, Congress' decision to define "employer"
> to include any "agent" of an employer, 42
> U.S.C. 2000e(b), surely evinces an intent to
> place some limits on the acts of employees for
> which employers under Title VII are to be held
> responsible.

Thus, while declining to issue a "definitive rule
on employer liability," the Court did make it clear that
employers are not "automatically liable" for the acts of
their supervisors. For the same reason, the Court said,
"absence of notice to an employer does not necessarily
insulate that employer from liability."

As the Commission argued in _Vinson_, reliance on
agency principles is consistent with the Commission's
Guidelines, which provide in section 1604.11(c) that:

> . . . an employer . . . is responsible for its
> acts and those of its agents and supervisory
> employees with respect to sexual harassment
> regardless of whether the specific acts
> complained of were authorized or even forbidden
> by the employer and regardless of whether the
> employer knew or should have known of their
> occurrence. The Commission will examine the
> circumstances of the particular employment
> relationship and the job functions performed
> by the individual in determining whether an
> individual acts in either a supervisory or
> agency capacity.

Citing the last sentence of this provision, the
Court in _Vinson_ indicated that the Guidelines further
supported the application of agency principles.

1)   Application of Agency Principles--"Quid Pro Quo"
Cases--An employer will always be held responsible for
acts of "quid pro quo" harassment. A supervisor in such
circumstances has made or threatened to make a decision
affecting the victim's employment status, and he
therefore has exercised authority delegated to him
by his employer.   Although the question of employer
liability for "quid pro quo" harassment was not at issue
in Vinson, the Court's decision noted with apparent
approval the position taken by the Commission in its
brief that:

> where a supervisor exercises the authority
> actually delegated to him by his employer, by
> making or threatening to make decisions
> affecting the employment status of his
> subordinates, such actions are properly imputed
> to the employer whose delegation of authority
> empowered the supervisor to undertake them.

Thus, applying agency principles, the court in
Schroeder v. Schock, held an employer liable for "quid
pro quo" harassment by a supervisor who had authority to
recommend plaintiff's discharge. The employer maintained
the supervisor's acts were beyond the scope of his
employment since the sexual advances were made at a
restaurant after work hours. The court held that because
the supervisor was acting within the scope of his
authority when making or recommending employment
decisions, his conduct may fairly be imputed to the
employer.   The supervisor was using his authority to
hire, fire, and promote to extort sexual consideration
from an employee, even though the sexual advance itself
occurred way form work.

2)   Application of Agency   Principles---"Hostile
Environment" Cases.
     a) Vinson --- In its Vinson brief the Commission
argued that the employer should be liable for the
creation of a hostile environment by a supervisor when
the employer knew or had reason to know of the sexual
misconduct.   Ways by which actual or constructive
knowledge could be demonstrated include: by a complaint
to management or an EEOC charge; by the pervasiveness of
the harassment; or by evidence the employer had
"deliberately turned its back on the problem" of sexual
harassment by failing to establish a policy against it
and a grievance mechanism to redress it.   The brief
argued that an employer should be liable "if there is no
reasonable available avenue by which victims of sexual
harassment can make their complaints known to appropriate
officials who are in a position to do something about
those complaints." Under that circumstance, an employer

could be deemed to know of any harassment that occurred in its workplace.

While the <u>Vinson</u> decision quoted the Commission's brief at length, neither endorsed nor rejected its position. The Court did state, however, that "the mere existence of a grievance procedure and a policy against discrimination, coupled with [the victim's] failure to invoke the procedure" are "plainly relevant" but "not necessarily dispositive." The Court further stated that the employer's argument that the victim's failure to complain insulated it from liability "might be substantially stronger if its procedures were better calculated to encourage victims of harassment to come forward."

The Commission, therefore, interprets <u>Vinson</u> to require a careful examination in "hostile environment" cases of whether the harassing supervisor was acting in an "agency capacity." Whether the employer had an appropriate and effective complaint procedure and whether the victim used it are important factors to consider, as discussed below.

b) Direct Liability --- The initial inquiry should be whether the employer knew or should have known of the alleged sexual harassment. If actual or constructive knowledge exists, and if the employer failed to take immediate and appropriate corrective action, the employer would be directly liable. Most commonly an employer acquires actual knowledge through first-hand observation, by the victim's internal complaint to other supervisors or managers, or by a charge of discrimination.

An employer is liable when it "knew, or upon reasonably diligent inquiry should have know," of the harassment. <u>Yates v. Avco Corp.</u>, (supervisor harassed two women "on a daily basis in the course of his supervision of them" and the employer's grievance procedure did not function effectively). Thus, evidence of the pervasiveness of the harassment may give rise to an inference of knowledge or establish constructive knowledge. Employers usually will be deemed to know of sexual harassment that is openly practiced in the workplace or well-known among employees. This often may be the case when there is more than one harasser or victim. Lipsett, (employer liable where it should have known of concerted harassment of plaintiff and other female medical residents by more senior male residents).

The victim can of course put the employer on notice by filing a charge of discrimination. As the Commission stated in its <u>Vinson</u> brief, the filing of a charge triggers a duty to investigate and remedy any ongoing illegal activity. It is important to emphasize that an employee can always file an EEOC charge without first utilizing an internal complaint or grievance procedure, and may wish to pursue both avenues simultaneously because an internal grievance does not prevent the Title VII charge-filing time period from expiring. Nor does the filing of an EEOC charge allow an employer to cease action on an internal grievance or ignore evidence of ongoing harassment. Indeed, employers should take prompt remedial action upon learning of evidence of sexual harassment (or any other form of unlawful discrimination), whether from an EEOC charge or an internal complaint. If the employer takes immediate and appropriate action to correct the harassment and prevent its recurrence, and the Commission determines that no further action is warranted, normally the Commission would administratively close the case.

c) Imputed Liability --- The investigation should determine whether the alleged harassing supervisor was acting in an "agency capacity." This requires a determination whether the supervisor was acting within the scope of his employment or whether his actions can be imputed to the employer under some exception to the "scope of employment" rule. The following principles should be considered, and applied where appropriate in "hostile environment" sexual harassment cases.

1. Scope of Employment --- A supervisor's actions are generally viewed as being within the scope of his employment if they represent the exercise of authority actually vested in him. It will rarely be the case that an employer will have authorized a supervisor to engage in sexual harassment. However, if the employer becomes aware of work-related sexual misconduct and does nothing to stop it, the employer, by acquiescing, has brought the supervisor's actions within the scope of his employment.

2. Apparent Authority --- An employer is also liable for a supervisor's actions if these actions represent the exercise of authority that third parties reasonably believe him to possess by virtue of his employer's conduct. This is called "apparent authority." The Commission believes that in the absence of a strong, widely disseminated, and consistently enforced employer policy against sexual harassment, and an effective complaint procedure, employees could reasonably believe that a harassing supervisor's actions will be ignored, tolerated, or even condoned by upper management. This apparent authority of supervisors arises from their power

392

over their employees, including the power to make or substantially influence hiring, firing, promotion and compensation decisions. A supervisor's capacity to create a hostile environment is enhanced by the degree of authority conferred on him by the employer, and he may rely upon apparent authority to force an employee to endure a harassing environment for fear of retaliation. If the employer has not provided an effective avenue to complain, then the supervisor has unchecked, final control over the victim and it is reasonable to impute his abuse of this power to the employer. The Commission generally will find an employer liable for "hostile environment" sexual harassment by a supervisor when the employer failed to establish an explicit policy against sexual harassment and did not have a reasonably available avenue by which victims of sexual harassment could complain to someone with authority to investigate and remedy the problem. (See Section E.) See also EEOC v. Hacienda Hotel, (finding employer liable for sexual harassment despite plaintiff's failure to pursue internal remedies where the employer's anti-discrimination policy did not specifically proscribe sexual harassment and its internal procedures required initial resort to the supervisor accused of engaging in or condoning harassment).

But an employer can divest its supervisors of this apparent authority by implementing a strong policy against sexual harassment and maintaining an effective complaint procedure. When employees know that recourse is available, they cannot reasonably believe that a harassing work environment is authorized or condoned by the employer. If an employee failed to use an effective, available complaint procedure, the employer may be able to prove the absence of apparent authority and thus the lack of an agency relationship, unless liability attaches under some other theory. Thus, even when an employee failed to use an effective grievance procedure, the employer will be liable if it obtained notice through other means (such as the filing of a charge or by the pervasiveness of the harassment) and did not take immediate and appropriate corrective action.

> Example --- Charging Party (CP) alleges that her supervisor made repeated sexual advances toward her that created a hostile work environment. The investigation into her charge discloses that CP had maintained an intermittent romantic relationship with the supervisor over a period of three years preceding the filing of the charge in September of 1986. CP's employer was aware of this relationship and its consensual nature. CP

asserts, however, that on frequent occasions since January of 1986 she had clearly stated to the supervisor that their relationship was over and his advances were no longer welcome. The supervisor nevertheless persisted in making sexual advances toward CP, berating her for refusing to resume their sexual relationship. His conduct did not put the employer on notice that any unwelcome harassment was occuring. The employer has a well-communicated policy against sexual harassment and a complaint procedure designed to facilitate the resolution of sexual harassment complaints and ensure against retaliation. This procedure has worked well in the past. CP did not use it, however, or otherwise complain to higher management. Even if CP's allegations are true, the Commission would probably not find her employer liable for the alleged harassment since she failed to use the complaint procedure or inform higher management that the advances had become unwelcome. If CP resigned because of the alleged harassment, she would not be able to establish a constructive discharge since she failed to complain.

In the preceding example, if the employer, upon obtaining notice of the charge, failed to take immediate and appropriate corrective action to stop any ongoing harassment, then the employer will be unable to prove that the supervisor lacked apparent authority for his conduct, and if the allegations of harassment are true, then the employer will be found liable. Or if the supervisor terminated the charging party because she refused to submit to his advances, the employer would be liable for "quid pro quo" harassment.

3. Other Theories --- A closely related theory is agency by estoppel. An employer is liable when he intentionally or carelessly causes an employee to mistakenly believe the supervisor is acting for the employer, or knows of the misapprehension and fails to correct it. For example, an employer who fails to respond appropriately to past known incidents of harassment would cause its employees to reasonably believe that any further incidents are authorized and will be tolerated.

Liability also may be imputed if the employer was "negligent or reckless" in supervising the alleged harasser. "Under this standard, liability would be imposed if the employer had actual or constructive knowledge of sexual harassment but failed to take remedial action." This is essentially the same as holding the employer directly liable for its failure to act.

An employer cannot avoid liability by delegating to another person a duty imposed by statute. An employer who assigns the performance of a non-delegable duty to an employee remains liable for injuries resulting from the failure of the employee to carry out that duty. Title VII imposes on employers a duty to provide their employees with a workplace free of sexual harassment. An employer who entrusts that duty to an employee is liable for injuries caused by the employee's breach of the duty. See, e.g., <u>Brooms v. Regal Tube Co.</u>, (employer liable for sexual harassment committed by the management official to whom it had delegated the responsibility to devise and enforce its policy against sexual harassment).

Finally, an employer also may be liable if the supervisor "was aided in accomplishing the tort by the existence of the agency relations". For example, in <u>Sparks v. Pilot Freight Carriers</u>, the court found that the supervisor had used his supervisory authority to facilitate his harassment of the plaintiff by "repeatedly reminding [her] that he could fire her should she fail to comply with his advances." This case illustrates how the two types of sexual harassment can merge. When a supervisor creates a hostile environment through the aid of work-related threats or intimidation, the employer is liable under both the "quid pro quo" and "hostile environment" theories.

E.   Preventive and Remedial Action
     1)   Preventive Action --- The EEOC's Guidelines encourage employers to:
          take all steps necessary to prevent sexual harassment from occuring, such as affirmatively raising the subject, expressing strong disapproval, developing appropriate sanctions, informing employees of their right to raise and how to raise the issue of harassment under Title VII, and developing methods to sensitize all concerned.

An effective preventive program should include an explicit policy against sexual harassment that is clearly and regularly communicated to employees and effectively implemented. The employer should affirmatively raise the subject with all supervisory and non-supervisory employees, express strong disapproval, and explain the sanctions for harassment. The employer should also have a procedure for resolving sexual harassment complaints. The procedure should be designed to "encourage victims of harassments to come forward" and should not require a victim to complain first to the offending supervisor. It should ensure confidentiality as much as possible and provide effective remedies, including protection of victims and witnesses against retaliation.

2) Remedial Action --- Since Title VII "affords employees the right to work in an environment free from discriminatory intimidation, ridicule, and insult", an employer is liable for failing to remedy known hostile or offensive work environments. See, e.g., Garziano v. E.I. DuPont deNemours & Co., (Vinson holds employers have an "affirmative duty to eradicate 'hostile or offensive' work environments"); Bundy v. Jackson, (employer violated Title VII by failing to investigate and correct sexual harassment despite notice); Munford v. James T. Barnes & Co., (employer has an affirmative duty to investigate complaints of sexual harassment and to deal appropriately with the offending personnel; "failure to investigate gives tacit support to the discrimination because the absence of sanctions encourages abusive behavior").

When an employer receives a complaint or otherwise learns of alleged sexual harassment in the workplace, the employer should investigate promptly and thoroughly. The employer should take immediate and appropriate corrective action by doing whatever is necessary to end the harassment, make the victim whole by restoring lost employment benefits or opportunities, and prevent the misconduct from recurring. Disciplinary action against the offending supervisor or employee, ranging from reprimand to discharge, may be necessary. Generally, the corrective action should reflect the severity of the conduct. See Waltman v. International Paper Co. (appropriateness of remedial action will depend on the severity and persistence of the harassment and the effectiveness of any initial remedial steps). Dornhecker v. Malibu Grand Prix Corp., (the employer's remedy may be "assessed proportionately to the seriousness of the offense"). The employer should make follow-up inquiries to ensure the harassment has not resumed and the victim has not suffered retaliation.

Recent court decisions illustrate appropriate and inappropriate responses by employers. In Barrett v. Omaha National Bank, the victim informed her employer that her co-worker had talked to her about sexual activities and touched her in an offensive manner. Within four days of receiving this information, the employer investigated the charges, reprimanded the guilty employee, placed him on probation, and warned him that further misconduct would result in discharge. A second co-worker who had witnessed the harassment was also reprimanded for not intervening on the victim's behalf or reporting the conduct. This court ruled that the employer's response constituted immediate and appropriate corrective action, and on this basis found the employer not liable. In contrast, in <u>Yates v. Avco Corp.</u>, the court found the employer's policy against sexual harassment failed to function effectively. The victim's first level supervisor had responsibility for reporting and correcting harassment at the company, yet he was the harasser. The employer told the victims not to go to the EEOC. While giving the accused harasser administrative leave pending investigation, the employer made the plaintiffs take sick leave, which was never credited back to them and was recorded in their personnel files as excessive absenteeism without indicating they were absent because of sexual harassment. Similarly, in <u>Zabkowicz v. West Bend Co.</u>, co-workers harassed the plaintiff over a period of nearly four years in a manner the court described as "malevolent" and "outrageous." Despite the plaintiff's numerous complaints, her supervisor took no remedial action other than to hold occasional meetings at which he reminded employees of the company's policy against offensive conduct. The supervisor never conducted an investigation or disciplined any employees until the plaintiff filed an EEOC charge, at which time one of the offending co-workers was discharged and three others were suspended. The court held the employer liable because it failed to take immediate and appropriate corrective action.

When the employer asserts it has taken remedial action, the Commission will investigate to determine whether the action was appropriate and, more important, effective. The EEOC investigator should, of course, conduct an independent investigation of the harassment claim, and the Commission will reach its own conclusion as to whether the law has been violated. If the Commission finds that the harassment has been eliminated, all victims made whole, and preventive measures instituted, the Commission normally will administratively close the charge because of the employer's prompt remedial action.

CHAPTER IX

THE FUTURE OF BUSINESS

INTRODUCTION

One aim throughout this text has been to prepare you
to think about the future of business and how business
will change over the next decades. As you read the
articles in this chapter try to formulate a statement of
the problems which you feel businesses are going to face
in the twenty-first century. Are the solutions proposed
by the authors in the text feasible, are they consistent
with the basic values of business society as described
in other selections? What assumptions regarding the
nature of business, and its values, are implicit in the
authors' remarks?

Thurow and Drucker ask you to consider alternatives
to revitalize capitalism. As in the earlier article on
institutionalizing unethical behavior, the authors are
critical of the emphasis of modern business management
on short term profits. Do you agree with their reasons
against short term profit taking, with their arguments
against taking shareholder interest as paramount over the
interests of other stakeholders? Are the authors arguing
that there should be new laws in order to implement these
changes, even though such laws will infringe upon the
market? In light of the competitive nature of business,
is it feasible for business to implement these changes
without government interference?

Professor Bowie suggests more radical problems and
solutions for modern business. Do you agree with him
that one of the most important function of business is
to provide meaningful work to employees? What if
meaningful work for employees limits an employer's short
term profits? Is the author's suggestion consistent with
a competitive society where if you want meaningful work
you must compete to create those opportunities for your
self?

Lastly, one ideology about the future of business which
continues to attract many persons worldwide is socialism.
I have included a section on socialism, because many
business persons with whom you will deal in the future
will consider themselves socialist. You should,
therefore, have some understanding of what is attractive
about this ideology. The selection from Professor Walzer
begins with a sympathic picture of socialism; yet he
raises important criticisms of a future socialist

society. In particular, he argues that socialism will "take too many evenings." What does he mean by that? Does modern representative democracy also take too many evenings? Is it possible to have a democratic society which requires that citizens spend a great deal of time in order to vote intelligently, along side a competitive business society which requires that citizens devote a great deal of time to business enterprises?

In conclusion, after this chapter you should tie together all the materials from the earlier sections and consider what business will be like in your future. How much of what you have learned will be changed by rapid technological and social developments; how much will continue to be valuable?

QUESTIONS AND PROJECTS

1.   Write a speech to a national business organization describing the future of American business with specific suggestions regarding desirable changes to be implemented and undesirable changes to be avoided.

2.   Write a dialogue between a socialist business person and a capitalist discussing the relative merits of these economic and political systems.

MANAGEMENT: The Problems of Success
Peter F. Drucker

Thirty years after City Manager Luther Gulick applied management principles to the running of a municipality, the Federal Government, which had grown out of control in the New Deal years, was finally organized more effectively. It was not until 1950 and 1951, that is, more than 10 years later, that similar management concepts and principles were systematically applied in a business enterprise to a similar task: the reorganization of the General Electric Company after it had outgrown its earlier, purely functional organization structure.

Today, surely, there is as much "management" outside of business as there is in business - maybe more. The most management-concious of our present institutions is probably the military, followed closely by the hospital. Half the clients of a typical management consulting firm are nonbusinesses: government agencies, the military, schools and universities, hospitals, museums, professional associations, and community agencies like the Boy Scouts or the Red Cross. Increasingly, holders of the advanced degree in business administration, the MBA, are the preferred recruits for careers in city management, in art museums, and in the Federal Government's Office of Management and Budget.

Yet most people still hear the word business when they hear or read the word management. Management books outsell all other nonfiction books on the best-seller lists, yet are normally reviewed on the business page. And while one graduate business school after another renames itself the School of Management, the degree they award has remained the Master of Business Administration. Most management books, whether for college classes or the general reader, deal mainly with business and use business examples or business cases.

From <u>Academy of Management Executive</u> (1987), 13-19. Reprinted by permission of Peter F. Drucker and the Academy of Management Executive. Copyright 1987. Endnotes omitted.

A SOCIAL FUNCTION AND ORGAN

Why is this so? Simply, the business enterprise, though not the first of the managed institutions, did not evolve gradually out of traditional organizations as the others did, but represented a fairly radical and highly visible development. No one could possibly have mistaken the new business enterprise, as it arose in the third quarter of the nineteenth century, for a direct continuation of the old and traditional "business firm" - the "counting house" with two elderly brothers and one clerk, which figures so prominently in Charles Dickens's popular books.

For one, the new business enterprise - the long-distance railroad that developed in the United States after the Civil War, the "Universal Bank" that developed on the European continent at the same time, the "Trusts" such as U. S. Steel, which J. P. Morgan forged in this country at the turn of the twentieth century - were not run by owners. Indeed, there were no owners, but shareholders. To accommodate the new business enterprise, a new and different legal person had to be invented: the corporation. In the "corporation," shares become a claim to profits rather than property. And capital is provided by large numbers of outsiders, each of whom holds only a minute fraction of the total and none of whom necessarily has any interest in or - a totally unheard of circumstance - any liability for the conduct of the business.

This new corporation could not be explained away as a reform, which is how the new army, the new university, and the new hospital presented themselves. It clearly was a genuine innovation. And this innovation soon came to provide the new jobs, at first for the rapidly growing urban proletarians and then for educated people as well. It soon came to dominate the economy. What in the older institutions could be explained as different procedures, different rules, became in the new institution a new function: management. An this function invited study, it invited attention and controversy. But even more extraordinary and unprecedented was the position of this newcomer in society. It was the first new autonomous institution in many hundreds of years, the first power center in society in hundreds of years that was independent of the central government of the national state. This was an offense, a violation of everything the nineteenth century considered (and the twentieth-century political scientists still consider) the "law of history" and, frankly, a scandal.

By now, almost a hundred years after management arose in the early large business enterprises of the 1870s, it is clear that management pertains to every single social institution. In the last hundred years every major social function - caring for the sick, education, and defense, for example - had become lodged in a large and managed organization. The identification of management with business can thus no longer be maintained. Management has become the pervasive, the universal organ of a modern society.

For modern society has become a society of organizations. The overwhelming majority of all people in developed societies are employees of an organization; they derive their livelihood from the collected income of an organization, see their opportunities for career and success primarily as opportunities within an organization, and define their social status largely through their position within the ranks of an organization. Increasingly, especially in the United States, the only way an individual can amass property is through the pension fund - that is, through membership in an organization.

In a society of organizations, managing becomes a social function and management the constitutive, the determining, the differential organ of society.

The New Pluralism

The society of organizations, then, is a pluralist society. The dogma of the "liberal state," still taught in our university departments of government and in our law schools, says that all organized power is vested in one central government. (The clearest modern formulation of this dogma is the "Pure Theory of Law," which the Austro-American jurist and philosopher, Hans Kelsen, developed in the 1920s, to worldwide renown.) However, in open defiance of the prevailing dogma, society contains a diversity of organizations and power centers.

The institutions of today's New Pluralism, though, are very different from those of the Old Pluralism - the princes and feudal barons, the free cities, the artisans, the religious institutions of Medieval Europe and Japan. Those institutions acted as separate governments. They levied taxes, for example, and established churches and schools.

The purpose of today's pluralist institutions - to make and sell goods and services, to protect jobs and wages, to heal the sick, to teach the young, and so on

403

- is nongovernmental. Each exists to do something that is different from what government does - or to do something so that government need not do it.

The institutions of the New Pluralism have no purpose except outside of themselves. They exist in contemplation of a "customer" or a "market." Achievement in the hospital is not a satisfied nurse, but a cured ex-patient. Achievement in the business is not a happy work force, however desirable that may be, but a satisfied customer who reorders the product.

All institutions of the New Pluralism, unlike those of the Old, are single-purpose institutions. They are tools of society to supply one specific social need, whether it be making or selling cars, giving telephone service, curing the sick, teaching children to read, or providing benefits checks to unemployed workers. To make this one specialized contribution, they need a considerable measure of autonomy: they need to be organized in perpetuity, or at least for long periods of time; they need to dispose of a considerable amount of society's resources - land, raw materials, money, and, above all, highly trained and highly educated people - and they need a considerable amount of power over people, coercive power at that. It is only too easy to forget that in the not-so-distant past, only slaves, low-level servants, and convicts had to be at the job at a time set for them by someone else.

This institution has - and has to have - power to bestow or to withhold social recognition and economic rewards. Whichever method we use to select people for assignments and promotions - appointment from above, selection by one's peers, even rotation among the jobs - these are always power decisions made for the individual on the basis of impersonal criteria related to the organization's purpose. The individual is at the mercy of a power grounded in the value system of whatever specific social purpose the institution has been created to satisfy. And the organ through which this power is exercised in the institution is the organ we call "management."

The features of the New Pluralism immediately raise a question: Who takes care of the Common Weal when society is organized in individual power centers, each of which is concerned with a specific goal rather than with the common good?

Each institution in a pluralist society sees its own purpose as the central and the most important. Indeed,

404

it cannot do otherwise. The school, for instance, cannot function unless it sees teaching and research as the tools that make a good society and good citizens. Surely nobody chooses to go into hospital administration or into nursing unless he or she believes in health as an absolute value. And, as countless failed mergers and acquisitions attest, no management will do a good job running a company unless it believes in the product or service the company supplies, and unless it respects the company's customers and their values.

Yet each of these "missions" is one, and only one, dimension of the common good. They're important, yes; indispensable, perhaps; yet a relative rather than an absolute good. As such they must be limited by, balanced with, and often subordinated to, other considerations. Somehow the common good must be made to emerge out of the clash and clamor of special interests. Can the New Pluralism do this? One solution is, of course, to suppress the pluralist institutions. The totalitarian state, whether it calls itself Fascist, Nazi, Stalinist, or Maoist, makes all institutions subservient to and extensions of the state (or of the omnipotent "Party"), stripping away all free thought and expression.

The State (or the "Party") is then indeed the only power center, as traditional theory preaches. But it can maintain its monopoly on power only as Lenin was first to realize, if it is based on naked terror. And even at that horrible price, it does not really work. As we all know - and the experience of all totalitarian regimes is exactly the same, whether they call themselves "rightist" or "leftist" - pluralist institutions persist behind the monolithic facade. They can be deprived of their autonomy only if they and society altogether are rendered unable to perform, such as through Stalin's "purges" or Mao's Cultural Revolution."

The opposite approach to that of the totalitarian state is the American system. Each of the "interests" in the United States is free to pursue its own goals regardless of the common good; it is indeed expected to do so. The American pluralist doctrine is, however, hardly adequate. Indeed, just as the Old Pluralism did, the New Pluralism has given birth to so many vested interests and pressure groups that it is almost impossible to conduct the business of government, let alone to conduct it for the common good. For the past two years, almost everyone in the United States has agreed that the country needs a drastic tax reform - with a few tax rates, and with exemptions eliminated - to replace an increasingly complicated and irrational tax code. Congress had a tough time enacting such a code this past year. Although not a drastic change, a new tax law was signed into law October 1986. The tax laws therefore have undergone change. Yet, vested interests will remain, no doubt, just in different forms.

Is there a way out? The Japanese seem to be the only ones so far able to reconcile a society of organizations with the pursuit of the common good. The major Japanese interests are expected to take their cue based on what is good for the country. They are expected to fit what will benefit them into the framework of a public policy designed to serve the national interest. It is doubtful, however, whether even Japan can long maintain this approach. It reflects a past in which Japan saw itself as isolated in a hostile and alien world - so that all of its interests had to hang together lest they hang separately. Will this approach have a chance in the West, where interests have traditionally been expected to behave as interests? Some will ask, "Is this a problem of management? Is it not a problem of politics, of government, or political philosophy?" But if management does not tackle it, then political solutions will almost inevitably be imposed. When, for instance, the health-care institutions in the United States did not take responsibility for spiraling health-care costs, the government imposed such regulations as the Medicare restrictions for the care of the aged in hospitals. And these rules clearly do not benefit health care at all; in fact, they may even be detrimental to it. They are designed to serve short-run fiscal concerns of government and employers - that is, to substitute a different but equally one-sided approach for the one-sided, self-centered approach of the health-care interests.

This must be the outcome unless the managements of the institutions of the New Pluralism see it as their job to reconcile concern for the common good with the pursuit of the special mission for which their institution exists.

The Legitimacy of Management

To be effective in any way, however, management must have legislative power - that is, power grounded in something transcending the organization that is accepted as a genuine value, if not a true absolute, by those subject to the power. Such values have included "Descent from the Gods" or "Apostolic Succession," the Consent of the Governed," "popular election", or what is so valued by so much of modern society, the magical "advanced

406

degree." If power is an end in itself, it becomes despotism, which is both illegitimate and tyrannical.

Here we encounter a puzzle. Management of the key institutions of our society of organizations is by and large accepted as legitimate. The single exception is the management of the business enterprise. Indeed, society is often more concerned with the survival of a large business or an industry than it is with that of any other single institution. And desperate attempts are made to salvage a major business in trouble. But at the same time, business enterprise is suspect. Any exercise of management power is denounced "usurpation," with cries from all sides for legislation or judicial action to curb, if not suppress altogether, managerial power.

One common explanation is that the large business enterprise wields more power than any other institution. But this simply does not hold water. Not only is business enterprise hemmed in - by government and government regulations, by labor unions, and so on - in exercising its power; but the power of even the largest and wealthiest business enterprise is insignificant next to that of the university, now that college degree has become a prerequisite for access to any but the most menial jobs. The university and its management are often criticized; but their legitimacy is rarely questioned. The large labor union in western European and U. S. mass-production industries surely holds more power than any single business enterprise there or here. But even its most bitter critics rarely question the union's legitimacy.

Another explanation - the prevalent one these days - is that the managements of all other institutions are "altruistic," whereas business is "profit seeking," "out for itself," and "materialistic." But even if, for many people, "non-profit" is virtuous and "profit" dubious, the explanation that profit undermines the legitimacy of business management is hardly adequate. In all Western countries the legitimacy of owners and their profits is generally accepted. Yet professional management obtains profits for other people rather than for itself - and its main beneficiaries today are the pension funds of employers.

And then there is the situation in Japan. In no other country, not even in France or in Sweden, was the intellectual climate of the post-war period as hostile to profit as in Japan, at least until 1970 or so. The left-wing intelligentsia of Japan in the universities or the newspapers might have wanted to nationalize Japan's big businesses, but it never occurred even to the purest Marxist among them to question the necessity of management or its legitimacy. The reason clearly lies in the image that Japanese management has of itself and presents to its society. In Japanese law, as in American and European law, management is the servant of the stockholders; the reality is that the behavior of Japanese big business management (even in companies that are family-owned and family-managed, like Toyota) is that management is an organ of the business itself. Management is the servant of the "going concern," bringing together in a common interest a number of constituencies: employees first, then customers, then creditors, and finally suppliers. Stockholders are only a special group of creditors, rather than "the owners" for whose sake the enterprise exists.

Of course, as their performance shows, Japanese businesses are not run as philanthropies. They know how to obtain economic results. In fact, the Japanese banks, which are the real powers in the Japanese economy watch economic performance closely and move in on a poorly performing or lackluster top management much faster than do the boards of Western publicly held companies. But the Japanese have institutionalized the "going concern" and its values through "lifetime employment," under which the employee's claim to job and income comes first, unless the survival of the enterprise itself is endangered.

The Japanese formulation presents real problems, especially now that rapid structural change in technology and economy demand labor mobility. Still, the Japanese example indicates why management legitimacy is a problem in the West. Business management in the West (and, in particular, business management in the United States) has not yet realized that our society has become a society of organizations, of which management is the critical organ.

Thirty years ago or so, when the serious study of management began, Ralph Cordiner, then CEO of the (American) General Electric Company, tried to reformulate the responsibility of corporate top management. He called it the "trustee for the balanced best interest of stockholders, employees, customers, suppliers, and plant communities" - the group that would later be called "stakeholders" or "constituencies."

As a slogan this caught on fast. Countless other American companies wrote it into their "corporate philosophy" statements. But neither Mr. Cordiner nor any

408

of the other chairmen and presidents who embraced his rhetoric did what the Japanese have done:institutionalize their professions. They did not determine what the "best balanced interest" of these different "stakeholders" would be, how to judge performance against such an objective, and how to create accountability for it. The statement remained a good intention, and good intentions are not enough to make power legitimate.

Underlying the wave of hostile takeovers that has been inundating the American economy these last few years - and is spilling over into Europe now - is the belief that the business enterprise exists solely for the sake of stockholder profits, and short-run, immediate profits at that.

By now it has become accepted widely - except on Wall Street and among Wall Street lawyers - that the hostile takeover is deleterious and in fact one of the major causes of the loss of America's competitive position in the world economy. One way or another, the hostile takeover will be stopped. No matter how, the solution will have tackled the problem of management legitimacy.

We know some of the specifications for the solution. First, the performance of a business - its market standing, the quality of its products or services, and its performance as an innovator - must be safeguarded. And financial performance must be controlled. If the takeover boom has taught us one thing, it is that management must not be allowed substandard financial performance.

Somehow the various "stakeholders" also have to be brought into the management process. And somehow the maintenance of the wealth-producing and job-producing capacities of the enterprise - that is, the maintenance of the "going concerns" - needs to be built into our legal and institutional arrangements. It should not be too difficult. After all, we built the preservation of the "going concern" into our bankruptcy laws all of 90 years ago when we gave it priority over all other claims, including the claims of the creditors.

Closely connected to the problem of management legitimacy is management compensation. To be legitimate, management must be accepted as a professional occupation. While professionals have always been paid well and deserve to be paid well it has always been considered unprofessional to put money ahead of professional responsibility and professional standards. This means

409

there must be limitations on managerial incomes. It is surely not "professional" for a chief executive officer to give himself a bonus of several million dollars when the pay of the company's other employees is being cut by 30% - as the chief executive officer of Chrysler did a few years ago. It is surely not professional for employees - who are not owners - to pay themselves salaries and bonuses greatly in excess of what their own colleagues in the organization receive. And it is not professional to pay oneself a salary and bonus so far above the norm that it creates social tension, envy, and resentment.

Work is needed on the preparation, testing, and selection of, and on the succession to, the top management jobs in the large business enterprise; on the structure of top management and the institutional arrangements for monitoring and enforcing them. Business must also determine what its "social responsibilities" are - and what they are not. Surely business - like any organization or person, for that matter - is responsible for its impacts. Responsibility for one's impacts is, after all, one of the oldest tenets of the law. And surely business is in violation of its responsibilities if it allows itself impacts beyond those necessary to and implicit in its social purpose, which is to produce goods and services. To overstep these limits constitutes a "tort," that is, a violation.

But what about problems that do not result from an impact or any other activity of business and yet constitute grave social ills? Clearly it is not a responsibility of business, or of any organization, to act where it lacks competence. But it can act in areas in which it has competence to treat social problems. When New York City was on the verge of self-destruction in the late 1960's and early 1970's, a small group of senior executives of major New York business enterprises mobilized the business community to reverse the downward slide.

Is there a message in this? There surely is a challenge. For management of the big business to attain full legitimacy while remaining "private," it will have to accept that it has a social, a "public," role and function.

The Job as Property Right

That social role applies to its relationship to its employees. Consider, for example, that in 1985 a fair-size Japanese company found itself suddenly

410

threatened by a hostile takeover bid made by a group of American and British "raiders," the first such bid in recent Japanese history. The company's management asserted that the real owners of the business, and the only ones who could possibly sell it, were not the stockholders, but the employees. This was considerable exaggeration, to be sure. But it is true that the rights of the employees to their jobs are the first and overriding claim in a large Japanese company, except when the business faces a crisis so severe that its very survival is at stake.

To Western ears, the Japanese company statement sounded very strange. But actually the United States, and the West in general, may be as far along in making the employee the dominant "interest" in business enterprise as is Japan. All along, of course, the employees' share of the revenues of a business, almost regardless of its size, has exceeded what the owners can possibly hope to get. It ranges from four times as large (that is, 7% for profits post-tax, against 25% for wages and salaries) to 12 times as large (that is, 5% for profits versus 60% of revenues for wages and salaries). The pension fund greatly increased the share of the revenues that go into the "wage fund" to the point that in poor years the pension fund may claim the entire profit and more. Moreover, American law now gives the pension fund priority over the stockholders and their proper rights in a company's liquidation, a provision way beyond anything Japanese law and custom give to the Japanese worker.

Above all, the West, with the United States in the lead, is rapidly converting the individual employee's job into a new property right - at the very time, paradoxically, at which the absolute primacy of stockholder short-term rights is being asserted in and by the hostile takeover.

The vehicle for this transformation in the United States is not the union contract or laws mandating severance pay, as it is in many European countries. The vehicle is the lawsuit. First came the suit alleging discrimination on grounds of race, sex, age, or handicap in the hiring, firing, promotion, pay, or job assignment of an employee.

But increasingly these suits do not even allege discrimination: they allege violation of "due process," claiming that the enjoyment of a job and its fruits - which include pay and any promotions expected - can be diminished or taken away on the basis of pre-set and

411

objective standards and through an established process that includes an impartial review and the right to appeal. This is how property has been treated in the history of the law. And as few managements yet realize, in practically every such suit the plaintiff wins and the employer loses. This development was predictable. Indeed, it was inevitable. And it is irreversible. It is also not "novel" or "radical." What gives access to a society's productive resources gives access thereby to a livelihood and to social function and status and constitutes a major, if not the major, avenue to economic independence. This independence, however modest, has always been a "property right" in Western society. And this is what the job has become, especially the knowledge worker's job as a manager or a professional.

We still call land "real" property. For until quite recently it was land alone that gave 95% or more of the population what property gives: access to, and control over, society's productive resources; access to a livelihood and to social status and function; and, finally, a chance at "estate" (the term itself meant, at first, a land holding) and, with it, economic independence.

In today's developed societies, however, all but 5 or 10% of the population gain access to and control over productive resources and access to a livelihood and to social status and function by being an employee of an organization. For highly educated people the job is practically the only access route. Ninety-five percent or more of all people with college degrees will spend their entire working lives as employees of an organization. The modern organization is the first, and so far the only, place where we can put large numbers of highly educated people to productive work and pay them for applying knowledge.

For the great majority of Americans, moreover, the pension fund at their place of employment is their only access to an estate - that is, economic independence. By the time the main breadwinner, white collar or blue collar, in the American family is 45 years old, the claim to the pension fund is likely to be the family's largest asset, exceeding in value by the far the family's equity in the home or such personal belongings as an automobile.

Thus the job had to become a property right - the only question was in what form and how fast.

Working things like this out through lawsuits may be as American as apple pie, but it is hardly as

412

wholesome. There is still a chance for management to take the initiative in this development and shape this new property right so it equally serves the employee, the company, and the economy. Above all, we need to maintain flexibility of employment. We need to make it possible for a company to hire new people and increase its employment. And this means we must avoid the noose the Europeans have put around their necks with severance pay mandates, making it so expensive to lay off anybody that companies simply do not hire. That Belgium and Holland have such extraordinarily high unemployment is almost entirely the result of these countries' severance pay laws.

Whichever way we structure this new property right, there will be several requirements that every employer will have to satisfy. First, there must be objective and equal performance standards for everyone performing a given job, regardless of race, color, sex, or age. Second, to satisfy the requirements of "due process," performance appraisals will have to be reviewed by truly disinterested parties. Finally, "due process" demands a right of appeal (something, by the way, as "authoritarian" a company as IBM has had for more than half a century).

The evolution of the job into a "property right" changes the position of the individual within the organization. It will change equally, if not more, the position of the organization in society for it will make clear what at present is still nebulous: organized and managed institutions have increasingly become the organs of opportunity, of achievement, and of fulfillment for the individual in a society of organizations.

Conclusion

In the next 50 years there is still important work ahead for the schools of management, management journals, and practicing managers themselves. Organization structures are changing rapidly under the impact of information. Indeed, we now know that a good deal of what traditionally have been considered parts of a structure in organization theory - especially management "levels" - are nothing but information relays rapidly being made redundant by information technology and information concepts. We also know that an information-based organization is likely to center in groups of professional specialists rather than in managerial generalists.

413

We know that the organization is rapidly shifting from one of manual workers to knowledge workers. But we know pitifully little about managing knowledge workers and knowledge work, about productivity with knowledge work, and about organizing knowledge work, integrating it, and measuring it.

And despite all the research done on motivation in the last 50 years, we really so far know very much about how to quench motivation and very little about how to kindle it.

There is work needed on how the multinational must be set up, organized, and directed in a rapidly changing world economy. We now know that management is a "culture" in itself and, as such, transcends national boundaries. Yet it has to be compatible with and supportive of distinct national cultures.

While there is thus a great deal to be learned in traditional management areas, the major challenges are new ones, well beyond the field of management as we commonly define it. Indeed, it will be argued that the challenges I have been discussing are not management challenges at all, but belong in political and social theory and public law.

Precisely. The success of management has not changed the work of management, but it has greatly changed its meaning. Its success had made management the general, the pervasive function and distinct organ of our society of organizations. As such, management inevitably has become affected with the public interest. To work out what this means for management theory and management practice will constitute the management problems of the next 50 years.

LET'S PUT CAPITALISTS BACK INTO CAPITALISM
Lester C. Thurow

We call ourselves a capitalist society, but there's something missing. We are rich in financial investors of every size and variety, from the man on the street to the giant pension funds to the get-rich quick speculators and the takeover artists. We have more corporate managers than we know what to do with - in recent years, the number of private executives has grown far faster than the rate of output has. What we lack are genuine, old-style capitalists - those big investors of yesteryear who often invented the technologies they managed and whose personal wealth was inextricably linked to the destiny of their giant companies.

A successful economy is one that generates a rising standard of living for its citizens. To so this it must have a healthy rate of productivity growth. Ours does not. U. S. productivity growth has averaged 0.8 percent over the past ten years and was 0.8 percent in 1987. In our economy, private business is responsible for productivity growth. If productivity is not rising at a healthy rate, then American business is not doing its job.

To put it bluntly, American capitalism needs a heart transplant. The financial traders who now control American capitalism need to be taken out and replaced by real capitalists who can become the heart of an industrial rebirth. But the regulations governing industrial organization - mostly antitrust laws and banking regulations - stand in the way. President Reagan has suggested some modest changes, but what's required is a wholesale rethinking of these laws. Our economy must be restructured to regain some semblance of its old-style capitalist energy.

The Problem: No Incentives for Productivity Growth

Most big corporations were once run by individual capitalists: by one shareholder with enough stock to dominate the board of directors and to dictate policy, a shareholder who was usually also the chief executive officer. Owning a majority or controlling interest, these capitalists did not have to concentrate on reshuffling assets to fight off raids from financial vikings. They were free to make a living by producing new products or by producing old products more cheaply. Just as important, they were locked into their roles. They could not very well sell out for a quick profit - dumping large stock holdings on the market would have simply depressed the stock's price and cost them their jobs as captains of industry. So instead they sought to enhance their personal wealth by investing - by improving the long-ruin efficiency and productivity of the company.

Today, with very few exceptions, the stock of large U.S. corporations is held by financial institutions such as pension funds, foundations, or mutual funds - not by individual shareholders. And these financial institutions cannot legally become real capitalists who control what they own. How much they can invest in any one company is limited by law, as is how actively they can intervene in company decision making.

These shareholders and corporate managers have a very different agenda than dominant capitalists do, and therein lies the problem. They do not have the clout to change business decisions, corporate strategy, or incumbent managers with their voting power. They can enhance their wealth only by buying and selling shares based on what they think is going to happen to short-term profits. Minority shareholders have no choice but to be short-term traders.

And since shareholders are by necessity interested only in short-term trading, it is not surprising that managers' compensation is based not on long-term performance, but on current profits or sales. Managerial compensation packages are completely congruent with the short-run perspective of short-run shareholders. Neither the manager nor the shareholder expects to be around very long. And neither has an incentive to watch out for the long-term growth of the company.

We need to give managers and shareholders an incentive to nurture long-term corporate growth- in other words, to work as hard at enhancing productivity and output as they now work at improving short-term profitability.

Why Minor Adjustments are Insufficient

The problem of slow productivity growth will not be solved by enforcement of existing antitrust laws, nor by throwing those laws out altogether, nor by encouragement of aggressive acquisition. Instead, the entire regulatory framework governing finance and industry needs to be restructured so that the biggest profits and highest incomes go to those who expand output, rather than to those who rejuggle financial assets.

Existing antitrust laws do not encourage productivity, as we have seen, and one could argue that they are downright harmful. General Motors is permitted to engage in a joint venture with Toyota that will attack Ford and Chrysler, but not in a joint venture with Ford that might repel the Japanese auto invasion. Private antitrust suits are now used as corporate blackmail - which was hardly what the laws were intended for. And since the current laws are not enforced by the Reagan administration anyway, no one is really even sure what the effective antitrust laws are.

Simply letting the market function without rules and regulations would not work, however. As the nineteenth-century robber barons demonstrated, there are all too often circumstances in which the most profitable activities lead to contracted output and redistributed earnings. Left to themselves, unregulated markets will inevitably focus on those activities - we need look no further than the current financial merger wars for evidence of this pattern. Profit maximization (which firms automatically shoot for, with or without government regulations) is not a synonym for output expansion.

Nor do financial speculations address the problem of slow productivity growth. In fact, they add to it, since they focus the attention of American business people on highly profitable activities that do not lead to industrial growth. When a company is acquired, its shareholders are certainly enriched, but the economy gains nothing. The productivity assets that the company had are still there - no bigger and no smaller. A redistributive activity - not a productive activity - has occurred.

In theory the assets might be better managed by the new owners and hence be more productive but no one has ever demonstrated that mergers lead to higher rates of productivity growth for the assets being reshuffled. (If financial rearrangements were the route to higher productivity the United States would have the highest rate of productivity growth in the industrial world - not the lowest - since it has rearranged more financial assets than any other country in recent decades.)

Mergers also load firms up with debt. As a result, there are fewer funds available for investment in new products, processes, or research and development. Companies are weakened financially and made more

417

vulnerable to financial collapse in the next recession, when they might not be able to meet their interest payments. Consequently, they become more risk averse - less willing to bet the company on new activities. The company has effectively already been bet.

Proponents of the takeover movement would argue that these criticisms miss the point: takeovers enrich shareholders, and firms exist solely to serve the interests of the shareholders, they would say. The enrichment part of the argument is certainly true - but do firms really exist solely to serve the shareholders' interests? If this view had been taken in the past, neither the antitrust laws nor the rules regulating the railroads would have been adopted. (There is no doubt that the activities being regulated in those instances enriched shareholders.)

Shareholders' rights are not paramount, in point of fact. Private firms exist in our society because collectively we have decided that they are the best way to expand the output available to everyone, shareholder and nonshareholder alike. If private firms fail to serve this social function, they will either be abolished and replaced with something that does serve it, or else they will be redirected (as they have seen in the past) with new rules and regulations that attempt to set them off once again on a productive path.

To achieve this redirection, real capitalists must be put back into the U.S. economy. And they must be boxed in so that their profit-making energies are focused on activities that raise productivity and output. Realistically, this means creating institutional capitalists, not expanding the supply of individual capitalists. Occasionally a brilliant entrepreneur will nurture a corporation until it becomes one of America's largest, but within one or two generations that corporation, like the rest of U.S. industry, will be without dominant shareholders. Startups are not a substitute for giant corporations that retain their vitality.

Regulatory Changes That Will Improve Productivity Growth
Today's short-term financial traders must be remade into tomorrow's long-term capitalistic investors. To accomplish this task, the following major changes should occur.

Get Shareholders Involved.....

The legal limits that now prevent financial institutions from acquiring a dominant or majority share-holding position should be removed.

Institutions should be encouraged to sit on the boards of directors of companies in which they invest, to actively hire and fire managers, and to worry about the strategies that will make their investments successful.

The regulations that prevent U.S. commercial banks from becoming merchant banks - banks that own and control industrial corporations - should be lifted. This proposed change deserves some discussion. In much of the rest of the world, the merchant bankers are the industrial capitalists who make the system work. When the Arabs threatened to buy a controlling interest in Mercedes-Benz a few years ago, for example, the Deutsche Bank intervened on behalf of the German economy and bought a controlling interest. The Bank now controls the board of directors. It protects the managers of Mercedes-Benz from financial raiders. It frees them from the tyranny of the stock market, with its emphasis on quarterly profits. It helps plan corporate strategies and raises money to carry out those strategies. It also fires managers if the company slips in the auto market, and prevents them from engaging in self-serving activities (such as mergers or golden parachutes) that do not enhance the company's long-term prospects.

This path has not always been closed to us. Some of what were once America's most successful companies - General Electric, U.S. Steel, International Harvester - were founded by merchant bankers before this practice was outlawed during the Great Depression.

In recent years, small-scale merchant bankers have reappeared in the guise of venture capitalists. They play a vital role in helping companies get started, but when the firms become middle-sized and offer their shares for sale to the public, the venture capitalist drops out, sells the stock, and starts over again with a new company. Venture capitalists are no substitute for merchant banks.

Today's laws draw too sharp a distinction between loans and equity. The institutions that provide major long-term loans to companies should take an active role in their strategic direction. To bring this about, long-term loans should carry voting rights. To avoid the

419

appearance of conflict, executives from banks and other lending agencies may now sit on the boards of only those firms to which they have not loaned much money. They are not supposed to be financially involved participants. This rule flies in the face of reason. Why not give long-term lenders voting rights? A $100-million long-term loan might, for example, entitle a lender to half the voting rights of a $100-million long-term equity investment. Major lenders, like equity investors, should not be absentee landlords.

As it now stands, bankers exert an influence on the management of a company to which they have loaned money only when the company is failing. How much better it would be if they were to help the corporation avoid mistakes that lead to failure.

Lock Them In...
We should also ensure that these institutions - or any shareholder with a dominant position in a company - cannot easily extricate themselves from that role. Finance and industry should not be at arm's length. They should be so entwined that their destinies cannot be separated. The United States needs an economy in which finance cannot succeed unless industry succeeds.

Anyone who holds a dominant position in any company - say, 20 percent or more - should be forced to give the public one day's notice of the intent to sell shares. While the ownership of a large block of shares constitutes a substantial lock-in all by itself (it is difficult to sell a large number of shares without depressing one's own stock price), this natural lock should be reinforced by requiring notice of intent to sell. Unless the announced sale could be explained to the satisfaction of the investing public on grounds other than expected future failures, any such notice would inevitably trigger a general rush to sell the stock before the major investor could do so, leaving the big investor to sell at much reduced prices. Like the old-time capitalists, he or she would think long and hard before trying to bail out of a troubled company.

To reinforce the distinction between traders and investors, the voting rights of equity shareholders should increase the longer the shares are held. Major investors subject to the 20 percent rule would become instant owners, but others would gain full voting rights only over a substantial period of time. No voting rights would be given to those who have owned shares for under two years, perhaps, and full voting rights would gradually be granted over the following three years: in year three, one-third of a vote for each share held, in year four, two-thirds of a vote for each share held, and in year five, a full vote for each share held.

...And Take Away Their Quarterly Statements

The tyranny of the quarterly profit statement should be abolished. When Japan resumed control of its economy after the U.S. occupation following World War II, it repealed the law requiring quarterly profit statements and substituted one requiring annual profit statements. The same should be done in the United States. Doing so might not change attitudes all by itself, but it would symbolize what needs to be done.

The importance currently granted quarterly profit statements puts managers in absurd and untenable positions. A recent example will illustrate this point. I was consulting for a firm whose cost-cutting program had substantially exceeded expectations. The firm had made 50 percent more money in one quarter than it had expected to make. This good news, learned too near the end of the quarter to be hidden by creative accounting, was treated as a disaster. Management was sure that stock prices would immediately rise and then plunge in the next quarter,, since the firm could not possibly duplicate this quarter's performance and so maintain market expectations about future profits. News that was in fact good for the company - and the economy - became bad news because of the short-term focus that quarterly reports reinforce.

The quarterly profit statement is supposed to improve the information available to investors. It may do this for short-run stock speculators (although even this is open to doubt, given the volatility of short-run numbers), but from a social point of view there is no payoff to this availability. Not knowing current profits might force short-term investors to understand the firm's technologies and its market position - it might even persuade today's short-term traders that they could make more money by becoming tomorrow's long-term investors.

Conclusion

The antitrust laws prohibiting interlocking directorates, joint research, and trading companies were all designed to avoid monopolistic industrial combines. If the same people were planning strategy in different firms, if products were being developed jointly, or if different firms were selling their products through a common sales organization, then the firms involved would not be totally separate and competitive. Strategies might be coordinated, joint development might lead to

421

joint production, the common sales force might eventually dominate the producing companies - in other words, de facto mergers might occur. There is some truth to such worries, but they are more than counterbalanced by the competition coming from abroad and the need to cooperate to meet that competition. National antitrust regulations are now simply obsolete. They don't recognize today's realities.

Merchant bankers, insurance companies, and pension or mutual funds managers should be encouraged to become capitalists who succeed or fail based on their ability to grow healthy industrial corporations. Their attention should be turned from something that is marginal to America's long-run success - the buying and selling of shares and the rearrangement of corporate financial assets - toward something that is central to U.S. success - the growth of productivity and output.

In any reformulation of our antitrust rules, one central goal must be kept in mind: put real capitalists back in charge of the American corporation and then box them in so that they have no choice but to improve the nation's productivity and competitiveness. Link their personal success to their corporation's productivity.

Without capitalists, capitalism can only fail.

THE PARADOX OF PROFIT
Norman E. Bowie

One of the more interesting philosophical paradoxes is the so-called hedonic paradox. Hedonists believe that happiness is the only good and that everything should be done with the aim of achieving personal happiness. The hedonic paradox contends that the more you seek happiness the less likely you are to find it. Consider the following situation. You awake at 7:00 A.M, and as a good hedonist you resolve to undertake each of the day's activities in order to achieve happiness. The achievement of happiness is your conscious goal in everything you do. I submit that if you adopt that strategy your day will be most miserable---probably long before noon. If you want to be happy you must pursue and successfully meet other goals. Happiness accompanies the successful achievement of those goals. To be truly happy, you must focus on consciously achieving your goals. In that way the hedonic paradox can be avoided.

I maintain that a similar paradox operates in business. Many business persons believe that profit is the only goal of business and that everything should be done with the aim of obtaining profit. I contend that the more a business consciously seeks to obtain profits, the less likely they are to achieve them. Let us call this paradox the profit-seeking paradox. What I suggest in this essay is that this paradox can be avoided only if there is a rethinking of the motives for making a business decision, the purpose of business, and the values that traditional business managers hold.

SERVICE RATHER THAN PROFIT

Perhaps the place to begin is with motivation. According to the traditional view, business persons are motivated to do well---well for themselves and well for the company. By the invisible hand this self-interested behavior of individuals and individual firms is coordinated by market forces to produce the good for all. Doing good is achieved by doing well.

From Papers On the Ethics of Management. Reprinted by permission of the Brigham Young University, Copyright 1988. Endnotes omitted

As several business persons said in <u>Ethics and Profits</u>,

> The American free enterprise system is not perfect, yet it has produced more benefits than any other system in history. We are the healthiest, wealthiest, best educated, most generous nation in the history of the world.

> The objectives of business and the achievement of social goals are the same. Without business, there is no money, no resources, no environmental protection.

> We believe our goals are compatible with the best interests in society.

Indeed, if business were motivated to do good it would be involved in an altruistic paradox. The more business sought to do good, the more harm it would do. This paradox arises if you believe that each individual is the best judge of his or her own needs and that attempts by institutions to "do good for people" rather than letting persons help themselves is actually harmful.

But the public does not accept the business person's analysis that in seeking profit business does good. They do not agree that the material success of business persons and business executives is necessarily advantageous to the public at large. That is because the public perceives the business person as someone who would do anything for a "buck"---if not for his own buck then for the stockholder's. Poll after poll has shown that the public has little respect for business executives. If business persons want respect they will have to convince the public that they are professionals rather than mere profit maximizers.

Traditionally the motive for professional conduct is the service motive; the professional skills are service skills, specifically skills that benefit humankind. Doctors, lawyers, teachers, and the clergy---the standard paradigms of professionals---exercise a special skill for the benefit of human beings. The Harvard Business School has as its motto, "To Make Business a Profession." However, I don't believe the Harvard Business School realizes just how radical that slogan is.

Business persons who view themselves as professionals are motivated to do good and in doing good the firm will do well. If a manager emphasizes the

production and distribution of quality products that
customers need and if she is honest and fair with
suppliers and lenders, and most importantly if she
provides meaningful work for employees, then both the
manager and the firm will be profitable. If the
profit-seeking paradox is to be avoided, the business
person must see herself as a professional and the service
motive must dominate. Business can only really do well
if its seeks to do good.

We now confront two competing paradoxes.
Traditionally the business person believes that business
does good by doing well (seeking profit) and that if
business were to consciously seek to do good, it would
neither do good nor do well. Business would be enmeshed
in the altruistic paradox. On the other hand, I contend,
as do other critics of the traditional view, that if
business is to do well, it must consciously seek to do
good. Otherwise business would be enmeshed in the
profit-seeking paradox. Who is right?

Let us begin by addressing that question indirectly.
The theory known as ethical egoism contends that each
person should act in his own perceived best interest.
On a traditional, but I believe mistaken, interpretation,
Adams Smith would support ethical egoism on the ground
that the invisible hand would coordinate egoistic
behavior so that the good of all was achieved. On the
other hand, Hobbes believed that life in an egoistic
world would be a war of all against all in which life was
nasty, brutish, and short. There is no invisible hand
to bring about utilitarian results. Instead, citizens
would rationally elect to place their hands in the power
of an absolute ruler (the Leviathan or state) so that the
state of nature could be avoided. Who is right, Hobbes
or Smith? Traditionally we have believed that Smith was
right and the empirical evidence seemed to support that
view. Lately however, Hobbes is having something of a
renaissance.

Similarly, the traditional wisdom and the empirical
evidence seemed to support the view that business should
consciously seek to do well rather than to do good.
Lately, however, the "business should consciously seek
to do good" view is being taken more seriously. In the
scholarly literature, Hayes and Abernathy's classic
<u>Harvard Business Review</u> piece, "Managing Our Way to
Economic Decline," pointed out how our excessive concern
with short-term profit was hurting our competitive
position internationally. In the popular literature,
Peters and Waterman's <u>In Search of Excellence</u> emphasized
that the profitable companies directed their concern to

425

their employees and their customers first and were profitable as a result. In essence, <u>In Search of Excellence</u> said that a company does well by doing good. Since the publication of these well-known works, a groundswell of supporting books and articles with supporting evidence has arisen. A significant number of scholars and practitioners from a diversity of disciplines and firms accepts the paradox. The more a corporation seeks to make a profit, the less likely it is to do so. Let us say that at this point the empirical evidence is inconclusive.

I do have difficulty with the two assumptions of those who argue that if corporations seek to do good they will run afoul of the altruistic paradox, namely that people are the best judge of their own interests and that in trying to do good you necessarily do harm. Certainly there is some truth behind those assumptions. People are often the best judge of their own interests. But not always. Society has correctly not honored the judgment of drug addicts. Moreover, persons who challenge the "do good by doing well" philosophy aren't necessarily asking business to "do good for people." Rather, business is being asked to create the conditions for persons to do one of the things they most want to do, specifically to have a challenging job that allows self-development and is useful to society. If business performed that function, I do not believe it would fall victim to the altruistic paradox.

Finally, I should like to address one ethical objection to the "do good in order to do well" theme. Some ethical purists would object to the "do good in order to do well" philosophy on the grounds that the only reason a business is motivated to do good is the belief that it will do well. This, the critics contend, makes moral behavior merely instrumental. Morality is simply a means for making a profit. The business person does not believe there is anything intrinsically valuable in doing good. What would (should) a company do if it can do well by not doing good or even by doing harm?

These ethical purists seem to forget that Plato actually believed that each individual reaped the benefits of ethical behavior. The virtuous man was the happy man; the tyrant was unhappy. For Plato, virtue clearly paid. While few philosophers would go as far as Plato, many (most?) agree that morality is good for society as a whole. In that sense, as Kurt Baier among others has pointed out, a society has a morality because it is rational to do so; and by rational Baier means in the interest of society's members. Similarly, morality

426

has been seen as one possible answer to prisoner dilemma situations. And recently, Robert Axelrod in his book, The Evolution of Cooperation, has shown that the limited "tit for tat" morality has a higher payoff than taking advantage of the altruistic behavior of others.

If morality was not of benefit to society, society would not have it. Indeed, many would argue that morality is required if there is to be a society at all. I think Kant's ethical theory can be pushed in that direction. Acknowledging that fact does not diminish the value of morality.

Of course, showing that morality is in the interest of society is one thing; to show that morality is always in the interest of each member of society is quite another. It seems obvious that on occasion doing the ethical thing is not in the interest of an individual (nor in the interest of an individual corporation). In such cases the individual or corporation ought to do what is morally correct even though they won't do well by doing so. On this point the ethical purists and I are in agreement. Where the ethical purist and I might disagree is on the attitude we should take toward those cases where doing good is not compatible with doing well. In the corporate context I would argue that we should manipulate institutional structures so that we decrease the likelihood of such occasions arising. For example, in a well-run company with adequate grievance procedures and the absence of an employment-at-will contract, whistle blowing would become unnecessary. An employee could be confident that her concerns would get a fair hearing and that she would not lose her job for raising her concerns. In such cases potential whistle blowers would not face the dilemma of doing good at the expense of doing well.

The ethical purist, on the other hand, might want to instill heroic attitudes in individuals---to give them the courage to sacrifice self-interest for morality. In the absence of such courage, persons will be tempted to protect their own interests to the detriment of larger interests. People should be prepared for the hard reality that doing good can mean not doing well. My approach, the purist would argue, tries to cover over the hard demands of reality.

I frankly believe the purists have a point. However, my view of the world and human nature leads me to think that individuals will face the hard moral choices often enough and that the likelihood of success in meeting them is enhanced when the number of times these choices must be faced is diminished.

I do not want to leave any doubt that I do believe doing good sometimes requires a sacrifice and that the sacrifice ought to be made. However, I am not concerned with such occasions here. Rather, I am concerned with the far greater number of cases where doing good really would lead to doing well. As a society I don't think people recognize the genuine value of moral behavior. Business leaders particularly need to be convinced that the profit-making paradox can only be avoided if business leaders see themselves as professional providers of a service. However, to adopt the service motive is to change one's view of the function of business.

MEANINGFUL WORK

In this section I argue that one of the main purposes of business is to provide meaningful work for employees. To get to this conclusion, we need to go through a two-step dialectic. First, the view that the sole function of business is profit making must be rejected; and second, various widely discussed alternatives to the profit-making function of business must be seen as incomplete. This prepares the way for my conclusion that the main function of business is to provide meaningful work.

The Friedmanite view that the purpose of a corporation is to maximize profits has already come under severe attack. The classical view ignores the negative externalities of the practices of the classical firm and it totally ignores effects on the distribution of income. Air and water pollution, noise pollution, and unemployment are but a few of the problems that have caused citizens to doubt that firms seeking to increase stockholder wealth actually do produce the greatest good for the greatest number.

Similarly, the classical profit-seeking firm unjustly treats labor as any other factor of production, that is, capital, machines, and land. When it pays to substitute machines for people, the profit-seeking firms should simply do it and that is the end of the matter. If the firm can hold down wages by threatening to move to another region or another country it should do so. In fact, if it pays to move a plant from one part of the country to another, the firm should do so whatever the reason. If the going wage in an industry is four dollars an hour and if it is extremely difficult for workers to live on $160 a week, that is not the concern of the

428

employer. In fact, he should seek to lower wages if he can. Even if an economic system with profit-making firms maximizes total income, that does not establish the justice of such a system. Hence, critics argue that the higher average wealth comes at the expense of the poor. And in any case, treating employees on a par with capital, land, and machines violates a fundamental moral maxim, that is, people cannot be treated like objects but are uniquely worthy of respect.

Moreover, even if Friedman, in his analysis in Capitalism and Freedom, is right in claiming that profit-making firms support political liberties, Friedman ignores the fact that the employee has few liberties within the corporation. As one commentator notes, the corporation is the black hole in the Bill of Rights. The Constitution simply does not apply. Moreover, the employment-at-will doctrine still predominates. In the absence of a contract to the contrary, an employee can be fired for any reason, be it a good reason, immoral reason, or indeed no reason at all. Since most people are far more involved with their job than they are with public affairs, it is not unreasonable to believe that many employees would trade some political freedom for more freedom on the job or would trade political liberties for increased job security. The classical view has a rather poor record protecting the liberties many people most want.

Of course, defenders of the classical view argue that the stockholders have rights employees do not have because stockholders are the owners of the corporation. However, the property rights argument won't do. First, property rights are not absolute. No individual can do what he wants with his property and neither can a firm. Second, from the moral point of view all property ownership is not equal. Consider the following dissimilarity between homeowners and stockowners. A homeowner who works on her home and perhaps improves it beyond what the improvements could return in resale is not judged to be irrational. A stockholder who treats his stock in that way is considered to be irrational. Which type of property ownership is most in need of restrictions? By the way, the manager and the employer usually have the most reason to treat the company as a homeowner treats her home. If the company does poorly, the costs fall more heavily on the managers and employees. They can lose their entire livelihood. Far less often does the collapse of a company mean that the stockholders lose their livelihood. Besides, analyses since the 1930s and 1940s have shown that most stockholders do not identify with the corporation in which they own stock. At this point in our history, the "big players" are the pension fund managers, and hence much of the outstanding stock is not even directly chosen by the individuals who own it. Therefore, if restrictions on personal property are legitimate for homeowners, they are even more legitimate for stockholders.

Third, if the stakeholder theory of the firm is correct, there is no moral justification for maximizing the interests of the stockholders at the expense of the other stakeholders. Indeed, if other stakeholders such as labor are at a greater risk if the firm fails, morality would support giving their interests greater weight.

In place of the profit maximization view, a number of alternative theories of the function of the corporation have arisen such as:
- Seeking profits so long as it does not cause avoidable harm or unduly infringe on human rights.
- Seeking to do social good (correct social problems) as well as seek profit.
- Seeking to produce life-sustaining and -enhancing goods and services.
- Seeking to maximize the interests of the various corporate stakeholders rather than simply the interests of the stockholder.

Each of these alternative definitions has much to be said for it. All recognize that there is more to business than making a profit. Yet I am convinced that each of the alternative views to a greater or lesser degree omits or gives insufficient emphasis to something essential---namely that the main purpose of the corporation is to provide meaningful work.

For example, the "seek profit while avoiding harm" view simply argues that corporations should follow a moral minimum required of all individuals and institutions. It puts constraints on the competitive profit-seeking game. There is a concept of unnecessary roughness in football. Similarly, there are concepts of unnecessary roughness in profit seeking. To recognize this fact is important, but under this view the essential function of business remains profit. Management is simply reminded of the rule against avoidable harm. As such, I think such firms and their managers remain vulnerable to the profit-making pardox.

The second alternative that urges corporations to do good by correcting social problems is vulnerable to the altruistic paradox, to all of Friedman's well-known criticisms, and to charges that the obligation to do social good is too open-ended.

The third and fourth alternatives require more extended discussion. Both avoid the paradox of profit making. For example, just as individuals can avoid the hedonic paradox if they pursue goals other than happiness, individual corporations can avoid the profit-seeking paradox if they pursue goals other than profit, and each specifies a goal for business other than, or in addition to, profit.

One of the criticisms of the third alternative is that it focuses on human beings as consumers rather than as producers. One of the common complaints against ethicists who criticize distributive justice under capitalism is that these ethicists ignore production at the expense of distribution. Goods can't be distributed unless they are produced. There is much merit in this criticism, but ironically the business community has forgotten its own insight. The focus is on selling to consumers; far greater attention is directed to increasing sales to consumers than it is to increasing the productivity of the employees.

Moreover, as the social commentator David Bell has pointed out, this attempt to increase consumption creates paradoxes that threaten capitalism itself. Specifically, the set of values business encourages in consumers is inconsistent with the values business wants to instill in its workers. The attitudes that make Americans good consumers are not the attitudes that make Americans good workers. Business wants workers who are loyal to the company, who will delay gratification, and who will exhibit the attributes associated with the work ethic. But business urges consumers to buy and enjoy now and to pay later on credit. Thus we have, in Bell's memorable phrase, "the cultural contradictions of capitalism."

Although In Search of Excellence argued that excellent companies focused on their employees, the point was diluted both by the anecdotal nature of that work and by the emphasis on being close to the customer. This dilution represents a danger of the fourth alternative. Should the interests of all the stakeholders be considered equal? I would argue that there are both economic reasons and ethical reasons why they should not all be considered equal.

431

Paradoxically, the focus of American business on consumer sales has hurt profits. The "productivity crisis" is a feature story in the popular business press. Recently a number of economists have addressed this problem and have argued that business must spend more time, money, and energy on employees. In an important recent book, The Next American Frontier, Robert Reich argues that the United States can only maintain its economic preeminence if we make a total commitment to investment in human capital.

Unlike high-volume production, where most of a firm's value is represented by physical assets, the principal stores of value in flexible-system enterprises are human assets. Specialized machines and unskilled workers cannot adapt easily to new situations. Flexible machines and teams of skilled workers can. Only people can recognize and solve novel problems; machines can merely repeat solutions already programmed within them. The future prosperity of America and every other industrialized country will depend on their citizens' ability to recognize and solve new problems, for the simple reason that processes which make routine the solution to older problems are coming to be the special province of developing nations. Industries of the future will not depend on physical "hardware," which can be duplicated anywhere, but on human "software" which can retain a technological edge.

Philosophers would argue that an emphasis on the individual employee is just what ethics requires. For example, Kant, in the tradition of Aristotle, recognizes that only human beings are capable of being motivated by moral rules. It is human beings that place values on other things; these other things have conditional value because they only acquire this value as the result of human action. Human beings, on the other hand, have unconditioned value, that is, value apart from any special circumstances that confer value. Since all human beings and only human beings have this unconditional value, it is always inappropriate to use another human being merely as a means to some end---as if they had instrumental value only. Hence, Kant argues, one should always treat a human being or a person with unconditional value as an end and never treat a human being merely as a means toward your own ends. Each person looks at himself or herself as possessing unconditioned value. If one is to avoid inconsistency, one must view all other

432

human beings as possessors of unconditioned value as well.

Kant's principle of respect for persons can be applied directly to business practice. A Kantain would take strong exception to the view that employees are to be treated like mere equipment in the production process. Human labor should never be treated like machinery, industrial plants, and capital, solely in accordance with economic laws for profit maximization. Any economic system that fails to recognize this distinction between human beings and other nonhuman factors of production is morally deficient.

It is one thing to argue that persons ought to be respected; it is quite another to specify how that is to be done in the employment context. A full discussion of this issue would take us into psychology---an area where I am at best an amateur---as well as into ethics. The psychological generalizations that follow may be controversial. However, they are common in the popular literature and are consistent with the "respect for persons" principle. I will take it is a given that people do not feel fulfilled unless they are gainfully employed in jobs that they find meaningful and important. If robots could do all our work, utopia would not have arrived. People would be unhappy and frustrated. People need to work.

However, not just any work will do. The work must first be seen as useful---as making a contribution to society. Second, it must challenge the worker. One of the problems with the assembly line is that it is hard to see how putting six bolts in a car door is useful work. It is also boring and fails to challenge the worker. Our foreign competitors discovered these truths before we did. Volvo never really had an assembly-line technique and the Japanese innovations are now widely discussed and often imitated.

Moreover, the employee must be able to exercise judgment and creativity. A job where the employee simply follows orders and where all the employee's actions result from orders has no autonomy. This denial of autonomy shows lack of respect. In the corporate context, autonomy can be honored through teamwork when each employee has some say in goal formation and implementation.

In summary, I take it as a psychological truth that all human beings need to be engaged in rewarding work where rewarding work is defined as work that is useful, challenging, and respectful of individual autonomy. Business does good when it provides jobs of these types. Moreover, that function of business is more important than the production of goods and services function. It seems obvious that a person can be deprived of nearly any product or even most of the products American industry produces without suffering severe psychological harm. But if a person is denied meaningful work, the psychological harm is very great. That is why I argue that it is morally more important for business to focus on the employee rather than on the consumer or the other stakeholders.

Suppose business sought to do good in the sense that it focused on developing those skills and attitudes that made people happier, healthier, and more cooperative human beings. Aren't those just the skills needed to make workers more productive? By doing good the corporation would also be doing well.

But isn't that just manipulative? Isn't the reason for doing good to do well? The companies behave morally because there is a payoff. We need to rethink our discussion in the first section of this essay to address this complicated question.

There are essentially three ways to seek happiness. First, one can set out consciously to do so. However, to seek happiness in that way leads directly to the hedonic paradox. Such behavior is self-defeating. Second, one can seek to achieve successful intermediate goals realizing "in the back of one's mind" that in so doing one will be happy. And third, one can seek to successfully achieve personal goals and in the process one will discover happiness. This later means to happiness clearly avoids the hedonic paradox.

What about having happiness in the back of one's mind? Is that sufficient for avoiding the hedonic paradox? Psychologically, I think we have a borderline case. Whether or not the paradox is avoided depends on how far "in the back of one's mind" the ultimate goal of happiness is.

Similar comments can be made about management's attention to employees. If the management is creating conditions for happy and healthy employees in order to make a profit, they are simply using employees as a means to their own end. They are not motivated by the respect and dignity of personhood. Hence, the motive of such managers is not moral even if the results are good. However, most employees recognize such motives and upon recognizing them undermine management's efforts. Many a quality circle has collapsed for just that reason. The result is that immoral motives that are supposed to yield good results frequently fail to do so.

On the other hand, if the firm consciously focuses on the individual self-realization of the employees, the employees are likely to recognize this and to respond appropriately. Will such moral motivation on the part of management yield good results? Within the firm, the answer, I believe, is certainly in the affirmative. Given a stable external environment, the firm will do best by focusing on the employee. Of course, changes in the external environment affect profit too. There is no guarantee that moral motives will yield good results.

Perhaps the best strategy is for management to focus on employee self-realization while keeping profits in the back of its mind. In that way management can respond to trends in the environment. But such an approach can be dangerous. If profits aren't sufficiently in the back of management's mind, the employees will develop the same kind of cynicism found when profit is the conscious goal of "moral" behavior.

Before leaping to the conclusion that this last strategy is the only practical one, keep in mind the following distinction:

1.   Management A says to its workers, "You will never be fired without cause, but if the economy turns sour, some of you will have to be let go" (moral behavior with profits in the back of the mind).
2.   Management B says to its workers, "You will never be fired without cause nor will you be fired in the event of an economic downturn. If the company should go under because of circumstances beyond our control, we will all go under together" (moral behavior with profits as a happy result).

Wouldn't the employees in company B be less cynical and more productive, and hence wouldn't the profit-seeking paradox be less likely to occur? I would invest my money in the stock of Company

B.
In this section I have rejected the classical view that the main purpose of the corporation is to maximize stockholder wealth. Moreover, I have argued that even the well-known alternatives to the classical view do not

435

place sufficient emphasis on what I take to be the most
important function of business---providing meaningful
work. The greatest contribution of business to human
well-being is to provide jobs rather than goods and
services for consumers. That is why firing a person
without cause is such a moral wrong. That is why layoffs
due to economic downturns are such personal tragedies.
If Weitzman's arguments in <u>The Share Economy</u> are correct,
his proposal is morally superior to current wage and
layoff practices.

However, if the notion that the chief function of
the corporation is to provide meaningful work is to be
implemented, the attitudes and values of American
business must change.

If the primary motive of managers ought to be
service and the primary purpose of business ought to be
providing meaningful work for employees, what are the
implications for traditional business values and business
practice?

First, we have to deemphasize competition. The
football and war metaphors have to be replaced.
Elsewhere I have suggested the family metaphor as an
appropriate device for seeing how a corporation ought to
function. We are not losing ground just because we are
not competitive enough. We are losing ground because we
are not cooperative enough. Cooperation must be
emphasized over competition because cooperation is
necessary to provide the cohesiveness necessary for the
practice of morality. It is harder to be a free rider if
you see your associates as colleagues or teammates rather
than as competitors. Much is now being written in
decision theory on ways to avoid zero sum games and
prisoner dilemma situations. This research needs to be
made accessible to managers and then applied to the
business context.

One change in corporate practice might be the
introduction of a notion of group merit to replace or
supplement individual merit. When an economic downturn
occurs, everyone could be put on a reduced work week
rather than placing the entire burden on the few who are
laid off. A profit-sharing system should supplement or
even replace the traditional wage structure. One of the
most developed suggestions is Martin Weitzman's. Worker
compensation is tied to a formula that makes it vary
inversely with the firm's level of employment. Although
these specific suggestions may have flaws, they capture
the flavor of the more cooperative collective approach.

More important than specific recommendations of the sort suggested above is a change in perspective on how the corporation is viewed. Rather than emphasizing the goals of the individual CEO, we must speak of corporate goals and organizational decisions. If we have better corporations we will have better individual corporate persons. Professor Kenneth Andrews's notion of a corporate strategy is extremely valuable in providing a focus for the ideas I have in mind.

Second, we must give up our excessive commitment to individualism. In a market economy it is very difficult to overcome free-rider problems. A rational individual, in situations that require cooperation, knows that he does best when everyone else cooperates and he does not; he then free-rides on the cooperative activity of others. But if everyone reasons this way, then the cooperative activity will not occur or will occur at a level below optimum. Since morality is essentially a cooperative activity, it easily falls victim to free-rider problems. This argument has been brilliantly made in Fred Hirsch's Social Limits to Growth and clearly stated in Reich's The Next American Frontier.

> The challenge of adapting to the era of human capital exemplifies the paradox of civic virtue. To the extent that people cooperate--- willingly sharing their knowledge, skills, and resources with one another--each person is rendered better off than he would be without such cooperation. The collective power of everyone's talents and resources is greater than the mere sum of the individual talents and resources involved. But each person is aware that he can be even better off if everyone but himself acts with an eye to the common good, so that he can benefit from the result without bearing any part of the mutual burden. If each person follows this logic and rationally opts for personal gain at the expense of everyone else, there will be no cooperation. Everyone will be worse off. What is rational for the individual is tragically irrational for the society as a whole.

Morality is particularly vulnerable when the pressure is on corporations to produce short-term gains. As I indicated earlier, one of the fatal flaws in the profit-seeking motive is the excessive emphasis on short-term profit. The solution to that problem is a collective rather than an individual one. What do I mean by that? I mean the problem rests in a deficiency of the

437

competitive system; it does not rest primarily with deficiencies in individual character.

Nonetheless, truth, trust, acceptance, and restraint---"canons of everyday face to face civility"---recognized by the classicist Theodore Levitt, is required for the conduct of business; yet the very practice of business undermines it. This is not mere academic theorizing. Observers in the field are commenting on the decline of morality and on its disastrous effects.

> Perhaps most troubling is that the atmosphere of insecurity and impermanence which characterizes all levels of American business has bred a selfish attitude among directors, managers, and employees, an egoistic mentality which is seriously undermining American enterprise. Within a productive system that increasingly depends on cooperation, good faith, and team spirit, the dominant ethic is coming to be cynical indifference and opportunism... We are witnessing an extraordinary increase in self-dealing within American enterprise.

As Hirsch argued, "The point is that conventional, mutual standards of honesty and trust are public goods that are necessary inputs for much of economic output." However, since they are public goods, their value cannot be fully captured in the market. If business is to conduct its activities in the public good, attention should not be directed to individuals. The emphasis on individualism is part of the problem.

> American society is now rife with other "beggar-thy-neighbor" tactics, many of which are rational from the standpoint of the individual actor but are tragically irrational for society as a whole: the asset rearranging undertaken through conglomerate merger, manipulation of balance sheets, and schemes of tax avoidance; the exorbitant salaries and bonuses provided to executives in America's largest companies; the rising incidence of employee theft and insider dealings; the political demands for tariffs, quotas, and bailouts to protect companies against foreign competitors; and the refusal by many middle-income taxpayers to foot any longer the bill for social services. The vicious circle has closed: As the economy continues to

decline, Americans grow more cynical about collective endeavor. Their consequential retreat into egoism merely accelerates the decline since collaboration is the only way to reverse it.

Rather, the emphasis must be on collective action; and that emphasis would require changes in business practice and corporate structure. As Reich said, "It is becoming clear that America's economic future depends less on lonely geniuses and backyard inventors than on versatile organizations."

Third, we should abandon the hierarchical view of management. Sharp criticism of the view that the manager is a boss and that employees should follow orders is now commonplace. Management teams, quality-of-life circles, are all the rage. But that kind of criticism is hardly new. It came in during the 1930s. The abandonment of the hierarchical view requires more than giving up all that is implied by the word "boss." It requires reducing the separation between those who plan work and those who execute it. As Reich has argued, to adapt to the new era of international competition we need to flatten management, eliminate hierarchy, stop producing by rules, ensure that those who plan and those who execute work together. The concept of the organization chart must be given up for the concept of the team.

There are strong moral and psychological reasons for abandoning a management tradition where a boss gives orders. If employees are to be convinced to develop institutional loyalty and to put the interest of the group ahead of their own self-interest, they must feel part of a team. Inability to participate in the setting of goals certainly doesn't contribute to a team concept.

In this case, psychology is buttressed by morality. In the absence of an opportunity to help set group goals, there is no moral reason for a person to sacrifice his or her self-interest for the interest of the group. Many autocrats talk the language of team loyalty, but the employees know that in such cases team loyalty is nothing more than loyalty to an autocratic boss. My arguments for team loyalty and firm loyalty must not be misunderstood. I am not calling for blind loyalty. I am calling for loyalty to a total cooperative enterprise. If the culture of the firm is autocratic rather than cooperative, loyalty to the firm can neither be expected nor morally demanded.

Fourth, we must bridge what Robert Reich calls "the cleavage between the business and civic cultures." Business people should see activity in the political process as a legitimate activity and even as activity required by morality. Citizens in a democracy should be active, not passive; living in a democracy brings civil responsibilities as well as benefits. For reasons already given, the notion of civic responsibilities is severely weakened in our culture. However, a limited sense of civic responsibility is strongly held by some corporate leaders. For example, business leaders usually chair the United Way and the boards of local artistic and educational institutions. Some companies actually allow employees to work for extended periods for charitable organizations. However, if business is to fulfill its aim of greater investment in employees and to emphasize full employment, government will have to be seen as a partner rather than the enemy.

But what about the charge of many conservatives, for example Milton Friedman and Theodore Levitt, that if government and business cooperate there is a danger that power will be abused? Some fear that a monolith will be created. Others pointedly remind us that corporate officials are not democratically elected. Still others argue that corporate involvement in the political process will only be self-serving.

Some thought has been given to this problem, particularly by public affairs professionals. Indeed, the profession has adopted a "Statement of Ethical Guidelines" that speaks directly to the concern of abuse of corporate power. Statement C speaks directly to our issue.

C.   The Public Affairs Professional understand[s] the interrelation of business interests with the larger public interests, and therefore:
   1.   Endeavors to ensure that responsible and diverse external interests and views concerning the needs of society are considered within the corporate decision-making process.
   2.   Bears the responsibility for management review of public policies which may bring corporate interests into conflict with other interest[s].
   3.   Acknowledges dual obligations---to advocate the interests of his or her employer, and to preserve the openness and integrity of the democratic process.
   4.   Presents to his or her employer an accurate assessment of the political and social realities that may affect corporate operations.

440

Of course, it is one thing to adopt a set of guidelines and quite another to live by them--- particularly when the guidelines are as general as these. However, the tone of the document represents the spirit of partnership I think necessary if business is to fulfill its function of providing full employment in meaningful jobs.

Fifth, we need to rethink the skills required for good management. Education of managers should move away from quantitative analysis to the traditional liberal arts. As Reich has charged:

> Professional education in America is putting progressively more emphasis on the manipulation of symbols to the exclusion of other sorts of skills---how to collaborate with others, to work in teams, to speak foreign languages, to solve concrete problems---which are more relevant to the new competitive environment.

Such calls for a greater emphasis on liberal arts education do not come solely from academics. A symposium held in conjunction with Harvard University's 350th anniversary celebration made a call for a liberal arts component in preparation for business careers. The call came from the Corporate Council on the Liberal Arts, an organization established in 1984 representing twelve major companies. Michael Useem gave as one reason for the call the fact that "so many managers are now expected to play a role in the firm's social and political programs, the liberal arts have acquired a new importance for the long range development of a corporation's human resources."

To emphasize the liberal arts is to send a signal as to what skills and attitudes the business community thinks are important. A knowledge of our history, some knowledge of other cultures, but most importantly some insight into what it means to lead a fully human life---these are the hallmarks of the liberal arts education and too often they have been missing from the education of business managers. Business can only carry out its function of providing meaningful work if it understands the ideals and aspirations of human life.

CONCLUSION

I have argued that, in order to avoid the profit-making paradox, American business must turn its attention to capital investment in individual employees---indeed, that business should see its essential function as providing meaningful work. By so doing, business will be doing good consistent with the demands of morality. Moreover, business will become more competitive as a result and, hence, in doing good, business will also do well. However, if business persons are to succeed in this task they will need to change some of their traditional attitudes and values.

A DAY IN THE LIFE OF A SOCIALIST CITIZEN
Michael Walzer

Imagine a day in the life of a socialist citizen. He hunts in the morning, fishes in the afternoon, rears cattle in the evening and plays the critic after dinner. Yet he is neither hunter, fisherman, shepherd, nor critic; tomorrow he may select another set of activities, just as he pleases. This is the delightful portrait that Marx sketches in The German Ideology as part of a polemic against the division of labor. Socialists since have worried that it is not economically feasible; perhaps it is not. But there is another difficulty that I want to consider: that is, the curiously apolitical character of the citizen Marx describes. Certain crucial features of socialist life have been omitted altogether.

In light of the contemporary interest in participatory democracy, Marx's sketch needs to be elaborated. Before hunting in the morning, this unalienated man of the future is likely to attend a meeting of the Council on Animal Life, where he will be required to vote on important matters relating to the stocking of the forests. The meeting will probably not end much before noon, for among the many-sided citizens there will always be a lively interest even in highly technical problems. Immediately after lunch, a special session of the Fishermen's Council will be called to protest the maximum catch recently voted by the Regional Planning Commission, and the Marxist man will participate eagerly in these debates, even postponing a scheduled discussion of some contradictory theses on cattle-rearing. Indeed, he will probably love argument far better than hunting, fishing, or rearing cattle. The debates will go on so long that the citizens will have to rush through dinner in order to assume their role as critics. Then off they will go to meetings of study groups, clubs, editorial boards, and political parties where criticism will be carried on long into the night.

Oscar Wilde is supposed to have said that socialism would take too many evenings. This is, it seems to me, one of the most significant criticisms of socialist theory that has ever been made. The fanciful sketch above is only intended to suggest its possible truth. Socialism's great appeal is the prospect it holds out for the development of human capacities. An enormous growth of creative talent, a new and unprecedented variety of expression, a wild proliferation of sects, associations,

From Dissent, 1968. Reprinted by permission. Footnotes omited.

schools, parties: this will be the flowering of the future society. But underlying this new individualism and exciting group life must be a broad, self-governing community of equal men. A powerful figure looms behind Marx's hunter, fisherman, shepherd, and critic: the busy citizen attending his endless meetings. "Society regulates the general production," Marx writes, "and thus makes it possible for me to do one thing today and another tomorrow." If society is not to become an alien and dangerous force, however, the citizens cannot accept its regulation and gratefully do what they please. They must participate in social regulation; they must be social men, organizing and planning their own fulfillment in spontaneous activity. The purpose of Wilde's objection is to suggest that just this self-regulation is incompatible with spontaneity, that the requirements of citizenship are incompatible with the freedom of hunter, fisherman, and so on.

Politics itself, of course, can be a spontaneous activity, freely chosen by those men and women who enjoy it and to whose talents a meeting is so much exercise. But this is very unlikely to be true of all men and women all the time - even if one were to admit what seems plausible enough: that political life is more intrinsic to human nature than is hunting and cattle-rearing or even (to drop Marx's rural imagery) art or music. "Too many evenings" is a shorthand phrase that describes something more than the sometimes tedious, sometimes exciting business of resolutions and debates. It suggests also that socialism and participatory democracy will depend upon, and hence require, an extraordinary willingness to attend meetings, and a public spirit and sense of responsibility that will make attendance dependable and activity consistent and sustained. None of this can rest for any long period of time or among any substantial group of men upon spontaneous interest. Nor does it seem possible that spontaneity will flourish above and beyond the routines of social regulation.

Self-government is a very demanding and time consuming business, and when it is extended from political to economic and cultural life, and when the organs of government are decentralized so as to maximize participation, it will inevitably become more demanding still. Ultimately, it may well require almost continuous activity, and life will become a succession of meetings. When will there be time for the cultivation of personal creativity or the free association of like-minded friends? In the world of the meeting, when will there be time for the tete-a-tete?

I suppose there will always be time for the tete-a-tete. Men and women will secretly plan love affairs even while public business is being transacted. But Wilde's objection is not silly. The idea of citizenship on the Left has always been overwhelming, suggesting a positive frenzy of activity and often involving the repression of all feelings except political ones. Its character can best be examined in the work of Rousseau, from whom socialists and, more recently, New Leftists directly or indirectly inherited it. In order to guarantee public-spiritedness and political participation, and as a part of his critique of bourgeois egotism, Rousseau systematically denigrated the value of private life:

> The better the constitution of a state is, the more do public affairs encroach on private in the minds of the citizens. Private affairs are even of much less importance, because the aggregate of the common happiness furnishes a greater proportion of that of each individual, so that there is less for him to seek in particular cares.

Rousseau might well have written these lines out of a deep awareness that private life will not, in fact, bear the great weight that bourgeois society places upon it. We need, beyond our families and jobs, a public world where purposes are shared and cooperative activity is possible. More likely, however, he wrote them because he believed that cooperative activity could not be sustained unless private life were radically repressed, if not altogether eradicated. His citizen does not participate in social regulation as one part of a round of activities. Social regulation is his entire life. Rousseau develops his own critique of the division of labor by absorbing all human activities into the idea of citizenship: "Citizens," he wrote, "are neither lawyers, nor soldiers, nor priests by profession; they perform all these functions as a matter of duty." As a matter of duty: here is the key to the character of that patriotic responsible energetic man who has figured also in socialist thought, but always in the guise of a new man, freely exercising his human powers.

It is probably more realistic to see the citizen as the product of collective repression and self-discipline. He is, above all, dutiful, and this is only possible if he has triumphed over egotism and impulse in his own personality. He embodies what political theorists have called "republican virtue" - that means, he puts the common good, the success of the movement, the safety of the community, above his own delight or well-being, always. To symbolize his virtue, perhaps, he adopts an ascetic style and gives up every sort of self-decoration: he wears sans-culottes or unpressed khakis. More important, he foregoes a conventional career for the profession of politics; he commits himself entirely. It is an act of the most extreme devotion. Now, how is such a man produced? What kind of conversion is necessary? Or what kind of rigorous training?

Rousseau set out to create virtuous citizens, and the means he chose are very old in the history of republicanism: an authoritarian family, a rigid sexual code, censorship of the arts, sumptuary laws, mutual surveillance, the systematic indoctrination of children. All these have been associated historically (at least until recent times) not with tyrannical but with republican regimes: Greece and Rome, the Swiss Protestant city-states, the first French republic. Tyrannies and oligarchies, Rousseau argued, might tolerate or even encourage license, for the effect of sexual indulgence, artistic freedom, extravagant self-decoration, and privacy itself was to corrupt men and turn them away from public life, leaving government to the few. Self-government requires self-control: it is one of the oldest arguments in the history of political thought.

If that argument is true, it may mean that self-government also leaves government to the few. At least, this may be so if we reject the disciplinary or coercive features of Rousseau's republicanism and insist that citizens always have the right to choose between participation and passivity. Their obligations follow from their choices and do not precede them, so the state cannot impose one or the other choice; it cannot force the citizens to be self-governing men and women. Then only those citizens will be activists who volunteer for action. How many will that be? How many of the people you and I know? How many ought they to be? Certainly no radical movement or socialist society is possible without those ever-ready participants who "fly" as Rousseau said, "to the public assemblies." Radicalism and socialism make political activity for the first time an option for all those who relish it and a duty - sometimes - even for those who do not. But what a suffocating sense of responsibility, what a plethora of virtue would be necessary to sustain the participation of everybody all the time. How exhausting it would be. Surely there is something to be said for the irresponsible nonparticipant and something also for the part-time activist, the half-virtuous man (and the most scorned among the militants), who appears and disappears,

446

thinking of Marx and then of his dinner? The very least that can be said is that these people, unlike the poor, will always be with us. We can assume that a great many citizens, in the best of societies, will do all they can to avoid what Melvin Tumin has called "the merciless masochism of community-minded and self-regulating men and women." While the necessary meetings go on and on, they will take long walks, play with their children, paint pictures, make love and watch television. They will attend sometimes, when their interests are directly at stake or when they feel like it. But they will not make the full-scale commitment necessary for socialism or participatory democracy. How are these people to be represented at the meetings? What are their rights? These are not only problems of the future, when popular participation has finally been established as the core of political and economic life. They come up in every radical movement; they are the stuff of contemporary controversy.

Many people feel that they ought to join this or that political movement; they do join; they contribute time and energy - but unequally. Some make a full-time commitment; they work every minute; the movement becomes their whole life and they often come to disbelieve in the moral validity of life outside. Others are established outside,, solidly or precariously; they snatch hours and sometimes days; they harry their families and skimp on their jobs, but yet cannot make it to every meeting. Still others attend scarcely any meetings at all; they work hard but occasionally; they show up, perhaps, at critical moments, then they are gone. These last two groups make up the majority of the people available to the movement (any movement), just as they will make up the majority of the citizens of any socialist society. Radical politics radically increases the amount and intensity of political participation, but it does not (and probably ought not) break through the limits imposed on republican virtue by the inevitable pluralism of commitments, the terrible shortage of time, and the day-to-day hedonism of ordinary men and women.

Under these circumstances, words like citizenship and participation may actually describe the enfranchisement of only a part, and not necessarily a large part, of the movement or the community. Participatory democracy means the sharing of power among the activists. Socialism means the rule of the men with the most evenings to spare. Both imply, of course, an injunction to the others; join us, come to the meetings, participate. Sometimes young radicals sound very much like old Christians, demanding the severance of every tie for the sake of politics. "How many Christian women are there," John Calvin once wrote, "who are held captive by their children." How many "community people" miss meetings because of their families. But there is nothing to be done. Ardent democrats have sometimes urged that citizens be legally required to vote: that is possible, though the device is not attractive. Requiring people to attend meetings, to join in discussions, to govern themselves: that is not possible, at least not in a free society. And if they do not govern themselves, they will willy-nilly, be governed by their activist fellows. The apathetic, the occasional enthusiasts, the part-time workers: all of them will be ruled by full- timers, militants, and professionals.

But if only some citizens participate in political life, it is essential that they always remember and be regularly reminded that they are...only some. This is not easy to arrange. The militant in the movement, for example, does not represent anybody; it is his great virtue that he is self-chosen, a volunteer. But since he sacrifices so much for his fellowmen, he readily persuades himself that he is acting in their name. He takes their failure to put in an appearance only as a token of their oppression. He is certain he is their agent, or rather, the agent of their liberation. He is not in any simple sense wrong. The small numbers of participating citizens in the U.S. today, the widespread fearfulness, the sense of impotence and irrelevance: all these are signs of social sickness. Self-government is an important human function, an exercise of significant talents and energies, and the sense of power and responsibility it brings is enormously healthy. A certain amount of commitment and discipline, of not-quite-merciless masochism, is socially desirable and efforts to evoke it are socially justifiable.

But many of the people who stay away from meetings do so for reasons that the militants do not understand or will not acknowledge. They stay away not because they are beaten, afraid, uneducated, lacking confidence and skills (though these are often important reasons), but because they have made other commitments; they have found ways to cope short of politics; they have created viable subcultures even in an oppressive world. They may lend passive support to the movement and help out occasionally, but they will not work, nor are their needs and aspirations in any sense embodied by the militants who will.

The militants represent themselves. If the movement is to be democratic, the others must be represented. The same thing will be true in any future socialist society: participatory democracy has to be paralleled by representative democracy. I am not sure precisely how to adjust the two; I am sure that they have to be adjusted. Somehow power must be distributed, as it is not today, to groups of active and interested citizens, but these citizens must themselves be made responsible to a larger electorate (the membership, that is, of the state, movement, union or party). Nothing is more important than that responsibility; without it we will only get one or another sort of activist or apparatchik tyranny. And that we have already.

Nonparticipants have rights; it is one of the dangers of participatory democracy that it would fail to provide any effective protection for these rights. But nonparticipants also have functions; it is another danger that these would not be sufficiently valued. For many people in America today, politics is something to watch, an exciting spectacle, and there exists between the activists and the others something of the relation of actor and audience. Now for any democrat this is an unsatisfactory relation. We rightly resent the way actors play upon and manipulate the feelings of their audiences. We dislike the aura of magic and mystification contrived at on stage. We would prefer politics to be like the new drama with its alienation effects and its audience participation. That is fair enough. But even the new drama requires its audience, and we ought not to forget that audiences can be critical as well as admiring, enlightened as well as mystified. More important, political actors; like actors in the theater, need the control and tension imposed by audiences, the knowledge that tomorrow the reviews will appear, tomorrow people will come or not come to watch their performance. Too often, of course, the reviews are favorable and the audiences come. That is because of the various sorts of collusion which presently develop between small and co-opted cliques of actors and critics. But in an entirely free society, there would be many more political actors and critics than ever before, and they would, presumably, be self-chosen. Not only the participants, but also the nonparticipants, would come into their own. Alongside the democratic politics of shared work and perpetual activism, there would arise the open and leisurely culture of part-time work, criticism, second-guessing, and burlesque. And into this culture might well be drawn many of the alienated citizens of today. The modes of criticism will become the forms of their participation and their involvement in the drama the measure of their responsibility.

It would be a great mistake to underestimate the importance of criticism as a kind of politics, even if the critics are not always marked, as they will not be, by "republican virtue." It is far more important in the political arena than in the theater. For activists and professionals in the movement or the polity do not simply contrive effects; their work has more palpable results. Their policies touch us all in material ways, whether we go or do not go to the meetings. Indeed, those who do not go may well turn out to be more effective critics than those who do: no one who was one of its "first guessers" can usefully second-guess a decision. That is why the best critics in a liberal society are men-out-of-office. In a radically democratic society they would be men who stay away from meetings, perhaps for months at a time, and only then discover that something outrageous has been perpetrated that must be mocked or protested. The proper response to such protests is not to tell the laggard citizens that they should have been active these past many months, not to nag them to do work that they do not enjoy and in any case will not do well, but to listen to what they have to say. After all, what would democratic politics be like without its kibitzers?